STUDIES IN
SOCIAL ANTHROPOLOGY

Studies in Social Anthropology

ESSAYS IN MEMORY OF
E. E. EVANS-PRITCHARD
BY HIS FORMER
OXFORD COLLEAGUES

EDITED BY

J. H. M. BEATTIE

AND

R. G. LIENHARDT

OXFORD
AT THE CLARENDON PRESS
1975

Oxford University Press, Ely House, London W. 1

GLASGOW   NEW YORK   TORONTO   MELBOURNE   WELLINGTON
CAPE TOWN   IBADAN   NAIROBI   DAR ES SALAAM   LUSAKA   ADDIS ABABA
DELHI   BOMBAY   CALCUTTA   MADRAS   KARACHI   LAHORE   DACCA
KUALA LUMPUR   SINGAPORE   HONG KONG   TOKYO

ISBN 0 19 823183 0

© *Oxford University Press 1975*

*Printed in Great Britain
at the University Press, Oxford
by Vivian Ridler
Printer to the University*

Preface

IN 1968 the teaching staff of the Institute of Social Anthropology
at Oxford University decided that an appropriate tribute to
Professor Evans-Pritchard on his retirement, then due in two
years' time, would be a collection of essays specially written for
him by social anthropologists who had taught at the Institute
during the years of his professorship. Almost all of the anthropologists eligible by this criterion accepted the editors' invitation
to contribute (a very few were editing or contributing to other
symposia for Evans-Pritchard, or were otherwise prevented).
This book is the somewhat belated result. It is a matter for regret
to editors and contributors that what began as a *festschrift* has
now, with the passage of time and with Sir Edward's death in
September 1973, become a memorial volume. But we may con-
sole ourselves with the knowledge that he was aware that the work
was in progress and was pleased by this.

The theoretical and regional interests of potential contributors
were so diverse that it was evidently not feasible to suggest a single
theme or topic for the volume. Instead, each was invited to write
on any aspect of his, or her, field of interest or research which was
linked, however tenuously, with Evans-Pritchard's own work.
In the case of some of the essays the connection is indeed so
tenuous as to be scarcely perceptible. But we do not think that
this matters. Evans-Pritchard's own immense achievement in
social anthropology ranges widely over the subject's many
branches, and the studies which follow may be said to reflect in
some measure this great breadth of interest. So they do not, and
could not have been expected to, exhibit any kind of organic
unity, either of theme or of region.

But diverse though the essays are, like most contemporary
social anthropology they do fall into one or other of a few very
broad categories, though these are not mutually exclusive and
indeed melt into one another. Most of the studies are 'ethnographical', in that they describe aspects of particular cultures or

communities, either contemporary or historical. In some, the emphasis is on social relationships, what actually goes (or went) on in these communities. In others, the main stress is conceptual; the central concern is rather with the ways in which people think, than with what they do. Obviously the two approaches cannot be divorced from each other, but the mixture may vary.

Thus in the first few chapters the focus is mainly on social action. Meinhard argues that for early Teutons unilineality was a more important determinant of social behaviour than has generally been recognized, at least by social anthropologists. Beattie describes a small African community where lineal descent and residence are—or were until recently—closely associated. Srinivas sets out and documents the claim that the Indian village can and should be seen as a more or less cohesive community, and not simply as the locus of a system of caste hierarchy. Burridge (in Chapter 4) discusses, in the framework of comparative ethnography, the importance in practical affairs in Melanesia of independent and respected negotiators or middlemen. Next, in P. A. Lienhardt's study, the political—and psychological—importance of rumour, especially in its more fantastic varieties, is analysed.

There follow a number of essays which focus mainly on belief-systems and their social implications. In Chapter 6 Fortes places Tallensi prayer and sacrifice firmly at the centre of that people's religious system. Next, Bohannan offers a factual account of Tiv divination and the ideas associated with it, and shows how it may be used as a means of group decision-making. Then Peristiany (Chapter 8) discusses some categories of ritual experts among the Pokot of western Kenya, and describes his own confrontation with one such expert. In the next chapter R. G. Lienhardt analyses the social and political implications of some Nilotic myths in which the return of a lost object (typically a bead) is demanded of the loser of it at unreasonable cost (typically the evisceration of a child who has swallowed it). Next, Jain demonstrates in the context of central India the importance of myth and traditional history in defining and sustaining a political order. And in Chapter 11 Pocock discusses the importance of territory in the first book of the Old Testament, and considers some of the spatial concepts which are entailed.

With Audrey Colson's account, in Chapter 12, of some institutions associated with birth among an Amerindian people of Guyana we return to the ethnography of contemporary pre-industrial societies, and in the next chapter the late Jean Buxton discusses the eager adoption by the Mandari of the Southern Sudan, from neighbouring peoples, of both the institution of age-sets and an accompanying fashion in bead-wearing.

In Chapter 14, the emphasis moves from ethnography to theory. In his discussion of *The Nuer* Dumont argues that most of Evans-Pritchard's successors have over-emphasized the territorial and political aspects of that work, at the cost of neglecting its more 'structural' concern with Nuer ways of thought. Next, Ardener discusses, in a West African context, how linguistic categories may affect the observer's perceptions of population as well as of 'ethnicity'.

Lastly, Needham (in conformity with an interest of Evans-Pritchard's own) describes his attempts to add to the very little that is known of the life of an important but neglected Victorian anthropologist, and reports the results of his investigation.

This brief and manifestly inadequate indication of the main themes of the studies collected here will at least give some idea of their variety and range. It certainly cannot be claimed that the association which all the contributors have had, over a period of many years, with the late Sir Edward Evans-Pritchard has left its mark on them in any kind of shared theoretical approach to their subject. Evans-Pritchard never founded a school, nor would he have wanted to. If these essays have anything in common (apart from whatever intrinsic interest they may possess) it is perhaps that in their very diversity they may communicate something of the tolerance, freedom, and breadth of interest which characterized the Institute during the years of Evans-Pritchard's headship of it. This, at least, both editors and contributors would like to think.

GODFREY LIENHARDT
JOHN BEATTIE

Contents

List of Plates

1

The Patrilineal Principle in Early Teutonic Kinship

H. H. MEINHARD

ONE of Professor Evans-Pritchard's lasting contributions to social anthropology has been the deepening of our understanding of the principle of unilineal descent and the stimulation of a great number of studies of lineage organization. The following essay attempts to review the literary evidence attesting the former existence of a system of unilineal descent, which, assailed by various adverse influences, gradually crumbled away, leaving only remnants or traces. The task is complicated by the virtual absence of contacts between historians and philologists on the one hand and social anthropologists on the other.

Let me introduce this survey with three quotations:

What is therefore unusual or rare . . . is the discovery of a people such as the Teutonic peoples of Europe (apparently alone amongst Indo-European speaking peoples) maintaining for some period, until the coming of feudalism and Roman law, a system in which there is considerable, if not quite complete, avoidance of the unilineal principle, in which a person derives similar and equal rights through the father and through the mother.[1]

The same (sc. agnatic) view of relationship pervades so much of the laws of the races who overran the Roman Empire as appears to have really formed part of their primitive usage, and we may suspect that it would have perpetuated itself even more than it has in modern jurisprudence, if it had not been for the vast influence of the later Roman law on modern thought.[2]

[1] A. R. Radcliffe-Brown in *Structure and Function in Primitive Society* (1952), p. 48.
[2] H. S. Maine in *Ancient Law* (1861; 1906 edn.), p. 156.

Ancient Roman law was agnatic, but the cognatic system was admitted by the later Praetorian law and is now practised by us. . . . It is a fallacy to argue that, because the Germanic system is cognatic, it must have been so from the beginning, and that it is impossible to suppose that it was at any time agnatic.[3]

The subject of early Teutonic kinship has been a prolific source of keen controversy for the last century and a half. As is well known, Radcliffe-Brown has developed his view of an essentially cognatic character of the Teutonic system, first expressed in 'Patrilineal and Matrilineal Succession' (quoted above), in his Introduction to *African Systems of Kinship and Marriage*, and in the years since then the Teutonic system has several times been referred to, on his authority, as a paradigm of the cognatic principle. Lorraine Lancaster's strictures[4] are directed against his generalizing tendency, especially his implication that the arrangement of kin by reference to the joints of the human body, which he has derived from the medieval *Sachsenspiegel* of northern Germany, is also relevant to Anglo-Saxon society.

Radcliffe-Brown's reliance on the kinship picture of the *Sachsenspiegel*, written by the East-Saxon knight Eike von Repgow about 1225, is unfortunate also in another respect. Eike has gleaned the substance of his kinship computation (*Ssp.* i. 3, § 3) not from current popular Saxon usage but from the conventional scholarship of his time. As has first been shown by Ulrich Stutz,[5] he has derived it, through a series of links—meticulously traced by the author—from Isidore of Seville's *Etymologiae sive Origines*, ix. 6,[6] confusing his source, however, with the patristic writer Origen. The proof of the literary relationship lies in the schematic parallelism, in both cases, of the six degrees of kinship with the six Ages of the World, the last beginning with the birth of Christ (*Etymol.* v. 39; *Ssp.* i. 3, § 1). The differences between the two versions are (1) that Eike substitutes the Germanic symbol

[3] P. G. Vinogradoff in *Outlines of Historical Jurisprudence* (1920–2), i. 206 f.
[4] 'Kinship in Anglo-Saxon Society', *British Journal of Sociology*, 9 (1958).
[5] *Das Verwandtschaftsbild des Sachsenspiegels* (1890), pp. 22 ff. See also *Sachsenspiegel Landrecht*, ed. K. A. Eckhardt (2nd edn., 1955), pp. 72 ff. (in the series *Monumenta Germaniae Historica*).
[6] See edition by W. M. Lindsay (O.U.P., 1911).

of the body and its joints for the Roman *arbor consanguinitatis*, (2) that in *Ssp*, i. 3, § 2, between the Ages and the kinship reckoning, he introduces another category of parallelism, that of the six orders of the *Heerschild* (army shield), the symbol of the gradation of feudal rank, and (3) that, following a later reckoning of Ages at a millennium each, he feels that he is living in a seventh Age of uncertain duration, to which correspond a seventh dubious order of feudal rank and a seventh equally dubious sib number, namely, the nail kinsmen. As Stutz puts it, for an answer to the question whether popular Saxon law recognized a kinship limit, and if so which one, the passage *Ssp*. i. 3, § 3, is of no use whatsoever.

Limits in the recognition of cognatic kin by reference to 'joints', 'little knees', etc., are already recorded in the folk-laws (*Leges Barbarorum*) of the post-migration period (fifth to early ninth century). Thus the Salian Franks reckon 'usque ad sextum genuculum', the Ripuarian Franks, 'usque quinto genuclo', the Thuringians, 'usque ad quintam generationem', the Lombards, Visigoths, and Baiuvarians, 'usque in septimum geniculum'. The differences are usually explained by variations in the mode of reckoning, e.g. including Ego as the point of departure so that the sibling represents the second geniculum, or beginning with the nearest collateral as the first geniculum.[7] There has been a great deal of controversy on the subject, but it would seem to be hazardous to rule out ecclesiastical influence. An opinion of Maine's[8] may be relevant in this connection:

Rude as are the Leges Barbarorum which remain to us, they are not rude enough to satisfy the theory of their purely barbarous origin; nor have we any reason for believing that we have received, in written records, more than a fraction of the fixed rules which were practised among themselves by the members of the conquering tribes.

The second half of the sentence might also have been pondered by writers on Anglo-Saxon and Scandinavian laws who have tended to imply that what is not on record cannot have existed.

---

[7] See H. Brunner, *Deutsche Rechtsgeschichte*, i (2nd edn., 1906), p. 325; S. Rietschel, art. 'Erbenfolge', in J. Hoops (ed.), *Reallexikon der germanischen Altertumskunde*, i (1913).　　　　　　　　　[8] Op. cit. (1906 edn.), p. 305.

The view taken by the majority of German philologists and historians of Teutonic law until fairly recently—although radical revisions seem to have been gaining ground in the post-war decades—may be briefly summed up as follows: In common with the rest of the Indo-European peoples, the ancient Teutons provide an example of 'father-right'. By far the greater part of Teutonic kinship terms are etymologically cognate with the equivalent ones in other Indo-European languages, which is at least an *a priori* consideration for the view that the ancient Teutonic kinship system was essentially similar to those of other Indo-European peoples. In the oldest times Teutonic society was structured on agnatic lines, with discrete corporate descent groups exercising political, legal, and other functions. Internally, the descent group was a 'peace community', protecting its members and exercising its own jurisdiction; externally it was a defensive and offensive body. It had the duty of the blood-feud; it received and paid compensation for homicide. In warfare its able-bodied men fought together as a group, though not necessarily forming a tactical unit of the tribal army. It was a separate settlement and land-holding community. At the time of the migrations, descent groups, occupying localities in newly conquered lands, named them with their own patronymic names (place-names with the suffix '-ing'). These are only some of the more important features ascribed to the old agnatic descent group, the last-mentioned being the most disputed.

This view is based, in the first place, on a few passages in Caesar's *De bello Gallico* and Tacitus' *Germania*. Though they have been quoted hundreds of times, it may be necessary to repeat some of them, however pedantic it may appear, since Radcliffe-Brown does not mention them. Caesar, vi. 22, speaking of a tribe on the move, says that the tribal authorities ('magistratus ac principes') apportion tracts of agricultural land to its 'gentes et cognationes' for temporary occupation. In the following chapter (23) he says that in times of war the tribe is led by an elected common authority ('magistratus') wielding power of life and death, but that in peacetime there is no common tribal authority, 'sed principes regionum atque pagorum inter suos ius dicunt

controversiasque minuunt'. After what has been said of the distribution of land in the previous chapter, it would seem probable
that the occupants of these territorial divisions were agnatic
descent groups, or at least assemblages of relatives clustering
round cores formed by such groups.

Tacitus, ch. 7, speaking of the constitution of tribal armies,
emphasizes as a special incentive of bravery the fact that a unit
is not built up by some kind of chance assemblage but is composed of 'familiae et propinquitates'. The word *familia* has of
course several rather different meanings, although the concept of
the group composed of husband, wife, and children does not
seem to be one of them. One of its technical meanings is that of
a major segment of the *gens*, but it is frequently substituted for
gens itself; Tacitus uses it interchangeably with *gens* as a matter
of course. Fustel de Coulanges[9] reminds us of Ulpian's dictum
'familiam dicimus omnium agnatorum'. What Tacitus says is confirmed, nearly 500 years later, by the Byzantine emperor Mauricius in his *Strategica*, saying that in battles the Franks, Lombards,
and other fair-haired peoples were drawn up by descent groups
("κατὰ φυλάς") and in accordance with mutual kinship and attachment (συγγένεια, προσπάθεια).[10] Speaking of compensation for
homicide, ch. 21, Tacitus says: 'recipit satisfactionem universa
domus.' The expression *domus* is of course indeterminate, but
presumably does not refer to the household community only,
which in any case among continental Teutons consisted of no
more than the nuclear family, perhaps with unrelated persons of
servile status who naturally would not be included in the compensation. From the opening of the paragraph, saying that a man
is bound to take up, or succeeds to, both the enmities (i.e. blood-
feuds) and friendships of his father or kinsman (*propinquus*), it
would appear that Tacitus thought of a larger grouping, the
propinquus probably not living under the same roof, though the
passage leaves it dark what kind of grouping he had in mind.
Nevertheless, German translations invariably render *universa domus*
by *Sippe*, by which ambiguous word they mean an agnatic group.

[9] *La Cité antique* (1864), p. 121 n.
[10] Rudolf Much, *Die Germania des Tacitus* (2nd edn., 1959), pp. 110 f.

A great deal of the semantic confusion in the discussion of early Teutonic kinship is due to the adoption, by German scholars, of this unfortunate word *Sippe*. This seems to have occurred at some time during the middle of the nineteenth century, and its use has continued to the present day. The argument for its choice seems to have been that of all the old words with a kinship meaning it is the most widespread in the various branches of the Teutonic languages and must therefore be assumed to be the oldest. I can only briefly refer to two dictionary articles on the word. Grimm's *Deutsches Wörterbuch* introduces its explanation with the definitions 'pax, foedus, affinitas, propinquitas', and continues, somewhat darkly, that the intrinsic meaning of the word is not descent from a common ancestor, the totality of those united by consanguinity, the parentele, but that primarily it designates, much more narrowly, relationship based on a compact ('die durch ein Bündnis begründete Verwandtschaft'). If I understand the compiler rightly, the interpretation rejected by him is what Radcliffe-Brown called a 'stock', while the primary, narrower meaning suggested by the compiler might well be that of a group having a corporate character. But with the word *Bündnis* ('union', 'compact') he may also hark back to the word *foedus* prefixed to the article, which, like *pax*, is a derivative meaning, introduced in Germany by the Anglo-Saxon missionaries who derived these connotations from the kind of relationship expected among kinsfolk. By a similar way of derivation, the Gothic Bible uses the adjective *unsibjis* in the meaning of 'unlawful', 'godless'. The second article, in Trübner's *Deutsches Wörterbuch*, begins with 'blood-relationship, degree of cognatic kinship', passing over to derivative meanings, but soon continues saying that 'in the oldest time the Sippe was a corporation based on agnatic principles'.

In fact this latter meaning is merely a learned convention, a heuristic construct of the nineteenth-century professors. There is not a scrap of evidence, in authentic old sources, showing the word to mean, unambiguously and exclusively, 'agnatic descent group'. We do not know the Germanic equivalents, in Caesar's and Tacitus' times, of the *gentes* and *familiae* of the *Interpretatio*

Romana. Nevertheless, most of the German students of the subject seem to assume that the term *Sippe* was originally applied to an agnatic descent group and only later, in historical times, changed its meaning to designate an impermanent Ego-centred cognatic body of kinsfolk, the type of grouping which we now usually style as 'kindred'. More precisely, noticing the vestiges of an earlier patrilineal alignment, they extended or retrojected the word, from its medieval meaning of 'kindred', to cover also the clearly traceable patrilineal descent group of the oldest time, distinguishing between the two different formations only by means of differentiating adjectives. Thus the *Sippe* as identical with the kindred, which confronted them in the medieval sources, was called *wechselnde* ('shifting', 'fluctuating') or *offene* (open) *Sippe*, while the earlier patrilineal descent group became the *feste* ('stable', 'solidary') or *geschlossene* ('closed') *Sippe*. The latter is sometimes also referred to as *agnatischer Sippenverband*, emphasizing its corporate character. Of course, the technical use of the same ambiguous term, only with differentiating adjectives which more often than not were omitted, to refer to two entirely different forms of grouping was bound to lead to considerable confusion.

In German ethnological usage, *Sippe* has been used in the sense of unilineal descent group at least since the late nineteenth century. An early definition is that by Ernst Grosse,[11] who uses the term in the sense in which legal historians spoke of the *feste, geschlossene Sippe*, avoiding any reference to their concept of the *wechselnde, offene Sippe*, but emphasizing that in ethnological usage the *Sippe* is either patrilineal or matrilineal. In this sense German ethnologists have predominantly used the term, thus identifying it with that of 'clan' as used in this country. But it is not at all rare to find the word used, in German ethnographical literature, in the sense of a cognatic kin-group, or even of denoting no more than an extended family. Some writers seem to be unable to keep the two meanings apart. This semantic confusion seems to be a heritage of the ambiguity of the term as used by the legal historians.

11 *Die Formen der Familie und die Formen der Wirtschaft* (1896), pp. 10f.

The present American use of 'sib' goes back, not to the *Sippe* of the ethnologists, but to that of the legal historians. When Lowie introduced it,[12] he recommended it for 'its alluring brevity and phonetic suggestiveness'. It may be as well to add that F. S. Philbrick, whom he cites as his authority, did not suggest the word of his own accord, but used it, in his translation of R. Huebner's *Grundzüge des deutschen Privatrechts*,[13] as the English equivalent of the author's *Sippe*. Lowie's later withdrawal of 'sib' in favour of 'clan'[14] may well be connected with Radcliffe-Brown's use of 'sib' and his explicit rejection of Lowie's different use, in 'Patrilineal and Matrilineal Succession'.[15] Murdock does not seem to have been affected by these strictures. He offers what is surely the most bizarre argument in justification of his use of the word: 'We have given preference to "sib" over "clan" primarily because the former has never been applied to kin groups other than consanguineal ones with unilinear descent, so that its use by us in this sense could lead to no confusion.'[16]

In short, I agree with Radcliffe-Brown's opinion that the word 'sib', if it is to be used at all, should be retained for the cognatic group of kindred to which it was historically applied; but since it is synonymous with the latter word, which is used more frequently, there would be no point in retaining it. I disagree with him on the question of whether or not the Teutonic peoples, at an earlier time, had a kinship system with agnatic descent groups as persistent segments of society, no matter what terms they may have used to designate them, which is of course an entirely different issue.

Another German word which was quite commonly used throughout most of the nineteenth century to denote a unilineal descent group, before it was superseded by the use of *Sippe* in the same sense, is the word *Geschlecht*, Old High German *slahta*. This word seems to express the notion of unilineality intrinsically and unambiguously and has, I believe, the best historical claim to

[12] *Primitive Society* (1921), p. 105.
[13] *A History of Germanic Private Law* (1918).
[14] *Social Organization* (1950), p. 237.
[15] *Structure and Function in Primitive Society* (1952), p. 39.
[16] *Social Structure* (1949), p. 67; see also ibid., p. 47.

be used, in German, as a designation of a patrilineal group. Unfortunately it has not, unlike *Sippe*, an etymological equivalent in Anglo-Saxon, nor is it represented in the Scandinavian branch of Teutonic languages. It has been adopted into Polish and Czech as *szlachta* and *šlechta* respectively, meaning 'aristocratic lineage', 'nobility', and 'noblemen' generally. In Italian it appears as *schiatta* (dictionary meanings: 'race, lineage, extraction, family, birth'); here as well as in Provençal (*esclata*) and in Alpine-Romance dialects (*šlata* and similar forms) it is believed to be derived from an unrecorded Gothic form. In south-western Germany and Switzerland *Geschlecht* is said to be still used as a synonym of *Familienname* ('surname'). In the nineteenth century and even in the first quarter of the present century, the term was more or less commonly used by historians as an equivalent of 'patrilineage'. Niebuhr used it for the Roman *gens*, so did Mommsen and later historians. In the English translation of Niebuhr's work, *The History of Rome*, the word *Geschlecht* is rendered by 'house'. Vinogradoff entitled one of his earlier essays[17] 'Geschlecht und Verwandtschaft im altnorwegischen Recht', using the word *Sippe* only rarely as a synonym of *Verwandtschaft*. As late as 1924 E. Mayer speaks of 'Germanische Geschlechts-verbände'. But the general trend is for *Geschlecht* to disappear. Gierke, in the first volume of *Das deutsche Genossenschaftsrecht* (1868), in which he describes agnatic descent groups as the earliest type of corporate bodies, uses *Geschlecht* and *Sippe* synonymously and interchangeably. In later discussion, *Geschlecht* drops out gradually, becoming increasingly replaced by *Sippe*. I do not know of any recent German writer using the word consistently and generally in preference to *Sippe*, with the exception of those specifically concerned with the *Dithmarscher Geschlechter*, corporate agnatic descent groups which survived beyond the Middle Ages and were actually known as *slachte* or, in later references, as *Geschlechte* (see further below).

As pointed out above, the majority of the earlier German legal historians took the view of an originally agnatic system being gradually replaced by a cognatic one. The main nineteenth-

[17] Reprinted in *The Collected Papers of Paul Vinogradoff*, ii (Oxford, 1928).

century dissenters, who both left a marked influence on Maitland, were A. Heusler[18] and J. Ficker.[19] More recently, F. Genzmer[20] has thrown doubts on the significance and corporate character of the *agnatische Sippe*, while K. Kroeschell[21] has, more radically, declared himself against the assumption of an original *agnatische Sippe* altogether. The latter has been strongly impressed, not to say dazzled, by Bertha S. Phillpotts,[22] whose book, by some chance, had remained virtually unknown in Germany for more than four decades. Indeed there are more signs that since the 1950s the current of opinion has turned against the hitherto central concept of the *agnatische Sippe*. The older German majority view of an original agnatic system has also been shared by J. M. Kemble,[23] Maine (see passage above, p. 1), Fustel de Coulanges,[24] and P. Vinogradoff.[25] The opponents in this country were F. W. Maitland,[26] B. S. Phillpotts (already mentioned), H. M. Chadwick,[27] R. H. Hodgkin,[28] and no doubt others. Considering that the subject has been thrashed out by generations of scholars for over a century, with the most searching inquiries and with controversies which even at the present time show no sign of abating, Radcliffe-Brown's assertion[29] that the theory of a prehistoric Teutonic system of patriarchy emphasizing agnatic descent is only a deduction from a general theory that originally all the Indo-European peoples had a patriarchal system, and that it is not supported by any historical evidence, really seems to be a somewhat cavalier dismissal of the matter.

[18] *Institutionen des deutschen Privatrechts* (1885–6), i. 258 ff., ii. 523 ff.
[19] *Untersuchungen zur Erbenfolge der ostgermanischen Rechte* (1891–1904), i. 253 ff.
[20] 'Die germanische Sippe als Rechtsgebilde', *Zeitschrift für Rechtsgeschichte*, Germ. Abt. (1950).
[21] 'Die Sippe im germanischen Recht', ibid. (1960).
[22] *Kindred and Clan in the Middle Ages and After* (1913).
[23] *The Saxons in England* (1849).
[24] 'Recherches sur cette question: Les Germains connaissaient-ils la propriété des terres?' *Séances et travaux de l'Académie des sciences morales et politiques*, N.S. 23 (1885), 705 ff.; 24 (1885), 1 ff.
[25] Art. on Old Norwegian law mentioned above; *The Growth of the Manor* (2nd edn., 1911), pp. 135 ff., 241 ff.; *Outlines of Historical Jurisprudence*, i (1920), pp. 206 f., 287 f., 302 f., 306 f.
[26] Pollock and Maitland, *The History of English Law* (2nd edn., 1911), ii. 240 ff.
[27] *The Heroic Age*, ch. xvi.
[28] *A History of the Anglo-Saxons* (1939), pp. 212 ff.
[29] *African Systems of Kinship and Marriage*, p. 18.

I am not qualified to dispute Maitland's and Phillpotts's general conclusions of the essentially cognatic character of Anglo-Saxon society. It may indeed be difficult to trace vestiges of an older agnatic system. It seems to be generally agreed that the conquest was effected, not by tribal armies in which members of descent groups fought side by side, but by war-bands, shiploads of fighting men following a war-leader to whom they might or might not be connected by kinship ties, the kind of grouping described by Tacitus as *comites, comitatus*. But some questions remain unanswered. If the *maegdh* is no more than a collective term for the *magas* (sing. *maeg*), describing a web of kinship links stretching from an individual to all his cognatic kin, its additional use for tribal and territorial divisions, e.g. *Westseaxna maegdh, Nordhanhymbra maegdh, Daera maegdh*, is somewhat surprising, and so is the compound *maegburh*. I would agree with Miss Phillpotts's view (p. 261) that an oversea migration, as in the case of the Icelanders and Anglo-Saxons, is bound to impair the kin-solidarity of those who venture on it, disrupting the cognatic kindred; but I would also maintain that an agnatic descent group system is no less vulnerable to such a venture, considering that it is not a group of agnates that builds and mans a vessel, but more probably a *comitatus*. As a general consideration, I would however be prepared to accept an argument put forward tentatively, as a possibility, by Maitland (p. 243): 'Others, again, may think that the great "folk-wandering" has made the family organization of the German race unusually indefinite and plastic, so that here it will take one, and there another form.'

However, some of Maitland's specific arguments may seem a little odd to social anthropologists. For example, he says (p. 241): 'So soon as it is admitted that the bond of blood . . . ties the child both to his father's brother and to his mother's brother, a system of mutually exclusive clans is impossible, unless each clan is strictly endogamous.' Or (p. 242): 'Now when we see that the wives of the members of one clan are themselves members of other clans, we ought not to talk of clans at all.' These passages are influenced by Heusler and Ficker, but the authority he refers

to specifically is Gierke. In a discussion of the causes of the dissolution of the agnatic system, Gierke says:

Recognition of cognation is absolutely incompatible with a descent
group system. When a married woman, although entering into her
husband's descent group, is still being protected by her own natal
group, when the husband himself is considered to be connected with
his wife's circle of kin, we have striking evidence of the difference
between the Germanic descent groups and the Roman gentes.

Indeed this fact that a woman's protectors were still her own
agnatic kinsmen, not those of her husband, appears to have been
a puzzle to most of the nineteenth-century scholars. They started
off from the presumption that the Teutonic agnatic system must
have been much the same as the early Roman one. In the older
Roman law, a woman, by passing into *manus mariti*, changed over
into another *patria potestas*, which meant legal severance from
her own natal group; a Teutonic woman, by contrast, continued
to be protected by her own agnatic kin.

There was a more general assumption, explicit or implicit,
that the prehistoric Teutonic descent group recognized as kin
only its own members; e.g. Rietschel[30] states: 'The oldest time
reckons predominantly, perhaps even exclusively, with kinship
transmitted through males.' The view that all societies recognize
cognatic kinship within certain limits, a commonplace to social
anthropologists, does not seem to have been shared by the older
generation of scholars; the failure to distinguish between the
categories of descent and kinship goes through the whole discussion, and is particularly marked in Heusler and Ficker. Tacitus'
reference to the close relationship between mother's brother and
sister's son (ch. 20: 'Sororum filiis idem apud avunculum qui
apud patrem honor' etc.) was often interpreted as the oldest
literary record of an agnatic society gradually admitting the
principle of cognation. One of many examples is Huebner:[31]

The special honour of the maternal uncle may have been merely a consequence of the fact that the maternal kindred came, in time, to be

[30] Art. 'Sippe', § 5, in Hoops's *Reallexikon*.
[31] *A History of Germanic Private Law*, trans. Philbrick (1918), p. 590. See also
pp. 114 f., 712 ff.

considered along with the paternal, who were at first exclusively regarded; in other words, a consequence of the fact that the family's purely agnatic structure was replaced by a cognatic organization. In this appearance of the idea of cognatic relationship, which transformed in the same manner the family and the sib, the maternal uncle naturally played the most important rôle: he was the link between the families of the father and the mother, and he was primarily the person upon whom was incumbent, as the representative of the maternal sib, the protection of the wife as against the husband.

Lowie, quoting the passage in his article 'The Matrilineal Complex',[32] remarks: 'My comment on this would simply be that it is unnecessary to assume the sequence from agnatic to cognatic institutions: matronymy is perfectly consistent with the assignment of definite functions to the father's group and patronymy is equally consistent with the avunculate.' But neither Lowie's nor Vinogradoff's comments have made German legal historians budge from their preconceived view of a system of exclusively agnatic kinship gradually changing to a cognatic one. One of the more recent examples is H. Conrad:[33] 'The increasing significance of blood-kinship can already be traced in the early Germanic period (preference given to the mother's brother).'[34]

The distinction between descent and kinship was first emphasized by Vinogradoff,[35] who seems to have anticipated Rivers on this issue. He says:

It would be wrong to assume that the predominance of agnatic organization necessarily implied a denial of all other modes of relationship.

It would not help to argue that the predominance of agnatic relationship must have entailed . . . the exclusion of all relationship through

[32] *University of California Publications in American Archaeology and Ethnology*, 16 (1919), 42.
[33] *Deutsche Rechtsgeschichte* (2nd edn., 1962), i. 34.
[34] It is true that the Tacitean passage has also been, as Radcliffe-Brown observes (*African Systems*, p. 18), the *pièce de résistance* of the 'mother-right' champions. However, the majority of writers interpreted it as meaning that the youth needed the protection of his maternal uncle against the claims of his half-brothers, either in the case of his father's polygynous marriage or in that of his remarriage after his first wife's death. Indeed it was generally assumed that the tie between a man and his sister's son could only have been a 'natural' one, an extension of the sibling tie, and without legal significance.
[35] *Growth of the Manor*, pp. 9 f., 90; *Historical Jurisprudence*, i. 306 f.

women, or vice versa, that the recognition of rights proceeding through women is to be considered a bar to any working arrangement of agnatic kinship.

. . . even so authoritative a historian as Maitland declared that as soon as men recognize the wide circle of cognatic relationship we had better cease to speak of clans. In reality it is erroneous to make the terms mutually exclusive in this rigid manner; for on examining the evidence we find that in innumerable cases the two formations overlap, as it were, and combine in all kinds of compromises suggested by utility . . .

Vinogradoff also emphasized the powerful influence, in the latter part of the nineteenth century, exercised by the new doctrine of a universal priority of 'mother-right', and the confusion it introduced into the study of Teutonic kinship. Its main protagonist, L. von Dargun,[36] adapted it to Teutonic prehistory. But by that time the new point of view had already led to a re-examination and reinterpretation of Teutonic kinship, a revision of hitherto commonly accepted assumptions, especially by Heusler and Ficker, who in their turn exerted a considerable influence on Maitland. Vinogradoff[37] on Maitland: 'In his analysis of kinship he protests against patriarchal theories, but goes a long way towards accepting matriarchal origins.' A marked 'mother-right' bias may also be detected in Miss Phillpotts's book.

A crucial issue for the question of the survival of the agnatic concept in the Middle Ages is the meaning of the Anglo-Saxon terms *spere-healf* (or *spere-hand*) as opposed to *spinel-healf* and of the corresponding German ones *swertmage* (more recent form *Schwertmagen*) as opposed to *spinelmage* (*Spindelmagen, Spill-magen, Kunkelmagen*) in relation to the distinction between patrilateral and matrilateral kin, in Anglo-Saxon *faedrenmaegas* and *medrenmaegas*, in Norse *foedhurfraendr* and *modhurfraendr*, in German *mage von vader* and *mage von muder* (*Vatermagen, Mutter-magen*). Radcliffe-Brown writes:

We have now to ask what use was made of the unilineal principle in the Teutonic systems. A man's kin were divided into those of the

[36] *Mutterrecht und Vaterrecht* (1892).   [37] *Historical Jurisprudence*, p. 149.

spear side (his paternal kin) and those of the spindle side (his maternal kin). In some of the Teutonic systems relatives on the father's side paid or received twice as much as those on the mother's side in a wergild transaction. This was so in the England of King Alfred . . . So far as the Teutonic peoples are concerned this may have been a late development. But in any case this did not mean the recognition of unilineal descent, but only that a father's sister's son was a nearer relative than a mother's sister's son.[38]

Similarly, Maitland (p. 242) writes under the heading 'Spear-kin and spindle-kin': 'It was so in England of Alfred's day; the maternal kinsfolk paid a third of the wer.' Thus he also equates the distinction with that between paternal and maternal kin. Phillpotts (p. 269) speaks of discrimination in favour of agnation in England, apparently referring to a fragment on wergild which she has quoted earlier (p. 224). The same fragment is quoted by Vinogradoff (loc. cit., pp. 312 ff.), who also comments on the 'marked preponderance of the agnatic element'. But the passage quoted by them does not use the word *spere-healf*. Bosworth and Toller in the *Anglo-Saxon Dictionary* explain under *spere-healf* and *spere-hand*: 'the male side or line in speaking of inheritance'; the Oxford Dictionary decides on 'the male line of descent'. As far as Anglo-Saxon evidence goes, it seems to be difficult to find a context in which the word is used unambiguously in the sense of *agnati* and clearly distinguished from that of *faedrenmagas*.

In the Norwegian Frostathing law, analysed by Vinogradoff[39] from the point of view of wergild payment, there is a clear distinction between agnates (*baugamenn, bauggildi*), who take the major share of the wergild, and non-agnates (*nefgildi*), who are relegated to a subordinate position. The term for the agnates is taken from the word *baug*, meaning a bracelet: wergild was paid in *baugar*, or gold bracelets. The *nefgildi* category is divided into the three sub-categories of the victim's own descendants through females but also including his sister's son; the *modherni* or maternal kin; and the *fadherni*, among whom his father's sisters' sons figure

[38] *African Systems*, p. 17.
[39] 'Geschlecht und Verwandtschaft etc.' Cf. above, p. 9 n. 17.

in the first place. All the *nefgildi* enumerated are males; a woman takes *baugar* only if she is a 'baug-woman' (*baugrygr*, the Teutonic counterpart of the Greek ἐπίκληρος), i.e. the brotherless daughter and appointed heiress of the slain man.[40] To avoid any misunderstanding, Vinogradoff is at pains to make it clear that he is not speaking of a society structured on lines of mutually exclusive descent groups. It is the usual medieval society with a pattern of intersecting kindreds (*aett*). But within any such cognatic circle of kin the individual standing in its centre distinguishes between his agnatic and non-agnatic kin, has a special relationship with his personal agnates. In other words, he can trace the outline of kinsmen with whom he would have been in the same descent group if the prehistoric descent group structure had survived.

This, then, means that, contrary to Radcliffe-Brown's view, there existed in medieval Teutonic society a clear recognition of unilineal descent. The German evidence confirms that of the Norwegian law. The sword is the symbol of the male sex, and therefore the *Schwertmagen* are defined, absolutely rigorously, as male kin connected with Ego exclusively through male links, they are not only *agnati* but *agnati masculi*; while Ego's *Spindelmagen*, or non-agnates, include all his female kin as well as male kin connected with him by a female link. A woman has *Schwertmagen*, but herself can be no man's *Schwertmage*. Thus the distinction has nothing to do with that between sides, patrilateral and matrilateral kin. I would venture to suggest that the distinction between *Schwert* and *Spindel* can only be understood as the imprint left by a prehistoric descent group structure on the medieval 'sibship' pattern.

The distinction has survived, at least in northern Germany, during the thirteenth century. It has been analysed, by H. Rosin,[41] on the basis of the *Sachsenspiegel* (c. 1225); Rosin has also traced it in other contemporary and later north German legal records. In the *Ssp. swertmage* and *andere mage* ('other kin'; the expression *spille* occurs only in a few manuscripts) are clearly distinguished from *mage von vader* and *mage von muder*. *Swertmach* is used,

---

[40] See a brief summary of the conclusions in *Historical Jurisprudence*, i. 30.
[41] *Der Begriff der Schwertmagen* (1877).

technically and consistently, in the sense of 'agnate'. One paragraph, saying that the heir of a man's war-gear (*herwede*) can only be an agnate, uses a synonym 'al ut von swerthalven to geboren' ('born to it throughout on the part of the sword'). The Latin translation, more than a hundred years later than the original, renders *swertmach* invariably by *agnatus*, e.g. *senior agnatus, proximus agnatus*, or with such expressions as 'qui ad eam jure agnationis pertinet', 'jure agnationis adhaerere', or with the tautology 'agnatus ex parte gladii'; while a non-agnatic kinsman is 'cognatus id est ex parte fusi seu mulieris'. By contrast, patrilateral and matrilateral kin, *von vader halven, von muder halven*, are translated as *ex parte patris* and *ex parte matris*. However, in the High German law books *Deutschenspiegel* and *Schwabenspiegel*, both from southern Germany and no more than fifty years later than the *Sachsenspiegel*, the two pairs of opposite concepts merge already, *Schwertmagen* now being used synonymously with patrilateral, *Spindelmagen* with matrilateral kin.

Another important point relevant to the question of the survival of the agnatic notion is the position of women in regard to the inheritance of land. As Vinogradoff[42] says, 'In the case of the Teutons the sword side has a natural and marked precedence in all matters concerning defence and ownership of land.' The laws of the post-migration period are at variance on the question of women's ability to inherit land. As far as Anglo-Saxon laws are concerned, there seems to be no direct rule against women holding land. Vinogradoff emphasizes that it was the Church that championed women's rights to the inheritance of land. This would seem to be confirmed by the complaint of the seventh-century Frankish monk Marculf, a compiler of legal decisions (*Formulae Marculfi*), that it is an old but heathenish custom to deny women their share in the inheritance of land: 'Diuturna sed impia consuetudo tenetur ut de terra paterna sorores portionem non habeant.'[43] The same influence shows itself in the *Lex Burgundionum*, which stipulates that a daughter who enters the Church

---

[42] *Historical Jurisprudence*, p. 302; see also pp. 286 ff.; *Growth of the Manor*, pp. 143 f., 248 f.
[43] Fustel de Coulanges, 'Recherches', p. 763 and n. 5.

is to receive the same share of inheritance as a son; whereas otherwise she can only inherit in the absence of a son, presumably as an
'appointed heiress'.

The ancient Teutonic rules seem to have been most faithfully
retained in the Frankish laws (*Lex Salica* and *Lex Ribuarica*) and
in that of the *Thuringians* (*Lex Angliorum et Werinorum, hoc est,
Thuringorum*), the latter as late as the early ninth century. The *Lex
Salica* (title 'De alodis') speaks of a man dying without leaving
sons. The first paragraphs refer to the inheritance of movable
property: if his mother survives him she inherits, if not, a brother
or daughter, etc. The last paragraph lays down that a woman can
never inherit his land, but that it must go to the male sex, his
brother or any kinsman of the male line: 'De terra vero nulla in
muliere hereditas non pertinebit, sed ad virilem sexum qui fratres
fuerint tota terra perteneat.' The passage is not too clear, but
'qui fratres fuerint' is probably to be understood as meaning 'of
the male line'. Many manuscripts write, instead of 'de terra', 'de
terra salica'. This has been explained as referring to the name of
the Salian Franks, and in this sense it must have been understood
by the authors of the fourteenth-century rule of French royal
succession, falsely named the 'Salic law', in harking back to this
passage of the genuine *Lex Salica* which speaks only of succession
to landed property.[44] Another interpretation of the adjective is
that it is derived from a Frankish word *sala* meaning 'house',
'homestead', thus *terra salica* would mean 'the land belonging to
the homestead'. This interpretation seems to receive support
from the *Lex Ribuarica*, the law of the Franks of the middle Rhine,
which excludes females from the *hereditas aviatica*, the inheritance
transmitted from the grandfather, or 'patrimonial inheritance':
'sed cum virilis sexus exstiterit, femina in hereditatem aviaticam
non succedat.'

The law of the Thuringians appears to remain closest to ancient

---

[44] The so-called 'Salic law' laid down the exclusion from royal succession not
only of women but also of their descendants; hence the maxim 'Le Royaume de
France ne tombe point en quenouille'. It seems clear that the lawyers who
derived this constitutional rule from the genuine *Lex Salica* must have understood
the passage as referring to males of the male line. Cf. H. S. Maine, *Dissertations on
Early Law and Custom* (1907 edn.), pp. 143 ff.

custom. The heritage of the deceased passes to the son, not to the daughter. If there is no son, the daughter takes the movable property ('pecunia et mancipia'). The land, however, is to belong to the nearest kinsman of the male line ('ad proximum paternae gencrationis consanguineum') . . . If there is no son nor daughter nor sister nor mother, the nearest kinsman of the male line takes everything, both movable property and the land. To whomsoever passes the inheritance of land, to him must also belong the suit of armour, the duty of avenging a kinsman, and the right to receive the composition ('Ad quemcumque hereditas terrae pervenerit, ad illum vestis bellica, id est lorica, et ultio proximi et solutio leudis debet pertinere') . . . The male line is to succeed down to the fifth generation.[45] However, after the fifth, the daughter may succeed to the whole of the inheritance, both from the father's and the mother's side; and then at last the inheritance may pass over from the spear to the spindle ('Usque ad quintam generationem paterna generatio succedat. Post quintam autem filia ex toto, sive de patris sive de matris parte in hereditatem succedat; et tunc demum hereditas ad fusum a lancea transeat').[46] Incidentally, the passage shows that in the older legal language the 'spear' seems to have been preferred to the 'sword' as the symbol of the male line.

I have already mentioned the late-medieval *Geschlechter* or *slachte* of Dithmarschen, the country along the west coast of Holstein between the mouth of the Elbe and the river Eider. The only reference to them in English known to me is in Bertha Phillpotts's *Kindred and Clan*.[47] In Germany, interest in this unique phenomenon has generated a whole spate of literature, from Neocorus's *Chronik des Landes Dithmarschen* (c. 1600)[48] down to the present day. Among more recent publications, Heinz Stoob's

[45] In the sense of 'begetting', 'procreation'. Rietschel, art. 'Erbfolgeordnung' (in Hoops's *Reallexikon der germanischen Altertumskunde*), §§ 13, 16, 18, assumes that the limit includes agnatic collaterals as remote as fifth cousins. I am not qualified to pronounce on the matter, but it seems clear that a daughter can inherit land only if there is no male claimant within a very wide range of agnatic kin.
[46] Cf. Fustel de Coulanges, 'Recherches', pp. 759 ff.
[47] C.U.P., 1913, pp. 125–34, 270 f. and *passim*.
[48] Ed. F. C. Dahlmann, 2 vols. (Kiel, 1827).

Die dithmarsischen Geschlechterverbände,[49] which summarizes the previous literature, is especially useful.

The Dithmarschers are, historically, a branch of the northern Saxons (Nordalbingi), subjected and Christianized, with the rest of the continental Saxons, by Charlemagne about 800. After the expulsion of the Danes from Holstein (1227), they passed under the nominal suzerainty of the archbishops of Bremen. Actually, they formed a peasant free-state, a confederation of semi-autonomous parishes. They defended their independence successfully against three major incursions, but were finally overthrown by the combined forces of the Danish king and the dukes of Holstein in 1559.

In older documents the descent group is usually designated as *parentela* or *progenies*, its members as *amici*. In the younger Low German sources, e.g. two codifications of the Dithmarschen law from the middle of the fifteenth century, the term *slacht* predominates, while the individual member is called *vrunt* ('friend') or *vedder* ('cousin', but only in the agnatic sense).

The names of the majority of the *slachte* are patronymics, e.g. Woldersmannen, Itzemannen, Bolinghemanni, Billemenni, etc. Their numerical size varied a great deal. The two first named are said to have been especially numerous, able to maintain military units of their own. On the other hand, Neocorus mentions several *slachte* which had dwindled down to a few surviving members. Each had its written statutes and its coat of arms. The *slacht* did not have an individual head; the only recognized internal authority seems to have been a full assembly.

A *slacht* of larger size was subdivided into segments. The primary segment was the *kluft* (the word etymologically related with English 'cleavage'),[50] which also had its written statutes and coat of arms, a modification of that of the *slacht*. Another division was the *temede* (the word said to mean 'offspring') or *brodertemede*. It does not seem to be quite clear whether the word was a synonym of *kluft* or denoted a secondary segment; Stoob assumes that the *kluft*, as a grouping intermediate between *slacht* and *temede*, came

---

[49] Heide in Holstein, 1951, 208 pp.
[50] In Dithmarschen law the word has a different meaning from the same word in Frisian law, which denotes the quarters of a personal kindred.

in only in the later period. Alongside these strictly agnatic bodies, also, the personal kindred was recognized as the *negheste sibblod* ('nearest sib-blood'), within which a 'sword' and 'spindle' side were distinguished. Legally, a man's closest kin were his agnates within this cognatic circle; they were reckoned up to the 'fifth generation'.[51] A man's more remote agnates, beyond this limit, were only fellow members of his *temede*. Generally, the functions and competencies of the *slacht* and its subordinate segments were clearly demarcated.

Slachte were not necessarily, nor even usually, spatially coherent bodies but more often distributed, in local nuclei, over several parishes. Even local groupings narrower than a parish, such as agrarian neighbourhood associations (*Bauerschaften, commarcani*), were not as a rule composed of fellow members of a descent group. However, it seems that dispersal was more characteristic of the later part of the period than of the earlier one, when membership of the descent group and membership of the neighbourhood group seem to have more frequently coincided.

Slachte had political functions in the sense that they concluded alliances among each other and, probably more rarely, also treaties with external powers, e.g. several *slachte* of the southern parishes are known to have settled a dispute over the wrecking of stranded vessels by negotiating, on their own responsibility, a pact of reconciliation with the city of Hamburg in 1316. But on the whole it seems that internal and external politics were rather more the province of the parishes. The *slacht* was very largely a protective organization. One of its main functions, as laid down in its statutes, was mutual aid among its members in cases of economic need, e.g. damage by fire or water, also impoverishment, illness, and death, etc. More important still was legal aid. The duty of a member to serve as helper in corporate oath-taking was explicitly emphasized. In the case of a member being killed by an outsider, the *slacht* was obliged to carry out the blood-feud, but should, however, in the first place try to come to an arrangement by blood-compensation. Wergild payments consisted of two parts, of which one went to the *slacht* as such,

[51] Cf. p. 19 n. 45 above.

while the other went to the victim's sword-kin, the nearest of his agnates. In Dithmarschen non-agnates were completely excluded from any share of wergild, while in all other Germanic laws, contemporary or earlier, they were entitled to varying shares. In inheritance law, non-agnates had a limited claim to chattels, while immovable property could only pass to agnatic heirs. Even after the conquest of their country, in 1560, the Dithmarschers were determined to maintain their agnatic inheritance law, refusing to accept a new law of the duke of Holstein which aimed at an improved position of women in the inheritance of land.

The *slacht* system appears to have been universal in Dithmarschen. A man not belonging to a *slacht* was virtually unprotected in law since he was unable to provide oath-helpers. Immigrant outsiders who wished to settle permanently tried to be admitted to a *slacht* by adoption, as emphasized by Neocorus.[52] Often also entire groups were accepted as a separate segment of a *slacht*, especially in cases where they were the surviving members of a *slacht* that had decreased too much to carry on by itself.

It seems to have been widely accepted that it was the great enterprise of the building of the dykes, supposed to have taken place between 1000 and 1200, which provided the incentive for the formation of the *slacht* system. Phillpotts, who did not believe in previously existing agnatic descent groups, regarded the system as a kind of agnatic freak within a general scenery of cognatic systems, indeed as an agnatization of a previously cognatic grouping necessitated by the task of the dyke-building.[53] One might object that the Frisians and the Netherlanders, too, managed to build and maintain dykes without adopting a similar system for the purpose. Stoob, who does assume the existence of earlier agnatic descent groups, considers the possibility of a reversion from a younger cognatic to an older agnatic system, but rejects it as being without parallel in legal history. His hypothesis is that an old Saxon system of 'stable sibs' survived Christianization, that

---

[52] See Phillpotts, p. 126.
[53] See pp. 270 f.: 'Is it not possible that the work of constructing and maintaining the great dykes . . . would result in an agnatic organization . . . ? For this reason Ditmarschen cannot be adduced to prove the existence of prehistoric agnatic clans . . .'

individual descent groups were, however, too small to cope with the task of dyke-building, which demanded the organization of larger groupings, and that the *slachte* came into being by way of merging pre-existing smaller descent groups.

This raises the question whether the enterprise of the dyke-construction really did have anything to do with the *slacht* system as such, which in any case is only an assumption on the part of both authors. Would it not be more likely that the Dithmarschers constructed their dykes, not *qua* members of their *slachte*, but *qua* members of their local agrarian associations or of their parishes? As another conjecture, the remoteness and relative isolation of the Dithmarschers from the rest of the world, and especially from external political influences, together with the absence of class distinctions and the virtual lack of an internal central authority, causing them to remain more conservative than their neighbours, seem to me to go a long way to provide an explanation of this singular longevity of an agnatic system.

Latin designations used for the descent group in the folk-laws are *genealogia*, *generatio*, and *genus*. A paragraph of the *Lex Alamannorum* (late seventh century) considers the case of two *genealogiae* disputing the landmarks of their respective estates ('Si qua contentio orta fuerit inter duas genealogias de termino terrae earum . . .'). The *Lex Baiuvariorum* (probably eighth century) contains a title 'De genealogiis et earum compositione', but names only the *genealogia* of the duke, which receives four times, and five noble ones entitled to twice the ordinary compensation payable for killing or injuring a member. The *Pactus Alamannorum* (earlier than the *Lex*) speaks of the *heris generationes*, the descent groups of the folk-army. A title of the *Lex Baiuvariorum* enjoins on the defendant in a particular case to swear an oath reinforced by those of twelve oath-helpers (*sacramentales* or *consacramentales*) 'de suo genere'. A defendant in a different kind of case is to swear with the usual twelve oath-helpers 'de leuda sua', a Latinized Germanic word obviously synonymous with *genus*.

A Teutonic term that virtually certainly has the primary meaning of 'descent group' is the Lombardic *fara*. It has of course been the subject of lively controversies. The main dispute took place, eighty years ago, between two philologists, Henning and Koegel.[54] In Henning's view the word represents the common Teutonic verb denoting 'to wander, move, travel' and noun 'a going, journey, voyage' (cf. the primary meanings of Anglo-Saxon *faran* and *faru*). He did not deny that Lombardic or other Teutonic armies had a descent-group structure (indeed that had been specifically emphasized by the emperor Mauricius, who had a great deal of trouble defending the Byzantine exarchate in Italy against the Lombards); what he denied was that the term *fara* meant 'descent group'. Koegel demonstrated on linguistic grounds that the quantity of the first vowel was long (*fāra*), that the word was etymologically different from Teutonic words meaning 'journey' but related to Latin *parere*, 'to bring forth, bear, beget', thus that its intrinsic meaning was 'offspring', 'descendants', and that it often assumed the derivative meaning of 'village' (see further below).

The star witness of this view has always been a passage in Paul the Deacon's *Historia Langobardorum* (eighth century), in which the author, a Lombard himself, relates that after the invasion of Italy King Alboin offered Friuli, a sensitive frontier area, to his nephew Duke Gisulf for settlement and defence. But Gisulf was only ready to accept on condition that the king allowed him to take with him the *faras* of his own choosing. After the word *faras* in the text, there follows a parenthesis, 'hoc est generationes vel lineas'. It is true that Paul wrote two centuries after the invasion, when the old *fara*-grouping had already become a mere memory. But there is also a contemporary Burgundian annalist, Bishop Marius of Aventicum, whose chronicle records, for 569, that in the previous year King Alboin, having left Pannonia with his whole army and people, 'in fara Italiam occupavit'. The addition of 'in fara' suggests that this kind of organization struck the Romanized chronicler as something noteworthy. An article of the *Edictus Rothari*, the first law of the Lombards (*c.* 643), declares that a free man is at liberty to migrate within the kingdom 'cum fara sua' wherever he wishes. In Henning's view, because of the context of a migration, *fara* stands for 'movable property', 'bag and

[54] *Zeitschrift für deutsches Altertum*, N.S. 24 (1892) and 25 (1893).

baggage'; against this Koegel argues that if a free man is at liberty to change his residence it may be taken for granted, need not be explicitly permitted by the law, that he can also take his movable belongings with him; so the words can only mean 'with his offspring'. A passage of the anonymous *Origo gentis Langobardorum,* older than Paul's *Historia,* refers to the dying out of the old dynasty of the Lethingi during the Lombards' brief occupation of Pannonia: King Waccho was succeeded by his son Waltari, a minor, who died, 'farigaidus', i.e. without issue. In documents of the Lombard period in Italy, the word *fara* is translated as *genealogia, generatio, parentela.*

Koegel's interpretation of *fara* as a descent group and at the same time an army unit has been accepted by philologists and historians, e.g. W. Bruckner,[55] L. M. Hartmann,[56] E. Gamillscheg,[57] and has been maintained by the majority of legal historians both before and after Koegel, while Henning's interpretation of 'wandering band' or 'travelling company' still figures in the writings of those who are either sceptical or unaware of the controversy. Bruckner also gives a list of Lombard personal names formed with the word, e.g. Farimundus ('Guardian of the *fara*'), etc. Hartmann and Gamillscheg have collected lists of Italian local names formed with the word, partly still existing, in which the word sometimes appears in a more or less modified form, partly taken from historical records, e.g. Fara Autarena, Fara Livani, Fara filiorum Petri, etc.

As a local name, the word, slightly modified, also appears in northern France, though only in the case of four localities: La Fère and Fère-en-Tardenois (Aisne), Fèrebrianges and Fère-Champenoise (Marne),[58] indicating that, as a term for a kin grouping and settlement unit, it was also familiar to the Franks. In compounds denoting personal and local names, *fara* is also widespread in the formerly Burgundian region of south-eastern France.[59]

[55] *Die Sprache der Langobarden* (1895), pp. 87 and 246 f.
[56] *Geschichte Italiens im Mittelalter* (1900), ii. 1, pp. 43 f., 52 f.
[57] *Romania Germanica* (1935), i. 235; ii. 62 f.
[58] Gamillscheg, i. 102; Auguste Longnon, *Les Noms de lieu de la France* (1920–9), p. 214; Ferdinand Lot, *La Fin du monde antique et le début du Moyen Âge* (2nd edn., 1951), p. 412; id., *Les Invasions germaniques* (1935), p. 203.
[59] Gamillscheg, iii. 55, 115 f.

Gamillscheg, whose *Romania Germanica* is a general investigation into the Teutonic residue left in the vocabularies of the
Romance languages, also states that the word spread, from the
earlier Pannonian seats of the Lombards, throughout the Balkans,
retaining its original meaning of 'descent group' and 'tribe'; he
finds it in the Transylvanian and Aromun dialects of Romanian,
in Albanian, in modern Greek and Bulgarian.[60] Unfortunately,
he does not give chapter and verse. In literary modern Greek
phara has a pejorative meaning, roughly corresponding to 'mob'.
However, confirmation of Gamillscheg's assertion, at least for
one area, comes from an unexpected source, viz. C. Fauriel's
Chants populaires de la Grèce moderne.[61] A series of war-songs in
his collection deals with the Souliotes, their exploits against the
Turks and eventual defeat and destruction in the early nineteenth
century. Fauriel introduces this section with a commentary
drawn mainly from a Greek source, a *History of Souli*, published
in 1815. The name is that of a village in a mountain refuge in
Epirus, the political centre of a total of eleven villages inhabited
by about 5,000 people, who depended for agricultural supplies
on a larger subject population in the plains, the 'Para-Souliotes'.
The free genuine Souliotes were divided into forty-seven *pha-
ras*, each composed of a varying number of families related by
common descent, and led by the head of the oldest or most
respected family; these forty-seven *phara*-heads formed a council
deciding public affairs.

Surely, in the case of the Souliotes, who stayed put in their
mountain fastness, except when raiding the Turks, the word
phara used for an aggregate of related families, is unlikely to be
derived from a word originally meaning 'wandering band' or
'travelling company'.

The facet of the subject on which controversy has been most
rampant is the meaning of the suffix '-ing' in topographical nomen-
clature. The patronymic function of the suffix is common to all
Teutonic languages. From this premiss J. M. Kemble[62] explained
a great many English place-names ending in simple '-ing', which

---

[60] ii. 260 f.   [61] Vol. i (Paris, 1824), pp. 225 ff.
[62] *The Saxons in England* (1849), i, ch. 2, and appendix A.

cluster most densely in the south-eastern counties, and the more widespread ones with compound '-ington', '-ingham', etc., as original settlements of descent groups. His hypothesis was later revised by the Swedish philologist Eilert Ekwall.[63] Place-names in '-ing' also abound in Bavaria and Austria, while in other German-speaking parts they end in '-ingen', clustering most densely in Baden-Württemberg. Localities with such names are generally held to belong to the oldest layer of settlements of the migration period, centuries before written records can be expected. The Bavarian historian S. Rietzler has in several publications[64] advanced the hypothesis that, in the case of demonstrably old villages, this type of name indicates original occupation by locally coherent descent groups known by distinct patronymics. Thus this hypothesis is essentially similar to Kemble's. In my view the conjecture of a whole named descent group occupying and sharing out a particular area would seem to be unnecessary; it would be sufficient to assume a single first occupant whose personal name is perpetuated, as a patronymic, by his descendants.

In northern France, Lorraine, and Burgundy, as well as in adjoining French-speaking parts, place-names with modified forms of the '-ing' suffix, varying regionally, are found in considerable numbers. The suffix is used, according to Ferdinand Lot, 'pour désigner la collectivité formée autour d'un chef par sa famille, sa descendance, ses gens . . . puis la localité habitée par cette collectivité.'[65]

This kind of interpretation received a heavy damper (according to Phillpotts, p. 244, 'its death-blow') from the philologist Friedrich Kluge.[66] He made the following points: (1) Patronymics with the '-ing' suffix are historically confined to aristocratic descent groups and especially ruling dynasties, e.g. Merovingi, Carolingi, the Bavarian Agilolfingi, the Lombardic Lethingi, etc., the

[63] *English Place-names in -ing* (Lund, 1923), esp. pp. 113 ff., 119, 121 ff.
[64] *Oberbayerisches Archiv* (1887); *Sitzungsberichte der Bairischen Akademie der Wissenschaften*, Phil.-hist. Klasse (1909 and 1920).
[65] *Les Invasions germaniques*, p. 204; see also pp. 176, 178, 200, 206, 219; id., *La Fin du monde antique*, p. 412; Longnon, pp. 197 ff., 205 f., 217 ff.; Gamillscheg, i. 63, 65 f., 70, 77; iii. 6, 31, 41, 180 f.
[66] 'Sippensiedelungen und Sippennamen', *Vierteljahrsschrift für Sozial- und Wirtschaftsgeschichte*, 6 (1908).

Anglo-Saxon Waegmundingas, Hrethlingas, etc., though this restriction does not apply to Old Norse patronymics of the type.
There is no evidence that in the period of migrations every free
Teuton belonged to a descent group with a distinctive name of its
own. (This argument is not quite conclusive, Ekwall points out,
as the custom of using such patronymics might have existed in
the migration period, but have been given up before the time of
written records, except in the case of royal and aristocratic
lineages.) (2) Among the swarms of local names in '-ing' and
'-ingen', there is only a small minority with a recognizable
Teutonic name, such as, e.g., Leoprechting, Sigmaringen, etc.
(3) The '-ing' suffix is not confined to the formation of patronymics, but is used for any kind of relation. It may be used for the
inhabitants of a country or town, the subjects of a ruler, etc. There
is no way of knowing whether a local name such as 'Sigmaringen'
refers to Sigmar's descendants or generally to his people, his
dependants, and in the case of other place-names of the type the
suffix may also refer to some natural feature or other peculiarity.

Obviously the suffix does not serve as a patronymic in names
such as Pfäffingen (referring to clerics, more specifically monks,
thus denoting a monastic estate), Bischoffingen (in a record of
c. 1000 'Piscofinga'), or Opolding (in the tenth century 'Abbat-
inga'), etc.

Kluge's strictures have been taken up by the more recent
students of place-names. According to Ernst Schwarz,[67] it is possible, in individual cases, to interpret the suffix as a patronymic,
but the over-all probability is that its meaning is 'people or
dependants of *X*'. It is likely that marked differences of wealth
and rank existed already in the period of invasions; there were
leaders and followers. It was apparently not the free-mark
association of equals sharing out a plot of land as every member's
absolute property. It is more likely that the main agents in the
annexation and allocation of land were the leaders, who became
the great landowners, apportioning parcels to their followers as
tenants. Thus this would be an early form of manorialism. The

---

[67] *Deutsche Namenforschung* (1950), ii, *Orts- und Flurnamen*, pp. 126 ff., 135,
137 ff., 141 ff.

place-name would refer to the owner of a domanial farm surrounded by dependent holdings.

To the unwary, this is a field strewn with pitfalls. It is a large area of historical interest, at least in Germany, studied by a number of medievalists specializing in this particular branch of research, with their own more or less specialized periodicals.[68] I am afraid I am not equipped to compete in this league.

None the less, even though this last argument may be deemed to be of doubtful value, I am sure that the various points brought together in this essay, though some of them are only salvaged from scraps of historical evidence, will add up to something more substantial than a mere mirage of a patrilineal descent system in prehistoric Teutonic society.

[68] e.g. *Zeitschrift für Ortsnamenforschung*, since 1925.

2

Tonya: A Lakeside Settlement in Bunyoro

J. H. M. BEATTIE

I F modern social anthropologists were asked to single out the most influential of Professor Evans-Pritchard's numerous important contributions to the subject, many would select his great study *The Nuer*, in which a segmentary socio-political system, articulated in terms of unilineal descent through men, was first fully described and analysed from first-hand field observation. Certainly his and Meyer Fortes's work impressed on me, as a graduate student in Oxford in 1950, the importance in many African societies of the principle of unilineal descent. When I went to Bunyoro in 1951, although I was aware that agnatic lineage organization was unlikely to play as pervasive a part in a politically centralized society like Bunyoro as it would in an 'acephalous' one, I expected it to have some, perhaps considerable, importance. So when I started work in the settlement of Kihoko in southern Bunyoro, I was gratified to hear constant references to clanship (*bunyaruganda*), lineages (*bitabu*), and 'clan heads' (*bakuru b'enganda*), and to a traditional close association between lineage membership and territorial distribution. In former times, I was constantly told, one lineage (*kitabu* or *ruganda*; the latter term was commonly used for both lineage and clan) used to occupy one *mugongo*—*migongo* are the slightly elevated areas of human settlement separated by small, shallow, usually swampy valleys— under the local authority of its head, the *mukuru w'oruganda*.

It may well be that in the past particular *migongo* were occupied by distinct groups of agnates, each constituting a localized lineage, probably shallow in genealogical depth. When pressed, however, Banyoro would agree that even then men of clans other than the occupying one might live on a *mugongo*. A man might live with his mother's people, for example, or, more rarely, with his wife's agnates; or he might take up residence in the area of his blood partner's group: a war captive (*munyagwa*) would live on his captor's *mugongo*. Evidently the matter was one of dominance, not of anything approaching exclusive occupation, and dominance is very much a matter of degree.

But in the 1950s little or nothing approaching even this modified pattern survived in upland Bunyoro (that is, all of Bunyoro to the south-east of the eastern escarpment of the Western Rift Valley). Though many *migongo* were still named after particular clans, usually the eponymous clan was scarcely, sometimes not at all, represented in the settlement named after it. In most settled areas many different clans were fairly evenly represented, and no special primacy attached to any. Thus the forty-one householders in the village of Kihoko between them represented eighteen clans, an average of just over two households per clan. The largest group of householders who were fellow clansmen was eight, and only five of these claimed any genealogical connection with one another. Everywhere the 'clan head' had virtually disappeared, though the term *mukuru w'oruganda* was still occasionally loosely used for the senior of a small group of brothers or half-brothers or, even more generally, for anyone of special eminence in a clan, without regard to any real or presumed genealogical connection with the speaker. Such of the *mukuru w'oruganda*'s traditional functions as still survived were for the most part divided between the lower grade of government chiefs, the *batongole*, and the *nyineka* or household heads. For most practical purposes clan and lineage membership were relatively unimportant.[1]

But when, at the very end of my field-work in Bunyoro, I spent a few weeks in the remote village of Tonya, on the eastern shore of Lake Albert about 25 miles south-west of the port of Butiaba, I found, to my surprise, what I had quite failed to discover elsewhere, a settlement in which lineages were more or less strictly localized, almost segregated, and in which lineage heads still played important roles. In this essay I offer a very brief description of Tonya and its pattern of settlement, and I raise the question

[1] For a fuller account of Nyoro clans and 'clan heads' see Beattie (1957), pp. 321–5.

why it, and to a lesser extent the two or three other lakeside settlements of Banyoro in the Rift Valley, should have differed so markedly in these respects from other Nyoro communities. A certain poignancy attaches to this exercise, as during the late 1950s and early 1960s the level of Lake Albert, like that of the other Great Lakes, rose several feet, and a great part of the village of Tonya was submerged. When I revisited the area by canoe in 1965 it was quite unrecognizable, and Tonya's population of ten years earlier, most of whom had lived there all their lives, was wholly dispersed.

The contrast between upland Bunyoro, with its lush growth of bush and elephant grass, its plantain groves, and its scattered fields of millet and sweet potatoes, and the arid Lake Albert littoral, 2,000 feet lower in altitude, is striking. Rainfall in the Western Rift Valley is minimal, and the only crop that can be grown there, apart from a few straggling fields of cotton, is cassava (*manioc*), which is planted in the sand close to the lake shore. There were no cattle in Tonya, and even goats did not thrive, but there were a few small flocks of scraggy sheep, at first sight hardly distinguishable from goats, and most people kept a few fowls.

The principal occupation of all Tonya men was fishing, with its ancillary activities, net-making (the nets were made from the cords extracted from discarded lorry tyres, and to make a single large net might take several months), and the manufacture and repair of the dug-out canoes which were at that time the normal means of transport by water, though in the late 1950s outboard engines and larger boats were beginning to appear. Lake Albert is rich in fish, and substantial quantities of Nile perch, tilapia, and other species were taken from it by Tonya fishermen. After being salted and dried, these were sold in Butiaba, the roadhead and port 25 miles north-east, and at Mahagi Port in the Congo, about 40 miles across the lake. Many Tonya fishermen made upwards of £50 a year from fishing (about five times the ordinary Munyoro peasant's annual cash income at that time); some made a good deal more. Tonya was quite a wealthy community by Nyoro standards, even by those of Uganda as a whole.

But life in Tonya was arduous, especially for the women. All the necessities of life, except fish and cassava, had to be carried down the steep escarpment, by a rocky and precipitous footpath, from the nearest shop and market at Biseruka, in upland Bunyoro, several miles inland. Most women made the trip, which took the best part of a day, once or twice a week; and it was a common sight to see a group of them, wearing their best and brightest clothes, climbing down the escarpment with huge bundles of millet or flour, bunches of plantains, sometimes pots of plantain wine, on their heads. In comparison with the upland people, who rarely ate meat and never fish, and whose diet was in consequence seriously deficient in protein, the people of Tonya were remarkably healthy and robust. In fact they regarded themselves as quite different from 'the people of the hills' (*b'ensozi*), an attitude which was reciprocated by the uplanders, who believed, not without some justification, that the people of Tonya were specially prone to sorcery. Although most Tonyans asserted that their ancestors had originally come from upland Bunyoro or further afield, they claimed that their immediate forebears had lived in Tonya for two or three generations at least. In fact most effective kinship ties of Tonya residents outside of Tonya itself were with the other, smaller lakeside communities which were scattered at considerable intervals up and down the coast, rather than with 'upland' Nyoro villages some of which were physically very much nearer.

In 1955 Tonya was a compact settlement of about 250 inhabitants, living in some sixty or so homesteads. By 'homestead' I mean an economically independent domestic unit, usually a man with his wife, or wives, and children, but sometimes also including a grandparent or a grown-up brother or sister. So some homesteads consisted of two or more houses. Most were of the rectangular mud-and-wattle type, thatched with grass (which had to be brought from a considerable distance), but there was a sprinkling of the old-fashioned 'beehive' huts, and a small number of larger houses with corrugated-iron roofs. There were a few men living alone during my stay in Tonya, but most of them regarded this as a merely temporary condition. There was a primary school with three standards, run by the Native Anglican Church (derived from the Church Missionary Society), which also had a thatched and very derelict church near the school. The Roman Catholics were not represented. Most Tonyans were nominal Christians, as their names indicated, but traditional Nyoro religious cults continued to flourish in Tonya even more vigorously (and very much less clandestinely) than in most parts of the country.

One of the first things I learned after I arrived in Tonya was that the village was divided into four sections or 'wards', each named after the clan whose members were numerically dominant in it. Further, each section had its head (*mukuru*), a member, not necessarily the most senior, of the dominant clan, and the heir (usually the son) of the former head. The four clans were the Basingo, the Basaigi, the Bango, and the Bahamba, and between them they accounted for just 70 per cent of all the household heads in Tonya. As was noted above, all four clans claimed origins in other parts of the country. Basingo and Bango claimed to have originated in Rugonjo, Ankole, more than 100 miles distant;[2] Basaigi derived their origin from the Congo, on the opposite side of the Lake: only the Bahamba (the smallest group) claimed to be original coastal dwellers, having come comparatively recently from a lake-shore settlement further to the north-east. The physical separateness of Kisingo, Kisaigi, Kingo, and Kihamba can be fairly easily discerned from the air photograph opposite, which was taken about four years after my visit; the divisions are clearly indicated on the accompanying rough sketch-map of Tonya households (Fig. 1). I now give a very brief account of each of the four wards.

I. Kisingo, though scarcely larger than Kisaigi in terms of population, was the most important ward. It owed its dominance

[2] In fact the Bango claimed to have originally been members of the Basingo clan, and to have separated off into a separate *ruganda* only when they first approached the lake. They explain the separation by reference to a dispute between two Basingo brothers, arising from the fact that the wife of one of them was left behind on the escarpment as, being pregnant, she was unable to descend it. After giving birth alone, she was befriended by a leopard (*ngo*); hence the new clan was called Bango, the leopard people.

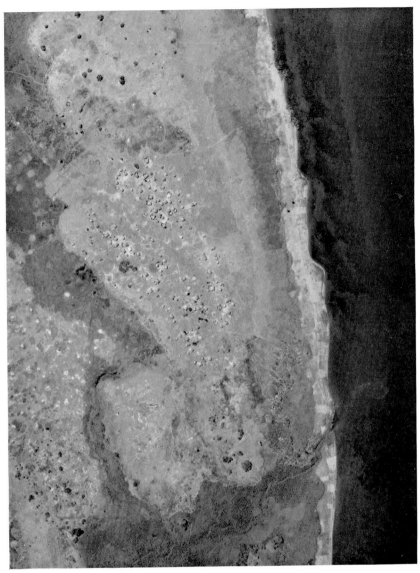

1. Tonya village from the air

partly to the fact that the 'parish chief' (*w'omuruka*, the second-lowest rank of the official chiefs), James Rubanga, was a Musingo. Much of the day-to-day business of local administration was

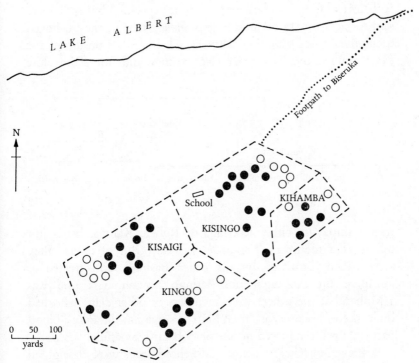

FIG. 1. Sketch-map of Tonya, showing 'wards' and households.
Shaded circles represent households of members of eponymous clan. Separate buildings, several of which may make up a household, are not shown. 'Ward' boundaries are approximations only.

carried out in, and in front of, his house. Also, Kisingo was the first part of Tonya one entered by the footpath along the lake shore, which provided the only route to Biseruka and upland Bunyoro. For most practical purposes James was the local head of the Basingo, but the formal lineage headship was vested in a younger man, Rubeni Kahwa, who had succeeded his father in 1953. Of the seventeen householders in Kisingo nine were members of the Basingo clan. Of these two were patrilateral half-brothers of James Rubanga and one was his married son. Three of the others were full brothers (the youngest of them was Rubeni, the new lineage head); their relationship to James Rubanga's branch of the lineage was not specified but they were said to be of the same 'house' (*kiju kimu*); that is, they believed themselves to be genealogically related, but were unsure of the exact connection. The other two Basingo did not claim close

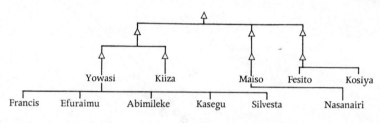

FIG. 2

relationship with either Rubanga or Rubeni Kahwa, being just fellow clan members (*b'oruganda kwonka*). But of course they were called 'brothers' by the other Basingo, and treated as kinsmen. Of the eight non–Basingo householders one was a Muhamba; the others were members of other clans who had built there because of 'friendship' (*bunywani*, literally 'blood partnership'), reinforced in one or two cases by affinal ties.

II. Eleven of Kisaigi's sixteen household heads were Basaigi, all of them members of the same four-generation lineage. The names and relationships of these eleven men are shown in Fig. 2. All of them, with their wives and children, lived in the Kisaigi ward, in the south-west of the village. Yowasi was the head of the Basaigi.

Of the remaining six householders in Kisaigi three represented an outpost of Basingo, one of whom, Kezironi, was married to one of Yowasi's daughters, with whom he was living uxori-locally. Close by lived Kezironi's full brother Yonasani, and a patrilateral half-brother. So a new segment of the Basingo had started to develop in Kisaigi. Another of Yowasi's daughters was also married to a Musingo man, but she was living virilocally in the Kisingo ward. The other three householders were of 'outside' clans.

III. The household heads in Kingo numbered eleven, of whom six were Bango. Five of these were the sons of one or other of two patrilateral half-brothers, Daudi and Paulo, both of them deceased; the sixth was Daudi's grandson. The lineage head, Yofesi, was the late Daudi's second son. Both of Yofesi's wives were Basingo from the Kisingo ward, one of them being the daughter of James Rubanga, the parish chief. Close to Yofesi's house (which was a large one, roofed with corrugated iron) were those of his elder patrilateral half-brother, Zakayo, and his younger half-brother, Ndyanabo. Zakayo, too, had married locally, one of his three wives being a Musingo and the other a Musaigi, both of them from neighbouring wards. Zakayo's married son, Yesi, also lived close by; his wife was a Musaigi. The two surviving sons of the late Paulo, Anderea and Ernesti, lived a little distance away but still within Kingo; Anderea also was married to a Musingo girl. So three of these men, Zakayo, Yofesi, and Anderea, exemplified the nearest the Banyoro have to a 'preferred marriage', for their paternal grandmother had been a Musingo, and Banyoro say that it is a good thing for men to marry their 'grandmothers' (i.e. women of their father's mother's clan) so long as she is not a close relative. For in this way 'the blood has come twice', and a fertile association established with a particular lineage two generations back has been renewed. The agnatic relationships of the Bango household heads are shown in Fig. 3.

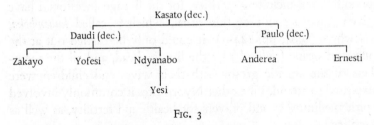

FIG. 3

Of the five non-Bango household heads in Kingo one was a Musaigi and one a Muhamba; the others were of 'outside' clans.

IV. Kihamba, the smallest of Tonya's four wards, contained five Bahamba households and three 'outsiders'. Of the five Bahamba four were sons of the former lineage head, the youngest being the latter's heir. The other Muhamba was not closely related to this group of siblings, though it was said that he was of the same 'house'. The three non-Bahamba householders in this ward comprised one Musingo (but not from Tonya's Kisingo ward), and two members of 'outside' clans.

Before I visited Tonya, I was told rather nostalgically by older Banyoro that in Tonya, differently from other parts of the country, members of the same clan were still 'close together'. Certainly these four descent groups, though they did not form extended lineages on anything approaching the scale of the Nilotic societies to the north of Lake Albert, exemplified to a degree not found anywhere in upland Bunyoro the Nyoro ideal that brothers should 'build together'. It is consistent with this that in Tonya, in contrast to the rest of the country, much stress was placed on the importance of the lineage heads (*bakuru b'ebitebe*, or *bakuru b'enganda*). The four Tonya lineage heads, with the possible exception of the Musingo head, who was overshadowed in practical affairs by his kinsman the parish chief, still wielded considerable influence in day-to-day matters. They settled disputes within their wards, supervised inheritance arrangements and installed heirs, and they received the 'goat of elderhood' (*mbuzi y'obukuru*) on the marriage of a girl of their group. But of at least equal importance in Tonya—though it had quite died out elsewhere—was the lineage head's ceremonial role in performing periodic rites, including sacrifice, for the lineage ancestors. I have given some account of this ritual, which is called *kubembeka*, elsewhere (1964, pp. 144–5); it could only be carried out at the ancestral shrine (*ebikondo*) by the lineage head, and all the members of the agnatic group with their wives and children were expected to attend. Like other Nyoro rites it commonly involved spirit mediumship and prayers for health and fertility, as well as sacrifice.

My data on the marriages of Tonya men are unfortunately very incomplete, but they are sufficient to show that, as one would expect, a considerable proportion of them are with women of neighbouring wards. Three of the four lineage heads had taken their wives from Tonya. Thus Yowasi (Musaigi) had a Muhamba wife, born in Tonya, and an earlier wife, since deceased, had been a Musingo; Yofesi (Mungo) had, as we saw, married two Basingo women; and Rubeni (Muhamba) had married a Mungo girl from the neighbouring ward. Of ten other marriages by Basaigi men about which I have information two had been to local Bango women and four to Bahamba; the other four had been to 'outsiders'. Of seventeen marriages by Bango men, five had been to Basingo, three to Basaigi, and one to a Muhamba girl; that is, just 50 per cent of the total had been to local women. Of the Bahamba, three had married Basaigi women, one each had married a Musingo and a Mungo, and five had married elsewhere; again a 50-per-cent breakdown of an admittedly minute sample. Unfortunately I was unable to obtain comparable information for any of the marriages of Basingo men.

Why did brothers tend to live together in Tonya, as they did also in the few other and smaller lakeside villages, in accordance with the Nyoro ideal, while so conspicuously they rarely and decreasingly did so elsewhere in Bunyoro? We should perhaps ask first of all why Tonyans lived in a compact village. The typical Nyoro residential pattern is one of widely dispersed settlements, each homestead surrounded by its plantain grove and gardens, and some distance from neighbouring households; this is indeed the pattern throughout almost all of the interlacustrine region. At least part of the answer appears to be straightforwardly ecological. In the baked and arid soil of the coastal strip there can be no gardens or plantain groves; virtually the only cultivation consists of small plots of cassava grown in the soft sandy soil by the lake shore. On the slightly higher ground where the houses of Tonya were built nothing grew except a few stunted bushes and, after the brief rains, a light covering of grass which was quickly cropped by sheep. Also, Tonya's main food crop came from the lake, which in the nature of the case lay apart from the homesteads. So there was nothing to prevent people building close to one another if they wanted to, as they evidently did.

There would have been no economic advantage in scattering their homesteads over a wide area, as there was for upland Banyoro, where the fields and gardens upon which the family depended were most conveniently disposed around the homestead. So the lake-shore region, unlike the fertile uplands, lent itself readily to an 'urban', or at least a village, way of life. People could, and did, choose to live in compact settlements, and in accordance with traditional Nyoro values they tended to do so on the basis of agnatic kinship.

It should however be said in conclusion that even in Tonya 'before the Flood' the neat correlation between lineage membership (for men) and residence pattern appeared to have been breaking down, if indeed it had ever existed in the degree generally claimed for it. Before I visited Tonya for the first time, and indeed during my first few days there, I was told firmly and repeatedly that the men of each clan occupied only and exclusively their own quarter of the village; and that 'outsiders' were not permitted to build in it at all, but would have to start their own settlements outside. We have seen that this was very far from being the case. In each of the four wards there were household heads who were not only not members of the clan traditionally associated with that quarter, but who were not even members of any of the other three 'resident' clans. Sometimes their presence was explained by reference to relationships of affinity or matrilateral kinship, but at least as often informants simply said that they lived where they did because they liked it there and got on well with their neighbours. So in Tonya, as elsewhere, ideal and real were at considerable variance, even though it is at least possible that the social organization of their community had changed more in recent years than most of its members realized. But it still preserved, in fact as well as in idea, a very much closer identification of lineage with territory than was to be found anywhere else in the Bunyoro kingdom.

REFERENCES

BEATTIE, J. H. M., 1957, 'Nyoro Kinship', *Africa*, 27 (4), 317–40.
BEATTIE, J. H. M., 1964, 'The Ghost Cult in Bunyoro',*Ethnology*, 3 (2), 127–51.

3

The Indian Village: Myth and Reality[1]

M. N. SRINIVAS

I

SINCE the beginning of the nineteenth century the Indian village has been the subject of discussion by British administrators, scholars in diverse fields, and Indian nationalists. The early administrators' reports, a few of which were included in documents placed before the British Parliament, obtained wide circulation owing to the fortuitous circumstance that two outstanding thinkers of the nineteenth century, Karl Marx and Sir Henry Maine, made use of them in the course of their reconstructions of the early history, if not prehistory, of social institutions the world over. Both the administrators' reports and the writings of Marx and Maine influenced the thinking of Indian nationalists and scholars. The first-hand and intensive studies of villages carried out by social anthropologists since the end of the Second World War have necessarily resulted in a critical appraisal of the earlier views and conceptions. Since some social anthropologists had themselves been influenced, consciously and unconsciously, by the earlier views their critical examination of them may be regarded as an attempt at self-exorcism.

Anthropologists who are active in researching into village India are subjecting to critical examination not only the views of earlier writers but also those of their colleagues. Thus, in 1957, Dumont and Pocock asked the question whether the village was indeed the '*social fact* which it has for so long been assumed to be' (emphasis mine; Dumont and Pocock, 1957, p. 23). Again,

[1] The writing of this paper was made possible by a fellowship at the Center for Advanced Study in the Behavioral Sciences at Stanford. I must thank Miss Miriam Gallaher, Research Assistant at the Center, for editorial help in the preparation of this paper.

'A field worker takes a village as a convenient centre for his investigations and all too easily comes to confer upon that village a kind of sociological reality which it does not possess' (p. 26). They conclude that 'the conception of "village solidarity" which is said to "affirm itself" seems all too often to be a presupposition imposed upon the facts' (p. 27). 'Village solidarity is nothing other than the solidarity of the local section of the dominant caste, and the members of the other castes are loyal not to the village as such but to the dominant caste which wields political and economic power' (pp. 27–9).

In contrast to the village, caste has 'social reality'. The village is only the dwelling-place of diverse and unequal castes.

Inequality, which the first [British] administrators did not stress because they found it natural and inevitable, disappears from the picture for many modern Indians, who assume a 'community' to be an equalitarian institution. In contrast to this widespread mentality are the outright statements of Percival Spear, of O'Malley, and of Srinivas: 'In a joint village, there are two classes of men, one with proprietary rights, and the other without them, power resting exclusively with the former.' (Dumont, 1966, pp. 75–6 n.)

The first influential account of the Indian village appeared in the celebrated *Fifth Report from the Select Committee on the Affairs of the East Indian Cy.* (1812), and Louis Dumont has traced its authorship to one of the great British administrators, Sir Thomas Munro (Dumont, 1966, pp. 70–1). After listing the various village functionaries the *Fifth Report* concluded:

Under this simple form of municipal government, the inhabitants of the country have lived from time immemorial. The boundaries of the village have been but seldom altered; and though the villages themselves have been sometimes injured and even desolated by war, famine and disease, the same name, the same limits, the same interests and even the same families, have continued for ages. The inhabitants gave themselves no trouble about the breaking up and divisions of kingdoms; while the village remains entire, they care not to what power it is transferred or to what sovereign it devolves, its internal economy remains unchanged. (*Fifth Report*, pp. 84–5.)

The above statement represented both an oversimplified and idealized account of the village in pre-British India and with slight alterations it was to be repeated by writer after writer for the next 150 years. The next influential account of the Indian village was in Sir Charles Metcalfe's Minute included in the *Report of the Select Committee of the House of Commons*, 1832 (Vol. iii, Appendix 84, p. 331). Metcalfe revived Munro's characterization of villages as 'little republics' which were 'almost independent of foreign relations'. Instead of the unchanging internal economy of the *Fifth Report*, Metcalfe used the expression, 'having nearly everything that they want within themselves'. (It is surprising to find even Dumont crediting the Indian village with 'economically almost perfect self-sufficiency'.) Finally, the village communities to which their inhabitants had a profound attachment as evidenced by their returning to them after periods of war, famine, and pestilence, were responsible for the preservation of the people of India, their freedom and happiness.

According to Dumont, 'For the observer of things Indian, there is something idyllic and Utopian about them [the descriptions], and a reader of Stokes' admirable book [1959] is tempted to father this idealization on the romantic and paternalist minds of the period: Munro, Elphinstone, Malcolm and Metcalfe' (Dumont, 1966, pp. 68–9). Romantic and paternalist they probably were, but how could they have failed to take note of the grinding poverty, disease, ignorance, misery, and inequalities of day-to-day living in the villages?

Both Marx and Maine made their own contribution to extant oversimplifications and misconceptions about the nature of Indian villages. According to Dumont, 'Although Marx and Maine are poles apart in other respects, they come together retrospectively as the two foremost writers who have drawn the Indian Village Community into the circle of world history. In keeping with contemporary—Victorian—evolutionary ideas and preoccupations, both saw in it a remnant or survival from what Maine called "the infancy of society"' (1966, p. 80). Both saw in nineteenth-century India the past of European society. Yet another point of agreement between the two was their belief in the absence of private ownership of land in India.[2] When pristine communal ownership of land was viewed alongside political autonomy, economic autarky, and vast numbers of people living in tiny republics which lasted while dynasties above them rose and fell, there emerged a picture of a happy pre-colonial past which educated Indians found nostalgic. Pristine communal ownership was interpreted to mean the absence of economic inequalities. The destruction of Indian handicrafts, especially handlooms, for which India was famous in the pre-nineteenth-century world, owing to their inability to compete with goods produced by the British factories and mills, provided a potent case for ending alien rule which had brought in so much misery.

Marx, who was totally preoccupied with economic and social change, found Indian villages singularly resistant to change. He made no attempt to conceal his dislike of them and all that they implied and stood for:

. . . these idyllic village communities . . . had always been the solid foundation of oriental despotism . . . they restrained the human mind within the smallest possible compass, making it the unresisting tool of superstition, enslaving it beneath traditional rules, depriving it of all grandeur and historical energies. We must not forget the barbarian egotism which, concentrating on some miserable patch of land, had quietly witnessed the ruin of empires, the perpetuation of unspeakable cruelties, the massacre of the population of large towns, with no other consideration bestowed upon them than that of natural events, itself the helpless prey of any aggressor who deigned to notice it at all . . .

[2] See in this connection Daniel Thorner's important paper, 'Marx on India and the Asiatic Mode of Production', *Contribution to Indian Sociology*, 9 (1966), 33–6. 'The key to understanding the history of countries like Persia, Turkey and India, he and Engels decided, was the absence of private property in land' (p. 42). 'Without private ownership of land and resulting class antagonism, Asia had never started on the road to development' (p. 43). But Marx seems to have had occasional doubts about the absence of private party in land: 'At other times, Marx was less sure that there had never been private property or at least private possession of land in India. He wrote to Engels that among the English writers on India the question of property was a highly disputed one. In the broken hill country south of the Krishna river, '. . . property in land does seem to have existed . . . In any case it seems to have been the Mohammedans who first established the principle of "no property in land" in Asia as a whole.' In some of the small Indian communities, Marx noted in the same letter, the village lands are cultivated in common. In most cases, however, 'each occupant tills its [*sic*] own field'. 'The waste lands were used for common pasture' (p. 43).

We must not forget that these little communities were contaminated by distinctions of caste and by slavery, that they subjected man to external circumstances instead of elevating man [to be] the sovereign of circumstances, that they transformed a self-developing social State into never-changing natural destiny. (Thorner, 1966, p. 41.)

All this explained the static nature of Indian society and its passivity, and British rule, while exploitative, had set in motion economic forces leading to the welcome destruction of traditional Indian society. Britain was producing 'the only social revolution ever heard of in Asia. [Marx] believed that England had a double mission in India: to annihilate the old Asiatic society and to lay the foundations of a Western society' (Thorner, 1966, p. 42).

According to Marx, the basis of the self-sufficiency of the village was in the 'domestic union of agricultural and manufacturing pursuits'. 'The "peculiar combination of hand-weaving, hand-spinning and hand-tilling agriculture" gives the villages self-sufficiency. The spinning and weaving are done by the wives and daughters' (Thorner, 1966, pp. 38–9). Again, 'the simplicity of the organization for production in these self-sufficing communities' provided the key to the secret of their immutability 'in such striking contrast with the constant dissolution and refounding of Asiatic States, and the never-ceasing changes of dynasty. The structure of the economic elements of society remains untouched by the storm-clouds in the political sky' (Thorner, 1966, p. 57).

Marx also noted the existence of caste and slavery in the context of the village. He referred to the prevalence of a strict division of labour within the village which operated 'with the irresistible authority of a law of nature' (Thorner, 1966, p. 56). But he was not able to weave slavery into his analysis of the village presumably because in his ideal scheme it was a characteristic of a later stage of economic development. It did not really belong there. He just contented himself with mentioning it.

Marx had no kind words for British rule either. He denounced the commercial exploitation of India by the East India Company.

India, the great workshop of cotton manufacture for the world, since immemorial times, became now inundated with English twists and cotton stuffs. After its own produce had been excluded from England, or only admitted on the most cruel terms, British manufactures were poured into it at a small and merely nominal duty, to the ruin of the native cotton fabrics once so celebrated. (Marx, 1853; Avineri, 1969, p. 106.)

Again,

It was the British who broke up the Indian hand-loom and destroyed the spinning-wheel. England began with driving the Indian cottons from the European market; it then introduced twist into Hindustan and in the end inundated the very mother country of cotton with cottons . . . British steam and science uprooted, over the whole surface of Hindustan, the union between agriculture and manufacturing industry. (Marx, 1853; Avineri, 1969, pp. 91–2.)

Marx was strengthening the armoury of the Indian nationalists.

The idea of primitive communism of property was a basic idea of the nineteenth-century evolutionists, and Maine saw in the village communities of North-Western Provinces (later called United Provinces) the prevalence of communal ownership. Generalizing from partial information he declared,

We have so many independent reasons for suspecting that the infancy of law is distinguished by the prevalence of co-ownership, by the intermixture of personal with proprietary rights, and by the confusion of public with private duties, that we should be justified in deducing many important conclusions from our observation of these proprietary brotherhoods, even if no similarly compounded societies could be selected in any other part of the world. (Maine, 1906, pp. 257–8.)

The 'Village Community' is 'known to be of immense antiquity', great stability, and it is 'more than a brotherhood of relatives and more than an association of partners'. 'It is an organized society, and besides providing for the management of the common fund, it seldom fails to provide, by a complete staff of functionaries, for internal government, for police, for the administration of justice, and for the apportionment of taxes and public duties' (Maine, 1906, pp. 252, 256).

After his experience as the Law Member of the Viceroy's Council (1862–9), Maine came to have a slightly better idea of the complexity of Indian villages: 'Even when the village-communities were allowed to be in some sense the proprietors of the land which they tilled, they proved on careful inspection not to be simple groups, composed of several sections, with conflicting and occasionally with irreconcilable claims' (Dumont, 1966, pp. 83–4).

Dumont has criticized Maine for his failure to understand that 'the constitution of the village had to be put in relation to caste on the one hand, and to political power or traditional kingship on the other' (Dumont, 1966, p. 85). Maine did regard villages as forming part of wider kingdoms but Dumont senses a 'contradiction' in the way in which the relation between the two was formulated: 'The contradiction comes up forcibly in another passage [of Maine]: "[the kings] swept away the produce of the labour of the village-communities and carried off the young men to serve in their wars but did not otherwise meddle with the cultivating societies." ' He concedes that 'Maine and other writers with him are probably right in assuming that kings did not interfere with the principles on which the villages were constituted, and one must distinguish between material or factual interdependence and juridical or moral intervention'. Since 'all over the country the villagers agreed to deliver to the king a substantial part of the produce' they did recognize their dependence on him. And Dumont concludes, 'Such a high degree of factual dependence cannot but be reflected, occasionally at any rate, in the constitution of the village and even in the ideology of its members' (Dumont, 1966, pp. 87–8).

In Section II, I shall be considering the question of the relation between the king or other higher political entity and the villages, and for the present I merely note that both Marx and Maine lent the weight of their authority to such misconceptions as economic autarky and political autonomy of the Indian village. Since both also thought that communal ownership of land was the pristine practice in Indian villages, it followed from this that villages were equalitarian communities. Though both mentioned caste, they do not seem to have understood how the institution worked or its implications for communal ownership.

The last quarter of the nineteenth century saw an upsurge in nationalist sentiment in India and it is understandable that Indian writers viewed the political and economic changes brought about by British rule from a nationalist angle. The economic exploitation of India, the continuous drain of wealth from India to Britain, the ruin of Indian handicrafts, and the consequent impoverishment of the peasantry became familiar themes with them.[3]

The general result of the nationalist interpretation of Indian economic history has recently been summed up by Mrs. Dharma Kumar in the following terms:

British rule, and the flooding of India with foreign manufactures, destroyed domestic industries, and so drove the artisan on to the land. The British introduced in certain areas a system under which land revenue was assessed at high rates and was payable in cash, and which held individuals responsible for payments. This led to the destruction of the old village communities. The British brought about changes in the law which made it possible to sell land; it went either to the State for non-payment of taxes, or to the money-lender for non-payment of debt. This turned the peasant into a landless labourer. Supporters of this theory concede that there were some landless labourers before the British took power, but their numbers, so it is held, were insignificant. (Kumar, 1965, p. 188.)[4]

Gandhi, who placed the peasantry in the forefront of the national consciousness by his political campaigns on their behalf in Champaran (Bihar) and Khaira (Gujarat) districts,[5] felt the need to do something immediately to lessen their poverty and misery. He urged Indians to use hand-spun and hand-woven cloth and converted its wearing into a national cult. It was part of his *swadeshi* movement and it included the boycott of foreign, especially British, goods. The *swadeshi* movement was a powerful weapon in the hands of a subject people who yearned for their freedom.

Certain elements in Gandhi's world-view made him a strong advocate of the village as against the State and the big city: he

---

[3] See for instance R. C. Dutt, *Economic History of British India under Early British Rule* (London, 1908), pp. 398–420.

[4] However, even during the British Period there were economists such as D. R. Gadgil who took a different view. See his *The Industrial Evolution of India in Recent Times* (O.U.P., London, 1948), pp. 36–42, and 140–1.

[5] See R. I. Crane, 'The Leadership of the Congress Party', in *Leadership and Political Institutions in India*, ed. R. L. Park and I. Tinker (Greenwood Press, 969), pp. 179–80.

was a philosophical anarchist[6] influenced by Ruskin, Tolstoy, and Thoreau. He had a deep suspicion of the power of the State, a hatred of the enslaving machine, and unlike most educated Indians was a staunch believer in the necessity of manual labour for everyone. He was also in the tradition of genuine spirituality, practising and preaching plain living and high thinking.

Gandhi's programme of rural reconstruction involved the revival of handicrafts and *panchayats*, and the removal of untouchability. He wanted *panchayats* to arrive at decisions on the basis of consensus, as he was convinced that ordinary democratic processes resulted in the suppression of minority views and interests.

To sum up: The erroneous, idealized, and oversimplified view of the Indian village first propounded by the early British administrators was later cast into the framework of universal history by Marx and Maine. Both of them, Maine more unqualifiedly than Marx, believed in the antecedence of communal ownership over the institution of private property, and Maine actually claimed to have discovered its existence in villages of the North-Western Provinces. It may be noted, in passing, that the theory of the primitive communism of property was popular with nineteenth-century Europeans who saw it everywhere around them. As against this, Marx supported, at least before he came upon Morgan's *Ancient Society*, the theory of the (east) Indian origin of communism in property:

A ridiculous presumption has latterly got abroad that common property in its primitive form is specifically a Slavonian, or even exclusively

---

6 See Geoffrey Ashe, *Gandhi* (New York, 1968). 'He moved toward the view that the State is evil, being coercive in its essence, an organ of privilege. Why should Indians be free from the vices of other rulers? *Better than any existing State would be a cooperative federation of village republics*' (pp. 242–3; emphasis mine). See also Gandhi's *Hind Swaraj* (Ahmedabad, 1944): 'I am not aiming at destroying railways or hospitals, though I would certainly welcome their natural destruction. Neither railways nor hospitals are a test of a high and pure civilization. At best they are a necessary evil. Neither adds one inch to the moral stature of a nation. Nor am I aiming at a permanent destruction of law courts, much as I regard it as a "consummation devoutly to be wished". Still less am I trying to destroy all machinery and mills. It requires a higher simplicity and renunciation than the people are today prepared for.' From the introduction ('A Word of Explanation') to the 1921 edition, pp. xi–xii.

Russian form. It is the primitive form that we can prove to have existed among Romans, Teutons, and Celts, and even to this day we find numerous examples, ruins though they be, in India. A more exhaustive study of the Asiatic, and especially of the Indian forms of common property, would show how from the different forms of primitive common property, different forms of its dissolution have developed. Thus, for instance, the various original types of Roman and Teutonic property are deducible from different forms of Indian common property.[7]

The communal ownership of land certainly has equalitarian implications. Marx loathed the Indian village and the kind of life which was possible in it, and he regarded its disappearance, as a result of the economic forces and technology introduced by the British, as both necessary and inevitable. It is therefore surprising to find a few Indian Marxists such as A. R. Desai presenting what Mrs. Dharma Kumar has aptly called 'Golden Age' descriptions of the Indian village (Kumar, 1965, p. 187). But against this there have been many others, Marxists and non-Marxists, who have refused to subscribe to the equality thesis.[8] Indian social anthropologists and sociologists who have carried out field studies of villages since Independence have certainly emphasized the existence of caste and other inequalities. In fact, there is a feeling among their colleagues in economics, political science, and history that they have paid too much attention to caste. In view of this it is surprising indeed to find Dumont writing that many modern Indians assume a community to be an equalitarian institution.

I shall consider in the next two Sections the concept of the self-sufficiency of the Indian village, first in the political and then in the economic sense. After that I shall take up the question whether the Indian village is a community or just an architectural and demographic entity.

---

[7] As quoted in Thorner, 1966, p. 51.

[8] See, for instance, *The Indian Rural Problem*, M. B. Nanavati and J. J. Anjaria (Bombay, 1944), pp. 74–5. See also the monographs on rural life in Gujarat and Maharashtra published in the 1940s by economists and sociologists in the Departments of Economics and Sociology of Bombay University.

II

Notwithstanding the frequency with which the term 'little republics' was used, neither the British administrators nor Marx or Maine regarded villages as self-governing in the full political sense. Such criticism as has to be directed against them pertains only to the manner in which they formulated the relationship between villages and the wider, inclusive political system.

It is, however, possible formally to acknowledge the existence of the State while ignoring it in actual discussions of the village community. Thus, while the fact of the payment of taxes by the village to the State finds mention generally, it is stated that but for this payment villages are autonomous.

To state, as many moderns have done, that 'apart from' this remittance villages were independent and the villagers the owners of the land, will not do. . . . [Elphinstone] went to the crux of the matter when he wrote: 'though under a settled government, it [the village] is entirely subject to the head of the State, yet in many respects it is an organized Commonwealth' (*History*, p. 68). The idealization begins when dependence on the State is forgotten, and the village is considered as a 'republic' in *all* respects. (Dumont, 1966, p. 74.)

It seems unlikely that villagers were entirely indifferent to the fate of the kingdom of which they were a part. They would have had a natural preference for a 'good' king and a distaste for a 'bad' one judged by such criteria as the share of the crop he collected by way of tax, and the effectiveness of the protection he offered them against robbers, marauding troops, etc. Apart from this, the fact that occasionally the king or chieftain hailed from a locally dominant caste resulted in his caste fellows in various villages in the kingdom rallying to his aid in a crisis. In medieval Gujarat, for instance, local Rajput chieftains and their allies, the Koli chieftains, fought, for a period of 400 years, the Muslim conquerors who had displaced the Rajput king of Gujarat (Srinivas and Shah, 1960, p. 1377).

The administrators also highlighted the great ability of the

village communities to survive temporary disaster, but this again
was an exaggeration as Baden-Powell pointed out:

As to the villages being unchangeable, their constitution and form has
shown a progressive tendency to decay, and if it had not been for
modern land-revenue systems trying to keep it together, it may well
be doubted whether it would have survived at all. No doubt there
are cases in which villages have been re-established by the descendants
of a former body driven out by disaster . . . but the invitation of the
ruler has much to do with the return: he desires to re-establish deserted
estates for the sake of his revenue; and old landholders are the best;
while an old headman family has an obvious capacity for inducing
cultivators to restore the village. When villages are refounded, it is
however just as often by totally different people. (Baden-Powell, i
(1892), 171–2.)

While one must conclude that there was a tendency to exagger-
ate the quantum of autonomy as well as the stability of the
villages, the early writers were only trying to characterize a situation in which the lowest level of the political system, viz. the
village, enjoyed a considerable measure of autonomy as well as
discreteness from the higher levels. It was also far more stable
than units at the higher levels. The latest scholar to comment on
this phenomenon is Frykenberg. His remarks on Guntur District
in Andhra Pradesh during the period 1788–1848 hold good for
other regions and periods as well:

Villages survived forces and innovations of central authority. Institutions above the villages were seemingly much less durable. Struggles
for village and district positions took place whenever a new regime
sought to enforce its authority; but power at high levels was much
more transient and its danger passed away. Perpetual strife, counter-
marching armies, and rapid rising and falling of fortunes are said to
have occurred as each king tried to spread the umbrella of his authority
over the plains. (Frykenberg, 1965, p. 14.)

One aspect of the relationship between the state and the village
which writers have generally commented upon is the former's
'extractive' role. According to Marx, the 'structure of government in Asia had consisted from time immemorial in only three
departments: that of Finance, or the plunder of the interior; that

of War, or the plunder of the exterior; and finally, the department of Public Works [for irrigation]' (Thorner, 1966, p. 40). Maine held a similar view (see p. 46 above).

Maine commented upon a further characteristic of the State in the British period: the State, '. . . with few doubtful exceptions, neither legislated nor centralized. The village communities were left to modify themselves separately in their own way' (Thorner, 1951, pp. 72–3).

O'Malley fills in some details on the relation between the pre-British king and the villages:

Except for the collection of land revenue there was little state control of the villages. The activities of the state did not go further than the primary functions of defence against external enemies, the prevention of internal rebellion, and the maintenance of law and order. The administrative machinery can scarcely be said to have extended to the villages . . . The only contact with the villages was by means of local officials having their headquarters in the towns, who were responsible for patrolling of the main routes, the suppression of organized crime, and the realization of the land revenue. So long as it was paid, and so long as there was no disturbance of the peace endangering the general security or outbreaks of crime preventing the safe passage of travellers and merchandise, the villagers were left to manage their own affairs, with headmen and councils of elders to try their petty cases and village watchmen to prevent petty crimes. (O'Malley, 1941, p. 12.)

While Maine and O'Malley were stating an important truth, we shall see later that the relationship between the king and his subjects was more complicated, and that the traditional king performed certain other duties as well. However, this is not to deny that British rule altered fundamentally the relationship between the rulers and the ruled.

The kind of relationship between the State and the village described above had its roots in primitive technology and the related phenomena of absence of roads and poor communications. In the first half of the nineteenth century, according to Gadgil, 'In most parts of the country roads as such did not exist, and where they did exist their condition was very unsatisfactory' (1948, pp. 3–4). There was an almost complete absence of roads in the Madras Presidency at the beginning of the nineteenth century. According to the Public Works Commissioners appointed by the Madras government,

... nearly the whole of the made roads (so called) are only so far made as to be just practicable for carts. They admit of carts moving in dry weather with light loads at a very slow pace and by very short stages. But by far the greater portion of these roads are unbridged and a heavy shower cuts off the communications wherever the stream crosses a line, and they are in many cases so unfit to stand the effects of the wheels while the surface is wet, that in the monsoon months they are out of use except for cattle or foot passengers. (Gadgil, 1948, pp. 3–4.)

Not until British rule was there an attempt to cover the country with a network of roads but their efforts were confined, more or less, to connecting the main towns. Inter-village communication improved, if at all, only incidentally. Only since 1947 has attention begun to be paid to rural roads. But the situation continues to be extremely unsatisfactory. According to J. M. Healey,

India has the lowest mileage of road per cultivated acre in the world. Large areas have no access to roads at all. Only 11 per cent of the 645,000 villages are connected by all-weather roads. One out of three villages is more than five miles from a dependable road connection. The isolation of many villages impedes the spread of new attitudes and techniques as well as movements of physical goods. (Healey, 1968, p. 168.)

Any portrayal of villages as helpless entities in their relationship with rulers in pre-British India would not be correct. There is here a need to emphasize the distinction between regular or continuing relationships between the village and the state, and individual instances of contact. In the latter situation, any cruelty or injustice could have been practised, whereas in the former there were several constraints on the king's power. I have already mentioned how geography and primitive technology favoured a measure of village autonomy. This was reinforced by the character of the pre-British political system. Any king who wanted to sit on his throne for a period of time had to win, in some measure, the support and goodwill of his subjects living in the villages of his kingdom. Otherwise he was inviting them to be disloyal to him during crises, which were only too frequent. Troops could certainly be sent to make an example of disloyal villagers but such a measure, one suspects, was resorted to only in an extremity. And, apart from other constraints, the king could not always take for granted the loyalty of his troops. Percival Spear writes of villages in the Delhi region during the last days of Mughal rule:

They [the landowners] acted as the representatives of the body of proprietors, and in the name of the rest of the village. They had first to fix the assessment with the government officials. This in itself required all the qualities of the diplomatist, the statesman and the soldier. If the Government was short of troops and they put on a bold front they might escape payment altogether. By judicious management, such as presents to soldiers mutinous through arrears of pay, they might turn the troops against their commanders, and even receive money for ransoms instead of paying up. If this was not possible they could retire behind their mud walls and defy the officers, hoping that the rains would break, that a party of marauding Sikhs would gallop up or that the troops might be called away before they had time to bring up the artillery. But they must not resist too long and allow the village to be stormed, when all would be lost in the general plunder. (Spear, 1951, p. 123.)

Villages paid some attention to their defence, and in the Delhi region villages of any size surrounded themselves with a mud wall, and had even watch-towers to protect their walls. Neighbouring villages came together to protect themselves against external attack (Spear, 1951, pp. 125–6). Generally, in most parts of India, the dominant peasant castes seem to have provided the pool from which chieftains were recruited, and some chieftains such as Shivaji even graduated to kinghood. An important criterion of dominance was the ability to field a certain number of men for a fight. Violence was an integral element in the tradition of the dominant castes, and the political conditions of pre-British India provided ample opportunities for violence. Further, the successful exercise of violence often resulted in a caste, or a section of it, being able to claim Kshatriya status.

It was the establishment of the *Pax Britannica* that effectively clipped the wings of the leaders of the dominant peasant castes. But even after a century of British rule many a peasant leader continued to have the attitude and outlook of a chieftain of yore. N. Rama Rao, during his lifetime a distinguished official of Mysore State, has presented the portrait of such a leader in his enthralling book of memoirs, *Kelavu Nenapugaḷu* (Rama Rao, 1954, pp. 149–50). Even today in Mysore it is not uncommon to refer to a powerful and autocratic village leader as a *pāḷegār*, a term referring to a chieftain of a group of villages.

Collective flight was another sanction available to villagers against oppression. The sanction was rendered more potent by the fact that labour was scarce in pre-British India while land was relatively abundant. There was also the likelihood that the flight of people in one village would have repercussions elsewhere, given the bonds of kindred and caste which frequently cut across villages. According to the Thorners,

so long as the peasants turned over to the local potentate his customary tribute and rendered him the usual services, their right to till the soil and reap its fruits was taken for granted. Local rulers who repeatedly abused this right were considered oppressive; if they persisted, the peasantry fled to areas where the customs of the land were better respected. As land was still available for settlement and labour was not too cheap, local chiefs had to be careful lest they alienate the villagers. (Thorner and Thorner, 1965, p. 52.)

Villages then, were, not helpless entities but had considerable resources of their own in dealing with higher political powers. An implicit recognition of this is to be found in the prevalence in pre-British India of a form of government which bore a close resemblance to what Lord Lugard termed 'indirect rule'. Tax-farming was an expression of indirect rule and its popularity was due to the fact that it relieved the king and his administration from preoccupation with the day-to-day problems regarding the villages farmed out. That the system had its dangers, grave ones at that, is not gainsaid. The tax-farmers could—and did—mulct the cultivators, and only a fraction of their collections reached the king. Again, the political system of pre-British India offered temptations if not opportunities for tax-farmers to transform themselves into chiefs. But there were also factors inhibiting their rapacity: the milch cows could run away, putting an end to the milk supply. There was also the likelihood of complaints reaching the king about the inhuman exactions. Punishment was likely to be swift and deterrent in such a case, as the act often provided the king with a chance to regain his popularity with the peasantry. Such punishment also conveyed an unequivocal message to other tax-farming officials.

I am aware that the 'joint' villages of the north have been called 'democratic'—in contrast to the 'severalty' villages elsewhere which have been dubbed 'autocratic'—on the ground that a relationship of equality characterized the representatives of the landowning lineages who formed the village council. The severalty villages, on the other hand, were dominated by the hereditary village headman who wielded enormous power. Leaving aside the fact that the democracy of the 'joint' villages did not include the members of the non-dominant castes, the distinction ignores a fundamental similarity underlying both types of villages, viz. the existence of dominant castes in both joint and severalty villages. This meant that the council of the dominant caste, comprising the elders of the different lineages, was important and even a state-appointed headman could not easily ignore its views.

The point I am making is that kings were willing to let villagers govern themselves in day-to-day matters, and wherever a dominant caste existed, its council, on which the leading landowners were represented, exercised power in local matters. The existence of the dominant caste was of greater importance than the fact that tax was collected either through a single hereditary headman or through a body of co-owners. The council of the dominant caste observed certain rules and principles which operated universally, such as respect for the customs of each caste, respect for the principle of hereditary succession including, in certain contexts, primogeniture, respect for males and elders, and for the authority of the head of a household.

In other words, something akin to 'indirect rule' seems to have

been built into the political and social structure. And yet, para-
doxical as it may seem, the king seems to have performed other
functions and duties besides those of collection of taxes and
conscription of young men during war. (This fact has not been
sufficiently recognized by the earlier writers.) A good king paid
attention to the condition of his people—he built roads, tanks,
ponds, and temples, gave gifts of land to pious and learned
Brahmins.[9] Disputes regarding mutual caste rank were ultimately
settled by him. Such a function was not restricted to Hindu
kings: under the Mughal emperors, the Delhi court was the head
of all caste *panchayats*, and questions affecting a caste over a wide
area could not be settled except at Delhi (Srinivas, 1966, p. 41).

   A good king also paid attention to the development of irrigation, though this is more evident in some parts of the country
than in others. In parts of modern Mysore, Tamil Nadu, and
Andhra Pradesh both canals and tank-systems have played
a significant part in agriculture. According to K. A. Nilakanta
Sastri, doyen among South Indian historians,

the importance of irrigation was well understood from early times;
dams were erected across streams and channels taken off from them
wherever possible. Large tanks were made to serve areas where there
were no natural streams, and the proper maintenance of tanks was
regularly provided for. The extension of agriculture was encouraged
at all times by granting special facilities and tax concessions for specified
periods to people who reclaimed land and brought it under cultivation
for the first time. (Nilakantha Sastry, 1966, p. 328.)

A feature of agriculture in many parts of South India is the
damming up of rain water in suitable places to form artificial lakes
which were constructed in such a way that the overflow water
from each tank fed one below till the excess eventually reached
a stream. Many of these tanks were large indeed, providing
irrigation water for hundreds of acres of land lying on the other
side of the embankment. The maintenance of these tanks was an
important duty of the king's. Irrigation tanks were also found in

   [9] See in this connection T. V. Mahalingam, *South Indian Polity* (University
of Madras, 1955), pp. 26–31; see also R. C. Dutt, 1908, pp. 196 ff.

other parts of the country such as Gujarat, Malwa, and Bundel-khand, though nowhere were they as numerous (O'Malley, 1941, pp. 233–41).

Thorner has, however, argued that '. . . canal networks have never been the outstanding feature of Indian crop production. Rather, Indian agriculture as a whole has always turned on rain-fall and the local wells or ponds of the villages' (Thorner, 1966, p. 40). If Thorner had looked below the all-India level to the regional, he would have found that irrigation, through canal and tank, was an important feature of pre-British agriculture in certain parts of the country. The bigger irrigation projects could not have come into existence without the king's active support and involvement.

The gist of my argument is that the relationship between the king and the village in pre-British India was a complex one. The villages were not without some resources in any continuing relationship between them and the king. The king's functions were not confined to collecting taxes and conscripting young men during war. He had also other duties.

Dumont has argued that Maine and other writers failed to understand the implications of the regular collection by the king of a 'substantial part of the produce'. This meant, in effect, that 'wherever the king delegated his right to one person there was a chance of this beneficiary and his heirs assuming the superior right and reducing its former enjoyers to subordinate status' (Dumont, 1966, p. 88). In other words, the king's power was effective enough to ensure that the rights of individuals who were recognized by him prevailed over other rights.

The payment of a substantial portion of the produce was then also a symbol of the village's dependence on the king. Dumont quotes Maine himself to make the point that Indian villagers exhibit their 'dependency' on the State by the importance they attribute to 'the sanction of the state, be it only in the form of the stamped paper on which an agreement between private parties is written' (Dumont, 1966, p. 88). My own field experience supports this. In 1948, I was surprised to find Rampura villagers frequently mentioning the existence of copper-plate grants listing the privileges, duties, and rank of particular castes. The copper plates were 'somewhere', with someone not available, near by; but what struck me was the fact of their being mentioned.

III

The myth of economic self-sufficiency or autarky of the pre-British village is one that is widely subscribed to, and it has persisted until very recent years. But no one, not even Dumont, has drawn attention to the contradiction between the fact of the subsumption of the village in the wider polity and the notion of its economic self-sufficiency. The former subtracted from self-sufficiency in that the State continually drained away a sizeable share of what was produced and left the village to make do with what was left over. There were also others such as tax-farmers and officials who came in for their share. And this was during times of peace. War not infrequently destroyed, at least temporarily, the economy of the village.[10]

However, it is not surprising that observers of the Indian village have been impressed with its appearance of economic 'self-sufficiency'. The crops provide food and seeds for the next season, taxes to the State, and the means to pay essential artisan and servicing castes such as the carpenter, blacksmith, potter, barber, washerman, and priest. In an economy which is non-monetized or minimally monetized, where poor communications confine the flow of goods and services to a limited area, the wants are few and are such as can be satisfied locally. The appearance of self-sufficiency was enhanced by caste-wise division of labour.

A closer look at the village will, however, reveal several loop-holes in self-sufficiency. Even a basic commodity like salt was not produced in most villages, and many spices also came from outside. Iron, indispensable for ploughs and other agricultural imple-

---

[10] Buchanan, for instance, mentions that a large tract of the country to the north of Tippu's capital of Seringapatam in Mysore had been laid waste at the time of Lord Cornwallis's invasion in 1792: '. . . the people had been forced by Tippu Sultan to leave the open country and retire to the forests where they lived in huts and procured provisions as best they could. A large proportion of them had perished of hunger, and the country was only sparsely populated even in 1800 . . .' (Dutt, 1908, p. 210).

ments, was not available everywhere, and iron-smelting was a localized industry. Sugar-cane was not grown in all villages (Gadgil, 1948, p. 60),[11] and it was the biggest source of jaggery, widely used by the peasantry. Betel leaves and areca nuts, coconuts, tobacco, and lime paste were other peasant wants not always locally met. Silver and gold were essential for wedding jewellery, and they had to be imported from the towns. And not every village had goldsmiths.

Weekly markets are a feature of rural India everywhere and they are a traditional institution. They dramatize the economic interdependence of villages and provide conclusive refutation of the idea of economic self-sufficiency.[12] It is indeed surprising that their existence has been ignored by most writers. The areas serviced by weekly markets seem to have varied from market to market, many having more than a purely local reputation. There seems to have been also a degree of specialization in weekly markets on the basis of the goods sold there.

The periodical fairs held on the occasion of the festival of the local deities or on certain sacred days (e.g. the full moon in Kārtik or Chaitra) were also visited by villagers in large numbers, and the fairs served many purposes, secular as well as religious. In southern Mysore, for instance, the annual fairs held in Chunchanakatte, Hassan, Mudukutore, and Madeshwara hills were well known for the buying and selling of cattle.

The concept of economic self-sufficiency also assumes that every village had living within it all the essential artisan and servicing castes. There can be some argument as to which are the essential castes, but those who have first-hand knowledge of rural India would probably agree that peasants would have a continuing need

[11] After making the usual bow to economic self-sufficiency, Gadgil proceeds to observe, 'There were only two important kinds of agricultural produce which, on account of their nature, could not be grown generally all over India . . . These were cotton and sugarcane. The trade even in these was of a limited extent and the area it covered was also limited.'

[12] Rivett-Carnac's description of a weekly market in Chinmoor in the former Central Provinces has been quoted by Gadgil, 1948, pp. 308–9. The date of the description is 1867–8, 'just after road building had vigorously begun'. Granting that a market such as this would have included fewer articles and attracted fewer persons before vigorous road-building, still its existence provides eloquent evidence of inter-village economic interdependence.

for the services of the carpenter, blacksmith, leatherworker, potter, barber, and washerman. This would mean that every village had to have at least seven castes. This was—and still continues to be—highly unlikely. The number of castes in a village is related to its total population, and according to Karan, 'In the north they [villages] are small with an average population of about 500; in the south they are large with nearly 1000 inhabitants. About one-fourth of all Indian villages have less than 500 inhabitants, another quarter have populations exceeding 2000 and the rest fall in between' (Karan, 1957, p. 56).

Kingsley Davis quotes from a survey, carried out in the early 1930s, by S. S. Nehru, of fifty-four villages in the middle Ganges valley, and Nehru found fifty-two castes inhabiting the area.

Not one of these castes, however, was represented in every village. The Chamars, one of the most pervasive, were found in only 32, and the Ahirs in only 30 villages. 'And yet, *a priori*, the Chamars should be represented in all villages, as they are the commonest type of *razil* population, supply all the labour in the village and are indispensable to village life.' There were Brahmins in 40 per cent of the villages. The Nai, or barber caste, was represented in less than half the villages. The average number of villages in which each caste, taken altogether, was represented was only 9·3.

Davis concludes that

. . . the rural village has by no means a full complement of castes, and that the castes it does have are generally represented by one or two families. The first fact means that each village must depend to some extent upon the services of persons in other villages, and the second that relations between caste members must be maintained by contact between villages. (Davis, 1951, p. 166.)

It is likely that the proportion of smaller villages was greater in pre-British India, for it was during British rule that large irrigation projects were undertaken in different parts of the country. And irrigation enables larger numbers of people to be supported on the same quantum of land through the intensive cultivation of more profitable crops. Irrigation increases the demand for labour and puts more money into the pockets of peasants; the money then becomes translated into new wants to be satisfied by new goods and services.

Individual villages, it is clear, are far from self-sufficient economically. It may be added that socially and religiously, also, villages were anything but self-sufficient. Caste ties stretched across villages, and in a great part of northern India the concept of village exogamy, and the existence of hypergamy on a village basis, constitute an advertisement for inter-village interdependence. The partiality of peasants for pilgrimages and fairs also highlights the fact that the Indian village was always a part of a wider network.

IV

Dumont and Pocock have argued that the Indian village is only an 'architectural and demographic fact' and that field-workers confer upon the 'village a kind of sociological reality which it does not possess'. Further, 'the substantial reality of the village deceives us into doing what we normally would not do in a social analysis and into assuming *a priori* that when people refer to an object by name they mean by that designation what we ourselves mean when we speak of it'. Dumont and Pocock argue that the 'village' has a different meaning for rural Indians: 'Whether a man is speaking of his own village or of another village, unless he positively specifies another caste by name, he is referring to his caste fellows' (1957, p. 26). 'Village solidarity', which many anthropologists, including myself, have reported as a reality is nothing else but a 'presupposition imposed upon the facts' (1957, p. 27). The lower castes do not possess a sense of loyalty to the village. They are clients of powerful patrons from the dominant caste(s), and the obligations of clientship force them to act in ways which are misinterpreted as arising out of 'village solidarity'. Speaking of Rampura in particular, Dumont and Pocock have asserted that 'if the solidarity of the village means anything it is the solidarity of the local group of Okkaliga [dominant caste]' (1957, p. 29). Caste, and occasionally, factional divisions, are so fundamental that they make a local community impossible.

As already mentioned, Dumont is critical of Indian scholars for ignoring the inequality inherent in Indian villages:

Caste is ignored or underplayed throughout, for in the prevalent ideology of the period a 'community' is an equalitarian group. This characteristic gains in importance as the conception spreads, becoming more and more popular. Dominance, and even hierarchy, are not absolutely ignored by all writers, but they do remain on the whole in the background, and the main current of thought sustained by the expression 'village community' goes against their full recognition. Indeed, the question arises whether this is not finally the main function of the expression. (Dumont, 1966, p. 67.)

If Indians have used the term 'community' to ignore inequality, to Dumont Indian villages are not communities because of the inequality of caste. He does not consider at all the question whether unequal groups living in small face-to-face communities can have common interests binding them together. It is assumed implicitly that equalitarianism is indispensable to community formation, and also that such communities are the rule in the Western world, or at least in Western Europe. There is no reference to the existence of economic and social inequalities in Western Europe. The assumption seems to be that when inequalities assume the form of caste they make community impossible.

In order to understand the part played by caste in the local community it is necessary to place caste against the background of the demographic, political, economic, and ideological framework of pre-British India. I shall now briefly list a few significant features of caste in pre-British India. In the first place, caste was generally accepted as well as ubiquitous. The idea of hierarchy, of the division of society into higher and lower hereditary groups was regarded as natural, and caste-like groups were to be found even in sects which rebelled against Hinduism, and among Muslims and Christians.

The demographic situation in pre-British India affected inter-caste relations in significant ways. Kingsley Davis has postulated that India's population remained more or less stationary 'during the two thousand years that intervened between the ancient and the modern period', and that 'the long-run trend would be one of virtual fixity of numbers. No real change could have occurred in this condition until the coming of European control, and then only slowly' (Davis, 1951, p. 24). One result of this demographic stagnation was the relative ease with which land was available for cultivation. According to Spear, reclaimable waste land was 'plentiful in the eighteenth century' in the Delhi region (Spear, 1951, p. 118). Extensive areas were available for cultivation in Madras Presidency at the beginning of the nineteenth century, and this was due to several factors such as the political instability of the preceding decades, high land revenue, and the existence of virgin lands (Kumar, 1965, pp. 107–8).

Maine has commented on the effects of a historical situation in which land was plentiful relative to available labour:

Right down to the last few generations there persisted a singular scarcity of indigenous law pertaining to tenures. Men remained of more value than land, the village communities continued to absorb outsiders in the hope of getting more land tilled and meeting the burden of revenue payments to political potentates, monarchs or emperors. The need for additional cultivators helped preserve a power of elasticity and absorption in the villages and kept them from becoming, with any rapidity, closed corporations. (Thorner, 1951, pp. 73–4.)[13]

The net result was a situation where landowners competed for the services of labourers, the exact opposite of that prevailing today in large and irrigated villages. The highly institutionalized nature of the employer–labourer relationship in pre-British India may well have represented an effort on the part of landowners to assure themselves of a steady source of labour. Such institutionalized relationships were characteristic of the country as a whole and not merely of a part. According to Daniel and Alice Thorner,

like other elements of the Indian agrarian structure, the relation between employers and labourers takes numerous diverse forms. We find in the literature hundreds of indigenous terms, each denoting a particular kind of labour or labourers. Even for a single such word, the

[13] As summarized by Thorner.

terms of employment, duration of the work, amount and form of payment may vary from district to district and village to village. (Thorner and Thorner, 1965, p. 21.)

The existence of institutionalized master–servant relationships not only assured each landowner of a steady source of labour but also helped to minimize competition between landowners for labour which might otherwise have split them into rival factions. There were also other factors which kept down factionalism. The threat to property and life from rapacious chiefs, freebooters, and dacoits and from such natural calamities as flood, famine, and epidemics emphasized the common interest of all villagers in sheer survival. It follows from this that British rule, bringing in law and order, and welfare measures, favoured the development of factionalism and at the expense of the village.

Strong employer–employee bonds provided a countervailing force to caste since generally the employers came from a high or dominant caste while the landless labourers generally came from the lowest strata. Mrs. Dharma Kumar has observed that

one of the most striking and important peculiarities of the Indian forms of servitude is their close connection with the caste system. Most types of servile status were hereditary, and in general the serfs and slaves belonged to the lowest castes. Although this group as a whole was at the bottom of the caste ladder, there were further gradations within it, each sub-group having its articulated rights and liabilities. In fact, the caste system not only confirmed the economic and social disadvantages of the agricultural laborer, but also gave him some rights, some economic, others of a social and ritual nature. (Kumar, 1965, p. 34.)

There is no reason, however, to think that landless labourers were always confined to the lowest castes, and it is likely that one of the results of the great population increase of the last hundred years or more has been the reduction of many individuals from the landowning hierarchy to the lower levels of peasantry. Here, the customary patterns of expenditure prescribed for weddings and funerals, and the hazards to which the subsistence agriculture of poor cultivators are subject, as, for instance, failure of the crops following drought or the death of a plough bullock during the agricultural season, played their part in pushing marginal land-owners down the economic slope. In any case, in rural India today landless labourers hail from a variety of castes, high and low, though it is even now true that the lowest castes generally provide the bulk of such labourers. Quite frequently, poor members from the dominant peasant castes are found serving their richer caste fellows as labourers and servants. It is only the Brahmin who does not substantially contribute to the ranks of landless labourers, this being particularly true of peninsular India.

In short, both political and economic forces in pre-British India converged to put a premium on localism, and to discourage the formation of horizontal bonds stretching across political bound-aries.[14] Movement across political boundaries was difficult for all, and especially for members of the lower castes. Besides, politically ambitious patrons had to keep in view the paramount need to acquire and retain their local followers. They had to be generous with food and drink, especially at weddings and funerals, and provide loans and other help when necessary. Also the fact that it was difficult to store grain or other foodstuffs for long periods in a tropical climate made necessary the distribution of surpluses. The far-sighted leader who gave, or loaned on interest, food-grains to his tenants and labourers earned their goodwill, which could be cashed in on a later occasion. Thus political factors com-bined with the ecological to favour an ethic of distribution which in turn was buttressed by ideas from the great tradition.

The tendency to stress intra-caste solidarity and to forget inter-caste complementarity is to ignore the social framework of agricultural production in pre-British India. Castewise division of labour forced different castes living in a local area to come together in the work of growing and harvesting a crop. Land-owners forged inter-caste ties not only with artisan and servicing castes but also with castes providing agricultural labour. These

---

[14] See in this connection E. Miller's 'Caste and Territory in Malabar', *American Anthropologist*, 56 (1954), 416–17: 'Movements of the military Nayar subcastes were similarly circumscribed by political boundaries. For all lower castes the chiefdom was the limit of social relations within the caste, while their relations with other castes were largely confined to the village' (p. 416).

last-mentioned ties involved daily and close contact between masters from the powerful dominant castes and servants from the Untouchable or other castes just above the pollution line. Again, in the context of a non-monetized or minimally monetized economy, and very little spatial mobility, relationships between households tended to be enduring. Enduringness itself was a value, and hereditary rights and duties acquired ethical overtones.

I have subsumed institutionalized relationships between a landowner and his labourers, and between him and households of artisan and servicing castes, in a single category, viz. patron and client. A characteristic of this relationship was that it became multi-stranded even if it began as a single-stranded one. It was such a strong bond that it attracted to itself a code of norms, and occasionally, the exceptionally loyal client was buried close to his patron's grave.

Thus, given a situation in which labour was scarce in relation to the available land, village society was divided into a series of production pyramids with the landlord at the apex, the artisan and servicing castes in the middle, and the landless labourers at the bottom. Rivalry between patrons was minimized by institutionalized relationships, and by the existence of external threats to the village community as a whole. A politically ambitious patron had to break through institutionalized arrangements if he wanted to achieve power at the higher levels of the political system, which was characterized by fluidity.

In pre-British India, both technological and political factors imposed limitations on the horizontal stretch of castes, while castewise division of labour favoured the co-operation of households from different castes. The relative scarcity of labour and the institutionalization of the master–servant relationship resulted in forging enduring bonds between households of landowners and landless labourers, hailing from different castes. Spear accurately characterizes the situation when he refers to '. . . the classes which, locked by economic, social and religious ties into an intimate interdependence, made up the village community' (Spear, 1951, p. 123). A most significant effect of British rule on the caste system was the increase in the horizontal solidarity of individual castes and the facilitation of their release from the local multi-caste matrix.

V

The members of a dominant caste are in a privileged position *vis-à-vis* the other local castes, and its leaders wield considerable power. These leaders have the greatest stake in the village, have command over resources and, generally, it is they who organize local activity, whether it be a festival, general protest, or fight. They dominate the traditional village council or *panchayat*.

However, the power exercised by the leaders of the dominant caste traditionally has been subject to some of the constraints to which the king's was in pre-British times. The leaders were required to show respect for certain values common to all castes, and for the customs of each caste even when they differed significantly from those of the dominant castes.[15] In addition, each leader of the dominant caste was bound by strong ties to his clients, and it may be assumed that he was not entirely impartial when matters affecting them came up before the council. The village council, then, had to acknowledge the existence of certain rules and principles, and also, of certain checks and balances which came into play when cases concerning non-dominant castes were being arbitrated upon. There was, however, considerable room for manœuvre, and this not unnaturally provided ground for charges of corruption, favouritism, etc., against the members.

The leaders of the dominant caste were expected to protect the interests of the village as a whole and were criticized if they did not. I have described elsewhere an incident which occurred in March 1948 in which the headman of Rampura played a leading part in preventing the government from taking away the villagers' right to fish in their tank (Srinivas, 1955a, p. 25). A petition was dispatched to the government stating that villagers had fished without hindrance from time immemorial, and that the government's sudden decision to set aside this right

[15] See in this connection my 'The Dominant Caste in Rampura', *American Anthropologist*, 61, 1 (1959), 1–16.

by an order was arbitrary. When the government ignored the petition and fixed a date for auctioning fishing rights, word was passed round to everyone, including leaders from neighbouring villages, not to offer bids at the auction. The boycott was successful, and the villagers experienced a sense of triumph.

In the above instance, the lead was certainly taken by the headman and other members of the dominant caste, but the matter affected the entire village, and in particular, the non-vegetarian castes. The idea is implicit that the leaders of the dominant caste have to work for the village as a whole and not for advancing their personal interests. It may be that the idea is more often respected in the breach than in the observance but that is a different issue.

Dumont and Pocock have also argued that 'even when disputes occur between "villages" it would appear from the evidence that these could be more appropriately described as disputes within the Okkaliga caste about land upon which the Okkaliga base their superiority' (1957, p. 29). In the first place, not all disputes between villages refer to land, and this is true of other villages besides Rampura. For instance, a big fight, in which armed police had to be called, occurred between Kere and Bihalli in October 1947 during the annual festival of the deity Madeshwara, and the subject of the dispute was the right to carry the portable icon of the deity in procession round the temple. There was a long queue and the party of Kere youths carrying the icon were asked to hand it over to others after their second trip round the temple. The youths replied that they would do so only after completing the third trip. There is a belief that odd numbers are auspicious while even ones are not. A few Bihalli youths tried to wrest the icon from the Kere youths, and a fight ensued involving injuries to several and premature closure of the festival. The dispute was settled only six months later, and Rampura and Hogur leaders played an important role in the tortuous peace negotiations. While it was true that Okkaligas took the lead in the fight, the fighters were convinced that they were fighting for the honour of their villages.

Even more interesting is the fact that Kathleen Gough has

reported the occurrence, over a period of twenty years, of four instances of fights between the lower castes in Kumbapettai and neighbouring villages. Members of the dominant caste of Brahmins were not involved in any of these fights (Gough, 1955, p. 46). It is surprising that this observation should have escaped Dumont and Pocock. Similarly, referring to the highly factionalized village near Delhi studied by Oscar Lewis, they raise the question, '. . . it would be interesting to see to what extent Oscar Lewis's account of the lack of even this kind of solidarity [of the local dominant caste group] is applicable elsewhere' (Dumont and Pocock, 1957, p. 29). But according to Lewis, even extreme factionalism did not prevent his field-village from acting as a unit on occasion: 'As we have seen earlier, there are occasions when the village acts as a unit. However, these are relatively infrequent and with the weakening of the old and traditional *jajmani* system the segmentation within the village is all the more striking, nor has it been replaced by any new uniting forms of social organization' (Lewis, 1951, p. 32). The ability of a village comprising a large number of castes, and also divided into factions, to function on certain occasions as a unit has impressed many observers. A. C. Mayer, for instance, is able to state, 'This account has shown how it is that a village containing twenty-seven different caste groups, each with its barrier of endogamy and often occupational and commensal restrictions, can nevertheless exist to some extent as a unit' (Mayer, 1960, p. 146).

It is possible for villages to function as units in spite of the various cleavages within them because everyone, irrespective of his caste and other affiliations, has a sense of belonging to a local community which has certain common interests overriding caste, kin, and factional alignments. It is likely that loyalty to the village was greater in the past than now, and future developments may weaken it even further. But the important fact is that it does exist in some measure today. Indian villagers have a complex system of loyalties: in an inter-caste context, identification tends to follow caste lines and this is often reinforced by castewise division of labour. In an intra-caste situation, on the other hand, affiliation follows village lines. This is dramatized in

Rampura, for instance, at weddings in the ritual of the distribution of betel leaves and areca nuts (*doḍḍa veelya*) to the assembled guests. Besides each guest receiving a set of betel leaves and areca nuts in his role as kinsman or casteman, some receive it also as representatives of their respective villages. The credentials of a person to represent his village are not always clear, and a man whose credentials are rejected feels humiliated. A few guests may claim precedence for their villages over the others, and this has often led to a heated debate. In 1948, elderly villagers spoke feelingly about the difficulties and dangers with which ritual betel-distribution was beset. The elders of Rampura had previously passed a rule which enabled anyone who paid Res 8·25 to the village fund to escape the cost and trouble of the formal distribution of betel.[16]

In the foregoing pages I have tried to adduce evidence to show that the village is not only an architectural and demographic entity but also a social entity in that all villagers have some loyalty to it. Rural Indians live in a system of complex loyalties, each loyalty surfacing in a particular context. It is presumable, indeed likely, that there are occasions when there is a conflict of loyalties but that is a different matter. The phenomenon of the dominant caste is indeed impressive, but it is not the whole story.

VI

The exclusion of Harijan castes from access to wells and temples used by the others is occasionally cited in support of the argument that the village does not really include all those living in it. It is relevant to point out in this connection that in traditional India relationships between people took place in an ideological framework that accepted caste. A person was born into a caste which was a unit in a hierarchy of castes, and relations among these were governed by the ideas of pollution and purity. This meant that in actual social life, the highly elaborated and systematized principles of inclusion and exclusion of individuals on the basis of caste came into play. Individuals from a particular caste were included in one context (e.g. living together) and excluded in

[16] See in this connection Srinivas (1955*a*), pp. 32–3.

another (e.g. endogamy), and this applied all along the line. Inclusion and exclusion were also matters of degree—for instance, the social distance between castes in Kerala was traditionally expressed in spatial terms.

The position occupied by a caste in the local hierarchy is not always clear, and a caste's own conception of its position frequently differs from that assigned to it by its structural neighbours.[17] In Rampura, for instance, each caste, including the Harijan, is able to point to another as its inferior. Thus the Harijan Holeyas are able to point to the Smiths as their inferiors, and as 'evidence' of their superiority, to the fact that they do not accept food and drinking-water from Smiths. They would also point to the Smiths being included in the 'Left-hand' castes while they themselves were included among the 'Right-hand' castes. Again, traditionally Smiths were not allowed to perform weddings within the village and were subjected to certain other disabilities. On their side, the Smiths would dismiss the Harijan claim as absurd, and point to their Sanskritized style of life, and to their not accepting food cooked by any except Brahmins and Lingayats as evidence of their high status. This kind of ambiguity regarding the position of several castes was not only a function of the flexibility of the system but also facilitated its acceptance.

I have stated that exclusion was not only contextual but also a matter of degree. An interesting instance of this has bearing on the question of membership of the village. One of the most important temples in Rampura—certainly, architecturally the most striking—is dedicated to the Sanskritic deity, Rāma. While its priest is a Brahmin, the temple is maintained by contributions from the entire village, and the headman's lineage not only has made substantial contributions in the past but also takes an active interest in the temple's activities. It came, therefore, as a surprise to me to find the headman (along with other members of the dominant Okkaligas) refusing to enter the *sanctum sanctorum* (in Kannada, *garbha gudi*) of the temple while he urged Brahmin devotees to stand there while the *puja* was being performed. Had he wanted to enter the *sanctum sanctorum* no one, certainly

[17] See in this connection Srinivas (1962).

not the Brahmin priest, who was heavily dependent upon him, would have prevented him. But the headman chose to remain outside. It did not occur to him that his full participation depended on his being on a par with Brahmin devotees. Given this kind of ideology, it should be clear that the exclusion of the Harijans from the temple cannot be interpreted as meaning exclusion from the village. The same can be said for other instances of exclusion of Harijans. Condemnation of the exclusion of Harijans (or any other caste) from the point of view of a new ethical system is a distinct phenomenon, and as such ought not to be brought in while trying to understand the meaning of exclusion and inclusion in the traditional system.

Again, exclusion has different connotations in different situations. For instance, in Rampura, four groups of villagers, viz. Brahmins, Lingayats, Harijans, and Muslims, are not called upon to make any contribution to the expenses of the Rāma Navami, the great annual nine-day festival at the temple of Rāma. Not only are the Brahmin, Lingayat, and Smith[18] households exempted from making contributions: they also receive the raw ingredients of a meal as their caste rules prevent them from eating food cooked by Peasants. The Lingayat may be regarded as a kind of Brahmin in view of his staunch vegetarianism and teetotalism, and in view of the fact that he acts as priest in two important village temples. In Sanskritic Hinduism, a gift made to a Brahmin confers religious merit on the giver. Not accepting contributions from the Brahmin, and giving him the ingredients of a meal, may be interpreted as conferring merit on those who make the contributions. No such consideration is applicable in the case of the Harijan or Muslim.

Harijans, however, perform many essential services at the festival. The hereditary servants run errands for the organizers, and Harijan women clean the rice and lentils for the ninth-day dinner. Harijan men, beating tom-toms, march at the head of the deity's procession. They also remove the dining-leaves on which the villagers eat the dinner. They are the last to eat.

[18] It appears as though the Smiths have won recognition in Rampura as a high caste. I do not know if this is also true in other villages near by.

Muslims also participate in the procession. In Rampura a fire-works man, invariably a Muslim, follows the Harijans, setting off fireworks. In 1948 one Muslim youth distinguished himself at the procession by a brilliant display of swordsmanship. The fact is that everyone looks forward to the procession with its music, fireworks, display of sword and stick (*lāthi*), fancy dress, and the monkey-god who walks on rooftops peeling green coconuts with his teeth and hands.

The traditional tasks performed by Harijans at village festivals had begun to be regarded by the middle of the twentieth century as degrading symbols of untouchability, and some Harijans attempted to refuse performing them. But the dominant castes used the twin sanctions of economic boycott and physical force to coerce them into conformity.

It is obvious that exclusion and inclusion need to be viewed over the whole range of contexts, religious as well as secular, in understanding the position of a caste. Thus, groups excluded in religious contexts may have important roles in secular contexts. For instance, individual households from the dominant or other high castes often have strong economic ties with households of Harijans. Thus, traditionally, each Harijan household served as 'traditional servant' (*halé maga*) in a peasant or other high-caste household.

This traditional servant had certain well-defined duties and rights in relation to the master and his family. For instance, when a wedding occurred in the master's family, then men of the servant family were required to repair and whitewash the wedding house, put up the marriage *pandal* before it, chop wood to be used as fuel for cooking the wedding feasts, and do odd jobs. The servant was also required to present a pair of leather sandals (*chammāligé*) to the bridegroom. Women of the servant's family were required to clean the grain, grind it to flour on the rotary quern, grind chilies and turmeric, and do several other jobs. In return, the master made presents of money and of cooked food to the servant family. When an ox or buffalo died in the master's family, the servant took it home, skinned it, and ate the meat. He was required, however, to make out of the hide a pair of sandals and a length of plaited rope for presentation to the master. (Srinivas, 1955*b*, p. 27.)

The institution of *jita* or contractual servantship was an important institution in which the servant worked long hours on the master's farm for a stipulated annual fee (Srinivas, 1955b, pp. 27–8). While many Harijans worked as *jita* servants for high-caste, landowning masters, all *jita* servants were not Harijans nor were all Harijans *jita* servants. Traditionally, *jita* servants did a great deal of the hard work on the land and they were indispensable to the economy. The situation described by Spear for the Delhi region in the early nineteenth century highlights the importance of the castes which normally provided the labour on the farm in contrast with the Brahmin priest whose services were symbolic:

Thus the lowly *Chamar*, the cobbler and dresser of unclean leather, received the highest allowance of all, while the priest or Brahmin was given by these hard-headed people the least. He had to make up as best he could by exacting presents on occasions like marriages and deaths when his presence was essential, and by soliciting gifts at festival times, when people were good-tempered and liked to stand well with the gods... The barbers and the water-carriers, two other despised occupations, were also rated highly. (Spear, 1951, p. 121.)

To sum up: In a society where the ideology of caste is fully accepted, and where the principles of exclusion and inclusion apply to everyone including the highest, the exclusion of a caste from particular contexts cannot be adduced as evidence of non-membership of the local community. To do so would be to misinterpret indigenous behaviour.

VII

I have so far looked at village unity or solidarity from the outside, and shall now turn to the villagers' perception of the problem. As it happened, I stumbled on to this while I was carrying out a census of village households in Rampura. From the villagers' point of view two factors seem to be crucial in determining who belonged and who did not: length of stay in the village, and ownership of real property, especially land. If a family had spent two generations in the village, and owned a little land and a house, then their membership had been established beyond question. Surprisingly enough, membership did not seem to have any connection with caste or religion. Exclusion from various activities was not viewed as being relevant to membership: it was something incidental to living in a caste society.

The question of membership in the village came up in the case of three groups, Basket-makers, Swineherds, and Muslims. There were seven Basket-makers in Rampura in 1948, and all of them, men as well as women, lived by making artefacts with bamboo bought in the market in Mysore. They made essential articles such as baskets, fish traps, partition screens, and winnows, and sold many of their products in the weekly markets around Rampura. Unlike the other village artisans they worked strictly for cash. They had the habit of never delivering goods on time, and this and their fondness for liquor had given them a reputation for undependability.

More importantly, all the Basket-makers were immigrants from the near-by town of Malavalli, and every few years a family would pack up and return home and its place would be taken by another. Only one household had spent about twenty years in Rampura. None of the Basket-makers owned any real property—indeed, all of them lived on the verandahs of houses owned by others. Verandah-dwelling (*jagali mēlé wāsa*) symbolized extreme poverty, and it was generally accompanied by the dwellers' doing casual labour (*kooli kamblạ*) for a living.[19]

While the Basket-makers made articles essential for the villagers, they were not regarded as properly belonging to the village. The Swineherds were another marginal group and had settled down in Rampura during the headman's father's days. They spoke among themselves a dialect of Telugu which was unintelligible to the others. During the rainy season they lived in a cluster of huts on the headman's mango orchard, and during the dry season moved to temporary huts erected on the headman's rice land under the C.D.S. canal. Their transhumance was a tribute to the power wielded by the headman's father: it was his way of ensuring that two of his fields were fertilized by pig manure.

[19] In 1948, out of a total population of 1,523, 31 lived on verandas, 14 being widows, 1 a divorcée, and the rest remnants of once fuller households.

The Swineherds had a herd of about sixty pigs, and a boy took them out 'grazing' every day. The pigs were scavengers and the low ritual rank of the Swineherds was due to their association with pigs. They also ate pork and drank toddy. Their women went round the villages begging and telling fortunes.

The Swineherds had regular relations with only the headman's household. They were tenants of the headman, cultivating 2·5 acres of his land. They occasionally borrowed money from him, and sometimes took their disputes to him. The rest of the village did not interact with them except when one of their pigs damaged plants in someone's backyard or field. They seemed to be in the village but not of it.

As a group, neither Swineherds nor Basket-makers were integrated with the village in the way the Harijans were. But Basket-makers, Swineherds, and Smiths all made contributions to the Rāma Navami festival, while Harijans, along with Brahmins, Lingayats, and Muslims, did not.

The Muslims were the third biggest group (179) in Rampura in 1948, and though they were scattered all over the village there was some tendency for them to cluster along the fringes of the high-caste areas. They were engaged in a variety of occupations, agriculture, trade—especially trading in ripe mangoes—and in crafts such as tailoring, tinkering, shoeing bullocks, and plastering. Many of them had migrated into Rampura in the 1940s but there was also a nucleus of earlier immigrants who owned land and houses, and did a little buying and selling of rice on the side. It was when I was carrying out a census among Muslims that I heard villagers use two expressions which I came to realize were significant: the recent immigrants were almost contemptuously described as *nenné monné bandavaru* ('came yesterday or the day before') while the old immigrants were described as *ārsheyinda bandavaru* ('came long ago') or *khadeem kuḷagaḷu* ('old lineages'). Only three households fell into the latter category and all of them owned land.

It was at this point that I realized the crucial importance of ownership of arable land in determining membership in the village. Villagers are acutely aware of the many ways in which land provides bonds with the village, and land once acquired cannot be disposed of easily, for public opinion is against the disposing of such an important and respected asset. Ownership of land enables owners to have enduring relationships with others in the village: they are able to pay the artisan and servicing castes and labourers annually in grain. Such payments are made on a continuing basis. The owners achieve the coveted status of patrons.

In their talks with me, my friends occasionally referred to such-and-such a Brahmin family as belonging to Rampura even though it had left the village two or three decades ago to settle down in Mysore or Bangalore. But the important fact was that they continued to own land in the village, and collected their share of the crop regularly. This kept alive their links with the village. I may add here that during the 1950s I talked to several Brahmin landowners in Mysore and Bangalore and all of them seemed to feel that land was not only economically profitable but also a link with the ancestral village. Selling land was not only improvident but almost implied a lack of piety toward the ancestors who had acquired the land with great hardship.

During the summer of 1952, when I visited the village a second time, a Shepherd sold all his land to settle down in his wife's village. While conflicts among grown brothers are a common feature of the kinship system of many castes, friendly relationships generally obtain between a man and his affines. The buyer of the land, an up-and-coming local Peasant, was represented at the transaction by an over-articulate affine, his wife's sister's husband. As the transaction was about to be concluded the buyer's representative made a pompous speech in which he said that his relative did not want to be accused later of having been responsible for depriving a fellow villager of all his land. The seller should consider whether he should not retain some property in the village, be it even a manure-heap, as a symbol of his belonging to the village.

While land indeed provides the passport to membership, not everyone has the resources to buy it. And in the case of a few artisan and trading castes in Rampura, preoccupation with the hereditary calling seemed to get in the way of acquiring land. Everyone, however, needs a house, and ownership of a house was also evidence of membership. There was a hierarchy in housing, the verandah-dwellers being at the bottom and the owners of large houses with open, paved central courtyards being at the apex. The hut-dwellers were just above the verandah-dwellers in the local prestige scale. The next rung was a house with mud walls and a roof of country-made tiles. Those who owned bullocks and buffaloes tended to live in courtyard houses (*toṭṭi mané*), one part of the inner roofed portion being reserved for cattle. It was the ideal of the villager to live in a house with a big central courtyard, with many bullocks, and milch-buffaloes and cows, and many children, especially sons and grandsons. Such a household indicated that its head owned much land, and his wealth and prosperity were regarded as evidence of divine favour just as verandah-dwelling and poverty embodied the worst fears of villagers.

It is significant that the question of membership of the Harijans in the local community never came up for discussion during my stay. In this part of India, as in several others, the hereditary village servant (*chakra*) came from the Harijan caste, and the holder of the office was traditionally paid in land by the government. In Rampura in 1948 the land allotted to the original *chakra* had been partitioned among his agnatic descendants. These households formed the core of the Harijan group and additions had accrued to this group through the immigration of affines and others from neighbouring villages. The Harijans were no doubt Untouchables by caste, and as such were subjected to several disabilities stemming from the idea of pollution, but there was no doubt that they were an integral part of the village, far more so than, for instance, the Basket-makers.

One way of conceptualizing the situation obtaining in Rampura and other villages would be to regard individuals from the dominant caste as first-class members, the Harijans as third-class members and those in between as second-class members. Though such a conceptualization would be too neat and schematic, and fail to take note of the phenomenon of the 'exclusion' of each caste, including the highest, in certain contexts, it would, on the other hand, make clear the inegalitarian character of the village, the differential rights and duties attached to each category of membership, and the inclusion of everyone from the dominant caste to the Harijan in the local community.

VIII

The historic descriptions of the Indian village, first given by the British administrators early in the nineteenth century, are now seen as having been somewhat idyllic and oversimplified. Yet they have influenced the perceptions and views of generations of scholars. It is only since Independence that a few social scientists, especially social anthropologists who carried out intensive field-studies of villages, have begun critically to examine the conventional representations of the Indian village. It needs hardly be said that this is essential not only to the correct understanding of village structure and life but of the dynamics of traditional society and culture.

What I have shown in the foregoing pages is that the traditional village was far from being economically self-sufficient. Besides, the fact of its being part of a wider political system made it even less self-sufficient: the government claimed a share of the grown crop as tax, and in addition the various officials imposed their own levies on the peasant. During periods of war, able-bodied villagers were likely to be conscripted with the result that yields declined on the farm.

Nevertheless, the village did give an impression of self-sufficiency: the villagers ate what they grew, they paid the artisan and servicing castes in grain, and a system of barter enabled grain to be used for obtaining various goods and services. There was an emphasis in the culture on getting the utmost out of the environment, every twig and leaf and the droppings of domestic animals being put to use. Castewise division of labour also added to the appearance of self-sufficiency. Moreover, the arrangements for internal or municipal government which existed in each village, and its capacity for survival in contrast to higher political entities, created the illusion of political autonomy. An incorrect understanding of the relationship between the king and the village helped to strengthen that illusion.

I have already suggested the reasons for the continuing influence of the views of the early British administrators. Social theorists such as Marx and Maine brought the Indian village into the forefront of the contemporary discussions on the evolution of property and other economic and social institutions. Marx's predominant concern with economic development the world over led him to discuss the phenomenon of the stagnation of Indian society. He perceived the source of the stagnation to be in the isolated and economically self-sufficient character of the village community, with its impressive capacity for survival while the kingdoms which included it rose and fell. Isolation and self-sufficiency went hand in hand with the absorption of the villagers in their own tiny world and their indifference to important events occurring outside. Such villages, he held, made tyranny possible, and the importance of British rule lay in the fact that for the first time in Indian history villages were undergoing fundamental changes as a result of the destruction of their self-sufficiency. Goods made in British factories, especially textiles, were displacing handlooms, and this was leading to the impoverishment of the countryside. The railways were aiding and abetting the factories in transforming village-based Indian society.

Indian nationalists used the argument of the impoverishment of the peasant and destruction of the village community to advance the cause of Indian independence. Beginning in the 1920s, Gandhi's attempt to revive the economic and social life of the village, and certain elements in his thinking such as his distrust of the power of the State, hatred of the enslaving machine, and his emphasis on self-reliance and the need for political and economic decentralization, led to a new idealization of the peasant and the village.

Perhaps it is in reaction to all this that there is now an attempt to deny that the village is a community. It is argued that the existence of caste and other inequalities make it impossible for the Indian village to be a community, for the community, it is assumed, has to be egalitarian.

But the argument that the village in India is only an architectural and demographic entity, and that it is caste that is sociologically real, does not take into account the true function of caste, which has to be viewed in the pre-British context. Given the scarcity of labour in relation to land and the resultant strong patron–client relationships, the social framework of production created bonds running counter to caste. Thus the paradox was that castewise division of labour was at the source of contracaste bonds. This was reinforced by the political system, which discouraged the formation of links across chiefdoms and kingdoms. The village was no doubt stratified along the lines of caste and land, but the productive process made it an interlocking community.

The power wielded by the dominant caste was real but it also respected certain common values, and observed the principle of 'indirect rule' *vis-à-vis* dependent castes. The leaders of the dominant caste had the maximum stake in the local community and they took the lead in all its activities. But the dependent castes also had a loyalty to the village, and were considered by the villagers themselves to have membership in it. Inclusion and exclusion operated (and continue to operate) at all levels of a caste society, and the exclusion of Harijans from certain important activities, areas, and facilities cannot therefore be interpreted as evidence of their not being part of the village community.

Finally, it must be remembered that in pre-British India there was a general acceptance of caste, and of the idiom of caste in governing relationships between individuals and between groups. Given such a framework of acceptance of hierarchy, it ought not to be difficult to conceive of communities which are non-egalitarian, their people playing interdependent roles and all of them having a common interest in survival. The argument that only 'equalitarian' societies can have local communities has to be proved, and cannot be the starting-point for evaluating hierarchical societies. Nor can an implicit assumption that 'equalitarian' communities do not have significant differences in property, income, and status be accepted as a 'sociological reality'.

REFERENCES

ASHE, GEOFFREY, 1968, *Gandhi* (Stein and Day, New York).

AVINERI, S. (ed.), 1969, *Karl Marx on Colonialism and Modernization* (Doubleday, New York).

BADEN-POWELL, B. H., 1892, *Land-Systems of British India*, vol. i (Clarendon Press, Oxford).

—— 1899, *The Origin and Growth of Village Communities in India* (Swann, Sonnenschein & Co., London).

CRANE, R. I., 1969, 'The Leadership of the Congress Party', in R. L. Park and I. Tinker (eds.), *Leadership and Political Institutions in India* (Greenwood Press, New York), pp. 169–87.

DAVIS, KINGSLEY, 1951, *The Population of India and Pakistan* (Princeton University Press, New Jersey).

DUMONT, L., 1966, 'The "Village Community" from Munro to Marx', *Contributions to Indian Sociology*, 9, 67–89.

—— and POCOCK, D. F., 1957, 'Village Studies', *Contributions to Indian Sociology*, 1, 23–42.

DUTT, R. C., 1908, *Economic History of British India under Early British Rule*, (Kegan Paul, Trench, Trübner, & Co., London).

Fifth Report, 1812, *Fifth Report from the Select Committee of the House of Commons on the Affairs of the East India Cy.*, dated 28 July 1812, 3 vols. (vol. 1, pp. 431 ff.).

FRYKENBERG, R. E., 1965, *Guntur District, 1788–1848* (Clarendon Press, Oxford).

GADGIL, D. R., 1948, *The Industrial Evolution of India in Recent Times* (Oxford University Press, London).

GANDHI, M. K., 1944, *Hind Swaraj* (Navjivan Press, Ahmedabad).

GOUGH, KATHLEEN, 1955, 'The Social Structure of a Tanjore Village', in McKim Marriott (ed.), *Village India* (University of Chicago Press, Chicago, and London), pp. 36–52.

HEALEY, J. M., 1968, 'Economic Overheads: Coordination and Pricing', in P. Streeton and M. Lipton (eds.), *The Crisis of Indian Planning* (Oxford University Press, London), pp. 149–72.

KARAN, P. P., 1957, 'Land Utilization and Agriculture in an Indian Village', *Land Economics*, 33, 1 (February), 53–64.

KUMAR, DHARMA, 1965, *Land and Caste in South India* (Cambridge University Press, Cambridge).

LEWIS, OSCAR, 1951, *Group Dynamics in a North Indian Village*, (Planning Commission, New Delhi).

MAHALINGAM, T. V., 1955, *South Indian Polity* (University of Madras, Madras).

MAINE, SIR HENRY SUMNER, 1890, *Village Communities in the East and West* (J. Murray, London, 1871) (ed. 1890).

—— 1906, *Ancient Law*, with Introduction and Notes by Sir Frederick Pollock (J. Murray, London. 4th American edn., New York, 1906).

MARX, KARL, 1853, 'The East India Company—Its History and Results', *New York Daily Tribune*, 11 July 1853. Cited in S. Avineri (ed.), *Karl Marx on Colonialism and Modernization* (Doubleday, New York, 1969).

MAYER, A. C., 1960, *Caste and Kinship in Central India* (University of California Press, Berkeley, Los Angeles).

MILLER, E., 1954, 'Caste and Territory in Malabar', *American Anthropologist*, 56, 410–20.

NANAVATI, M. B., and ANJARIA, J. J., 1944, *The Indian Rural Problem* (Indian Society of Agricultural Economics, Bombay).

O'MALLEY, L. S. S., 1941, *Modern India and the West* (Oxford University Press, London).

RAO, N. RAMA, 1954, *Kelavu Nenapugaḷu* (Jeevana Prakatanālaya, Bangalore).

Report 1832: *Report from the Select Committee in the House of Commons*, Evidence, III, Revenue, Appendixes (App. No. 84).

SASTRI, K. A. N., 1966, *A History of South India* (Oxford University Press, London, 3rd edn.).

SPEAR, PERCIVAL, 1951, *Twilight of the Mughals* (Cambridge University Press, Cambridge).

SRINIVAS, M. N., 1955a, 'The Social Structure of a Mysore Village', in M. N. Srinivas (ed.), *India's Villages* (Asia Publishing House, Bombay), pp. 21–35 (1st edn.).

—— 1955b, 'The Social System of a Mysore Village,' in McKim Marriott (ed.), *Village India* (University of Chicago Press, Chicago and London), pp. 1–35.

—— 1959, 'The Dominant Caste in Rampura', *American Anthropologist*, 61, 1–16.

—— 1962, 'Varna and Caste', in M. N. Srinivas, *Caste in Modern India and Other Essays* (Asia Publishing House, Bombay), pp. 63–9.

—— 1966, *Social Change in Modern India* (University of California Press, Berkeley, Los Angeles).

—— and SHAH, A. M., 1960, 'The Myth of Self-Sufficiency of the Indian Village', *Economic Weekly*, 10 September 1960, 1375–8.

STOKES, E., 1959, *The English Utilitarians and India* (Oxford University Press, London). [Cited in Dumont 1966.]

THORNER, DANIEL, 1951, 'Sir Henry Maine (1882–1888)', in H. Ausubel, J. B. Brebner, and E. M. Hunt (eds.), *Some Modern Historians of Britain* (Dryden Press, New York).

—— 1966, 'Marx on India and the Asiatic Mode of Production', *Contributions to Indian Sociology*, 9, 33–66.

—— and THORNER, ALICE, 1965, *Land and Labour in India* (Asia Publishing House, Bombay).

4

The Melanesian Manager

K. O. L. BURRIDGE

I

THE basis of my topic, a discussion of the Melanesian 'Big man', or 'manager' as I persist in calling him, is the way in which Evans-Pritchard has spelt out how and why people such as the Leopard-skin chief,[1] the divine king of the Shilluk,[2] and members of the Sanusiya order,[3] make the social process possible. For, not simply a local entrepreneur,[4] the manager seems to me to belong to a series which, in addition to those mentioned above, also includes, for example, the Dinka Master of the fishing-spear,[5] the Hindu Sanyasi,[6] and the shaman[7] among others. That is, we are talking about someone who is an individual, singular, and a symbol as well.

Involved in community life, a manager does the tasks that other men do. Formally, he has a restricted domain in which he

[1] E. E. Evans-Pritchard, *The Nuer* (Oxford, 1940), esp. pp. 152–75; and *Nuer Religion* (Oxford, 1956), esp. pp. 171–2, 293–304.

[2] E. E. Evans-Pritchard, 'The Divine Kingship of the Shilluk of the Nilotic Sudan', in *Essays in Social Anthropology* (London, 1962), pp. 66–86.

[3] E. E. Evans-Pritchard, *The Sanusi of Cyrenaica* (Oxford, 1949).

[4] From an abundant literature on the subject perhaps I may be allowed to refer to the following selection: K. O. L. Burridge, *Mambu* (London, 1960), pp. 72–112; H. Ian Hogbin, 'Social Advancement in Guadalcanal, Solomon Islands', *Oceania* 8 (1937), 62–89; Phyllis M. Kaberry, 'Law and Political Organization in the Abelam Tribe', *Oceania* 12 (1941), 79–95, 209–25, 331–63; Margaret Mead (ed.), *Co-operation and Competition among Primitive Peoples* (New York, 1937); H. A. Powell, 'Competitive Leadership in Trobriand Political Organization', *Journal of the Royal Anthropological Institute*, 90 (1960), 118–45; K. E. Read, 'Leadership and Consensus in a New Guinea Society', *American Anthropologist*, 61 (1959), 425–36; Marshall D. Sahlins, 'Poor Man, Rich Man, Big Man, Chief: Political Types in Melanesia and Polynesia', *Comparative Studies in Society and History* 5 (1963), 285–303.

[5] Godfrey Lienhardt, *Divinity and Experience* (Oxford, 1961).

[6] Louis Dumont, 'The Modern Conception of the Individual', *Contributions to Indian Sociology* 8 (1965), 13–61.

[7] Mercea Eliade, *Shamanism* (New York, 1964).

can realize his private being, his personal ambitions and desires. But he is also an individual. And if everyone is compounded of both social and private being, an individual is one who, both of and also in a sense outside or set apart from the moral order, makes his private being sociologically relevant. Not only is he essential to the social process, but it is through him that the social process can be understood. At this point he becomes a particular kind of category of understanding, a symbol, one who both embodies and transcends the inherent and recurrent conflicts, whether of action or idea, to which his community is subject, and who reveals to others the kinds of moral conflict in which they are involved.

In a monetized or industrialized economy many of the values and conflicts epitomized in the kinds of people I am talking about will have been differentiated into the variety of activities, categories, and offices typical of the open society. But whatever the type of society, and although differentiation makes it possible to resolve operationally those conflicts which, otherwise, have to be transcended, some conflicts remain which must be transcended. Since what gives rise to conflict may be necessary or thought highly desirable, the conflict itself becomes necessary or desirable, and its consequences can only be controlled by that which transcends it. That is, rather than deny the values that give rise to conflict, and so run counter to the imperatives on which the moral order is based, the consequences of conflict are mitigated or transcended by recourse to an authority, typically religious, which stands aside from the moral order proper. In Melanesia the manager is such an authority. Appreciating the relations of the parts to the whole, he is singular, one who stands by himself, who has it in him to initiate. But because in order to do or be these things a manager has to venture outside what is normatively moral, he demonstrates, I think, an essentially religious value.

II

Writing of the traditional rather than of the contemporary scene, and attempting a synthesis which, I hope, will bring together the principles underlying cultural variation, everywhere in Melanesia the basic situation was, and to some extent still is, determined by the relations implied in a subsistence economy. Without money, all or most of the members of a community participated in common in a series of selected subsistence activities, the basic measure of prestige and status being relative competence in these activities. While other capacities and qualities, such as oratory, fighting skills, magical knowledge, dreaming, myth-making, and technical skills were also taken into account, the basic measure of man was related to the production of food in particular ways for prescribed purposes. While most adults were masters of specialist crafts, these were part-time if necessary auxiliaries to the main task of subsistence. With a simple division of labour based upon age and sex, there was no significant full-time specialization. For this comes with money, a common measure of man as well as a common medium of exchange and social differentiation. In some communities, it is true, there might be a magical or technical full-time specialist. But in such cases the specialist was usually isolated or insulated from the main prestige system. His expertise carried its own prestige, and he could not, as a full-time specialist, make his productive effort compare with those of others. If he could, at times, exercise political influence, this generally went with the ability to organize subsistence activities. Only rarely, too, do we find such organizers who were not also themselves workers. For, to organize others a man had first to show that he could organize himself. And this he did by demonstrating industry and skill in foodstuffs harvested, and fish and other animals caught and appropriately treated.

Produce was distributed through defined types of exchange, specific kinds of goods passing between affines, friends, trading partner-rivals,[8] and co-operative and local community groups. Generally, exchanges entailed continuing moral obligation: when *A* gave to *B*, *B*'s repayment to *A* made the latter again beholden to *B*.[9] And, whether giving or receiving, the manner and timing

8 Exchange 'partners' is sometimes misleading. For us a 'partner' is usually someone with whom we co-operate 'against' others. In Melanesia those with whom one exchanged were as much 'rivals' as 'partners'.
9 This is a quite different state of affairs from that existing in a monetized

of executing a passage of goods, or rendering a service, bespoke attitudes of respect or contumely, involved personal pride and integrity, and resulted in the gain or loss of relative prestige and status. To give appropriately was to receive power and virtue, to receive appropriately was to acquiesce and eat. But since exchanges, whether carried out *en bloc* or in a series of instalments, had to be more or less equivalent, deemed a fair swap in the circumstances, skilful and industrious workers found a relevant prestige in a more rapid turnover of transactions within larger networks of exchange and trading relationships. Expanding the personality by thus increasing the range of his interactions with others, an ambitious man put his integrity at risk and increased the opportunities for rebuffs. Effective influence depended on his selection of priorities within a general complex of obligations and credits. And since, for the most part, obligations had to be redeemed in perishable foodstuffs, attempts on either hand to enforce repayments or postpone redemption days were integral moves in a game in which the advantages of realizing credits at some times were matched by the inconvenience of having them realized for one at other times. The activity of exchanging, particularly in the way in which material losses and benefits were met, reflected personal and moral qualities. Even where kin groups coincided with co-operative groups as corporate bodies, since each man had a unique set of affines, and a unique personal network of exchange relationships within which he had to manœuvre to gain his maximum advantage, ambiguity and risk were built into the system. While relative prestige and influence depended on the sizes and ranges of exchange networks actively maintained, the larger the range the greater the risks of affronts to moral integrity by failures to meet obligations at specified times.

The manipulation of credits was to a certain extent stabilized by ceremonial exchange cycles.[10] And as these exchanges, and

economy. For in the latter, in principle, even within a moral relationship, a single *do ut des* can complete the transaction. Thus: money economy: $A \rightleftarrows B$. Subsistence economy: $A \rightleftarrows B$.

[10] There is of course a vast literature on this subject. Perhaps I may be allowed to refer simply to: F. R. Barton, 'The Annual Trading Expedition to the Papuan Gulf', in C. G. Seligman, *The Melanesians of British New Guinea* (Cambridge,

the feasts which accompanied them, were phased to the seasonal rhythms of horticultural and climatic cycles, and so had to be planned in advance, they provided regular occasions when it was known that credits were going to be called in and obligations would have to be met. Ceremonial exchanges entailed the exchange—more usually only against each other—of valuables such as trochus-shell ornaments, pigs' tusks, dogs' teeth, strings of ground shell, gold-lip oyster-shells, or feathers, treated and made up in certain ways. Unless obtained on the security of foodstuffs provided in order to enter the system, these valuables, though appropriate to bride-price and compounding a homicide, were ordinarily not purchasable in other commodities, and were not, in general, used to buy other kinds of goods. Existing beside, but apart from, the organization for producing, distributing, and consuming the real wealth of the community, its foodstuffs, the valuables had associative, historical, and aesthetic values certainly. But their main significance in the present context is that, not money, they were tokens indicating prestige. Obtaining possession of them depended on performance in producing foodstuffs and manipulating exchanges. On the other hand, this possession was inescapably linked to parting with them, and while keeping such a valuable overlong could be detrimental to prestige, and could erode a man's moral standing, holding on to one and then making a more advantageous exchange increased prestige. Continually asked to put prestige and moral standing at risk, no one in Melanesia succeeded like the successful risk-taker. He demonstrated that he was better than others at solving the basic problem of his culture: the management of exchange relationships wherein each participant had a different and competitive set of priorities, and where failure to meet an obligation reflected on both giver and receiver.

The feast, which could be combined with other activities such

1910), pp. 96–120; Ralph Bulmer, 'Political Aspects of the Moka Ceremonial Exchange System among the Kyaka', *Oceania* 31 (1960), 1–13. G. A. M. Bus, 'The *Te* Festival or Gift Exchange in Enga', *Anthropos* 46 (1951), 813–24; George Dalton, 'Primitive Money', *American Anthropologist*, 67 (1965), 44–66; George Dalton (ed.), *Tribal and Peasant Economies* (New York, 1967), pp. 171–284; Bronislaw Malinowski, *Argonauts of the Western Pacific* (London, 1922); R. F. Salisbury, *From Stone to Steel* (Melbourne, 1962).

as dancing, sacrificial ceremonies, initiation or mortuary rituals, or an important phase in the ceremonial exchange cycle, was the central institution which knitted together the many unique networks of exchange obligations. But the Melanesian feast was competitive rather than an expression of solidarity.[11] In the latter, contributions are made to a central figure who, in organizing the feast, enhances or maintains his prestige. Participants join together in a unificatory meal punctuated by self-congratulatory speeches and exhortations to revivify the values they are taken to hold in common. Competing interests and divisions of opinion tend to be obscured in the solidarity ritual of commensality. In the Melanesian feast, however, rivalries were dominant as interested parties attempted to gain ends not available to all at once. Food was generally provided by several allied organizers or managers, and handed over to affines and rivals in exchange to eat. Food providers did not join in commensality. The speeches accompanying the feast were mutually opposed and competitive: subtly derisory or mocking, teasing, or needling, even when overtly bland. Providing the occasion for attempting temporary resolutions of disputes concerning theft, trespass, adultery, homicide, or sorcery, these matters went with attaining or confirming status and prestige. Further, consistent with the general nature of exchange in Melanesia, any one feast was but a single example in a series of feasts in which co-operative groups took it in turns either to provide food, or engage in an appropriate activity such as, for example, building a new house, performing an initiation ceremony or mortuary ritual, or making a ceremonial exchange of valuables. If, in the field situation, elements from both types of feast might be identified, the distinction between them as types or models is crucial. In the one the unity of the parts which make the whole is emphasized, and an attempt is made to transcend the oppositions and conflicts between the constituent parts. In the other, mutual oppositions, conflicts of interest, rivalry, and discord are revealed in their entirety, sometimes obviously, at

11 Cf. Helen Codere, *Fighting with Property: A Study of Kwakiutl Potlatching and Warfare*, Monographs of the American Ethnological Society, xviii (New York, 1950).

other times more subtly. And if, in this mutual opposition, relative prestige was at issue, so was moral integrity.

For managers a feast was the occasion for demonstrating their
managerial qualities in competition with others before the
assembled community. Their productive capacities were seen by
the greatest number which could be gathered together at the same
time and place, they had every opportunity to show their auxiliary
skills. At feasts, a manager earned or lost that confidence which,
placed in him by others, could either strengthen or diminish his
network of credits. A good performance enabled him to participate
more fully and relevantly in ceremonial exchanges, and attracted
those further exchange partner-rivals whom he needed to make
his productive capacity earn him even more prestige and influence. On the other hand, an organizational mistake, a feast
held too soon or delayed too long, spoiled or messy foodstuffs,
clumsy dancing, poor oratory, the rash or hasty word, loss of
temper—such blunders resulted in losses of confidence and entailed the manager's entering a downcurve.[12]

Generally in Melanesia, children were apprentices who learned
the tasks associated with their sex in a more or less free, easy, and
permissive ambience. At puberty, particularly in the case of
males, permissiveness gave way to harsh discipline, trials of fortitude and restraint, and training in the warrior values:[13] a dia-
chronic expression of that tension between self-willedness and
self-restraint which, permeating Melanesian society, was most
acutely manifested in homicide. A few years later, upon marriage,
a man and his wife started to work up their productive potential.
Resolving conflicts of claims over land, the household engaged
in exchanges with close affines, and allied itself to a co-operative
group making group exchanges with a similar group. Competing
in productivity and manipulating exchanges, an ambitious man
began to show both co-operators and exchange partner-rivals
the sort of man he was. In time, marrying again and so increasing

[12] Cf. K. O. L. Burridge, *Mambu* (London, 1960), pp. 72–111.
[13] Cf. R. M. Berndt, *Excess and Restraint* (Chicago, 1962), p. 110; and Marie
Reay, *The Kuma* (Melbourne, 1959), p. 172.

the number of his affines, he himself became the organizer or manager of a co-operative group. But his status did not solely depend on his co-operators: it was qualified or enhanced by those with whom he maintained exchange relationships, particularly his affines.

Assuming that he married with purpose, choosing his affines with care and handling his exchanges with acumen, a manager succeeded in gaining the confidence of both allies and rivals. On the other hand, since these men would themselves be engaged in unique networks of exchange relations within which they would have to allocate priorities, and would be seeking the same goals of prestige and influence, outside a small group of dependent kin no manager could be quite sure just how others might react to his initiatives. Each had his own interests to secure. While allies might help him forward his own arrangements, they, being prudent, had to gauge the developing situation in relation to those others who wished either to obstruct the projected arrangements, or so to qualify them that they could reap advantage from them. Far from controlling a permanent corporate group of kin, a manager had particular kinds of relations with numbers of households some of which he could recruit to a task at certain times, others of whom he could not. Since all were playing the same game, and a sharp finesse might make the difference between failure and success, a manager had to be prepared for surprises while doing his utmost to forestall them. He had to recruit to an occasion not only co-operators, but affines and rivals as well. And to succeed in this he had to both find and create an optimum area of consensus. On the one hand he had to restrain self-willedness and conform to the moralities, on the other hand—if he was to remain in control of a developing consensus—he had to cheat a little, go outside the normative moralities.

Continuing exchange within moral relationships involved not so much the certainty that a repayment would be made as the risk that, made at an inappropriate time, or placed low on another's priorities, it would prick a man's pride and lower his prestige. The choice between assuaging hunger and meeting this or that exchange obligation was a constant moral problem which did not cease being a moral problem because the choice was linked to advantage and status. On the contrary, work done, organizing ability, prestige, influence, and moral virtue grew out of each other. Since 'wrongdoing' and 'rightdoing' both related directly to the conduct of exchange relations, the wrongdoer was as limited in his fashion as the good man in his. Whilst the temporary possession of valuables indicated risks successfully taken, the significant wealth produced, perishable foodstuffs subject to vagaries of soil, climate, and pests, was consumed as its handling and apportionment translated work into moral qualities. In a good year a jubilant manager had jubilant rivals, and in a bad year rivals were similarly morose. A man made his mark by the way in which he managed larger numbers of approximately equivalent exchanges. And if these capacities could be rationalized by fellow villagers in relation to the ways in which his skills in dealing with exchanges and people were matched by his knowledge of magical spells, his interpretations of dreams, his relationships with tutelary deities, and married to his experiences with his father's ghost— experiences which are accurately summed up as 'wrestling with his conscience', or attempting to resolve the tension between self-willedness and self-restraint[14]—the man who won out could not but be considered more capable than others at solving or transcending the moral dilemmas that grew out of the circumstances of making exchanges.

Apart from the categories of kinship and friendship, a traditional Melanesian community could be divided into four sorts of persons: managers, sorcerers, ordinary men, and rubbish-men. Ordinary men were those who conformed with the prescriptions and restrictions of the moral order, who held their private beings on a leash, who could or would not project their private domains into a relevance outside the bare demands of conformity. While managers were initiators, accepting the risks of initiative and exulting in success, ordinary men were careful followers who

[14] See R. F. Fortune, *Manus Religion*, reprinted from *American Philosophical Society*, Memoir vol. 3, Philadelphia, 1935 (Bison Books, 1968); and P. Lawrence and M. J. Meggitt (eds.), *Gods, Ghosts, and Men in Melanesia* (Melbourne, 1965).

sought the comforts of conformity and played it safe. Rubbish-men,[15] on the other hand, were men who had either opted out of the status competition, or who habitually failed to meet their obligations. Often, they lived on the fringes of a settlement, between the village proper and the forest or bush outside: a placement which reflected their position in the moral order. Because they had failed to meet their obligations, or were unable or had chosen not to participate in the process whereby proper men were supposed to demonstrate their moral nature, they hardly rated as men, were not fully moral beings in the locally recognized sense. Treated with a charitable contempt which they accepted with resigned equanimity, rubbish-men were generally left to their own devices, working by and for themselves at a markedly lower level of subsistence than others. Where managers interacted with others and lived in a vital, creative, and positive sense, rubbish-men did not respond to the call to make their morality explicit in competitive interaction. Severally and as a pair of opposites, managers and rubbish-men defined the generality of community values as they were expressed by ordinary men: the one by an intense expression, the other by a void.

Like the manager and rubbish-man, the sorcerer, too, was an individual. But he made his private being relevant by flouting the moral rules. Unlike the rubbish-man, who merely stood aside from the rules of the moral order, unable or unwilling to cope with an intricate web of exchanges, a sorcerer used the rules, cheated, infringed the rules—and could get away with it. Believed to have access to a variety of mystical techniques, he was thought to have both the positive desire and ability to induce sickness in others, kill—mystically or more obviously—thieve, trespass, or commit adultery. Certainly interacting, he did so nastily and spitefully. His self-willedness ran counter to the general will, contravened the normative moralities, vitiated the generality of projections relating to exchange, and generated indignation and counter-activity. Yet while some sorcerers were 'known', fair

[15] 'Rubbish-men' were not refuse-disposal operatives, as is sometimes thought. 'Rubbish-man' is the anglicization of the Pidgin *rabisman*, an impoverished person, where *rabis* itself, taken from the English 'rubbish', means poor, of no value.

game if and when caught in the act, any man who behaved in a sorcerer-like way might in that context be treated as a sorcerer. Murderer, criminal, witch, thief, adulterer, trespasser, and scapegoat, 'sorcerer' was often a label looking for a man. And he who was 'known' as a sorcerer, who defiantly pinned the label on himself, was feared and deferentially treated.

A sorcerer exacted obligation out of fear; and though he could be, he was not necessarily a manager. But a manager could become a sorcerer, or like a sorcerer. For a manager, having influence and power, might become arrogant, venture outside the moralities a little too far in self-willedness, and become contemptuous of the moral rules by which the majority lived. Moreover, since there were limits to productive capacity, and so to the number of exchange relations a man could maintain, when a manager began to reach these limits it was almost inevitable that he would attempt to increase his prestige and status by using the methods associated with sorcerer: intimating or threatening loss, injury, sickness, or death by mystical or pragmatic means. Consequently, as a man reached the peak of his managerial career, and as rivals lessened the distance between him and themselves, he was more and more readily suspected of having become a sorcerer. Yet a manager did not necessarily lose power and influence by becoming a sorcerer. On the contrary, since the confidence he now commanded was coloured by fear, he could gain more power. But to retain it he had to tread a delicate path between the arrogance associated with an unmitigated sorcerer and the shame expected of an ordinary man who was discovered in a transgression of the normative moralities.[16] And in so doing he set himself aside or apart from the moral order whilst continuing to participate in the social order.

As categories, manager, sorcerer, ordinary man, and rubbishman were distinct co-ordinates by which any man could define himself to himself and others. But, particularly as between manager and sorcerer, the situation on the ground frequently involved

---

[16] See, for example, H. Ian Hogbin, 'Shame: A study of social conformity in a New Guinea village', *Oceania*, 17 (1947), 273–88; and K. O. L. Burridge, 'Tangu Political Relations', *Anthropological Forum*, 1, nos. 3–4 (1965–6), 393–411.

ambiguity of persons in relation to category. Yet though it was possible for an ordinary man to show sudden zeal and become a manager, or fall away and become a rubbish-man, or spurn the moralities and become a sorcerer, on the whole he remained an ordinary man, a good conformist, the measure of average integrity. For while becoming a rubbish-man involved either failure, infrequent in a thriving culture, or rare purpose, but in any case withdrawal, becoming a manager or a sorcerer seems to have required an inherent and purposeful ability to interact, take risks, and handle ambiguities. As categories, manager and sorcerer represented, respectively, active respect and active contempt for the moralities as observed by ordinary men. But the man who wanted to be either a manager or a sorcerer, and who also wanted status and influence, had to make his own resolution of the opposition between them.

Political relations in Melanesia, effectively between territorial groups composed of villages or clusters of settlements, were characterized by opposition and mutual dependence. Oppositions were expressed directly in homicide, ambushes, and war—events which were usually the consequences of sorcery. The sorcerer who was most actively feared came from another village, another territorial group. And though sorcerers in the home village might at any time direct their spite against members of the in-group, a feature constantly borne in mind, it was supposed that they generally concentrated on the members of other territorial groups: thieving, trespassing, inducing sickness, killing, and vitiating domestic arrangements and affinal exchanges by committing adultery. Consequently losses, impaired exchange relationships, sickness, or death in the home community usually mobilized aggressive energies which a manager would organize into an expedition with homicide and revenge as its object. In turn, a counter-attack or ambush could be expected. Few deaths were not either attributed to sorcery, or did not result from a revenge killing for a death attributed to sorcery. Sorcery was the rationale of death, and, since most deaths were thought to be homicides, of homicide too. Yet if a sorcerer was a killer, so was a manager.[17] And while all killers were not necessarily managers, any killer was feared and respected. Killing was a positive value in itself.[18]

Mutual dependence between territorial groups was expressed in trade and exchange, and the creation of moral relationships within the categories of kinship and friendship. But if in some instances the economic interdependence could be said to be necessary for survival, in other cases it was a rationale for the moral relationships. The constant in the situation was, rather, the notion and activity of exchange, the desire—for purposes of prestige—to expand and maintain networks of exchange relationships. So that though killing was the kind of positive value which could be cited as an irreducible imperative, the facts that homicide was reciprocal, that peacemaking involved the reciprocal invoking of conventional rules for controlling the rate of homicide, and that both homicide and peacemaking can be derived from exchange, point to exchange as the basic value. Sorcerers who might be managers provided the initial provocation by theft, trespass, adultery, inducing sickness, or killing; managers who might be sorcerers organized the counter-attack; and the same men took the initiative in organizing the return to a period of peaceful coexistence.

Before the members of different territorial groups could make exchanges it was first necessary to establish binding and continuing moral relationships. Thus men and women formed friendships with men and women in other villages. This gave them trading and exchange partners in other territorial groups, and some assurance of sanctuary from the sorcerers believed to live there. At the kin level the same sorts of sanctuary and trading

[17] Albert Maori Kiki writes (in *Kiki* (Melbourne, 1968), pp. 5, 15): ' The very first thing I can remember is the day on which they brought back my dead uncle. Like a hunted boar, they had tied his hands and feet to a long pole . . . There was a large gash across his clavicle and the blood was still red and fresh . . . I have sometimes been asked by Europeans whether there was any way of breaking the vicious circle of revenge and counter-revenge and arriving at some kind of peace. I think we did not really want peace because we *enjoyed* [sic] the fighting. The village leader was always the man who had killed the most people.'

[18] Cf. J. A. Barnes, 'African Models in the New Guinea Highlands', *Man*, 72, 2 (1962), 9: 'In New Guinea a greater emphasis appears to be placed on killing for its own sake rather than as a continuation of group policy aimed at material ends.'

and exchange relations were effected by intermarriages or the assumption of kin relationship by procedures equivalent to adoption. Still, sorcerers were by no means wholly disarmed by these relationships, and the more frequent the intercourse between members of different territorial groups the more scope there was for the accidents and irregularities which engendered accusations of sorcery. On the other hand, the presence of friends and kin in other villages also laid the basis for coming to a temporary accord and making peace.[19] And, since managers had the most extensive and effective networks of kin, friends, and trading partners, they were well placed both to provoke incidents which could lead into homicide, and also to control the consequences of accusations of sorcery and alleged or real homicides.

At the more explicitly political level—which included the personal and kin levels—both opposition and dependence were expressed in the ceremonial exchange cycles. Often carried out as a peacemaking ceremony after a phase of fighting or acute tension accompanying accusations and counter-accusations of sorcery, or in order to compound a series of homicides, ceremonial exchanges, organized by managers, were explicitly situations of sanctuary in which trading and exchange relations might be resumed in an atmosphere of integrity and implicit resolve not to resort to sorcery. But of course the resumption of trading and exchange relations set the scene for just those events which, seen as affronts to personal dignity and moral integrity, and regarded as all the more dastardly and informed with spite when it seemed that a smooth roguery was being answered by a sorcerer causing sickness, would lead into gathering tensions, accusations of sorcery, and an injury or homicide followed by making peace and a further ceremonial exchange.[20] Going with a generalized political instability in which distinct political groups could not know precisely when yesterday's allies would become enemies, ceremonial exchange cycles also seem to go with a situation in which mutual suspicions of foul play, cheating, and provocative

[19] For an account see K. O. L. Burridge, 'Disputing in Tangu', *American Anthropologist*, 59 (1957), 763–80.
[20] See especially Ralph Bulmer, loc. cit.

finesse, inevitably attached to trading and exchange relationships, coincide with moral relationships and cross the boundaries of political groups: a cycle of moral dilemma in which, chiefly, adultery and sickness and death brought on those crises of conscience which revivified the values of exchange.[21]

Recognized by his position in relation to the categories of manager, sorcerer, ordinary man, and rubbish-man, and defined by his initiatives and responses towards affines, productive ability, general exchange, group exchanges, feasting, ceremonial exchange, sorcery, and homicide, the man who was a manager generally had to be physically strong, well-muscled and well-proportioned, energetic, athletic, agile, a good dancer—though physical presence was more important than mere bone and muscle.[22] With a prominent nose, deep chest, and broad forehead—rule-of-thumb indicators of sexual potency and capacities for work and thought —and with darting, watchful eyes that missed nothing, he was expected to give an immediate impression of bottled energy, of being fit, healthy, and truly alive. No one subject to recurrent sickness could become a manager. Sickness prevented a man from working and organizing, was evidence of vulnerability to sorcerers. And, since a manager was expected to take the initiative in dealing with sorcerers, he could hardly do so if he himself was continually sick. Besides, sickness could be evidence of a prior transgression, might indicate a bad or weak conscience, and was easily attributable to unsatisfactory relations with the father's ghost. Moreover, it was desirable that a manager should show the positive outward marks of inward integrity: a clear and shining skin. Not that those with skin diseases were necessarily without integrity, but, since skin ailments were generally thought to stem from debilitating conflicts within a man, it was difficult to place any confidence in such a man. If a clear-skinned man might turn out to be a rogue, he would not, as those with skin diseases

---

[21] But the cycle does not seem to *depend* on sickness and death (see Burridge, *Mambu*, pp. 59–71).

[22] See in particular K. E. Read, *The High Valley* (New York, 1965), pp. 56–94; and H. B. Watson, 'Tairora: the politics of despotism in a small society', *Anthropological Forum*, 2, 1 (November 1967), 53–103.

were thought prone to do, accompany a failure to meet his obligations with a string of sincere and apparently adequate excuses.

A manager had to succeed, meet his obligations, produce the goods. Otherwise he lost ground and was forced to yield to another. Relentlessly pursuing the advantageous exchange, never leaving until tomorrow what could be done today, a manager had to apply his own standards to others, dealing ruthlessly with those who failed to meet their obligations to himself. Generally expected to act fairly, much of his power depended on his capacity to retain general confidence in spite of particular treacheries. Personal loyalties to others were subject to the political and economic demands entailed in maintaining exchanges. Kindly and considerate to children, particularly his own, a manager had to be aggressively sensitive of his good name, commanding a wholesome respect—and fear if need be—rather than seeking warmth and affection. While women could point to a manager as the sort of man most women would want for a husband, he might well be a permitted adulterer[23] and was also the kind of man who could deal decisively with a lazy or troublesome wife, killing her if necessary.

In contrast with the rubbish-man who was truly independent, without allies, a manager had to command that confidence which would draw dependants—kin, allies, friends, trading partners— and yet, in interacting with others, preserve that mien which indicated that dependants could rely on him only as long as he could rely on them. Because he generally was that type of man, young men tended to ask him for help in making marriage payments, became beholden to him, and, if they themselves were to rise in status, had to meet their obligations to him. Well travelled because he had a far-ranging network of affines, friends, and trading partners, a manager had to be capable of accepting the considerable risks from sorcery and ambush that travelling entailed. A fighter with the sorcerer's capacity for killing, he also had to have that command of language and smooth words which could either persuade men into combat, or soothe ruffled plumes, arbitrate, and make peace. Proving his reciprocal nature,

[23] See H. B. Watson, loc. cit.

and honouring his obligations to others, a manager still had to show himself as singular, as the sort of man who, comprehending the relations of the parts to the whole, could act non-reciprocally and initiate.

III

For all the cultural diversity that is subsumed under the term 'Melanesian', and though the managers of particular communities differ in a variety of features from the general and inclusive sketch I have drawn, the structural similarities are striking. That is why it has been possible to speak of the manager as a general category. For though he may take his place on an evolutionary scale, or in a typology of political roles,[24] he is, I think, the more significantly intelligible by being defined by the relations of opposition and dependence which are contained in affinal relationships, networks of personal exchange relationships, competitive feasting, ceremonial exchange cycles, sorcery, and homicide. And all of these are interdependent parts or refractions of exchange. Because these relations appear to obtain throughout Melanesia, the same kind of manager is bred out of a variety of resource bases and arrangements for the recognition of kin and formation of descent groups. Even if it could be shown, rather than existentially asserted, that exchange arose from significant differences in the resource bases of neighbouring communities, and that the same differences together with endemic and environmentally determined causes of sickness and death could account for the rate of homicide, sociologically, I think, the primacy of exchange cannot be doubted.

Malinowski long ago drew attention to the importance of 'reciprocity' in Melanesia;[25] Mauss[26] and Lévi-Strauss[27] have refined the category as a universal in human affairs; and Sahlins has attempted

[24] Cf. Marshall D. Sahlins, 'Poor Man, Rich Man, Big Man, Chief: Political Types in Melanesia and Polynesia', *Comparative Studies in Society and History* (1963), 285–303.
[25] Bronislaw Malinowski, *Argonauts of the Western Pacific* (London, 1922); and *Crime and Custom in Savage Society* (London, 1926).
[26] Marcel Mauss, *The Gift*, trans. Ian Cunnison (London, 1954).
[27] Claude Lévi-Strauss, *Les Structures élémentaires de la parenté* (Paris, 1949).

to define types of reciprocity.[28] But my main point is not so much exchange itself as the way in which the sets of relations found in Melanesian exchange, bearing out Malinowski's and Mauss's more subtle points on the subject, define the manager. Because of these relations it would be possible, I think, so to dub in the detail of the manager that all the major conflicts in being to which Melanesian peoples are heir would be found in him. That is why he is worth noticing and usefully brought into a context which includes divine kings, leopard-skin chiefs, and the rest. Measuring a total available awareness, the manager resolved the dilemmas of continuing moral obligation without money by taking his capacities for self-restraint and self-willedness outside the normative moralities and into an area of special permissiveness. While a manager's adultery might be almost an honour, he transformed the gross impulses of killing, fighting, and cheating into ideals of heroism, peace, and transactional shrewdness. He combined opposites and brought them to cognition, he condensed meanings and transcended moral conflicts. An 'eternal object' in the sense that, like others of his genre, he embodied and revealed the leitmotives of his culture, he was also an individual, filling out the meaning of individuality.

The advent of Europeans has seen a significant addition to the list of Melanesian individuals: the prophet, the man or woman who plays the central part in a cargo movement. But though these prophets start similar kinds of movements—movements which readily lend themselves to being called 'cargo' movements, a feature which carries its own message of cultural similarity and distinctiveness—it is not so much the prophets themselves as the responses to their initiatives that are distinctively Melanesian. For the prophets have very different personal make-ups, emerge in different ways from situations of stress born of specific European experiences, and take their places more comfortably with the general run of millenarian prophets wherever they may be found. They show forth and symbolize a new man, they attempt syntheses of what they find vital in tradition and worth while in

[28] Marshall D. Sahlins, 'On the Sociology of Primitive Exchange', in *The Relevance of Models for Social Anthropology* (London, 1965), pp. 139–227.

the new Europeanized environment that is taking shape. Themselves compounded of European and Melanesian characteristics, they have for many years been initiating experiments in new ways of living, ways which envisage increased differentiations and entail a generalization of individuality. And a new kind of manager, in part a product of these prophets' endeavours, has been taking his place in national legislative assemblies. But what is important here, I think, is that whatever new ideals of salvation or spiritual or transmondane enhancement may have been in a prophet's mind, the Melanesian concern for translating a mystical, emotional, or intellectual experience into a moral relationship expressible in an exchange of material stuffs comes uppermost. That is, whether we go to the symbolic or more obvious and apparent values in a cargo movement, the import of a prophet's teaching is shaped by the relations predicated by Melanesian exchange. Until money begins to differentiate the parts, morality, demonstrated through exchange, holds the spiritual on a rein.

5

The Interpretation of Rumour

PETER LIENHARDT

I

THERE was an outbreak of cholera in Iran in 1964, but in 1965 it was widely believed, in Isfahan at least, that there had not been. The Persian government had feared a serious epidemic and they had given the cholera maximum publicity so as to persuade as many people as possible to have themselves inoculated. Because of the government's precautions, taken with impressive speed and thoroughness, the outbreak was far less serious than had been feared.

Arriving in Isfahan in 1965, I myself had no doubt that there had been cholera in Iran the year before. One of my friends had caught it in Tehran. In Isfahan, however, people said that the Persian government had invented the epidemic. It provided an excuse for failing to send Persian troops to support the Americans in Vietnam—a gesture which would have been unpopular in Iran. The Persian government, said the Isfahanis, had been able to tell the Americans that they thought it better not to send troops to Vietnam because with a cholera epidemic at home there would be a risk of spreading the disease among their allies.

This rumour has something of a typically Isfahani flavour, calling to mind Sir Reader Bullard's suggested Persian answer to the question, 'Why did the chicken cross the road?'—'Because it wanted you to think that it wanted to get to the other side.' But it also has something in common with rumours from the very different culture of the Arabian shores of the Persian Gulf, which I wrote about first in 1957,[1] and with some rumours from other parts of the world. One of the Persian Gulf rumours spread in

[1] In a thesis written under Sir Edward Evans-Pritchard's supervision.

Bahrain in 1955 was a complete fabrication. It was to the effect
that the British government had forced the Ruler of Bahrain to
accept a proposal to legalize the sale of alcohol to Muslims in
Bahrain. Another rumour, which spread along the Trucial Coast
in the same year, arose from an actual incident when British-
officered troops took up positions outside the town of Dubai
and two warships were seen lurking off the coast. The rumour
spread that the British had landed troops from the warships and
were expelling the Ruler of Dubai and all his family; they were
handing the town over to the sheikhs of Abu Dhabi who had
agreed to appoint a British adviser to organize Dubai as Sir Charles
Belgrave had organized Bahrain. It was a complete misinterpreta-
tion of the original situation. The troops had, in fact, been asked
for by the Ruler of Dubai himself in order to block the escape
route to Sharjah whilst he sent some refractory members of his
family into exile.

Among the things these rumours had in common was that they
were not only untrue but they were fantastically unlikely. Being
untrue, they must have been invented. If they had been invented
consciously, those who invented them had apparently taken little
care for plausibility, and if invented through an unconscious
process of misunderstanding, misreportings, and distortion, they
had been subjected to very little rational criticism in the course of
it. But they seized the public imagination. They gained a wider
currency than other rumours which were much more realistic.
For, of course, not all rumours were fantastic like these. To
instance one from the Trucial Coast in the same period, there
was a rumour that some bedouin of Abu Dhabi had raided some
bedouin of Dubai. The Abu Dhabi group in question had a serious
grudge against the others and it was always possible that some
little incident might spark off a serious fight. The rumour might
easily have been true. Had it, in fact, been true it would have
surprised no one.

False but realistic rumours raise no problem as to why reasonable people should be deceived into believing them. I am told
that in Ethiopia would-be realistic rumours are intentionally put
about for both private and public purposes. Little private rumours

are perhaps better classed as gossip or stories, but they seem, in the context, to resemble some rumours of a political kind. When Amhara parents want to arrange a marriage for a son or daughter and are afraid that a direct approach might provoke a rebuff from the family they have in mind, or if, for the sake of family solidarity or money, people less directly involved want a particular marriage to take place, it is hoped that putting a story about that the marriage has been arranged will plant the question in the minds of the principals and evoke some reaction from them. The Ethiopian government is thought to set rumours afoot about matters of public policy such as the appointment of a particular official or the release of a particular political prisoner to test out public opinion before reaching a final decision. In the case of the rumours believed to be officially inspired, it is, apparently, noticeable that those spreading them are important people, the sort of men who are usually secretive and discreet.

The rumours officially fabricated in Britain as 'black propaganda' in the Second World War seem to have stopped short of the wilder fantasies.[2] They also seem to have had relatively little practical success[3] as compared with the stroke achieved in America in the 1930s when people never identified spread the rumour that a leper had been found working in a factory manufacturing Chesterfield cigarettes. This was serious enough for the manufacturers to offer a reward of 25,000 dollars to anyone identifying the culprits.[4] In one country area of Iran, when a young unmarried girl became pregnant her parents took her to Tehran and came back with the story that a specialist had blamed it on the girl's habit of constantly chewing Adams chewing gum. Sales of the chewing gum dropped.[5]

---

[2] Sefton Delmer, *Black Boomerang: An Autobiography*, vol. ii (1962).

[3] Daniel Lerner, *Psychological Warfare against Nazi Germany, the Skyewar Campaign, D-Day to VE-Day* (1971), p. 305.

[4] Tamotsu Shibutani, *Improvised News: A Sociological Study of Rumor* (1966), p. 193, taken from David J. Jacobson, *The Affairs of Dame Rumor* (1948), which I have not managed to see. According to Shibutani, two-man teams would enter a crowded subway carriage from opposite ends, move inwards and carry on a conversation about the leper whilst others were still between them.

[5] If the name *Adam* had any significance here, it is the same in Persian as in English.

Some of the more interesting modern studies of rumour discount the quality of fantasy[6] within the sort of rumours that become notorious. In his fertile and impressive study, *Improvised News*, Tamotsu Shibutani takes the view that it is only people who 'do not share the perspective of the participants' who are amazed at 'wild' rumours. He says that 'even when a rumour seems bizarre to an outside observer, it is quite plausible from the standpoint of the public.' And he thinks it important to emphasize that some rumours are true. Falsehood 'is not a necessary feature' of rumour.[7] In another significant book dealing with rumour, Leon Festinger goes further and prefers not to concern himself with the truth or falsehood of the information conveyed by rumours.[8] Two other psychologists writing on the subject, Allport and Postman, who do distinguish rumour from news, do so mainly in terms of the absence of 'secure standards of evidence'.[9] The question of fantasy disappears from these inquiries.

But fantasy is one of the things one remembers—even characterizes—rumours by. To this extent it is part of the data of the subject. It is true that it would be hard to imagine a rumour circulating if it were devoid of all plausibility for those who spread it. But this does not mean that plausibility has to be the main criterion: entertainment value might conceivably count for much more than truth. A few years ago, in an aristocratic English divorce case given much space in the press, part of the evidence was a photograph of a naked man with the head omitted. A rumour spread identifying the 'headless man' by detailed—and no doubt false—circumstantial evidence with a prominent public figure, to be followed by another rumour to the effect that he and another equally well-known man had both had medical examina-

---

[6] A notable exception is Sir Raymond Firth, who gives full importance to 'the fantastic, the untoward event, the extraordinary' in 'Rumour in a Primitive Society', an article first published in the *Journal of Abnormal and Social Psychology*, 53 (1956), and reprinted in *Tikopia Ritual and Belief* (1967).

[7] Tamotsu Shibutani, *Improvised News: A Sociological Study of Rumor* (1966), pp. 77 and 17.

[8] Leon Festinger, *A Theory of Cognitive Dissonance* (1957), p. 196.

[9] Gordon W. Allport and Leo Postman, *The Psychology of Rumor* (1947), pp. ix–x.

tions to prove that it could not be a photograph of them. My impression, in the circle in which I heard these rumours, was that we entertained them mainly because we found them intriguing, not because they were plausible. No doubt the ground of plausibility had been prepared by the Christine Keeler case, then fairly recent. Our attitude, however, was largely frivolous. And it is common enough for the same people to accept a rumour one day and dismiss it as an absurd falsehood the day after. They could scarcely change their 'perspectives' quite so abruptly if by 'perspectives' one means lasting attitudes. The association of rumour with falsehood in common parlance and in literature cannot be without significance:

> Rumour is a pipe
> Blown by surmises, jealousies, conjectures,
> And of so easy and so plain a stop
> That the blunt monster with uncounted heads,
> The still-discordant wavering multitude,
> Can play upon it.

'Only a rumour', 'just a rumour', reflect a ready assumption of falsehood and it seems a pity to discount for purposes of analysis an association to which the very idiom of the language insistently draws attention.

In this paper I shall not consider truthful rumours and shall only discuss rumours that could be called realistic in as far as they have a place in hypotheses that have been put forward about rumour in general. My direct concern is with the interpretation of some rumours which I call fantastic. And my main questions are, why should people entertain them, and, what do they reveal about the communities in which they circulate?

II

By excluding the distinction between true and false from the terms of inquiry, Festinger treats rumour not as a special issue but as a body of data relevant to the very broad question of why people accept or reject information of any sort. Festinger considers the way people behave as receivers of information. What sort of information are people prepared to receive and how do they process it for themselves? But he pays little attention to the related question, very important for rumour, of why people communicate or fail to communicate the information. It is perhaps a result of this approach that what can be interpreted as being psychologically reassuring, or at least confirmatory of existing states, has an immeasurably more important role in his explanations of behaviour than what could be classed as intriguing, interesting, or entertaining. And yet, even in a context which recognizes the deep psychological need for security that human beings have, a taste for these latter qualities should not be discounted as being merely superficial. They go with curiosity on the one hand and the urge to communicate on the other. To neglect them is to neglect the whole orientation of human beings towards learning and informing, so important even at an animal level to the survival of the species.

Festinger advances the theory that a person's opinions and attitudes tend to exist in 'clusters' that are internally 'consonant', by which he means 'consistent', but not necessarily in a logical way. 'Dissonance' occurs when the consonance of a cluster of opinions and attitudes is disturbed. Dissonance, Festinger says, is 'psychologically uncomfortable'. Hence when a person is so affected he will try to achieve consonance again. He will try both to reduce the dissonance and to avoid situations and information that might increase it.

The explanation is oriented to individual psychology, but Festinger naturally has a good deal to say about the social group. For him the social group is both a 'major source' of cognitive dissonance for the individual and a 'major vehicle' for eliminating dissonance. Other members of a group may introduce information and opinions dissonant with the individual's present cognition. But also, says Festinger, 'one of the most effective ways of eliminating dissonance is to discard one set of cognitive elements in favour of another, something which can sometimes only be accomplished if one can find others who agree with the cognitions one wishes to retain and maintain'.[10]

[10] Leon Festinger, op. cit., p. 177.

This brings us to rumour. A rumour that spreads widely, Festinger says, needs to convey information that has a similar effect on a large number of people. He asks his readers to imagine a situation in which many people have heard some undeniable information which conflicts with opinions or beliefs they hold. The new information causes dissonance. The dissonance may be removed in various ways. Either the opinion may be 'not very resistant to change' and so may be discarded; or, if it is resistant to change, then people may reject the new information. Otherwise, the recipients of the information may either 'attempt to acquire additional cognition consonant with the belief in question' or else attempt to change the cognitive elements corresponding to the new information. The attempt to regain consonance will receive support from others, and this will assist the acceptance of the new cognition. Dissonance will thereby be reduced.[11] Festinger provides an illustration of people acquiring additional cognition consonant with a preconceived belief in his account of a rumour of the sort that I should call fantastic. After the Japanese had surrendered to the Americans, a rumour spread among some Japanese that the Americans had specially chosen an unhealthy position for a relocation centre for Japanese evacuees so that as many as possible of them would die there. Festinger's explanation is that the Americans' good treatment of the Japanese was, for the Japanese, dissonant with their attribution of hostility to the Americans.[12] The same explanation is given by Tamotsu Shibutani for a rumour that spread in Japan during the American occupation to the effect that General MacArthur was of part Japanese descent. According to Shibutani, the Japanese supposed that the Americans hated them and that MacArthur (I presume because of his earlier defeats) had extra reasons for hating them. But instead of treating people badly, MacArthur did a lot of good for the Japanese and was very popular. 'This', says Shibutani, 'was difficult to understand. But if the general were part Japanese, everything would fit together; he would not be an outsider at all.'[13]

[11] Leon Festinger, op. cit., p. 197.   [12] Ibid., p. 242.
[13] Tamotsu Shibutani, op. cit., p. 79.

Festinger's theory of the existence of effectively discrete clusters of opinions and attitudes in the individual mind is an interesting one, but he does not itemize the constituent parts of any of the clusters in question. If clusters exist and are so firmly tied together as to resist change, then it would be interesting to have examples of what is tied together and how. A knowledge of the precise configuration of the relevant cluster would then make it possible to demonstrate that one particular interpretation of a rumour connected with the cluster was diagnostically correct and others were inadequate. But this does not happen: Festinger provides no discussion of alternative interpretations.

This cannot be because none are possible. Reading the two Japanese rumours I have just mentioned, one might put forward an alternative interpretation significantly different from those given but still within the possible framework of the cluster theory. The interpretation would be to the effect that the Japanese hated the Americans who had defeated them and so expected them to behave in a hateful way. In the case of the relocation centre, the rumour invented a hateful way of behaviour. In the case of General MacArthur, if the Japanese found they had to respect him or approve of him, the invention of Japanese ancestry enabled them to do so without including other Americans in their more favourable opinions. I am not arguing at the moment that this interpretation is better than the others, but simply that it is tenable within the theory and yet different. It attributes the rumours to the hatred of the Japanese for the Americans instead of attributing them to the fear of the Japanese that the Americans hated them. It might have been helpful for those directing American policy in Japan to know which was the better assessment of the situation. If so, they would have been disappointed by a theory of rumour that stopped short of the most practically significant point.

There is no doubt, however, that many rumours can be fitted into Festinger's scheme. It will be remembered that when he relates his theory to rumour Festinger asks his reader to imagine 'some undeniable information' impinging on the cognition of many people. In the First World War, when people in England became aware that the position at the front was precarious, the still famous rumour spread of the arrival of 100,000 Russian reinforcements from Archangel. The rumour had a slender basis in fact, in that there were a large number of Russian military and naval staff officers in Edinburgh and also 6,000 or 7,000 Russians were returning to Europe for the war from America and Canada through Liverpool, though they were not easily identifiable because they were wearing civilian clothes. The next year, 1915, another rumour spread: angels had appeared at Mons to save British troops from a German attack. The rumour arose out of an article by a woman writer who was, it is said, apparently copying a story called *The Archers* published the year before. In the story, St. George and a band of heavenly archers defended some British soldiers who were being outflanked by the Germans.[14] In the case of both of these rumours, what would have to be regarded as the 'undeniable information' would be information about British weakness at the front, which would be counterbalanced by the more hopeful cognitive material supplied by the rumours.

But other rumours can be fitted into the scheme only with excessive strain. For example, it is difficult to suggest what 'undeniable information' of a psychologically uncomfortable sort was responsible for the rumour which Edgar Morin and his colleagues investigated a few years ago in Orleans concerning the abduction for the white-slave trade of women being fitted for clothes in Jewish shops. And yet, according to Morin it was not an isolated case: similar rumours occurred in various places from 1959 onwards. And it is even more difficult to fit in the rumours I have mentioned about cigarettes and leprosy and about chewing-gum and pregnancy. A girl getting pregnant outside wedlock should not disturb any 'cluster' in the minds of the general public. It is the chewing-gum that is surprising. Nor do the rumours

[14] Sir Charles Oman, *The Unfortunate Colonel Despard and Other Studies* (1922), pp. 60–1. Oman does not say whether the description of the Russians 'with snow on their boots' (in August) was included in the rumour from the start, or whether it was added as a memorable absurdity later when the rumour had ceased to be believed. Indeed he altogether misses out the snow, the very thing that has made the rumour remembered.

about Persian cholera and about the legalizing of alcohol in Bahrain fit at all comfortably with Festinger's theory.

It also happens in some cases that one can interpret a rumour in a way that is in keeping with the theory but possibly less in keeping with the facts of the situation. I have already suggested how, by using Festinger's theory in the Japanese examples, one can diagnose two significantly different states of public opinion. In an Irish example, the application of his theory would suggest an assessment of public opinion at variance with other very respectable evidence. In April 1972, *The Times* gossip column reported a rumour current in Dublin to the effect that the Irish Government had undertaken to pay £150,000 compensation for the burning of the British Embassy in Dublin and, as *The Times* put it, 'Furthermore—and here is the twist—as the building was supposedly leased from an I.R.A. supporter some of the money would eventually filter through into the I.R.A.'s coffers.'[15] The implication of the rumour that some of the money was to go to the I.R.A., according to Festinger's theory, would clearly be that public opinion in Dublin was supporting that organization. But Conor Cruise O'Brien describes the burning of the embassy as the point at which the I.R.A. overreached themselves.

In particular, [he says] the burning of the Embassy had been a mistake from the I.R.A. point of view. People were afraid of lawless violence 'coming down here'. They didn't want any kind of war with England, even an economic one, from which Ireland would suffer more than England. They knew the burning of the Embassy would have to be paid for, in terms of jobs and trade and tourists and they were not in any such mood of exaltation as would induce them to accept sacrifices.[16]

Two of the more interesting early studies of rumour appear in essays by Sir Charles Oman and C. G. Jung. It is not only the

[15] The truth of the matter was, according to *The Times*, that no sum had been agreed and indeed talks on compensation had not got any further than the Irish government's original undertaking to have the building fully rehabilitated. The building had been owned by the father-in-law of a woman who was a supporter of the official Sinn Fein and had earlier stood bail for an I.R.A. leader. It was now held by trustees on behalf of her children and she had nothing to do with it.
[16] Conor Cruise O'Brien, *States of Ireland* (1972), p. 284.

psychologist who makes psychological comments on the phenomenon of rumour. Indeed, to some extent Oman's explanations
prefigure those of Festinger. Festinger explains that his initial
problem was to understand why, after an earthquake in India in
1934, rumours spread that even worse earthquakes were on the
way.[17] Why were 'anxiety provoking' rumours widely accepted?
It occurred to him that they might not be so much 'anxiety
provoking' as 'anxiety justifying': 'Perhaps these rumours provided people with information that fit with the way they already
felt.'[18] Oman, on whose essay I have already drawn for accounts
of rumours of the Great War, remarks of rumours in general,
'The old fashioned rumour was generally "tendentious", *i.e.* bore
witness to a psychological state of expectation of certain desired
or dreaded events, and declared that they had actually taken
place.'[19] And he elaborates a little on this in discussing the rumours
of 'La Grande Peur' in France in 1789: 'In this case we may say
that a phase of national psychology was the real explaining cause—
the attitude of fear, anger, and suspicion was the parent of the
necessary legend to justify its existence.'[20] In a later study of *La
Grande Peur*, Georges Lefebvre shows how these rumours of
widespread brigandage, which was believed to have been
organized and encouraged by the aristocracy in order to punish
the people of France for their insubordination, were first spread
by word of mouth but later gained another kind of authority by
being copied by the newspapers.[21]

In Jung's paper, a rumour enables a group of schoolgirls to talk
about a mildly salacious subject which they might otherwise

[17] Perhaps people there were only being realistic because it seems to be all too
common for earthquakes to follow each other.
[18] Festinger, op. cit., pp. vi–vii.
[19] Oman, op. cit., p. 50.
[20] Ibid., p. 60.
[21] Georges Lefebvre, *La Grande Peur de 1789* (1932), p. 87. Another kind of
confirmation of rumours by beliefs, on the principle of *petitio principii*, was
described by Fernand van Langenhove discussing German stories of atrocities committed against their troops in Belgium by *francs-tireurs*, priests, and other civilians:
'If the German soldier is dead, must it not be the civilian enemy who has slain
him? If the civilian is dead, is not that proof that he was guilty? Thus each attitude
and each thought obeys the magnetism of a common suggestion and finally
creates a reality conformable with itself.' (*The Growth of a Legend* (1916), p. 184.)

have found it difficult to discuss. The paper,[22] written in 1910–11, shows the marks of Jung's still-remaining closeness to Freud. Jung had been asked to investigate the rumour because of the trouble it caused. The rumour had spread in a girl's school and proved to be an elaboration of a dream that one of the pupils had told to other girls who had then passed it on as an account of a true happening. In her dream the girl had been bathing naked with one of the male teachers. Jung's conclusion was that the rumour had 'analysed and interpreted' the dream. And the dream itself was 'le vrai mot de la situation', giving expression to something already in the air. The girl, he found, had been fond of the teacher, but the teacher had criticized her work in a way she resented. Hence she had entertained fantasies of doing him damage. By depicting a sexual involvement with the teacher, the dream compensated for her fantasies; but also the telling of the dream served the purpose of revenge because it caused the teacher much embarrassment. Thus it appears from Jung that the rumour was an interpretation of the dream and the dream was the true expression of an *ambiguous* emotional situation, though he does not actually use the word 'ambiguous'. This seems to have been Jung's first and last contribution to the study of rumour, and it could be read today as rather commonplace popular Freudian psychology. Nevertheless, as Oman foreshadows 'anxiety justifying' rumours, Jung foreshadows the consideration of rumour in relation to ambiguity, to which I now turn.

III

Both of the more elaborate studies of rumour already referred to, the one sociological and the other psychological, regard ambiguity as one of the basic conditions of circumstances in which rumours come into being. In *Improvised News*, Tamotsu Shibutani regards rumour as arising when men are 'caught together in an ambiguous situation'.[23] And in *The Psychology of Rumour*, Gordon

---

[22] *The Collected Works of C. G. Jung*, vol. 4, ed. Sir Herbert Read, Michael Fordham, and Gerhard Adler (1961), pp. 35–48.
[23] Shibutani, op. cit., p. 17.

W. Allport and Leo Postman lay down as two basic conditions for the spread of rumour that 'the theme of the story must have some *importance* for the speaker', and that 'the true facts must be shrouded in some kind of *ambiguity*'.[24]

'Ambiguity' itself is a not unambiguous word, for it can mean either the capability of being understood in two or more ways or else, more simply, uncertainty. In the case of the fire of Rome in Nero's time, which serves Allport and Postman as a historical example with which to illustrate their conclusions, the ambiguity as it relates to the 'basic facts' may be no more than uncertainty. In the authors' commentary, the fire had an enormous bearing on the lives of the people of Rome. This establishes 'importance'. Its cause was unknown. This establishes 'ambiguity'. One could say, though Allport and Postman do not do so, that ambiguity in the more common sense of the word applied, in that people must have had to choose between attributing the fire to accident and attributing it to design. Allport and Postman's interpretation, in terms of psychological motivation that led the people of Rome to accept rumoured attributions of the cause of the fire, is that the people hungered for an explanation and for the relief that fixing the blame for the fire would bring. They

[24] Gordon W. Allport and Leo Postman, *The Psychology of Rumor* (1947), p. 33. The authors join these two conditions into the quantitative formula $R \sim i \times a$, which means that 'the amount of rumour in circulation will vary with the importance of the subject to the individuals concerned times the ambiguity of the evidence pertaining to the topic at issue'. A noticeable weakness in this formula is that although it manages to look precise it is made up of three things each of which is only arbitrarily quantifiable. The formula also suggests that importance and ambiguity are somehow or other equivalent or interchangeable, at least beyond some unspecified point. The proposition seems to be that if a rumour about a particular subject gains wide currency in a particular community, then either the story must be very important to members of the community, or else the evidence about the basic facts must be highly ambiguous, or both. Put another way, if one finds a rumour about a particular subject widely current in a particular community and the evidence about the basic facts is only fairly ambiguous, then the story must be of great importance to the members of the community; and if it is only fairly important to members of the community, then the basic facts must be highly ambiguous. If one tries to test this proposition out on some actual rumours, one soon runs across two difficulties: that of deciding what to regard as the 'basic facts' and that of judging in the same scale of value the importance of, say, sex as compared with politics or earthquakes. The authors also say that rumour thrives *only* in the absence of secure standards of evidence. In the case of the Orleans rumours, the standards of evidence were there but people disregarded them.

already hated Nero and so at first they favoured a rumour that blamed him for the fire. But they also feared Nero, and so when Nero set about a counter-rumour blaming the fire on the Christians, the people of Rome accepted it in preference to the earlier (and less convenient) one.[25]

The tendency of human beings to prefer blaming their misfortunes on other people, against whom they can react, rather than on accident is scarcely to be doubted. And it is hard to have to blame some terrible thing on something trivial. In the matter of attributing blame, Lefebvre draws attention to the common tendency to fear that a party or a social class threatens the life and goods of the majority.[26] But what is a little surprising here, according to the terms mentioned by Allport and Postman, is that having experienced the psychological relief of fixing the blame on Nero the Romans should then have disturbed themselves again in order to reapportion the blame.[27]

In the case of the fire of London in 1666, it was the Catholics who got the blame. But the rumour seems to have taken some time to crystallize. The fire broke out on the night of 1 September, and it is only on 5 November that Pepys notes that Sir Thomas Carew

do, from what he hath heard at the Committee for examining the burning of the City, conclude it is a thing certain that it was done by plots; it being proved by many witnesses that endeavours were made in several places to increase the fire, and that both in city and country it was bragged by several Papists that upon such a day in such a time

[25] Allport and Postman, op. cit., p. 160.

[26] Georges Lefebvre, op. cit., p. 64.

[27] Allport and Postman seem aware of the difficulty when they raise the fear of Nero, but they do not explain why the Romans did not blame the Christians in the first place. An account which might be convincing in the case of an individual changing his mind is less so when it deals with a large number of people. If the Romans had behaved in accordance with Festinger's theory of cognitive dissonance, they would not have changed their minds; see his summary of chapter iii, in which he says: 'Following a decision there is an increase in the confidence in the decision or an increase in the discrepancy in the attractiveness between the alternatives involved in the choice, or both. Each reflects successful reduction of dissonance . . . The successful reduction of post-decision dissonance is further shown in the difficulty of reversing a decision once it is made . . .' (Festinger, op. cit., p. 83). But this has more to do with his discussion of advertising than with the present example.

we should find the hottest weather that ever was in England, and words of plainer sense.[28]

In view of the Romans' change of opinion over their own fire, it is curious to note that in the same year as that of the fire of London, another plot to burn the city was blamed on the Dutch, a country whose interest was opposed to that of the Catholics. On 13 December 1666 Pepys writes:

... W. Hewer dined with me, and showed me a Gazette, in April last, which I wonder should never be remembered by anybody, which tells how several persons were tried for their lives, and were found guilty of a design of killing the King and destroying the Government; and as a means to it, to burn the City; and that the day intended for the plot was the 3rd of last September. And the fire did indeed break out on the 2nd of September . . .[29]

The *Gazette* to which Pepys refers adds that

one Alexander, not yet taken, had likewise distributed money to these conspirators; and, for the carrying on the design more effectually, they were told of a Council of the great ones that sat frequently in London, from whom issued all orders; which council received their directions from another in Holland, who sat with the States . . .[30]

In the case of the fires of both Rome and London, then, there is not only ambiguity as to whether the fire happened by accident or by design, but also evidence of equivocal attitudes in the public among which the rumours circulated. In Rome the culprits are the Emperor or the Christians, two interests very much opposed to each other who must have represented very different things to the Roman populace; similarly the Catholics or the Dutch are the culprits in London.

Of course, not all rumours, and perhaps even not many rumours, are changeable like this. But any general theory needs to take such cases into account. The occasional changeability of rumour does accord with a formulation produced by Warren Peterson and Noel Gist in 1951.[31] Peterson and Gist treat rumour

---

[28] H. B. Wheatley (ed.), *Pepys Diary* (1949), vol. vi, p. 49.
[29] Ibid., pp. 93–4.   [30] Ibid., p. 94 (footnote).
[31] Warren A. Peterson and Noel P. Gist, 'Rumor and Public Opinion', *American Journal of Sociology*, 57 (1951).

as a form of public opinion, defining public opinion as 'temporary and fluctuating attitudes and beliefs resulting from collective efforts to interpret constantly emerging new situations', to be contrasted with 'more static concepts like "culture" '. The formulation allows at least for rumours being able to succeed each other without consistency. Members of a population through which a rumour spreads are regarded as trying to interpret new events and form an attitude towards them, rather than as trying to relieve some Pavlovian tension which the novelty sets up in them.

In *Improvised News*, Tamotsu Shibutani incorporates the ideas of public opinion and of ambiguity of circumstance into one theoretical proposition, which he states in the form of a definition. 'In this book', he says, 'rumour will be regarded as a recurrent form of *communication through which men caught together in an ambiguous situation attempt to construct a meaningful interpretation of it by pooling their intellectual resources.*'[32]

On this definition hinges a great part of a very interesting book. But as a definition or theory I do not think it will do. To take a further case: a year or two ago, a rumour spread that a new and particularly virulent form of venereal disease was about in Addis Ababa. It was thought to have originated in Vietnam and to have been brought back to the main Ethiopian Air Force base near Addis Ababa by Ethiopian airmen who had caught it while training in America. The effect of the disease was to make erections of the penis continue to swell until the penis burst and the sufferer died. The disease also had lethal effects on women. The rumour was taken seriously enough for prostitutes in Addis Ababa to stop working for weeks. To calm the fears of the public, the Ethiopian government eventually made an official announcement that a medical investigation had proved conclusively that the new disease did not exist.

It is not very surprising that people should be credulous enough to believe such a rumour. But can we really suppose that a significant part of the population of a large city had to pool their intellectual resources in order to produce it? Can we suppose this

[32] Shibutani, op. cit., p. 17.

of most of the rumours I have mentioned? Some very inferior
material, to say the least, must have gone into the pool. One
inevitably asks why the idea that the group produced should be
so much sillier than what many individual members of the
group could have produced by uncooperative private speculation.
And two further questions arise when we apply Shibutani's
definition to the foregoing rumour. What was the 'ambiguous
situation' in which people were caught—can one even say whether
it was ambiguous in relation to politics or in relation to public
health? And also, in what sense could this rumour about a
non-existent disease provide a 'meaningful interpretation' of anything?

The expression 'meaningful interpretation' is a crux in the
whole subject. In Shibutani's account, rumour comes into being
when people are caught together in an 'ambiguous' or 'inadequately defined' situation. Their collaborative social interaction
produces a collective formulation which defines the situation.
Through rumour (or in it—this is not quite clear) people make
up their minds. In a crisis, says Shibutani, much of the situation
is already 'defined' in the sense that there are a number of known
facts. But not all the facts are known and between the known
facts there are many possible relations. Rumour provides the
'missing' facts which establish a particular relation between the
known facts. 'Events', says Shibutani, 'are not disjointed affairs,
but chapters in a united outlook; hence, an interpretation becomes
understandable only when the gap is filled in a manner that makes
it an integral part of an ordered conception of the world. The
definition most likely to be accepted is one that fits in with pre-
suppositions held more or less in common within the public.'[33]

There is obviously a great deal of truth in that account of
collective representations, but when people reach a 'meaningful'
formulation of what has hitherto been an ambiguous situation, is
the formulation meaningful simply in the sense of not being
'meaningless', or something more? Shibutani suggests that it is
something more. Reading his book, one has indeed the feeling,
from time to time, that having spent a long time studying it he

[33] Shibutani, op. cit., p. 77.

has become a partisan of rumour. 'The reality to be studied', he says, 'is not distortion in serial transmission but the social interaction of people caught in inadequately defined situations. To act intelligently such persons seek news, and rumour is essentially a type of news.' This is a large claim—not with regard to news but with regard to people's wanting the news in order to act intelligently. I will not labour the point that the claim does not accord with a number of the instances of rumour already mentioned. But it is a conspicuous fact that in situations of crisis, when a rumour stimulates a group of people to action, the action taken is not only often very foolish: it is also action of a type that would have been foolish *even if the rumour that stimulated it had been true.*

In a number of countries in the world at present, the spreading of rumours is a criminal offence. This is, of course, a very awkward kind of criminality on which to legislate. How does the citizen know that what has been told to him as a true fact is actually a rumour which it would be a crime to pass on further? And one is inclined to suspect the motive of the legislation. Many of those who have written about rumour have said that it comes into being when there is an unsatisfied demand for information; a statement formulated as a hypothesis by Shibutani, who says, 'If the demand for news in a public exceeds the supply made available through institutional channels, rumour construction is likely to occur.'[34] When governments impose legal penalties for the spreading of rumours, one suspects them both of fearing to tell the truth themselves and of intending to silence others.

But I can quote one modern case at least in which a government's campaign against rumour seems indisputably justified. It concerns the Malaysian government's attempts to prevent any recrudescence of the Malay anti-Chinese and Chinese anti-Malay rumours which contributed to the very serious civil disturbances of 13 May 1969. Since then in Malaysia there have been government notices in shops and offices and on the outsides of private houses saying, 'Do not believe in rumour'. Intercommunal strife

---

[34] Shibutani, op. cit., p. 57. The idea was also very much in the minds of those who set up the Ministry of Information in Britain in the Second World War.

could scarcely result from the wish to act intelligently in relation to the other community. It is associated much more with the aggression, fear, anger, and hatred that are bound up with the collective representations of those concerned. And thus I think it would be wrong to speak of a 'meaningful' interpretation in any sense beyond what could equally well be expressed as a *coherent* (as distinct from incoherent) interpretation. The substitution of the word 'coherent', it will be noticed, would take us a distinct step closer to the psychological coinage 'consonant'. And it would not implicitly exclude from consideration the possibility that some rumours may be tied up with some lowest common denominator of mental processes within the people who make up a community. Moreover it would not have such a strong underlying suggestion of function, not to say of utility.

IV

The approaches of the social psychologists and sociologists on the one hand and of the historians on the other, as they have appeared so far in this paper, reveal a notable difference. The social scientists are inclined to treat rumour as purposive—sometimes even therapeutic—for the public within which it spreads, whereas the historians, on the other hand, tend to treat it as being symptomatic. For Sir Charles Oman, rumour 'bore witness' to a psychological condition. For the social scientists, rumour resolves psychological tensions caused by the ambiguities of new situations, gives psychological relief, enables people to form or remodel their world into a coherent pattern, or, even, allows them to act.

It is to be observed that the generally 'purposive' interpretations of rumour tend to assume a clearly marked division between people and the circumstances in which they live, whether the people are considered as individuals or as groups. In this view, people are exposed to an outside world that is always changing. Hence their intactness is constantly threatened with the ambiguous stimuli that a confusing outside world produces. They interpret and supplement the stimuli that impinge on them from the 'outside' and thus adapt them to their 'inside'. This may, perhaps, be an appropriate way of conceiving of individual psychology—though one wonders again whether it implies a cocoon-like intelligence at the centre of things, in the place of a brain evolved to the very end of receiving stimuli and often, as in the case of pain, cruelly unable to blunt them. But it is not an entirely appropriate way of approaching the group, since as well as receiving stimuli from the outside the group can produce its own stimuli. If this is admitted, then we are not obliged to speculate on the elusive external stimuli that might have been needed to provoke rumours I have quoted which have proved in some way or other intractable—for example, the rumour of venereal disease in Addis Ababa. One can try instead to search for the whole explanation within the community where the rumour spread, inquiring what there is in it that connects with the details of the rumour. But one problem then becomes more complex— the problem of ambiguity, and where the ambiguity lies. Does it lie in the events or in the people?

The complexity stands out in Jung's essay. In the girls' school rumour he investigated, events seem to have thrown up no special ambiguity. The ambiguities of which we are made conscious are those of the dreamer and her fellow pupils the rumour-mongers, girls who are at a more advanced stage of physical development than society will recognize socially. Where in this case can we find an 'outside' distinguishable from an 'inside'?

An inquiry into the issues associated with the Addis Ababa rumour already mentioned reveals a state of affairs more closely akin to that of Jung's case study than to the idea of ambiguities in external circumstances. But here there is no dream at the back of things but a conflict in the minds of members of the group. When I heard of the rumour, my first reaction was to suppose that it was an expression of public opinion, opposed to any involvement of Ethiopia in the Vietnam war. A wish among the general public to keep out of the war had certainly been a significant part of the rumour about cholera and the Vietnam war in Iran. But I was told that in the Ethiopian case few people, if any, feared that Ethiopia might be drawn in.

The association of ideas and situations was not such as a stranger to Ethiopia could have made up by guesswork. It was a good deal more interesting, and though it had some bearing on Vietnam the question of venereal disease proved to be a better key to the matter. An Ethiopian explanation of the relevant situations was as follows: there were never any Ethiopian troops in Vietnam and it was never thought likely that any would be sent there. Many Ethiopians, however, objected to the war and also disliked any close military involvement with the United States. To that extent the rumour could be about foreign politics. But at home the high rate of prostitution in Addis Ababa was a controversial issue. Students blamed the government for not increasing industrialization or providing poor women with the opportunity of earning an honest living. They also claimed that the government encouraged prostitution so as to keep the students occupied in the brothels and leave them no time for political activities. Moreover, since it was out of the question to criticize the government directly in Ethiopia through the public media, an expression of concern about prostitution was an oblique way of using the media to criticize the government for failing to modernize the country. The irony of the rumour was that the government should have had to produce a denial, thus implicitly suggesting that potential political activists could return to their dissipations. And lastly, returning to the foreign aspects of the rumour, for all the modernity of the United States itself, people associated close ties between their own country and the United States with impediments to progress.

Once a commentary is provided on the relevant social situations, the ambiguities hitherto embedded in the Ethiopian rumour speak for themselves. The commentary on the rumour illuminates the society in something of the same way that a dreamer's comments on his own dream reveal his personality. There only remains to be added as a final detail of ambiguity a note of the ambiguous state of conscience in those who criticize the government but at the same time feel that they themselves are letting dissipations distract them from their ideals. They are in the circumstances and the circumstances are in them. And indeed, all the ambiguities that appear here lie as much in the people as in the situation: the two cannot be separated.

In the Ethiopian case we find an undoubted example of a bundle (to use Festinger's word) of associations. It seems highly unlikely—indeed it is impossible—that the separate details should belong in this bundle and no other. So perhaps a tangle would be a better term. But, bundle or tangle, the group of associations is of some interest. At the very least, a rumour like this one shows the associations, or some of the associations, in people's minds at a particular time. It is a key to inquiry. But, in addition, the specific details that are associated together are of interest. Working outside logic, the associative process of thought disregards the usual classifications—politics, morality, economics, and so on— within which analytic thought usually takes place, and is the more 'structural' (in Evans-Pritchard's sense of the word) for doing so.

But is ambiguity a necessary part of the formation of all rumours? I think not. It is observable that when the argument needs to connect rumour with external stimuli, ambiguity and doubt have an important and perhaps indispensable part to play. They are part of the circumstances which rumour supposedly readjusts or resolves. If one considers society as being capable of producing its own stimuli, ambiguity remains a possible feature of the case, but it is no longer indispensable. In Isfahan again, I heard one of those rare rumours whose content is entirely happy and reassuring. In a penitential month, one of the holy personages from early Islam miraculously appeared and brought help to an Isfahani family when the supplies of refreshments needed for entertaining a pious congregation had run out. No ambiguity was involved. I should, however, regard this particular rumour as being bizarre or fantastic only to those who are not in tune with popular local thought. In local devotional terms, the rumour was realistic. Apart from this, I doubt whether much more can be said positively of the rumoured miracle than that it was an expression of, and an encouragement to, faith. Negatively, however, to go back to another theory, instead of having anything to do with Peterson and Gist's 'temporary and fluctuating attitudes and beliefs', it would seem rather to have had to do with 'culture'.

The abandonment of the idea that all rumours are connected with doubt or ambiguity naturally raises a further question. If there does not have to be anything for rumour to readjust or resolve, do all rumours have to be purposive? There is one good reason for supposing that they do not. It is that if rumours do serve an important purpose it is surprising that there should be so few of them. For once one starts trying to remember rumours one has heard oneself in order to test one hypothesis or another, one realizes that rumour is far from being an everyday phenomenon. The world is full of doubts, difficulties, and ambiguities, all societies suffer stresses and contradictions, and yet rumour is, comparatively speaking, rare.

It might be objected that in a society like that of modern Britain where the public media produce an ample supply of news, there is little place for rumour. The objection is not altogether convincing. In a comparable society, there seems to have been no absence of news at the time of the white-slave rumours in Orleans, and people, especially women, believed the rumours in spite of evidence to the contrary. Why, then, should there have been that rumour rather than a lot of rumours on other subjects? But in any case, the Trucial Coast, when I was there between 1954 and 1956, would have seemed an ideal place for rumour. There were no newspapers and there was no local broadcasting. The majority of people were illiterate. Local people quite often misunderstood the news they heard broadcast in Arabic from foreign radio stations because of differences of pronunciation and of idiom. And there were all sorts of changes and crises. And yet rumours were few and far between. This suggests that if rumours can be considered to have a function, then it must be a function which is usually fulfilled by something else. And that is rather more difficult to believe than that they do not necessarily have a function, or, to return to my earlier vocabulary, that they are not all purposive.

But this is not to say no rumour is more than symptomatic. One can still suppose that when rumours happen they sometimes

do something (whether valuable or not) for the people who entertain them. From the examples I have quoted, it seems to me that
this is commonly so when the rumour has to do with ambiguities
in people's attitudes and in the society. In conclusion, I will try to
interpret some of the rumours I have mentioned.

The simplest is the Dublin rumour. In a position where people
were divided in their own minds over the question of the I.R.A.
and Britain, the rumour that the Irish government was going to
pay compensation for the burning of the British Embassy and
that some of the money would find its way to the I.R.A., seems
to me to allow people to reconcile their conflicting sympathies for
the moment and to have their cake and eat it, in the sense that they
could think at one and the same time of making peace with
Britain and continuing to sympathize with the I.R.A.

If I am right about this, what appears is a set of images expres-
sive of public feeling and public attitudes. It is, no doubt, in one
sense 'public opinion', as others have said. But if one regards it
as being public opinion, one must be careful to distinguish it
from the more logical, analytic, or reasonable part of public
opinion. It cannot be regarded as an attempt to understand or
evaluate. The rumour has its associations much less in the field of
logical thought than in the field of metaphorical thought. It is
not found by rational speculation. It is figurative. Hence the
attitudes it expresses do not have to be consistent with each
other. A bizarre set of 'facts'—and it has to be bizarre here for
the rumour to work—is invented to fit in with the attitudes of
the public. The bizarre story provides the logic, appearing as an
exceptional conjunction of facts, not a characteristic one. It
keeps the public's attitudes co-present even though they are not
consistent. In this sense they form a 'coherent' whole. And not
being rational, what is formed is not controversial in the same
way as its elements could be. The attitudes are potentially controversial in that some people will have a greater measure of
sympathy for the I.R.A. and some will have a stronger desire for
reconciliation with Britain. In discussing the rumour, however,
people can have common ground and keep each other company
in conversation without quarrelling, because the rumour caters

for both attitudes. It must have been something of a relief while
it lasted.

The rumour that the Persian government had invented a cholera
epidemic as an excuse for not sending troops to Vietnam I would
interpret as follows: the announcement that there was an epidemic
of cholera had caused considerable alarm and yet there had been
no epidemic in Isfahan. People thought that government statements were often untruthful, but they did not suppose that the
government was capriciously untruthful. People in Iran very
much disliked the Vietnam War. There had been a strong
polarization between the left and the right wing in Iran, and people
could imagine the bombs being dropped on Vietnam being
dropped on them. But the situation was becoming milder in Iran
at that time. If, after the 'white revolution' the government was
being cooler towards America, there was further cause for relief.
And all the worry over the cholera would not have been wasted.

The background situation of the Dubai rumour, in which the
British were supposed to be turning out the sheikhs of Dubai and
handing the town over to their traditional enemies the sheikhs of
Abu Dhabi in order to introduce a British adviser who would
modernize the running of Dubai, would unfortunately take far
too long to relate. But I will quote the conclusion I reached in
1957:

The conclusion suggested . . . is that here there is a desire to have
modernization such as could be achieved by the appointment of a
British adviser, but that it would be apprehended that the appointment
of an adviser would place the British in active, practical control of
local affairs. We are given the picture of the British removing the
whole ruling family by force and handing over their state to their
enemies for the sake of introducing a British adviser: which is to say
that the bringing in of an adviser is to be done with the maximum
display of British power and with the maximum offence to local
feeling. Hence, we reach the conclusion that the Dubai rumour is an
expression of a desire to have a more modern type of government in
the Trucial Coast but at the same time an expression of the hostility
felt by local people to the prospect of having control of local affairs
taken out of local hands, an objection to any further extension of
British influence even though the extension of this might be the only

way in which more orderly administration might be introduced at the present time.

I have saved the most curious example until last. The case is probably exceptional. The rumour was that the British government had forced the Sheikh of Bahrain to legalize the selling of alcohol to Muslims. At that time in Bahrain there were many conservative-minded and pious Muslims who thought drinking alcohol very wicked, and at the same time there were many modernists who drank illicit alcohol, which was expensive, in secret. The rumour was more current among the modernists than among the conservatives. One might have thought it was simple wish fulfilment. And no doubt to some extent it was. But it was conspicuous and surprising that the form taken by the rumour, raising as it did the question of outrageous interference in religious affairs by the British government, meant that the very people who would have liked to be able to drink legally and were passing the rumour around expressed great anger over the matter. Their political attitude was one of strong opposition to the dominant British position in Bahrain. This again, then, was a matter of having one's cake and eating it. But more significantly, like the Irish rumour discussed above, the Bahrain rumour had something in it for two points of view. It was suitable both for the conservative Muslims who objected to alcohol and the modernists who objected to colonialism. The rumour did not raise the question of whether it was good or bad to legalize alcohol. For the conservatives, the rumour invented a British outrage in that the British were spreading anti-Islamic evil, and it invented a British outrage for the modernists in that the British were interfering in Bahrain's internal affairs. Thus it provided an opportunity for conservatives to unite with modernists for motives that were not only ambiguous but incompatible and even opposite.

I suggest, then, that rumours of the more fantastic sort can represent, and may generally represent, complexities of public feeling that cannot readily be made articulate at a more thoughtful level. In doing so, they join people's sympathies in a consensus of an unthinking, or at least uncritical, kind. And perhaps this explains why the word rumour has a bad connotation that goes beyond mere foolishness. It suggests a surrender to the irrational. Rumours which produce integration in terms of feeling without thought are the voice of the mob before the mob itself has gathered.

6

Tallensi Prayer

MEYER FORTES

'THERE can be no doubt at all', says a famous authority on the subject,[1] 'that prayer is the heart and centre of all religion.' In Tallensi religion, as among the Nuer, prayer is normally associated with sacrifice or libation, and it is this complex as a whole that is the centre of their ritual system. Tallensi religious beliefs and ritual practices presuppose personality analogous to that of humans in all the significant agents and powers of their supernatural domain. The dead (*kpiinam*) participate in the existence of the living (*vopa*) as identified ancestors, not in collective anonymity; the Earth (*teŋ*), the complementary pole of their mystical and moral universe, participates in the affairs of mankind in the form of personified, named, and particular sacred localities or shrines (*toŋbana*). The religious system is pervaded by the personified representations of the ancestral dead and of the Earth. These draw all other agencies and objects and instrumentalities of ritual cult and action into their orbit. Medicines, for example, whether overtly magical or supposedly physical in action, are believed to be impotent without the concurrence of the ancestors and the Earth.

Given this system of beliefs and ideas, it is consistent for Tallensi ritual normally to include an interpersonal transaction between worshippers on one side and personalized mystical agencies on the other. Sacrifice and prayer are particularly apt media for such transactions and relations.[2] The Tallensi have terms for both. The verb for 'to sacrifice' is *ka'ab* and it embraces every kind of

---

[1] Friedrich Heiler, *Prayer* (originally published 1932), trans. and ed. Samuel McComb, Galaxy Books (O.U.P., New York, 1958), p. xv.

[2] I am reminded of Tylor's remark: 'As prayer is a request made to a deity as if he were a man, so sacrifice is a gift made to a deity as if he were a man.' E. B. Tylor, *Primitive Culture*, vol. 2 (1871), p. 375.

ritual offering or libation at a consecrated place or altar. It is commonly used in the expression *ka'ab ba'ər* which can best be translated as 'to sanctify' or 'to worship at' the consecrated place or shrine by prayer, libation, and blood sacrifice. The implication is that it is a ritual act directed at the altar to the supernatural recipient. The associated word *ka'* is what I am translating as 'prayer' but it is a verb and can more accurately be glossed 'to invoke' or 'call upon' mystical agencies. Both *ka'ab* and *ka'* are restricted in usage to their ritual context. One cannot in Talni 'sacrifice' oneself or one's time for a cause or address a prayer to a living person. One can however, plead with (*bɛləm*) or beg (*soχ*) living persons as well as mystical agencies.

I shall refer to sacrifice only indirectly since my theme is prayer among the Tallensi. And the first point of importance is that Tallensi prayers or invocations, from the simplest and shortest that occur in the setting of ordinary family life, to the long, elaborate, and rhetorical orations in the ceremonies of the Great Festivals, though stylistically distinct, are couched in the language of everyday discourse, easy to be understood.[3] They have no esoteric or liturgical language reserved for ritual occasions, as is to be expected in the absence of a church organization or a professional priesthood, or a written scripture in their religious system. Interestingly enough it is most conspicuously in the Talis cult of the External *Boγar* that hymn-like invocations occur, and this is clearly associated with its esoteric structural status as a prerogative of descent-restricted congregations of initiated males.[4] The ancestors and the mystical Presence of the *Boγar* are summoned by the chanted exhortation of the officiants accompanied by the rhythmic hand-clapping of the congregation. But the prayers which announce and explain the subsequent offerings, though ritually fixed, use the same colloquial language as do ordinary domestic prayers.

There are well-defined, customary procedures for libations and offerings but it is characteristic of the Tallensi that they are not

---

[3] In the spirit of 1 Cor. 14: 9, 'So also ye, unless ye utter by the tongue speech easy to be understood, how shall it to be known what is spoken?'

[4] Cf. M. Fortes, *The Dynamics of Clanship among the Tallensi* (1949), pp. 108 ff.

sticklers for minutiae. It would be unthinkable for a sacrifice to be repeated because some detail in the ritual sequence was omitted through carelessness or ignorance, though the lapse would not escape criticism. Nevertheless, the patterns are fixed and are well known to responsible adults.

Prayers, analogously, have some fixed features of form.[5] They commonly begin with an invocation summoning the ancestors or other mystical agencies, and end with petitionary exhortations usually made up of stock phrases. There are routine sacrificial situations when prayer follows a stereotyped formula—as when the ancestral shrines are apprised, on the first sowing-day of the year, that the time for sowing has arrived and the customary pleas for propitious sowing and well-being are pronounced. But in most sacrificial situations, even those that pertain to the Great Festivals and therefore have a fixed location and calendrical incidence, there are distinctive incidental features related to the personal histories, circumstances, anxieties, and hopes of the officiants, to chance events such as abnormal drought or rain, to the public mood, and to communications from diviners. For, as Tallensi frequently insist, the future cannot be foreseen. One never knows when misfortune may strike or good luck supervene. This signifies that one cannot know from day to day or year to year what the ancestors and the other occult powers and agencies are demanding and expecting.[6] Hence it is normal for those responsible to consult diviners before making any offering, even if it is one that is regulated by routine or by calendrical fixture. Even if the offerings demanded by ancestors prove, empirically, to be the same—as does in fact happen—year after year in the same situation, they must on every occasion have the authorization of commands from the ancestors transmitted through the diviner. The norm is thus honoured and also adapted to the current circumstances of the donors. Tallensi, unlike Nuer,[7] never in the

---

[5] Heiler's analysis of 'primitive prayer' remains a useful guide and I have benefited from consulting it. The articles s.v. 'Prayer' in *Hastings Encyclopaedia of Religion and Ethics* are less relevant to my theme but also make a useful introduction to the subject.

[6] See M. Fortes, *Oedipus and Job in West African Religion* (1959).

[7] Cf. E. E. Evans-Pritchard, *Nuer Religion*, p. 21.

face of misfortune 'ponder how it may have come about' in order to trace the fault in themselves to which it must be due. Tallensi become anxious, assume that some responsible person has been at fault, and hasten to a diviner for a diagnosis that identifies both the offender and the offended mystical agencies and prescribes the piaculum. In keeping with this, the body of a prayer is apt to be a free and *ad hoc* construction reflecting the particular features of the occasion, though stock phrases will be used and stock sentiments and attitudes exhibited.

It was this aspect of Tallensi prayer that chiefly held my attention at the beginning of my field research in 1934. It was in the middle of the dry season and ritual activities were at their peak; and as they were commonly public, carried out in daylight with no particular reticence, it was easy for me to attend. At this stage, being still ignorant of the language, I was dependent on informants for the reproduction of the prayers I had heard and seen delivered; and they invariably gave me shortened, conventional formulas. 'He called his ancestors', they would say, 'to come and accept their goat and to permit peaceful sleep to be slept and livestock to breed and farming to prosper and women to be married and to have children . . .' It required no knowledge of the language to doubt the adequacy of this summary of a prayer that lasted fifteen minutes or more. Later, I learnt for myself that it was by no means easy to record (in those days before the advent of the tape-recorder) let alone reproduce, the whole flow of a prayer, full of personal allusions and eloquent exhortations such as normally accompany a sacrifice.

I must, however, explain why the flexibility and the apparent informality of prayer so early aroused my interest. Evans-Pritchard had just published his paper[8] contrasting the Trobriand insistence on strict adherence to the verbal formulas in magical spells and their monopolization by the rightful owners, with the verbal laxity and freedom and the indifference to ownership of Zande magic, with its emphasis on the material substances used

[8] E. E. Evans-Pritchard, 'The Morphology and Function of Magic', *American Anthropologist*, 31, 4 (1929), 619–41. This paper, it should be noted, by the way, does not raise objections to Malinowski's theory of magic; its concern is with the structure of the ritual performance.

in the ritual. The theoretical issues this raised were much discussed in our circle of postgraduate students. Was the essential point of difference merely that in one system magical power lay in the spoken spell whereas in the other the same power was embodied in material substances, or did it lie in the qualities and character attributed to the supernatural agencies mobilized? The evidence from African ethnography available at that time seemed to confirm Evans-Pritchard's analysis without, however, answering all the questions raised by it. This was the stimulus that directed my attention to the form of Tallensi prayers.

In describing Tallensi prayers as flexible or free or *ad hoc* or informal, that is, like Nuer prayers of 'no set form',[9] I do not mean to suggest that they are casual. To be sure the Tallensi do not have verbally fixed prayers like the Christian Lord's Prayer or the Hebrew *Shema*, or the Muslim *Shalaat*; nor do they have stipulated times of worship during the day, or week.[10] They do not offer a prayer on rising in the morning nor do they say grace at meals. Nor, however, do Tallensi ever utter prayers spontaneously. It would be inconceivable for a Tallensi in trouble to do as a Nuer does and 'pace up and down' in his homestead in the open uttering a supplication to the Earth or to his ancestors. As I have noted, his reaction would be immediately to have recourse to a diviner. Such pious ejaculations as *Naawun bɛme*—Heaven (God) is there (to protect and bless), *Naawun nna mari*—God will guard you, *banam ni yaanan bɛme*—our fathers and ancestors are there (to protect or bless), may be addressed to anybody at any time. But these no more count as prayers than does the corresponding curse *i na nye*—you will see. And, as I have already implied, there are no sacred words in Talni reserved for the proper ritual context and forbidden in mundane situations.

What regulates Tallensi prayers in their incidence, style, and general shape, is their normal association with sacrifice (*kaʿabɔr*) and altars (*bayɔr*). The beings or powers to whom prayers are addressed are invoked to attend at a particular shrine or place of

---

[9] Evans-Pritchard, op. cit., p. 22.

[10] Christian and Muslim prayer and ritual are designated *poʿox, Nayin*—which, literally translated, means to salute or give thanks to God.

sacrifice and the invocation is aimed, as it were, at this visible and tangible material focus, and not launched towards heaven or into space. An audience is assumed to be present, and the postures and attitudes of the officiants and participants reflect this situation.

A diviner's shrine (*bakologo*) is one of many that are upright, standing four or five foot high. In sacrificing to it a man stands and speaks as if addressing another person face to face. Other ancestral altars, and Earth shrines, are on the ground or low down. In sacrificing to these a man squats, likewise addressing the recipient as if face to face on the same level. Sacrifice and prayer are offered thus in the idiom of mutually courteous everyday intercourse with elders. It is as if in salutation to an elder or chief that heads are bared and eyes lowered by the participants in solemn sacrificial ceremonies, and it is as a gesture of special respect that in certain sacrifices given during funerals the officiant washes his hands first (for 'you are offering food and drink to the dead'). A tone of intimacy and frankness runs through the supplication and confession. Tallensi may bow the head but they do not abase themselves either in prayer, or in the presence of living superiors by status.

I have said that spontaneous individual prayer is not a Tallensi practice. Perhaps the main reason for this is that freedom to offer sacrifice and prayer is not general. Women, being jural and ritual minors, are permitted to officiate in prayers and sacrifice only in special circumstances, and this applies also to youths and even to men of mature years whose 'fathers are still alive'.[11] Similarly, the right and duty of officiating in worship of the Earth shrines and of the founding ancestors of the lineage at the altars dedicated to them is regulated by age and office. There are also ritual restrictions on freedom to offer sacrifice and prayer. It is, for instance, ritually prohibited for the officiants, and all other participants, in a sacrifice at an Earth shrine or an External *Boɣar* to wear a cloth upper garment; a man whose wife is pregnant or menstruating may not officiate in mortuary and funeral rituals; and there are many other ritual restrictions of this type.

[11] Cf. M. Fortes, *The Web of Kinship* (1949), pp. 147 ff.

Lest, however, the impression be conveyed that prayer is no more than a variant of ordinary respectful discourse, I must emphasize that it is clearly distinguished by its context of association with sacrifice and its focus in an altar, as well as by its style and contents; and an examination of some specimens will make this clear. We must bear in mind that there is no priesthood or scripture to ensure uniformity or conformity in prayer.

I begin with an example of a prayer as it was reported to me by an informant before I knew enough of the language to follow it myself. A minor headman had offered a chicken on the altar consecrated to his father's *Yin*.[12] According to my informant his prayer ran as follows:

My father, you begot me, and then you died and you said that if I gain the headmanship I must give you [in sacrifice] a cow. I gained the headmanship and you said I must give you a cow. Today, I have been to thatch the white man's house and the District Commissioner has paid me. But people, some of them, have gone to Gambaga to report that I have withheld their money from them. If, when they return, no evil matter [i.e. prosecution by the District Commissioner] befalls me, I will buy a cow and offer it to you; but if, when they return I am put to shame, I will not give it to you.

This potted version of a long and repetitive prayer does scant justice to it. It does not convey the undertone of anxiety in the speaker's voice and leaves out all the details of his story, of his invocation, and of his expostulations. But it suffices to indicate what is the most striking feature of Tallensi prayer.

Prayer is a cathartic exercise. Let me explain what I mean by this. Prayer is the central element of a ritual act calculated to master what Tallensi represent to themselves, in the idioms of their customary beliefs and ideas, as a crisis or a threat of a crisis. To the observer the crisis might seem trivial and ephemeral or no more than a remote contingency, or even, in reality, non-existent. It is none the less experienced as a real and compelling one by the Tallensi themselves. Prayer serves, then, as the main cathartic element of the ritual by making public and thus bringing into the open of social acceptability the state of affairs that is believed to

[12] For an account of this notion among the Tallensi cf. Fortes, op. cit. (1959).

lie behind the crisis. Now, in general all of this is known to the responsible participants, that is to say the lineage and family elders and the close relatives of the principals by whom or on whose behalf the offering is made. In many cases the relevant circumstances will also be known to a wider public. But revealing them in public in what amounts to a kind of confession, giving them explicit utterance in the ritually legitimizing situation of the sacrifice, gives the prayer its cathartic value. It enables the crisis to be grasped and interpreted and finally mastered. The fears and compunctions evoked by the crisis are openly expressed, the faults in question are admitted; and promises of the appropriate ritual services for restoring amity with the ancestors and other mystical powers are announced. On the other side, too, benefits received can be praised, triumphs flaunted, rights in relation to these powers asserted, and hopes of future benevolence declared. Piety is mobilized in action.

This explains why prayers always begin with an account of the reasons for the sacrifice, though it is well understood that they will be known to the main participants and, of course, by definition, to the mystical recipients. The past events that led to the demand for the offering, and the circumstances that compel submission to it, are rehearsed. The catharsis may be personal for the individual making the offering on his own behalf, or it may be vicarious when an offering is made on behalf of others. The prayer, however, is always a public and open utterance, directed as much at the company present as at the mystical powers addressed. Secret ritual activities are assumed to be associated with private medicines and charms that belong to the sphere of sorcery and magic and not to religion. It is a rule that legitimate religious activities must have witnesses entitled and obliged to share in them.

Though I am stressing the cathartic value of prayer it is, of course, the rite as a whole to which this pertains. The bustle of movement, argument, and cheerful conversation, when the sacrifice is shared in termination of the rite coming after the respectful silence during the prayer, is the best evidence of the relief experienced by the participants. But the prayer is the primary medium for the catharsis because it puts into words what the act of sacrifice can but symbolize. In particular, it affords expression to the ambivalence in the relations of the living with their ancestors and the other mystical powers which is of critical importance in Tallensi religion. The threat, in the prayer I have quoted, to withhold promised or commanded offering if a desired boon is not granted is a typical instance. Attempts at mutual coercion phrased in quasi-legalistic terms are characteristic of the relations of men with their ancestors. The public exposure of these relations in prayer is a way of trying to impose on the ancestors moral accountability to the living equal to the accountability of the latter to the former. Of course this never works. In the long run, death supervenes and this is interpreted as the victory of the ancestors or the Earth over the intractable living.

In the following prayer the catharsis is in part vicarious. To understand it one must bear in mind that a wife cannot offer prayer or libation on her own behalf; it must be done for her by her husband. One must also know that it is a sin for an infant to die in the arms of its mother. If this happens she must be ritually purified when she next gets pregnant or else the following infant will die in her arms when she first nurses it.

Daamoo's wife suffered this misfortune and when she was advanced in her next pregnancy the owner of the appropriate medicine was sent for to purify her. After spreading his paraphernalia in the courtyard, he took up the chicken provided for the offering and a dish of water. Handing the water to Daamoo he invited him to 'pour the customary libation'. Daamoo, squatting, spoke in a quiet conversational tone as follows;

My father Y., I am calling you hither, do you call your father N. and let him call his father P. and when you have gathered, do you then call J. and O. and all other fathers and forefathers. This woman bore a child and it died in her arms. I have no mother of my own and not even a stepmother. Indeed, there was nobody at home then who could have taken the child and that is how it happened. Now it is said that when such a thing happens and when the woman conceives again it is customary to perform a certain sacrifice and it then finishes. I therefore sent for the people to come and perform the ritual. Accept this water for you to drink and now that this young woman has this pregnancy, do you permit her to have a safe delivery and may the baby take the breast satisfactorily so that well-being may come about.

Then he poured some water on the ground calling out, 'accept, accept, accept this water and drink'. This done, he turned aside and splashing some water on another spot spoke:

O Zubiung Earth, I pray you, too, to accept this water, and you, all you departed Zubiung tendaanas, do you too accept this water so that you may support these medicine roots from before and from behind and permit this [mishap] to be like a light rain that passes quickly and not like a heavy downpour that goes on and on.

This prayer needs no gloss. However, it is revealing to put beside it the prayer spoken by the medicine owner. Taking this dish of water and addressing himself to the small bundle of magical material—the so-called 'roots'—he said, speaking in the same quiet conversational tone:

My father A., I am calling you, do you call your father M., and he call his father T., and he call D. and O. I am calling upon you by reason of your having begotten me, for you have no concern with these roots. It is only that you may come and sit here and give support as I do what is to be done with these roots, so that it turns out to be a light and passing rain and not a heavy and endless downpour. My mother, come and sit here by your roots and do you call my grandmother, your mother, and she call her mother and all of you assemble and sit by these your roots. You died and left this medicine to me. I, for my part, don't care to go about performing this ritual but it is you who said that it delivers people from trouble. That is why I am sitting here. An infant had remained in this woman's arms and that is why they have summoned me to come and perform this sacrifice. If you are really effective [as you claim] do you permit her to bear her child so that no sound [of pain] is heard, so that not even the mice hear a sound. Permit the child to be sitting in her lap so that they all realize that your roots do indeed exist [i.e. have magical power].

He then nicked the middle toe of the chicken's right foot, dripped some blood on the roots, and added 'here is your chicken, here are your money and your guinea corn too. Accept water and drink, accept your chicken, and permit everything to go well.'

These prayers are so typical of situations in which therapeutic
or magical treatment takes place that they can be regarded as
routine in form. It is noteworthy and characteristic of Tallensi
religion that the power assumed to be inherent in medicine is
inert until it is released and permitted to work by its original
owners and transmitters. But they cannot be effective without
the concurrent help of all the ancestors of all the principal participants. The patient's representative and the doctor have to solicit
the help of their respective ancestors independently though it is
in the same cause, for one cannot call upon ancestors other than
one's own. The Earth, too, must be invoked to aid the cure.

It is essential that both the client and the doctor must make the
circumstances which have led to the situation explicit in their
prayers. The full significance of this would require a longer
exegesis than is appropriate here. It is enough to note that it is
not merely the words spoken that mobilize the mystical powers,
but the words spoken by the person responsible for, and entitled
to perform, the ritual. The medicine, its original owners, and the
doctor's ancestors are not deemed to be present until the doctor
himself invokes them; but they cannot succeed unless the patient's
mystical guardians permit them to. And it is worth adding that it
is always taken for granted that the ancestors, the Earth, the
medicines, and so on must and will respond to the pleas. They
will become spiritually present. It may turn out later that they
have not given the help solicited—but this would be for reasons
as yet unknown to the supplicants, not through absence from the
occasion.

Note further that when both the patient's representative and
the doctor thus invoke their respective ancestors they are also
explaining the situation to others present. These are normally
kinsfolk or persons otherwise entitled to be present, not random
spectators, and the prayer enlists their participation in a very
direct sense. It is a two-way catharsis—in relation to the ancestors
and other mystical powers, and in relation to the living who have
interests in and commitments to the principal parties. Prayer
exculpates, on the one hand by relieving the worshipper's conscience, and on the other by affirming his moral standing in the

community. What cannot be over-emphasized is that the crisis thus dealt with is real and urgent to the actors. Babies do die in the way they fear.

The communal orientation of prayer is most in evidence when the officiant acts in a representative rather than a personal capacity. Then sacrifice is often accompanied by what could as well be described as an allocution addressed to the congregation as a prayer, though its ostensible reference is to the ancestors and other mystical powers. The following is an example: Buntuya died, rich in years, in children, in grandchildren, and in possessions, having thus attained the fulfilment that every Tallensi aspires to. But at the mortuary divination it emerged that he had been slain by his own Destiny ancestors on account of a white bull he had promised and failed to sacrifice to them. It emerged also that if this bull was not offered before the obsequial ceremonies, there would be further deaths in the family. Thereupon Buntuya's sons procured a white bull and summoned kinsfolk and clansfolk, friends, and neighbours to attend. They came, a great throng, packing the inner courtyard in which the altar that was to receive the sacrifice stood. The bull was dragged to the altar and the dead man's oldest son, addressing the senior lineage elder, spoke as follows (I omit the repetitions and elaborations):

Bulug, listen: Buntuya as a young man went to live at Biung. He farmed, he farmed immensely; he gained wives and more wives and children. But all the time he lamented saying that he was getting no returns for his work, that his Yin ancestors must be powerless else they would help him to farm profitably and get wives and children. But his Yin ancestors declared that he would farm and gain wealth and buy cows and be replete with wives and children and grandchildren. And they said that when he is thus satisfied he must give them a white bull, a spotless white bull. Buntuya promised, and he did indeed farm and get wealth and marry wives and abound with children and grandchildren and his Yin ancestors said let him give them a white bull, one that is spotless for they had prospered him and he again promised. Then he left Biung and returned to Tongo. Presently one of his wives conceived but became ill. He went to his Yin shrine and pleaded—permit this woman now lying in her room to get well, for if she were to die he himself would die and if she did not die he would with his own hands slaughter his bull for his Yin ancestors. But the woman died. So he said that he himself could not slaughter the bull for his Yin ancestors, it would be for us to give it and send it after him. He did not kill the bull and then he died and it emerged that his Yin ancestors had come and slain him and were commanding us to procure the bull to send after him. Thus indeed has it come to pass. Now we have found the bull and we offer it to Buntuya. May he accept his white bull at his Yin ancestors' shrine, to give to them, and be gathered to his fathers, so that this house may grow cool again and we be permitted to celebrate his funeral propitiously and be granted peaceful sleep to be slept and wives to accrue and children to be born.

This was no conversational piece. It was declaimed loudly and rhetorically, phrase by phrase, with mingled pride and piety, emphatic repetitions, and evident feeling. The congregation sat or stood in complete and attentive silence throughout its long-drawn-out periods. Then Bulug responded in a similar but more sober and solemn tone (again I abbreviate):

Buntuya's Yin ancestors [he said] had spoken fittingly. He had indeed farmed and gained wealth and wives and children. Now let him accept his bull and permit peaceful sleeping and grant that those who do not yet have wives get wives this very month and that children are born, so that this house may grow even larger than it is now. May the guinea corn now sprouting ripen properly and may we be permitted to slaughter this bull for him without mishap and to perform his funeral rites propitiously.

This was the climax. One of the younger sons of the deceased, who had been squatting on the flat surface of the altar all the time, now poured a libation and slaughtered a chicken as a preliminary sacrifice and waited for the bull to be killed. He carried out these acts in silence. The exchange of speeches between his older brother (for whom he was deputizing) and Bulug here took the place of the more usual form of prayer. Buntuya dead was thus reconciled with his ancestors by the pious action of his sons, and the mystical security as well as the moral standing of the family was thus re-established.

I have space for but a part of one more of the many dozens of prayers I recorded. One of the most dramatic ritual events I have ever witnessed was the acclamation of the most hallowed Earth and *Boyar* shrines of all Taleland and the ancestors, in supplication of well-being for the coming year, by the assembled Hill Talis *tendaanas* during the Golib festival. It took place just before dawn at the site of their most sacred Earth shrine *Doo*. The dance, attended by a vast concourse of perhaps 5,000 people, had gone on all night. Then as the first glimmer of light appeared, the senior *tendaana* cried out that it was time for the dance to stop. Within minutes complete silence descended and the multitude sat down on the ground. Then the *tendaanas* spoke, each in turn, standing on the rocks which are the altar of *Doo*, dimly visible, and seeming to tower above the audience. They hurled their invocations towards the audience at the top of their voices, with many dramatic pauses, with insistent repetition of the key phrases, and with many figurative variations. The effect was that of a reverberating incantation; and the audience, though well acquainted with this ceremony, sat as if spellbound in complete silence.

I will not attempt to reproduce any of the invocations spoken, even to the extent of the incomplete records I was able to make. But their flavour can be indicated by some excerpts from the opening allocution of the Wakyi *tendaana*. Turning first to the assembled *tendaanas* he cried loudly, 'Speak for me—will you not speak for me? Are we not all equal to one another? Does not each of us have power over each and thus we abide together?' This was a gesture of courtesy for he continued at once, addressing the audience at large:

Pardon me then. Our fathers, our ancestors of yore used to send out the call [at this time] telling people that *Doo* was inviting them, strangers and all, to join in the ceremonies by day and by night. It is ordained that there shall be no quarrelling, that the people who congregate here shall not strike blows—these are forbidden on pain of fines and penalties.

The *tendaana* dwelt on this topic at some length as the danger of fights breaking out between the dancing groups and among the spectators is ever present. Then he continued in a tone of high exultation: 'Well then, I now call upon my father the Tendaana, to call upon his father [and so on, in the usual manner enumerating a long line of ancestors] for all to come and take their place here, for it is *Doo* that calls them.' Then followed a long sequence of further invocations to ancestors of the other Hill Talis *tendaanas* and to all the Earth shrines and External *Boyar* shrines of the Talis. Then his voice and manner changed. A personal, protesting note crept in as he continued, ostensibly addressing the ancestors and other mystic powers.

Consider my coming here. How many years is it that I have been coming here [to this ceremony]? My coming up here, it is four years since I first came here and you permitted me to speak. I said long ago that I wanted a house [i.e. a family and many descendants].

Though he uses the first personal pronoun it is understood that he is speaking for the community as a whole.

I want to live to see such a house. Have you given it to me? [He added further reproaches in the same vein and continued] I call upon you to take heed. First about farming, we beg for early millet and for guinea corn. We beg *Doo* to grant us a cow, to grant us a sheep, to grant us goats and chickens. It is *Doo* that must grant peaceful sleep, grant marriages and children to all of us [and so on with repetition and variations]. Next, rain, let there be one sufficient rain, one rain, [and so on with repetition], one rain, so that we need but one sowing for our early millet, so that orphans may have food, widows may have food, women and children may have food. Next, locusts. May they go down into holes. Let them not come to this land, let them go down into holes, go down into holes [with further elaborations]. Once more, I want to call upon you to take heed as I have called upon you in the past. Let the early millet be well rooted, let the guinea corn be well rooted [and so on]. We want wives and children, we want things of all kinds to be gathered together for us.

This allocution, as I have called it, needs little exegesis. Though addressed to the Earth and the ancestors it smacks of magical intention. It is as if its declamation at that ritually sanctified place and at that symbolically suggestive hour of dawn, in that taboo-marked period of the sowing-festival, expresses the deepest longings, hopes, and fears of the whole assembled multitude. They come from the whole of the Tallensi country and beyond, not only to dance but to receive, by their presence, and to take back with them, the blessings solicited in the prayers of the *tendaanas*. But in characteristic Tallensi fashion the appeals are couched in terms that appear to demand rather than to supplicate and they are addressed to the ancestors and the Earth, not to magical substances.

The other *tendaanas* now followed with their allocutions in turn, trying to outdo one another in eloquence, dramatic iteration, and indirect allusion to their relative superiority in the rank order of the *tendaanas*.

No libations or sacrifices accompanied this ceremony. They had, in fact, been made earlier at a ceremony in which only the *tendaanas* and their elders had participated. This gave added point to the prayers themselves. It brought home vividly to me what I have previously noted about the hopes and fears, wishes and aspirations voiced in them. They are not to be thought of as figures of speech or flourishes of rhetoric. They reflected what, for generations, had been the hard realities of their existence for the Tallensi. Erratic or insufficient rainfall at the right time of the year was a frequent occurrence and the result was often a failure of the crops which, even in the 1930s, spelled famine. Locusts came often enough at the height of the growing season to ruin the guinea corn and reduce people to starvation. Periods of drought and disease killed off livestock most years. And above all, sickness, food shortage, and lack of medical and hygienic knowledge conduced to a chronically high death-rate, especially among infants and the aged. The complex of divination, sacrifice, and prayer among the Tallensi cannot be properly understood without taking into account their experience of living under what had for generations been to them the shadow of perennial and inescapable uncertainty, unpredictability, and threat in the management of their personal and social life. They believed, as they recognized in their religious ideology, that these dangers came from external forces and agencies; and they were not wholly unjustified in this. Environmental conditions, added to lack of the necessary skills and knowledge and to the limitations of their political and social organization, gave some objective foundation to their beliefs. This has a direct bearing on the significance of divination, sacrifice, and prayer in their worship of their ancestors and the Earth. Given their system of religious thought, it is quite realistic for Tallensi to solicit the things they ask for in their prayers.

7

Tiv Divination

PAUL BOHANNAN

THE Tiv of Nigeria, like many African peoples (the Azande remain, after a third of a century, the best recorded),[1] rely on oracles to answer questions to which there can be no pragmatic answers. They use several kinds of oracle: a rubbing-horn, administration of sasswood to chickens (rare enough when we studied Tiv from 1949 to 1952 that we did not see such a seance), and several contrivances that Tiv themselves consider of doubtful authenticity.[2] By far the most commonly used oracle is the divining-chain.

The Divining-Chains and How to Use Them

The chains are made from the pits of the *ive* fruit or segments of the pods of the silk-cotton tree. Most chains have four such pods, held together with heavy cotton twine on to which snake bones have been strung. Tiv sometimes tell inquirers that the bones must be from poisonous snakes, but different diviners in several parts of Tivland have confided that in fact they are made from any sort of snake bones that may be available—and may, in fact, be filled out with fishbones, though that is something like stretching yam porridge with cassava.

The diviner usually uses four chains, tossing them, one at a time, end over end so that they fall to the ground in front of him. The pod furthest from the diviner is called the head, the second is the belly, the third is the genitals, and the pod nearest him the feet. The chains are 'read' from cues derived from whether the pods

---

[1] E. E. Evans-Pritchard, *Witchcraft, Oracles, and Magic among the Azande* (Clarendon Press, Oxford, 1937).

[2] Fuller descriptions of Tiv oracles are to be found in Paul and Laura Bohannan, *A Source Notebook in Tiv Religion* (Human Relations Area Files Press, New Haven, 1969), pp. 669–88.

fall 'open' (concave side up) or 'shut' (convex side up). An open pod represents a 'good thing'—not necessarily an affirmative response to a specific question. A closed pod represents a bad or dangerous thing. If one of the pods lands and remains tilted upright on its side, it is a sign that a grudge is involved.

The way in which the chains are read varies widely from one diviner to another. It is simply wrong to assume, as Downes did,[3] that there are 4^4 responses (or $4^4 \times 2$ if you count the grudge, as Downes did not). It is context that is all-important.

After the seance has begun[4] the usual procedure is to have a question in mind and then to throw all four chains, most often from left to right, until the 'heads' of all chains fall closed or else all fall open. The first chain is thrown, then the second. If the head pods are in agreement, the third chain is thrown. If not, the second is rethrown once or twice. If it insists on coming down with the opposite indication from the first, the first is rethrown. The throwing continues until all head pods are the same. Whatever the probabilities, this usually occurs with very little re-throwing— even when I throw the chains myself.

Tiv tell me that the reason they use four chains is so that each 'man' can check on the others. One man (or chain) can lie or be contrary (*nyiman*), but it is more difficult for four men or four chains to maintain a concerted lie.

The answer to the diviner's question or proposition—which may have been stated aloud, but may not have been—is derived from the head pods. Cues for the next question are picked up from the fall of the rest, and the next question always depends on context. In a seance about a woman's barrenness, for example, if the controls come down closed, thus indicating a 'bad thing', and if even one of the chains has all its pods closed, then the situation is serious enough to indicate that the woman may never again bear a child (although conditions *may* change). If, on the other hand, the chains come down with all the head pods closed and most of the belly and vagina pods open, but the feet all

---

[3] R. M. Downes, *The Tiv Tribe* (Government Printer, Kaduna, 1933), pp. 68–70.

[4] For details and further cases see Paul and Laura Bohannan, *Source Notebook*, pp. 712–34.

closed, then the indication is that there is some *akombo*[5] concerned; if a proper ritual is carried out, she will immediately be able to conceive again.

Oracles as Quasi-Communication

Linguists and folklorists have created a model which is of considerable assistance in analysing the way in which Tiv use oracles. In their model of communications, there must be 'an *addresser* who encodes, according to specific statistical constraints, a *message* out of a *code* which, to permit decoding, must be shared by an *addressee*; the message also requires a *referent* and a *channel* tying the participants into a semistable unit'. Just as Sebeok has adapted this model to the more special task of analysing Cheremis charms and incantations[6] so we too may adapt it to purposes of analysing Tiv oracular revelations.

Tiv themselves consider the divining-chains to be a sort of prosthesis that might be compared to a Geiger-counter: that is, an artificial extension of the senses that will convert forces that cannot be detected with the senses, but nevertheless affect human life, into a form which the senses are able to deal with. With a Geiger-counter, physicists or physicians can detect radioactivity. With an oracle, Tiv can detect the sources of misfortune. In order to use this instrument, Tiv establish a sort of quasi-communication between the diviner and his oracles, which in fact *hides* the sources of actual communication among the petitioners of the oracle.

Using the units suggested in Sebeok's model, there can be said to be two kinds of communication and one of quasi-communication occurring in the course of a seance. First of all, the diviner can ask the petitioners for any information that he requires—genealogical information, the state of health of anyone,

---

[5] *Akombo* has never been translated in the literature—it is a material thing in which a force is said to exist; it is a symptom of disease; it is a medicine for that disease; it can be used mystically to cause harm, and it can be repaired in order to counteract that harm. See Laura and Paul Bohannan, *The Tiv of Central Nigeria* (International African Institute, London, 1953), pp. 85–90.

[6] Thomas A. Sebeok, 'The Structure and Content of Cheremis Charms', as printed in Dell Hymes (ed.), *Language in Culture and Society* (Harper and Row, New York, Evanston, and London, 1964), pp. 356–71. The quotation is on p. 363.

political persons and changes of administration, grudges within
the household. The petitioners answer these questions freely—
they say that the oracle cannot tell you the truth if you lie to it;
their attitude reminded me of the notion in our own society that
we must tell medical doctors the truth about our symptoms if we
expect the best service from them. Therefore, at that level, there
is a free flow of information.

Second, and at another level, there is another flow of information: this can only be seen in terms either of intuition or of what
psychoanalysts study under the rubric of 'empathy and introspection'[7] or—better—of both. It is certainly no accident that
successful Tiv diviners are intelligent and sensitive men—many
are even 'nervous' types—because they are called upon at a more
or less pre-conscious level to garner information about feelings as
well as information about overt events. By focusing the attention
of his petitioners (and, perhaps, his own attention as well) on
the *oracle*, he frees himself to use his intuition and his 'unconscious'
perception of feelings and affects, as well as more obvious paralinguistic signals among the petitioners. A good diviner does
something comparable to the kind of association that a good
psycho-analyst makes and describes as 'free-floating attention' to
his patient, the while he allows his own fantasies and feelings to
emerge into consciousness. The oracle itself facilitates this process
by giving a point on which the attention of all can be focused.

Therefore, there is a first set of communications carried on as
conversation among the principals and the diviner. A second set
of communications includes all this as well as paralinguistic and
empathic messages. The overt channel for the second set is created
by narrowing attention to the oracle to allow widening of a
covert channel among the petitioners and the diviner.

Third, the act of consultation itself is made to resemble a
communication to the point that some diviners actually cock
their heads to 'listen' to a reply. Tiv do not engage in anything
they describe as contact with spirits or familiars—another form of
quasi-communication that is common in Africa. Obviously,

---

[7] Heinz Kohut, 'Introspection, Empathy and Psychoanalysis', *Journal of the
American Psychoanalytic Association*, 7 (1959), 459–83.

none of these cases is 'real' communication. The Tix diviner, using his oracular equipment, and with a thorough knowledge of the factual situation through interview, a good knowledge of the affective situation through empathy, and his sureness of the principles of Tiv culture, engages in introspection. From the intuitive introspections of the diviner (based, obviously, on referents and codes well known to all those present), a 'reply' is forthcoming.

Tiv say that almost any diviner can learn to 'hear' (*ungwa*—but the word more generally means 'to sense') the messages. However, it takes one with a great deal of courage actually to *relay* these messages to the petitioners in words. A diviner's findings imply fault and guilt and sometimes actually cite specific individuals as guilty of witchcraft. As one diviner put it, 'After you have called about so many people in the community witches, you begin to wonder whether you should walk down the paths.'

The messages which a diviner 'receives' from his oracles *always* involve situations past and present—never future, except in so far as the future can be implied causally (using Tiv ideas of cause) from the present. Put another way, the answers a diviner gives are 'answers' to questions that have no pragmatic answers: what *akombo* has been used to cause the illness or barrenness or misfortune of the person about whom we are inquiring. Since there are no pragmatic answers, only mystical means of quasi-communication will yield the desired non-pragmatic answers. Tiv say they must know what rituals to perform in case of misfortune. The oracles tell them.

At the same time, however, oracles tell you something else: they tie down to an overt situation the vague and diffuse feelings of fear, anger, or dread that exist in the extended household. When these feelings are so pinned down, they can be ritually or jurally countered, and psychically abreacted.

Ende's Age-Set Consult the Oracles[8]

The age-set of men in their middle twenties in MbaGôr lineage of MbaDuku met in Chenge's compound (a large one

---

[8] A more detailed, but preliminary, account of this seance is to be found in Paul and Laura Bohannan, *Source Notebook*, pp. 712–26. The true name of the

where two members of this age-set lived) in the middle of a morning in March of 1950. Ende, one of their age-mates, was ill. Within this span of lineage, there were only seven other members to go to the diviner to inquire about his difficulty. The age-set had already made several unsuccessful attempts to get enough of their members together to consult the oracles. Today they managed to convene what they considered to be a sufficient group. Ende had fallen ill several weeks before. Pus had run out of his eyes, his belly ached, and sores appeared on his scrotum, which also swelled and was painful. Gbe, one of the age-set, told me that although Ende's 'lineage' (*nôngo*) were subject to hydroceles, this was no mere hydrocele. Gbe said that they expected to discover from the oracles what *akombo* to repair in order to make Ende's recovery possible. He added that the oracles can tell you who has used that *akombo* to bewitch the victim, but it is difficult to find a diviner who is willing to divulge this information, even when he knows.

The age-set members and I went first to a young diviner who was a guest at Tyuna's compound—within their own lineage area. He got out his chain oracles and tossed them a few times, but very soon said that the problem was 'beyond' the power of his oracle. The diviner refused even to consult about the *akombo* involved, saying that he was afraid.

The age-set sat on at Tyuna's discussing other diviners. They finally decided to go to Katsina in MbaYongo lineage, geographically close (little over a mile) but genealogically distant. When we arrived there, Katsina was not at home—he had gone to the chief's compound, and we were the second group of people to have come there this morning for consultations. The other party had gone on. We also left. Gbe forked off to the chief's to get Katsina to return. We proceeded to another diviner, Kôson.

To carry out the consultation, Kôson sat down in his reception hut beside a mound of plastered mud, with a pot sunk into the top of it. He spread a cow-skin out before him, put a bit of

<hr/>

diviner I have here called Kôson is 'Hindan', and so appears in the *Source Notebook*. I have changed it because that is also the name of one of the *akombo* involved in the case. The name of the diviner does not really matter, and the change makes the description easier to follow.

medicine into the pot, and then took his divining-chains and horns and ringers down from above his head—he stores them so that he can reach them without standing up. He chewed more of the medicine, spat it on the wall behind him, and inserted the rest of it in a hole in the top of the mound into which the pots are set.

Kôson divines with three single divining-chains and one double chain. As in all seances, Kôson 'warms up' by chewing

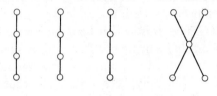

melegueta pepper and other medicines which activate those that he swallowed at the time of his initiation as a diviner. The chewed medicines are put on all of the apparatus as well as on the various parts of his own body—his chin, his elbows, his knees (this varies from one diviner to another). Then—and again this is usual—he begins by ringing the short metal tubes that are attached—perhaps thirty of them—to the base of each of two antelope horns. He taps or beats the points of the horns on the ground in rhythm, getting a response from the metal 'bells'. The stated purpose is to activate the medicines and to establish contact: to wake up the oracles. Kôson chanted during this performance—but the chant was mumbled, for it was a 'communication' between Kôson and his apparatus and not meant to include the petitioners. He made a considerable show of listening for a response.

Kôson, after having made his contact with the chains and apparently hearing an answer that everything is all right, asked the age-set what their problem was. He asked for specific genealogical information and asked to know the mother's agnatic lineage of Ende and of all members of his compound. Adzembe gave this information. He was some years older than the rest of

us—an agnatic kinsman of Ende's who had accompanied the age-
set as the 'witness' of Ende's small agnatic lineage (which was
hooked to MbaGôr by an uterine link). As he listened, Kôson
stared at two small stones held in his hand (this is the only time
I ever saw a diviner use this particular 'listening device'). When
Adzembe finished talking, Kôson said, 'There are two lineages
involved here, and a death has occurred.' He then turned to the
age-set and asked, 'Where is Ende?' The reply was, 'He is sitting
at home in his compound. He has not gone any place.'

Kôson then flipped the chains once, looked into the water, and
began to chant: 'Ende. It is he that I am talking about and asking
about. It goes on different paths. That path is good. That path
too is good.' He then turned and said in a natural voice, 'We
shall zero in on it.' (Literally, 'We move by foot into the centre.')
He returned to flipping the chains and muttering such things as
'Is it that which bested this man?... I understand, it is his father...
Again, I understand.' Again, Kôson seemed to listen and then
turned back and asked more questions: 'Is Adem his great father
or his little father?' (that is, 'Is it his grandfather or his father?').
Answer: 'His little father.'

Q. *Is his father dead?*
A. Yes.
Q. *Is his mother alive?*
A. Yes, she is living.
Q. *And what is she called?*
A. Jen.

Kôson went into another spasm of bell-ringing, and looked into
the water again. He again flipped the chains, saying, 'Is something
going to come toward me about his mother?' He listened. 'His
mother Jen...' He listened again. 'Is it his father? His father died
here among us.'

He then seemed to listen again, and turned for more information. 'Where has this man been?' Adzembe answered, 'He has
always been at home.'

Kôson then listened again, and said that if this man has a
strong heart, he would be all right.

There followed a short, but very mixed-up and many-sided conversation from which it emerged that what originally hurt Ende was not finished, and that now his swollen scrotum was the trouble. At the end of the discussion, Kôson announced that the *akombo hindan* was to blame. Akise (an age-set member whose

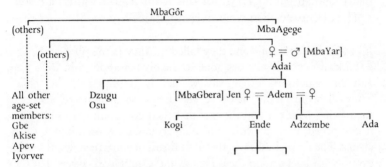

FIG. 5. Genealogy of Ende, his Agnates and his Age-set

father was a diviner) asked, 'What must we do about the *akombo hindan*?' The diviner tossed the chains. We were interrupted by women bringing food. When eating was finished, Adzembe turned back to the diviner and said that the *akombo hindan* had given their compound a great deal of trouble. He said that his father had a *twer*, but that nobody there has now, and the *twer* was part of the *akombo hindan*, was it not? (Everybody knows that it is.) The diviner replied, 'The *twer* and the *chigh* together make up the *akombo hindan*. You have to repair the whole thing.'

Akise now asked a question, 'Didn't they do more than that?' The diviner chanted, tossed the chains, and said, 'An argument either has broken out or will break out.'

Adzembe looked up in some concern and said, rather unbelievingly, 'An argument?' (The word is *yôsu*—it is rather stronger than an argument, but not as strong as fighting.) The diviner: 'Yes. What about the money and what about that woman?' (Two items about which Tiv—as well as some other people we know—fight constantly. Therefore, a safe ploy.)

Adzembe's answer was drowned in a general hullabaloo. The

diviner, however, understood it and made a second mark on the ground (he had made the first one after he had hit upon the *akombo hindan*). This second mark meant that there was a woman involved in this. Therefore he must next determine whether it is a bride or a ward. Adzembe took care of the matter by saying that they had paid £1.15s. for this woman—obviously, a bride.

The discussion then went over my head. My rough notes read:

Jiji's wife had one child and they killed it. Apev [a member of the age-set] asks if anybody else has gone to the diviner about this. Bells ring, and the response is 'Apev, this woman is mourning for her child'. They all begin talking at once. The discussion includes references to their being MbaYar and the fact that their compound has split. This, it is assumed, must be the result of an argument. More flipping of the chains. The diviner asks whether Ada forms one marriage ward sharing group with his two kinsmen, Dzugu and Osu. He discovers that they are separate, forming two such groups. He finds that Ada is now the oldest member of the group who is living, and discovers to his apparent astonishment that Dzugu's father's fields had bounded his own lineage area, where MbaYongo and MbaDuku come together.

When the noise had died down, a member of the age-set asked, 'Is it Ada who has spoiled the land? Is it indeed Ada himself?'

Kôson tossed the double chain, which falls thus (x means closed; o means open):

FIG. 6.

Several onlookers gasped: 'ah' and 'oh'. Someone in the age-set muttered, 'It is Ada who keeps it. MbaGôr will never agree to this.' (He had, in this statement, read Ada out of MbaGôr and back into MbaYar—a position that the MbaAdai were trying to avoid because they wanted their agnatic link forgotten and their female link into MbaGôr to be agnaticized, as it were.)

The diviner then said, 'It is very dusky [like twilight] and I am afraid.' He flipped his chain again, and it comes up:

FIG. 7.

'We are on the right road. There is a quarrel here.'

Adzembe spoke up loudly, 'There is no quarrel! Never! There is no quarrel!' They then recapitulated what was known already: there are four brothers, of whom Ende is next youngest. The diviner took over: he has shown them that 'something seized Ende' but that it would not kill him. He had then shown them which *akombo*. Apev interrupted to say that they have two mothers (i.e. the group of brothers is divided into two sets of half-brothers). Then one of the age-set said, 'Ask about their kinsman Nyugu from MbaGbera!' The diviner had no opportunity—or need—to consult the oracle because everybody began talking at once. The diviner listened carefully—so did I, but the sheer quantity was beyond me (and perhaps him too). In the old days they were fighting about their children—a reference to difficulties and grudges consequent to reassigning children of complementary exchange marriages. At the height of the noise, a member of the age-set took out money and said, 'This thing is finished', throwing the money on the cowhide. Akise and Apev both said to their age-mate that this was not a thing of money, but a thing of witchcraft (*tsav*). He took the money back.

When the word *tsav* was muttered there was a long pause. The silence was broken when Akise noted that Ende had two children —what about them? Another age-set member corrected him— Ende had three children. Confusion again broke out. Akise eventually 'got the floor' and summed up by listing four *akombo* that were concerned.

The age-set then withdrew slightly to discuss what its problems were and what its next move should be. During their conference, the diviner threw his oracle chains again, and one of the pods stood on edge, indicating a grudge. He said rather simply that there was indeed a quarrel—nobody could deny it when they saw the indication of the pod on its edge. After another pause, the diviner started off again with bells and staring into the water. The age-set was quiet, and I noted at the time they seemed so be giving him time to screw up his courage. But instead of sticking with this case, he side-tracked the discussion by asking Iyorver (another age-set member) whether his wife had a belly-ache. Iyorver responded that she did indeed, and moreover she was not pregnant. Kôson threw his oracle chains, but made no reply.

The next ten minutes or so were taken up with genealogical discussion about positions within MbaGôr. The argument was about the agnatic position of the MbaAdai (see Fig. 5). For Kôson there was a difficulty—not in understanding the genealogies, but in determining whether or not he would split the divining-chains and reveal the name of the witch (or *mbatsav*). He took considerable time running down all the genealogies with his chains to see whether he could find the place where things were wrong. Just behind me, Akise said to Apev, 'This man is not asking the right questions. Let's go.' Akise paid Kôson two pence. He tried to get more money, but none was forthcoming.

We all left and took the ten-minute walk back to Katsina's. He had his divining-apparatus spread out. Both he and Gbe were asleep in the reception hut, waiting for us.

Katsina's equipment was much more elaborate than any I have seen in this area. Instead of a water-pot, he has a mirror sunk into the top of a mud pillar, surrounded with feathers that are obviously those of the nightjar and *swande*, as well as those of sacrificed chickens. As we settled in, he started by pounding a rhythm with his ringers on the leather in front of him. He pounded a great deal more and a great deal better than Kôson. Akise put sixpence on the leather before him—a large fee, which I now think meant that they wanted no small favours, but rather that Katsina should proceed to 'split' the oracle and tell them the name of the guilty man.

Katsina tossed one chain, and then dipped something (I do not know what) into water and touched the chains, the bells, three of the various charms hanging behind him, and his own knees and shoulders. Then waving whatever it was he had dipped in the water (I never did see it) in front of him, he started to toss the chains. He then asked what they wanted to know—who is it? Apev answered that it was Ende u Adem. Katsina knew these people and turned to Adzembe to ask what had happened. Adzembe replied that during the last rainy season a wife of Ada had gone down to the stream early in the morning to fetch water. It was raining. Sitting in a tree, she saw a bird that had not yet learned to fly. (This was an evil omen, called *mnyam* by Tiv, the same word as 'dream'.)

The diviner asked Adzembe and found out that Ende's mother was from MbaGbera; he made mention of the *akombo gbande*, but was told that they had killed a young goat on it. Without ado, the diviner gave Apev four stick tallies. The first, he said, was for the *akombo gbande*, and he said no more about it. The second was for the *akombodam*, and he agreed that this would also be passed over. The third was for the *akombo hindan*. They paused on this one; Adzembe spoke up saying that their father had a *twer*, but that nobody had taken it up after his death. In the exchange, the *twer* was referred to as an *akombo mbatsav*—an *akombo* used by witches and hence demanding human sacrifices or human body parts in its construction. This point was to become essential in the reconstruction that was created after the end of the seance. The fourth tally was never named.

Katsina then tossed his chains and chanted unintelligibly, except that he broke in with 'Praise/thank you' (*M wuese*) every time the chains seemed to give information that was unknown to the rest of us.

Katsina turned to the group and said that he was going to 'split the oracle'. He turned back to his chains and flipped, muttering: 'Is it the mother? The child? Is it an agnate [*wanter*]?' On the last question, his single chain came up:

FIG. 8.

and he shouted 'I praise you', and turned to the age-set. There was silence.

After an impressive pause, Katsina turned back to his divining-chain and, using only one, he chanted to it and alternately asked Adzembe for information in a very rapid exchange. Adzembe gave him a list of all the 'agnates' beginning with four girls of his own generation. He then went to Ada. Adzembe's father 'bought' (*yam*) a wife/woman from MbaKaange, and [some agnate] then came to live in MbaItyo [lineage of MbaDuku—which contains MbaGôr but not MbaYar, their true agnatic segment]. How about Harga from Gaav? And what did this have to do with Nombua? [a red herring]. Adzembe said there were five of them [MbaAdai] in MbaGôr, and that Ada had received £3 [for a marriage ward, but it was not said which] and with this he 'bought' (*kem*) Dzugu and Osu. [This material came this way—what sense it makes can be garnered below.]

During a pause, the diviner turned to the age-set and said, 'Your age-mate will die.' Apev began to object because the other diviner had said he would not, but was shut up by Akise. [This discrepancy was later interpreted as fear on the part of Kôson, the first diviner.]

The diviner announced, at some length, that this was a matter of an *imborivungu*—Harga's *imborivungu*. [The *imborivungu*, or 'owl pipe' is a voice disguiser made either of the human tibia or of a bronze tube. It is a part of the equipment of the *mbatsav*, is associated with the *akombo* called *po'or*, and sometimes, as in this case, with the *twer* aspect of the *akombo hindan*.][9] The diviner turned to Gbe and told him that he (Gbe) obviously knew the things of the *mbatsav*, and knew what this meant. Gbe looked at the ground and said nothing [standard Tiv behaviour in such a situation—to admit it is unthinkable, to deny it is to protest too much].

Adzembe now said that Harga was caught having intercourse with a daughter of Adem's line—it was their daughter (*wan kwase*). Harga had paid a cow as a fine, and a dispute had erupted

[9] Henry Balfour, 'Ritual and Secular Uses of Vibrating Membranes as Voice Disguisers', *Journal of the Royal Anthropological Institute* (1948).

about how the ownership of the cow was to be determined within the compound.

Gbe then asked the diviner: 'Is it Ende himself who is at fault?' The diviner replied, 'It is concerning the mother of Adzembe.' Akise asked, 'Aren't they killing our age-mate?' Diviner: 'Yes' (*Mmmmm*—with the affirmative gesture).

There is a dilemma: the problem is that Adzembe came along as witness, but now he turns out to be the culprit, or one of them. What is to be done? No solution to this was reached. Katsina could not say more, and the group wandered away in twos and threes.

That evening, Gbe and Iyorver summed it all up for me. The version they had 'reconstructed' said that Jen also bore a son named Kôgi, who had stolen the *imborivungu* of their father's father Adai, and taken it off to Ikurav lineage, where both he and it had stayed until Kôgi had died. Then Adzembe had gone off to Ikurav and fetched the *imborivungu* back. They 'know' this because Adzembe had, without being asked, given Ende £1.15s. to 'walk around the market'—and that is unheard of unless there is something on his conscience. Moreover, Ende has three children and Adzembe has none. Harga inherited Adem's wives away from Ada [this is in contradiction with what I had been told earlier in the day about Harga's being a man from Gaav]. Thus, Adzembe is trying to kill Ende so that he (Adzembe) can pour Ende's blood into the *imborivungu* pipe.

A month later I saw Ende walking through our compound. He said he had almost recovered, and that his age-set really did him a good turn by going to the diviner for him.

Summary

Given Tiv ideas about illness, Ende's condition had to be explained and the mystical causation of it corrected before the physical causes could be medically counteracted. The seances turned up the mystical explanation: the illness was due to tension between half-brothers. The story about the *imborivungu* and the 'reasons' assigned to the 'guilty' half-brother were something of an afterthought, a poetic statement of the tensions. Although the story was complete by evening, it certainly had not been part of the seance. Age-set members took the 'information' they got from the seance (including references to *tsav* and the *hindan*) and, by a process of 'secondary elaboration', turned it into stories about *imborivungu* pipes, revenge, and murder. The underlying message in all such stories deals with the constant tensions in daily relationships, and ways to expiate them. Tiv said that, after being 'exposed', Adzembe should have desisted. He and Ende could thereupon 'discuss' their problems, with the rest of the compound present or even call a moot to discuss them before the entire lineage.[10] After their grudges and suspicions had been aired, the principals (and probably everyone else in the compound) should have performed the ritual of 'blowing out the grudge' (*hamber ifan*). This particular instance did not end in a public moot, and I do not know whether or not a discussion was carried out or the ritual was ever performed. From the Tiv point of view, the matter is almost irrelevant. Once they 'know', then their 'hearts' are at ease: they know the source of the danger, realize that it is domesticated and can hence be dealt with. Ende was not afraid of Adzembe; they were half-brothers and such things are to be expected from half-brothers.

This particular case shows several points clearly: there is a scale of 'bravery', and therefore of efficiency, among diviners. The first diviner would not even tackle this problem; he said his oracle was inadequate to the task. The second diviner, Kôson, revealed the *akombo* which had been used to make Ende ill, but he could not or would not proceed to the problem of the underlying social relationships that had gone wrong and hence 'motivated' the *akombo* to cause the illness. The third diviner, Katsina, quickly reviewed the *akombo*—his list was not identical with that of Kôson, but the questioners very quickly and without much thought disposed of the inconsistency: Katsina came up with the *akombo gbande*, which Kôson had not mentioned—only to be told that that had already been taken care of (i.e. the ritual had been carried out) at an earlier date. He did come up with the *akombo*

---

[10] Such moots are described in Paul Bohannan, *Justice and Judgment among the Tiv* (International African Institute, London, 1957), pp. 160 ff.

hindan, which coincided with Kôson's statement. And Katsina never did put a name to the fourth *akombo* tally he handed the age-set (when I asked later, it was said to be the tally of the witchcraft). Therefore, the 'reconciliation' of the two diviners was done by the questioners themselves—different diviners 'always' come to the 'same' solutions, because different façades of the question are revealed by each, and it is up to the questioners to put it all together.

What Katsina added, then, was the completion of the task—actually naming the 'witch'. This stage is not often reached—most seances stop where Kôson stopped, after which the questioners perform the *akombo* ceremonies indicated and do not ask about the specific witch unless the illness persists.

Tiv, unlike Azande,[11] seldom ask the oracles about practical steps in the business of living, and they even brand their neighbours, the Uge and the Udam, who do so, as superstitious. Although the oracles can indeed determine that there may be dangers that have not yet come to light—and in that sense 'predict' the future—Tiv never go to the oracles for that purpose (the assurance that you will not 'perish on the path' is sometimes thrown in by the diviner as an extra). Rather, they consult oracles to determine which particular social relationships are to be patched up right now, and which curing ceremonies are to be performed.

It can be seen that communication among the age-set and the diviners was, at the pragmatic level, open. The diviners got all the practical information they needed, merely by asking for it. In addition, however, by knowing the patterns of tension common in Tiv households, by noting the composition of the group consulting the oracle (age-sets never consult an oracle except in case of illness of a member; when two men of father–son generations consult an oracle, the problem is always the illness or barrenness of the wife of the younger, etc.), and by calling on a general knowledge of the culture, the diviners 'sense' additional information. Then, by focusing on the oracle itself, they further allow themselves to pick up innuendoes from the members of the

---

[11] Evans-Pritchard, op. cit.

consulting group (Adzembe gave himself away)[12] and to play their own hunches. The oracle itself is primarily a distracting device that allows the principals to construct an explanation that can be handled.

To call the 'interaction' between the diviner and his oracle a 'quasi-communication' because diviners like Kôson cock their heads and 'listen' may be to interpret the Tiv point of view a little too literally. The analogy to prosthesis—hearing aids or Geiger-counters—is more apt, especially since Tiv do not and will not speculate about the nature of any thing, person, or force that 'sends' the message.

Without the divining apparatus, the Tiv mode of group decision could not be utilized so effectively—someone would have to take the authoritarian position of 'dictating' the answer. Sometimes influential elders can and do merely 'tell' their juniors what *akombo* are involved and occasionally even what relationships are to be 'repaired'. But such authoritarianism is both rare and distasteful to Tiv. Whereas some African peoples use divining chains to underwrite the authority of leaders, Tiv use them to protect their non-authoritarian social organization and its way of taking group decisions. Through it, and through the ritual that follows consultations, the community is 'repaired'.

[12] See Theodore Reik, *Myth and Guilt* (G. Braziller, New York, 1957).

8

The Ideal and the Actual: the Role of Prophets in the Pokot Political System

JOHN G. PERISTIANY

IN writing about Pokot[1] prophets, concerning whom our only knowledge is the presumption of their non-existence,[2] I have had to draw solely on my own personal experience,[3] exposing, sometimes in narrative form, the roots of this knowledge as it was revealed to me.

I propose to discuss the actions of prophets and the beliefs concerning them, in relation to the conceptual framework, the institutional structure, and the system of values of the Pokot people. In so doing a number of discrepancies between Pokot ideals and everyday reality come to light. The compromise which transmutes the ideal into the actual is an index to the latent values of the Pokot and to the moments in their social existence when these values become operational.

In order to clarify the role of the prophet I shall draw in outline the three types of world within which the Pokot have to function. These are the world of the gods, the world of the spirits, and, finally, the social and physical world, the world-which-throws-shadows, all three being elements of one conceptual framework

[1] The Pokot (sing. Pochon or Pechon) were better known as Suk (see Peristiany, 1954, for an outline of their ecological and political divisions). I use throughout the name Pokot as though this were both the singular and the plural form.

[2] In his preface to Beech's book on the Pokot (Beech, 1911) Sir Charles Eliot writes: 'Mr. Beech informs me that though he is not prepared to deny the existence of medicine men among the Suk, he has never heard of any, which comes to much the same thing. But I confess that I feel sceptical as to this complete anarchy in a tribe of raiders who must have required some kind of leader in a fight. Tradition says that a Suk wizard bewitched the Samburu.' Beech himself (Beech, 1911, pp. 56 and 127), in the grammatical and the vocabulary sections, states that the Pokot word for medicine man is *werkoyion*.

[3] I carried out field-work among the Pokot in 1947 for a period of approximately six months as a sociologist to the Government of Kenya.

whose hierarchical gradations are reflected in the Pokot perception of time.

1. *The World of the Gods*

In order to understand who they are and why they act as they do the Pokot situate themselves in relation both to the gods who created them and to their fellow creatures, be these Pokot, aliens, animals, or plants.

The basic distinction and, therefore, evaluation is reflected in the Pokot conception of the Above and the Below.[4] The second, which may be said to represent but one of its facets, pertains to the order of appearance of beings. Highest and first are conterminous as are lowest and last, the extremes of each borderline category being endowed with the ambiguity of marginality. The nearest to two orders of beings, divine, human or spirit, participates in the nature of both and being both and neither mediates between the proximate orders, exerting its greatest power in relation to the lower order, which it partly transcends.

The three Pokot gods, all gods of the Above (*Yim*), are the Sky, the Sun, and Lightning.

Primacy of appearance in time is the main measure of the deity's relative greatness, first being equated with greatest. The opposite holds true with reference to the divinity's physical proximity to man and to man's perception of the divinity's signal characteristics. Thus, the god who is nearest to man, with whom man holds most frequent converse and of whom man is most intimately aware, is also the god lowest in the scale of the divine order.

The Sky, Tororut, father or master of both the Sun and of Lightning, is the greatest of the Pokot deities, the most distant from the earth, the most remote and most unknowable to man. The Heavens, a fluid and amorphous representation, are identified with Tororut, whose likeness no one has ever contemplated. Not only the Heavens, but the very notion of the Above, are equated with Tororut. Mt. M'telo, Tororut's abode on earth, is the most venerated Pokot site. When the deity dwells there, he mingles with the heavens. This mountain may not be scaled and no fire

---

[4] A similar belief exists amongst the Kipsigis.

may be ignited in its vicinity. Should a fire, nevertheless, be lit, no human hand may extinguish it. During great festivals, only the elders—only those, that is (and the Pokot are explicit on this matter) who are nearest to death, may sit facing in the direction of the sacred mountain.

Tororut's epithets are indicative of his function: *Pturei*, the one who listens, *Lumei*, the one who understands. Having created the world he observes its affairs but he seldom intervenes unless invoked, acting then in defence of the righteous person, of the one who has used recognized means of acquisition, as against those who have used unjust force. I note, in passing, that unjust force is to be distinguished from trickery (that is, from the devious manipulation of socially acceptable behaviour in order to gain illegitimate ends), as trickery seldom attracts divine retribution. Tororut, the Sky, listens and understands both in the sense of knowing what is in the 'hearts' of men and of having followed the sequence and the pattern of events. It is sometimes said that Tororut may be incensed by the wrongdoing of his children and that, in this case, he may visit on them various calamities, more as a warning than as a punishment. The form and the extent of the warning varies with the social range of the offence. Individual wrongdoers or, preferably, patrilineal descendants of a common grand- or great-grandfather, the more distant the more adequate for this purpose so as to give the sinner time to apprehend the warning and repent, may suffer in their health or their herds, a large territorial section may be stricken with an epidemic, with drought or rinderpest. In the first instance the rites of invocation, atonement, and blessing may be performed by any local *tilil* elder, that is by an elder known for the purity of his way of life; in the second, that is, in the case of wide-ranging afflictions connected with a large number of human and/or animal lives, the services of a widely renowned specialist should be used, especially when collective prayers have failed. In the first instance the sacrifice of a black goat accompanied by the performance of uniform rites should effectively atone and placate; in the second the discovery, *inter alia*, of the deep-lying cause of the affliction should be matched to the colour of sacrificial cattle appropriate to its removal; detection of both cause and remedy necessitating, in this case, qualities beyond those of an ordinary, if respected, elder.

Asis, the Sun, is almost equally remote. He is described as *Munung po Maril*, the Child of Whiteness, of purity, and, by extension, of purification with which the colour white is always associated, and as *Piwun po Nyung*, the Torch, the Firebrand, of the Earth. His main role is to be *Kong po yim*, the Eye of Above, the All-Seeing Witness. It is mainly in this capacity that he is invoked, thus: 'Asis, you saw my cattle being stolen. You see everything, Eye of Above. Punish the thief, make him return my cattle!' Asis—and this applies mainly to the traditionist hill section of the Pokot—may be solicited as amongst the Kipsigis and the Nandi: 'Asis, give us health, give us cattle, give us children . . .' Asis may give without his stock, so to speak, being depleted, but he grants requests only on his own singular terms.

Asis, like Tororut, does not succour human beings unless involved in their affairs through an invocation. Succinctly put, the attitude of the Pokot on this point (and not in relation to divine retribution, which sin sets in motion) is: 'Why should Asis help us if we do not ask for his help?' Does he, then, assist all those who entreat him through the performance of the appropriate rites? Asis 'sees', as Tororut 'listens', when the invocation is addressed by an elder whose heart (*mukulogh*) is pure (*tilil*), the 'purity' being made manifest not only through his good reputation but through the overt signs of divine favour, mainly long life, numerous grandchildren, a healthy herd; qualities necessary in the intercessor, advantageous but not essential in the suppliant. The main difference between Asis and Tororut is that Asis is said to behave like a 'father' towards humans (and not only the Pokot). His visitations are minor and personal, rather than major and wide-ranging.

The third member of this trinity of celestial beings is Ilat. The root *rel* (or *lel*) is used in words denoting the kindling of fire, light (as opposed to dark), lustre, effulgence, cleanliness and purity in the sense of being free from sin.

Ilat has a variety of epithets each reflecting one of the actions ascribed to him and the forms under which he becomes manifest. *Kerial*, lightning, *Ketil Ilat*, thunder, (*Ketil* denotes an abrupt explosive sound, a clap), *Kechogha*, thunderbolt, *Terchon* (from *torkina*, gradually, slowly) when Ilat has manifested his presence in the sky through thunder and lightning, while his other sign, rain, tarries in their wake, *Ngussurin*, when rain follows them apace.

Ilat, like Tororut and Asis, is a god of the Above. At the same time many of the tangible signs of his riparial existence are to be found on earth. Of Ilat it is said *ma chil pa, chil moro*, 'he does not cook grain, he cooks mud'.

Through rain, rivers, lakes, mud, Ilat is intimately connected with the earth, his works forming part of the earthly cycle of activities. Ilat fertilizes the soil and causes life to sprout from it. Present in rain, watercourses, and the rain-soaked soil, Ilat is the only deity to descend from the heavens when, assuming the form of a handsome and radiant warrior, he consorts with, and impregnates, the daughters of man.

Originating from the action of a god on a human female, the children of Ilat partake both of his divine nature and of their mother's limitations. Thus, in the case of their father, lightning is said to be produced by the flapping of 'Ilat's vast wings'. The godlings' overt sign is the lightning that issues from their armpits, should their arms, while they are children, be suddenly and inadvertently raised; indeed this accident may cause their death if their entire potency is released through this single act. Ilat's lightning is a precursor of rain. The demigods' lightning is mainly a sign of their origin. Ilat may fly through the air, as the Above is his element. During sleep the half-human children of Ilat have the daemonic capacity of releasing their head, or the power contained within their head, which then propels itself through the air, while their body retains its human nature and lies still on its couch. In this state they may not only come to witness actual, if spatially distant, events but their disjointed head may venture into the future and return to relate its course.[5]

---

[5] Care should be taken when waking any sleeping person as, although few are either children of Ilat or prophets (as we shall see later), sleep is so near death that a sudden awakening may result in one's spirit departing from the body.

The life of the consorts of Ilat and that of his children (*munung*, or *wer'po*, Ilat, son of Ilat, *chepto chepai*, Ilat, daughter of Ilat), are marginal to two worlds. The human wives of Ilat,[6] having consorted with a god, are separated from humanity by a number of ritual prohibitions, the most important being the danger that attends, for ordinary humans, contact with those who are physically connected with a god. This also applies to the children of Ilat. They have to be specially treated and even the woman who has ministered to their special needs[7] is heavy, *nyikis*, in her relations with other men. Not only her body but her shadow should be avoided, thus ensuring her effective separation from all humans who do not share her special condition.

One of Ilat's specific functions is to act as the messenger of Tororut. When people are bad (*ya*) they are warned by Ilat to change their ways, his warnings often taking the form of droughts or of verbal remonstrances.

Grown men and women are usually addressed by him in the dark, so that only his voice may be heard. His appearance, that of a radiant warrior in the full flush of youth, is usually reserved for uninitiated girls who have neither menstruated nor slept with men.[8] Ilat also appears to uncircumcised boys 'whose testicles are not yet heavy'. These youths Ilat holds to be *keltet* (clean, in a physical and moral sense) and he uses them, after addressing them in a melodious voice, as his intermediaries with the sinful adults.

When there is no rain, a 'clean' girl of a clan answering to the name of Ilat, Ngussurin, or Terchon, is taken to any permanent and clear pool (*ka po Ilat*, home of Ilat), and while one of her hands is grasped by that of an equally 'clean' man (see p. 174), she is immersed in the water. On emerging, and while water is still dripping from her body, the maiden pours milk, beer, and dung

---

[6] Ilat is said not only to court girls but to transfer to their father the normal bride wealth. He also works in the fields of his mother-in-law whenever custom warrants this action for a human son-in-law.

[7] Special care when coming into physical contact with the daemonic parts of their body, care, during sleep, when head and body might be separated, etc.

[8] I found no word for virginity and little understanding of the hymen.

in the water and invokes Ilat's help on behalf of the people.⁹ At
the same time this quality of purity, which is used to invoke and
appease Ilat (and which Ilat, on behalf of Tororut, aspires to
extend to all tribes), is made to serve Ilat's own sexual desires.
For the Pokot these two types of behaviour are not antithetical.
In the innumerable tales concerning the amorous encounters of
Ilat, the maidens invariably court his favours and the parents
frequently waive their normal demands for bride wealth so as to
secure more readily the divinity as their son-in-law.

One final reference to Ilat's predilections will assist my exposition. The three colours mainly connected with Pokot ritual are
white, red, and black, the first two, in particular, being associated
with Ilat. White is said to be light as opposed to both dark and
heavy (it is *rel* and *koskos*) and it tastes 'sweet' (*anyin*), these three
qualities forming, with *yim*, above, the complex of things
auspicious. White is invariably the colour decorating initiates so
as to single them out as protégés of Ilat. This colour protects
them, at the appropriate time, against the heavy (*nyikis*) and dark
(*togh*) powers. Warriors are decorated with both white, the 'light',
the 'pure' colour of Ilat, and also with red, Ilat's 'dangerous'
colour, which is associated with blood and with Ilat's thunderbolt, the arm used by Ilat to smite and destroy. White protects

⁹ This is the usual invocation by the maiden:
    Mengarach, pich a Kugo.
    You help, people of grandfather.
    Kewonyo tich ngo pich.
    Are finished the cattle and the people.
    Achono chego ngo kumi ngo eghyande. Kokoniyi yee. Ngaracha!
    This is milk and beer and dung. I give you now. Help!
When the maiden has poured the milk, beer, and dung in the water, the assembled
people sing:
    Terchon eoe, ngaracha kor, Terchondenyo.
    Terchon eoe, help the country, our *Terchon.*
    Ngaracha kor, ngaracha kor, Terchondenyo.
    Help the country, help the country, our *Terchon.*
    Ngaracha kor.
    Help the country.
It will be noticed that the supplication 'help the country' is repeated four times.
The number four (and in other contexts the number three) has a ritual value
which may be translated into an invocative and compulsive power.
    Women whose first child was a daughter may also pray to Ilat and even the
husband of such a woman may address directly his prayer to Ilat.

the wearer. Red both destroys the enemy and preserves the wearer when it has been prepared and applied by the charismatic specialist. I should add that both green and blue have symbolic affinities with white. They are included, in an auxiliary capacity, in the same auspicious category. Green is the colour of fresh grass which sprouts after rain; it is also the colour of the underside of Ilat's white wings. Blue is the colour of the sky.

Black is the usual colour of animals chosen for bloodless strangulation during the exorcism of 'heavy' spirits. It is a 'heavy' colour, but this very 'heaviness', which acts as a potent apotropaic and exorcizer for the evil spirits (the *ouget* and *cheptoimu* which are themselves dark and heavy (see p. 182), does not affect human beings.

Thus, the only colour considered as inherently dangerous is red as it attracts human strife and the thunderbolt of the god.[10] Ilat himself advises humans not to use it in decoration unless they have good cause.[11]

To recapitulate the operational arguments: the overt signs of the favour of Tororut and Asis, long life, good health, numerous cattle (and cattle and wives are, in a way, conterminous, as cattle wealth leads to numerous wives and children), indicate that a man is *tilil*, pure, blessed. Such a man is fit to invoke the gods and to act as an intercessor on behalf of his creatures. His very contact, especially through his spittle used in blessing, communicates his condition and may cause the sharing of the effects of his blessedness. This pure man derives his power from his being attuned to the will of his creator, from his acting out the divine order in his daily life. One case, in particular, escapes the ministrations of the blessed man, the case of the wide-ranging afflictions,[12] such as rinderpest or widespread disease, which have not been remedied by formal prayers. Only a charismatic leader with a particular type of transcendent gift may then avert annihilation.

The 'cleanliness' which appeals to Ilat may be achieved not

[10] Ilat asks humans not to wear red decorations or apparel during heavy rain or thunderstorms.
[11] It would be interesting to compare the beliefs concerning the potency and the associations of the colours red and black amongst the Pokot and the Masai.
[12] As against those which strike one man or one descent group.

through a long life of purity and of resistance to the transgression of custom (*poghisio*) but by acting as a vehicle for a particular condition, e.g. membership of a particular clan coupled with extreme youth, or the bearing of a daughter as a first child, this last being an inversion of the socially approved pattern of male primogeniture. Again, Ilat is the only divine progenitor. His daemonic children owe their powers not to their way of life but to special (in this case, inborn) qualities which become manifest in certain situations characteristic of their dual origin.

Tororut is the only Pokot demiurge. Asis is his themiscopos, a divinity whose role is to ascertain that the divine precepts are observed, and Ilat is the divine emissary, the go-between from Tororut to his creations. He carries both water and messages from the sky, his close proximity to man pervading his divine nature.

The Heavens and the Sun are clear and unambiguous gods and so is Lightning, while he remains in the sky. In their celestial capacity these three gods are linked with humans through men who either keep, in their daily life, the laws of the divine order, or, as in the case of Ilat's intercessors, are 'clean' mostly through ascription. Ambiguity manifests itself when a celestial god becomes the progenitor of earthly children, thus confining two worlds in one being. To shield oneself from these ambiguous daemons, purity is not enough. A special type of knowledge is required and this knowledge may be heightened by a gift, a charisma, which vouchsafes its owner not only protection against, but also power over, the daemons. Further, the male daemons themselves may become the progenitors of children of either sex whose inherited qualities render them apt to enact an exceptional role in Pokot life.

As we descend, both literally and metaphorically, from gods to daemons and from daemons to equivocal forms of life, the area of perilous ambiguity increases. Survival amongst these hazards necessitates both knowledge of correct comportment and inborn qualities attuned to the needs of all possible levels of being.

The exceptional person participating in the nature of these plural worlds holds the key to the understanding of the causality affecting human existence.

II. *Appearance of Life on Earth*

Having outlined the works of the gods and their relations with humans, I now turn to the appearance of life on earth.

Kenyisiok, a long time ago, denotes, for the Pokot, the dawn of history. This marks the beginning of things below the sky. At first, no living thing grew on, or trod, the earth. Then Tororut, the Sky, who pre-existed all living things, created earthly life, an undifferentiated form of life, from which plants, animals, and humans evolved. Primeval life, whose uniformity excluded sex differentiation, contained, at one and the same time, elements which, later, characterized plants, animals, and man. Those destined to be humans gradually shed their plant and animal characteristics in the same way as plants and animals, through a process of individuation, came to look and to function as they do today. While this was taking place, while this process was unfolding, the elemental beings, which had as yet remained undifferentiated, were prone to attack those who were assuming an increasingly human form. During this vulnerable chrysalis stage the peril was extreme. Only those who retained the memory of the ritual formulas in the language of their previous existence while straining to attain their new form, beings, that is, in whom these two moments of existence were conjoined, could ward off the attacks of the sylvan beings. The first humans, serving as links between the past and the present, communicated with all living things. Those who have preserved the gift to this day, the mediators, at the level of nature, between humans, animals, and plants and at the level of time between the past, the present, and the future, are destined to preserve their people from calamity and to lead them to new pastures. Again, those who know the nature or the language of animals and plants may also prevail on them to do their bidding. Thus the various types of warlock[13] address their familiars—usually lions, hyenas, and rhinoceroses—in the language of long ago, bending them to their will through this channel of common awareness.

[13] The most powerful warlocks are said by the Pokot to be either Karimojong or of Karimojong origin, or even Karimojong-trained. The warlock known as Kabulokion is now tending to assume other functions in imitation of the practices of neighbouring tribes.

III. *Specialists of ritual and magic*

There are numerous intermediaries between human and other phenomena. I shall examine them briefly to situate the prophet in his natural perspective. The ritual and magical specialists I group under three classes.

First, the *auguries*, of whom I know five types: the *p'kwanian* (m.), a respected local elder, who examines the entrails of (usually sacrificial) cattle for omens, the *kakorokion* (m.) and the *amoross* (m.), both venal haruspices, the first operating through the entrails of cattle and the second of goats, the *istoindokwe* (m.), who educes portents from the position of pitched sandals and the *chepokopo* (m./f.), who uses water mixed with milk as a medium of divination.

Second, *the wizards and medicine men*, some with ambivalent powers; powers, that is, which can be used for either good or evil. These are the *kabulokion*, the *kaworokion*, the *chebsogeyon*, and the *mutin*.

The *kabulokion*, a word of Karimojong origin, is a warlock (m., female only in an area known as *Kasauria*). The good *kabulokion* acts only as an executant of the *kokwa*, the council of elders. The bad *kabulokion* uses his familiars to further his own ends. Closely resembling the *kabulokion* is the *kaworokion* (m.), also a warlock, but one who almost invariably uses his familiars in order to threaten, extort, and inflict harm. His main service to the community resides in his power to counteract the harm inflicted by another *kaworokion*. Another point of interest is that the *kaworokion* operates with red-tinted clay,[14] the colour of blood, of anger, and of threatening Ilat, whereas the good *kabulokion* uses white, the colour of purity, as well as green and blue, the colours of the deities of the above and especially of Ilat in their benevolent mood. The *kabulokion* also uses yellow, an auspicious colour

---

[14] Red-tinted clay is made by mixing clay with the juice of a plant of the nightshade family and with animal blood. The idea that the power of the *kaworokion* is so highly specialized or so great that only two *kaworokion* may cancel each other out together with the use of red clay points to the *kaworokion* as a possible imitator of the *werkoyon*. The additional similarity between these two names also points to this possibility, which is enhanced by the Pokot habit of slightly altering the appellation of dangerous practitioners, either as an apotropaic or to point to a variant of the main category.

The witch, *mutin*, procures the appurtenances of a person (such as blood, excrements, hair, nails, footprints, etc.) and inserts them in a log from the *kipes* tree.[15] The rotting of the wood or its destruction by ants is said to be attained by a similar physical deterioration in the bewitched person. Here again the distinction between good and evil is one of social utility. A good *mutin* (m.) acts as a servant of the *kokwa*, while a bad *mutin* (m./f.) aims only at furthering his own ends.

The *ponin* (m./f.), an exclusively evil witch, both uses and sells his magic. One of the more frequent accusations brought against him is that, on encountering a person who resists his exactions, the *ponin* opens his legs, swings his body under them while throwing handfuls of earth at his opponent, the while muttering spells such as 'may your wife be sterile, may your child die, may it get lost in the bush'.[16] Of all accusations of witchcraft those of being a *ponin* is the most frequent, as the *ponin* is said to be usually motivated by envy and no one, however powerful, is free of this emotion, not even government chiefs. The only person to stand above such an accusation is the prophet.

Finally, we come to the *chebsogeyon*.[17] The good *chebsogeyon* (m./f.) is a doctor, a herbalist. The bad *chebsogeyon*, invariably a female, by adding her faeces, her urine, or her menstrual blood to her concoctions renders man pliant to his wife's desires while limiting his potency to his relations with her.

The third class comprises *exorcizers and purifiers*, both beneficent.

The most important of these is the *parparin* (m.), who is said to kill (*par*) whatever harms the country he inhabits and to clear up evil as a field is 'cleared of rubbish' (*parpar*). The twisting of a stick in a special contraption, in order to reproduce the voice of the spirits (said to be *wu-wu*), is also called *parpar*. The *parparin* performs purificatory ceremonies on behalf of those who have wilfully or unwittingly committed antisocial or unnatural actions (e.g. committed adultery or given birth to twins) and in so doing

[15] *kipes*, 'thigh', to denote a large tree.
[16] The curse can be cancelled by the *ponin* reversing his earth-throwing and his spell. Another usual practice of the *ponin* is to place earth on a rock while uttering a curse of sterility. [17] *sogei* = medicine.

he cleanses the land of his fathers and renders it 'pure'. His power is hereditary and is, ideally, transmitted through primogeniture[18] through males from a male ancestor who was the first occupier of the land protected by his descendants. The great *parparin* live in the hills where the population is sedentary so that the pastoral Pokot have to return to the hill homes, from which they originated, for the performance of the *parpar(a)* ritual.[19]

Some general conclusions may be drawn from this discussion. First, that only male practitioners operate in relation to cattle; thus all haruspices are male. Second, that whenever both males and females can perform a certain magical action, only males may act on behalf of a politically constituted body or of a large gathering such as an ox-feast, so that, even when a female is more gifted than a male, the male exercises wider power. Third, the arcana of all wizards and medicine men, although some may be inherited while others are handed down orally from generation to generation, may also be purchased. The only exclusively hereditary gift we have so far listed is that of the *parparin*, the purifier of the land of his ancestors. Finally, and perhaps most significant, the power of each specialist is limited by his speciality. We have not as yet encountered any single individual with universal and transcendent powers.

IV. *Ancestral Spirits and the Pokot Concept of Time*

I shall now discuss beliefs concerning spirits in relation to the concept of time before focusing our over-all conclusions on Pokot prophets.

In attempting to probe Pokot conceptions concerning the world of the gods and the position of humans within it I have continuously referred, albeit in an indirect way, to the Pokot concept of time. I shall take this up briefly as it is a key element in the understanding of what is to follow.

We have seen that any attempt to delimit the time of the

---

[18] Ideally male primogeniture of the first wife in each generation.

[19] There are a number of other minor practitioners in this class, I shall only mention the *liokin*, a male or female exorcizer of evil spirits and of the evil eye.

appearance of the gods is so inconceivable[20] that the gods are said to have existed before all else, that is, before the very act of creation. The beginning cannot be dated. Life began—the Gods did not. When, then, did life begin? This beginning is conceivable not in absolute terms but in terms of moments in the process of creation. Thus, the process begun by the gods ended in all beings attaining their present form. This is a closed system of reasoning in which estimates of the passage of time can only be made by reference to internal stages.

May the Pokot, then, date the events of their own social history? Can they situate events which came to pass more than, say five or six generations ago, in a certain sequence marked by a 'before', a 'during', and an 'after' in such a manner that this sequence will remain unique and never be repeated? More simply the question I am asking is: 'Do the Pokot share our concept of historical time, which may be represented by a sequence stretching onwards and never retracing its steps?' The answer, with some qualifications relating mainly to kinship memory, is: 'No.'

For the Pokot, especially for those living in the conservative hill homeland, the past, the present, and the future are encompassed by eight time-reckoning units, each of a duration of approximately ten to fifteen years. These eight time-units are repeated through eternity, with the same names rotating in a cyclical order. Thus 1 is followed by 2, 2 by 3, until the cycle of eight is repeated in the traditional order, each unit taking up to fifteen years to surrender its position in the cycle. Each time-unit we call an age-set, to denote, *inter alia*, that those who are recruited into it (through initiation at adolescence) are considered as social coevals. Parents and sons may not belong to proximate sets. Ideally first sons should be members of their father's alternate age-set, so that both Ego's grandfather and Ego's grandson, especially in the socially significant case of primogeniture, should, again ideally, be members of a homonymous age-set or, as the Pokot see it, of the 'same' age-set. Thus, age-set regulations should normally prevent young men from being initiated *before* the initiation

---

[20] The appearance of the gods can only be dated with reference to their own order of appearance. Thus Tororut appeared first, then Asis, and then Ilat.

period of their father's alternate age-set, while a man aspires for membership of this set for his male first-born. Self is then separated from either his grandfather or his grandson by four age-sets, four

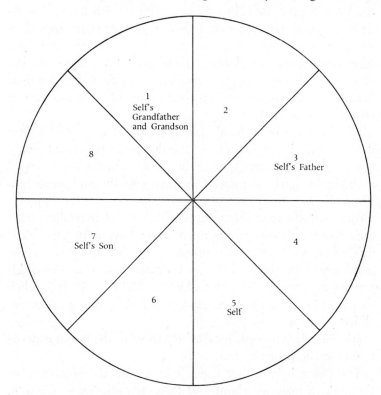

FIG. 9. In the 8-circumcision age-set cycle the minimal distance, which is also the ideal distance, between father and son should be one intervening age-set. Thus, in Fig. 9, 5 *should* ideally be the son of 3 and the grandson of 1, while he should be the father of 7 and the grandfather of 1. Thus, again ideally, one's grandfather and one's grandson should have the same age-set name. The ideal and the actual draw especially close together in the cases of male primogeniture through first wives.

'ascending' and four 'descending', eight remaining the total number of named sets as the grandfather's and grandson's age-sets bear the same age-set name.

I shall not examine further the mechanics of this system but I shall draw from it the conclusions which bear directly upon my subject.

(1) The Pokot believe that death is followed by the separation of the shadowless spirit from the shadow-forming body. The spirit, *onyet* (pl. *oi*), thereupon joins the neighbourhood spirits in the bush, a cave, or below ground. Spirits with living descendants anticipate reincarnation in their issue, they watch over their living kinsmen, appearing to them in dreams or generating signs forewarning of danger. These well-disposed spirits, the *chepkaramu*, literally 'the good ones', coexist peacefully with their kinsmen, from whom they accept libations of milk and beer as an overt indication of their goodwill.

(2) If, on the other hand, a long period of time elapses after death and no living member of the deceased's patrilineal family has called out the spirit's name during the naming ceremony of a child, the spirit despairs of returning to life and turns into a *cheptoimu*, literally a 'black one'. The 'black ones', vagrant spirits unattached to a lineage or neighbourhood, in retaliation for their receding hopes of reincarnation, endeavour to harm their living kin, who are in turn protected by their spirit allies, 'the good ones', by those, that is, who have a stake in the child-bearing capacity of their living kinsmen. The black ones, when they have lost even the memory of their kin, become a menace to all living people.

(3) The relation borne by these doctrines to the Pokot conception of cyclical time is clear.

The Pokot believe that a man who enjoys the protection of the gods, a man-on-whom-rests-the-eye-of-the-Sun-in-Heaven, will not die without leaving behind him male progeny. The length of his life-span, an expression of divine favour, results in his coming to know his grandfather and to witness the birth of at least one male grandchild. In terms of generations, tempered by primogeniture, this is equal to the revolution of the full cycle of eight age-sets. In terms of human memory, the last person who may reasonably be expected to call the name of his grandfather, at the naming ceremony, is his grandson, so that one of the important functions of a man is to provide his grandfather's spirit with a corporeal substance, that of his own grandchild, in whom rests the grandfather's almost last hope of reincarnation.

Thus, the eight-age-set cycle encompasses the most significant social expectations of any one person in relation to his ancestors and to his unborn children, the living vehicles of his ancestors' spirits.

(4) Finally, and this point is of capital importance, for the Pokot the past, the present, and the future are encompassed, not only for the individual but for the whole nation, by eight age-sets whose names are repeated through time in the same cyclical order. No point in the cycle, no age-set name, may be used to mark the beginning. Extreme points of reference within the cycle (for there is no way of referring to a 'previous' cycle) may be established with reference to the self, or to its homologue, the present. Within this cycle, and through the sole use of age-set names, no event may be dated more than three generations ago. It may come, then, as no surprise that the repetition of the names of the age-set cycle is equivalent to a recapitulation of tribal history. Each age-set is linked with a number of events, events whose form will recur when this age-set name is repeated. The history of the Pokot (I am tempted to say of man), the history of his actions since he assumed his definitive human form, is encompassed by the cycle of eight age-sets. Only the appearance of the gods, and their acts of creation, lie, in terms of time, beyond the confines of this cycle. Divine history (at least before the creation of man) is open-ended, social history is cyclical.

v. *Encounter with a Pokot prophet*

The events now to be described took place in 1947 during the Kerongoro age-set.

Kerongoro is the most nefandous Pokot age-set name, and I use 'nefandous' in its literal sense, a word that must not be spoken. The previous Kerongoro age-set periods were said to have been marked not only amongst the Pokot but also amongst their southern kin, the Kipsigis[21] by droughts, rinderpest, the infection of circumcision wounds, the disobedience of the young Kerongoro warriors, the folly of their leaders, and defeat at the hands of their enemies.

[21] And, I believe, in a number of tribes with similar age-sets.

How may one ward off the repetition of these calamities, the overtaking of the tribe by these evils? Through the elimination of the Kerongoro name from the age-set cycle, which would then progress to the immediately following age-set, thus intercepting the re-enactment of the pattern of events connected with the inauspicious age-set. This seems to have been the Kipsigis'[22] solution—a precedent unknown to the Pokot elders, who were pressing their young warriors to accept it. But the headstrong young men, standing fast in the belief that the name 'Kerongoro' was the property of their age-set, refused to be known by any other name. Faced with this predicament Pokot expectations centred on the appearance of a great leader, of a seer, of a prophet who would arise from amongst them and avert the calamities which were at hand.

I shall now turn to the description of the emergence of a Pokot prophet and of my own participation, or, rather, of the use that was made of my presence, in the events that I shall describe. This narrative may serve to anchor in some form of reality what might otherwise have centred around a discussion of concepts.

The time is that of debating the naming of the age-set which, according to the order of the age-cycle, should have already been named Kerongoro. The place is the vicinity of the Marich Pass, notorious for a massive defeat suffered by the Pokot at the hands of the Masai.

We were progressing in single file—a long line of porters, of tribal friends, as well as of hangers-on and of loafers invariably attracted by the anthropologist's party, especially during a long march, as we provided entertainment, food, and novel subjects of conversation for their homecoming. Small mounds of stones marked the side of the path; graves of brave Pokot warriors whom one honoured and placated by adding a stone to the memorial. When were their battles fought? A 'very long time ago'. During which age-set? Kerongoro, of course, for during what other set could such calamities have befallen the Pokot?

[22] See Peristiany, *The Social Institutions of the Kipsigis* (1939), p. 42 n. 3: 'Some of my informants were of the opinion that the first set of the Kipkoymet were traditionally called Kerongoro until some unlucky event befell these last and the name dropped out.' We now see that Kerongoro was an age-set in its own right.

To have asked 'which' Kerongoro would have been, as we know, a meaningless question, unless it could have been connected with known and authenticated genealogical information.

Suddenly the shrill song of a bird froze us all into immobility. Was this a bird of omen and, if so, did it 'aim' its song at the left or the right side of our column? If this song was a portent, was it auspicious or inauspicious? Long discussion. But we were on a peaceful journey; why should omens, used mainly for war, affect us? The argument carried little weight with those wishing to turn back. Had not the path we stood on been trodden by innumerable warriors, friends and foes? Did this not occur during the inauspicious age-set, the same as the one of this day? The bird stood guard and warned of what was to come. Of what significance would be the peaceful rather than warlike present condition of this area if harm was to befall us? Who could best answer these questions, who could interpret the omen? Certainly none of us. We lost some members of our group and the others marched on. On the way I asked what had happened at the Marich Pass, but I was warned that one did not speak of these matters near the Pass, especially at dusk. The next day we reached the Wei-Wei River. On the opposite bank crocodiles were basking in the sun while their attendant birds were picking their teeth. There was no argument as to our next move. We hurled stones at the crocodiles who eased themselves into the river, and thereupon we waded in, as if to meet them, towards the bank they had just vacated, the water rising no higher than our chests. If, following Pokot animal ethology, one enters the water at the same time as the crocodiles, being careful, as one advances, to thrash the surrounding waters with a stick, no harm should come to one. Here, Pokot opinion was unanimous. There was no hesitation and no controversy. Arrival on the river bank, sighting of the crocodiles, stone-throwing, simultaneous wading in of crocodiles and humans from opposite river banks—these events succeeded each other as in a well-rehearsed act.

At dusk our party camped near the river. I was settling before my working-table, preparing to demonstate how to administer anti-snake-venom injections, when I sensed that something out of the ordinary was taking place. Following the startled look of the Pokot standing on either side of me I saw what turned out to be a six-foot black mamba moving towards me at great speed. I scarcely had time to rise from my chair and to push away the Pokot standing by its side, before the mamba glided through the legs of my table and, continuing on its course, into my tent where it emmeshed itself in my mosquito-net before being shot through with Pokot poisoned arrows. The next day I was stung by two small scorpions while inspecting my shoes against such an eventuality.

The Pokot who had continued the journey with me were deeply shaken. Did not the bird try to warn us? And was it not unusual for a mamba to attack men, sallying forth from a considerable distance? This was no ordinary snake. It was the familiar of a warlock who wished us ill. Who, amongst us, both attracted this ill will and had the power to withstand it? These and other matters were debated during this journey, the topic of conversation always moving to more mundane matters at dusk. As for the scorpions, opinion was divided. It is usual for scorpions to rest in dark places—but odd that their active encounter should have followed upon that of the mamba.

These were the highlights of our expedition to the hills of Cheptulel, the heartland of the Pokot tribe. Nothing out of the ordinary followed these events, which were soon forgotten, until we returned to our main camp at Kongelai near the Turkwel River and the Uganda border. Here, of course, our minor adventures were dramatized for the benefit of our visitors. The spirits of those among the dead warriors who had not been reincarnated for many generations, which inadvertently we had not placated by placing a stone on the mounds, were credited with clawing at us, as we traversed the Marich Pass, as some had already become evil spirits while others wished to remind us of their existence and of their present unhappy state. Various deep lacerations and wounds were shown as proof of this assertion. And then—always in a hushed silence—the story of the attack and the death of the black mamba—a story, unlike that of the spirits, never told after dusk. As for the crossing of a river teeming with crocodiles, this was only mentioned as an amusing incident of the journey.

I had been planning to visit the *kokwa*, that is the assembly-place, of Ptoyo. On hearing this place-name there were hurried consultations amongst those present. Alternative journeys were proposed and there was unquiet when these were rejected. We left for Ptoyo on the morrow.

Following due north the course of the Turkwel River, we found the path meandering towards the highlands of Ptoyo, an easy and pleasant walk but for the combination of torrential rains and scorching sun which alternately drenched and baked us. A sentiment of strain, as when one 'feels' that something is about to go wrong, pervaded our party and increasingly dispirited it as we approached Ptoyo. I had myself the uneasy sensation of being followed by one or more persons who took great pains to remain out of sight. Our destination was reached before nightfall and after lighting a large fire we all gathered round it exhausted and shivering. 'Sit as near the fire as you can,' I was advised, ' we don't want the women of this place to throw their shadow on you.' I thought that this advice referred to the usual care taken by Pokot to guard against the shadow of menstruating women from falling upon them. As night advanced it became increasingly clear that the normally carefree atmosphere of our camps did not prevail here. Conversations were monolectic. My companions sulked, choosing to stare, doggedly, into the fire, rather than look into my face. I felt compelled, as one sometimes does in the dark, to look over my shoulder. Two eyes, glowing with the reflection of the camp-fire, seemed to have fastened on me. Yet another hyena? I turned in for the night.

When I awoke, it was early morning and I was weak with fever. I called out, but my Pokot had fled the camp. Realizing that I was alive and well they drifted back explaining that, as they thought that I was about to die, they had run away having no wish to be blamed for my 'murder'. Why should I die? And why 'murdered'? Because I was delirious and burning with fever; 'Why should illness strike so suddenly a man who seemed so well until then?' But people do fall ill suddenly, especially after a long march in the rain. This and other matters were debated until we eventually returned to our base camp in the arid plains of Kongelai. At sunrise my camp presented a picturesque sight. Not a Pokot was in sight. The thorn trees adjoining my tent were festooned with serval cats, hyenas, and rats, all hanging dead from their necks. My tent itself was encircled by small mounds. This made it impossible to take a step in any direction without treading on, or stepping over, one of them. At least that made sense as I knew, even then, that the Pokot, in order to prevent marauders from neighbouring tribes from trespassing on their pastures, bury various medicines in small mounds in the belief that whoever steps on, or over, them, forfeits his life or his mind. There was, of course, another alternative; to dig them up. I did, turning up a number of dead mambas and scorpions. When I had stepped clear my friends returned, solicitous for my health and testing, somewhat blatantly, my reactions to their questions. I must have seemed my usual self for they took down the dead animals from the trees amidst as much excitement as they would have mustered on the announcement of a neighbouring ox-feast. I kept my peace. Questions so near an event whose repercussions were unpredictable would have been side-stepped. I did go, though, to an *adongo* dance that night to broadcast what, I felt, was some kind of achievement. The gathering seemed glad to see me, but then the Pokot are a delightful people.

A few days later I returned to my highland station. In the morning I found a bearded man, naked but for the grey monkey skins covering his shoulders, squatting by my door. After the usual preliminaries, and in the presence of my Pokot assistant Aperit, he delivered himself of a long monologue. I have tried to preserve its meaning and some of its lilt.

'I am Riamanyan, son of Rionokol, son of Psielei, son of Pusien, son of Okomdi, of Okomdi *wōoo*, the one who first burnt the bush and cleared the land of Sòòk, driving the enemies before him.

'My father, Rionokol, and my grandfather Psielei and our ancestors before him are buried in Sòòk. Who can dig new fields, who can open new pastures without asking me? Who can utter

2. Portrait of Riamanyan

the oath of death [the judicial oath] without my consent? And who dare travel in these lands, looking at the well-fed cattle with envy in his *mukulogh-na-togh* [heart-which-is-black]?

'I shall be the Eye of my people by day. I shall be the Ear of my people by night.'

'This is "the-time-which-is-bad"'—and here he stood up, spitting, to ward off the evil of having had to mention, albeit indirectly, the Kerongoro age-set—'and here you come, "elder-of-the-stories"'—this nickname given me by the Kipsigis followed me amongst the Pokot—'speaking this *ngwen*, this bitter, name, and writing it in your papers. You have come back with the enemies of long ago to take away our land. I, Riamanyan, have worked hard to kill you. I sent the black mamba to bite you, I told the scorpions to sting you, and when you came to my land I asked the ghosts of our ancestors to take you away with them, but you did not die, so I came by night to your camp at Kongelai and made magic (*pan*) to kill you or to make you foolish.

'Elder-of-the-stories, if you are our enemy, put me in the House of the King [that is, in prison]. If you are our friend, make peace and teach me your magic, as I shall teach you mine.'

I was deeply moved not only because I was about to enter a world which would, otherwise, have remained sealed to me but also and, I hope, mainly because I was honoured by a brave man showing his trust in me.

What Riamanyan was stating unambiguously was not only that he was a prophet with great magical powers but that he claimed, through his gifts, to lead his people in times of danger. Prophets amongst a number of neighbouring tribes had, in the past, been rounded up and exiled. The Pokot had been successful in concealing their own prophets. The disclosure to me not only of the existence of prophets but of a personal claim to this gift, was a proof of desperate courage bordering on temerity.

Riamanyan, in the opening sentences of his statement, asserted his position as provincial arbitrator and buttressed its legitimacy by claiming to be the descendant, in an unbroken line of agnatic filiation through the primogeniture of first marriages, of the first Pokot to have ritually occupied the land of Ptoyo in the

wider area of Sòòk. As such, he claimed to be the supreme
Arbitrator of the people living in Sòòk and of the destinies of that
land in the name of the ancestors who made it habitable and who
lay buried in it. It is clear, that is, that Riamanyan appealed to
a status woven by his family links with local tradition.

The long association with Riamanyan which followed this
meeting, together with further field-work in this area, proved
that his assertions concerning his actual power were undisputed
but that its infrastructure of legitimacy was, in parts, tenuous.
Riamanyan's aspiration to an extension of his influence rested on
his as yet untested power as a major *werkoyon.*

Riamanyan stated in his claim that he was descended from the
original settlers in Ptoyo. In reality only his grandfather, Psielei,
had settled in this area on his arrival from Leila, when the first
Pokot settler Pchemua (grandfather of Manna, who was the great-
grandfather of young Lorkino, the present purifier of the land (see
Fig. 10)), had already ritually taken possession of the land (p. 193)
and was recognized as the purifier and arbitrator over a wide area.
At the time, Psielei was a young married man and Pchemua an
elder. Pchemua, on his death-bed, asked Riamanyan's grandfather,
Psielei, to be the *kitoghoghin* (the leader, the instructor) of his
infant son Masop, until Masop could grow up and stake his claim
before the *kokwa*: *kamenagn kerebeto paponyan* ('I have come [for]
the foodbasket of my father').

Indeed, Psielei became the 'leader' of young Masop and as such
he stepped into the position of Pchemua, that of federation and
provincial arbitrator. The only office vested in Pchemua that
could not be transferred to Psielei was that of *parparin*, or purifier,
as this is a ritual status that can almost never be disconnected
from the agnatic descendants of the first occupier of the land.
Now Psielei acted, for a time, as both federation and provincial
arbitrator. When Masop grew up he found Psielei's authority over
an area extending far beyond Ptoyo so well established and so
entrenched that it would have been foolhardy for an inexperienced
man to dispute it. Psielei's power was due to the revelation—and
recognition—of his prophetic gifts. As an established prophet
(*werkoyon*) he was consulted on important matters (see p. 208)

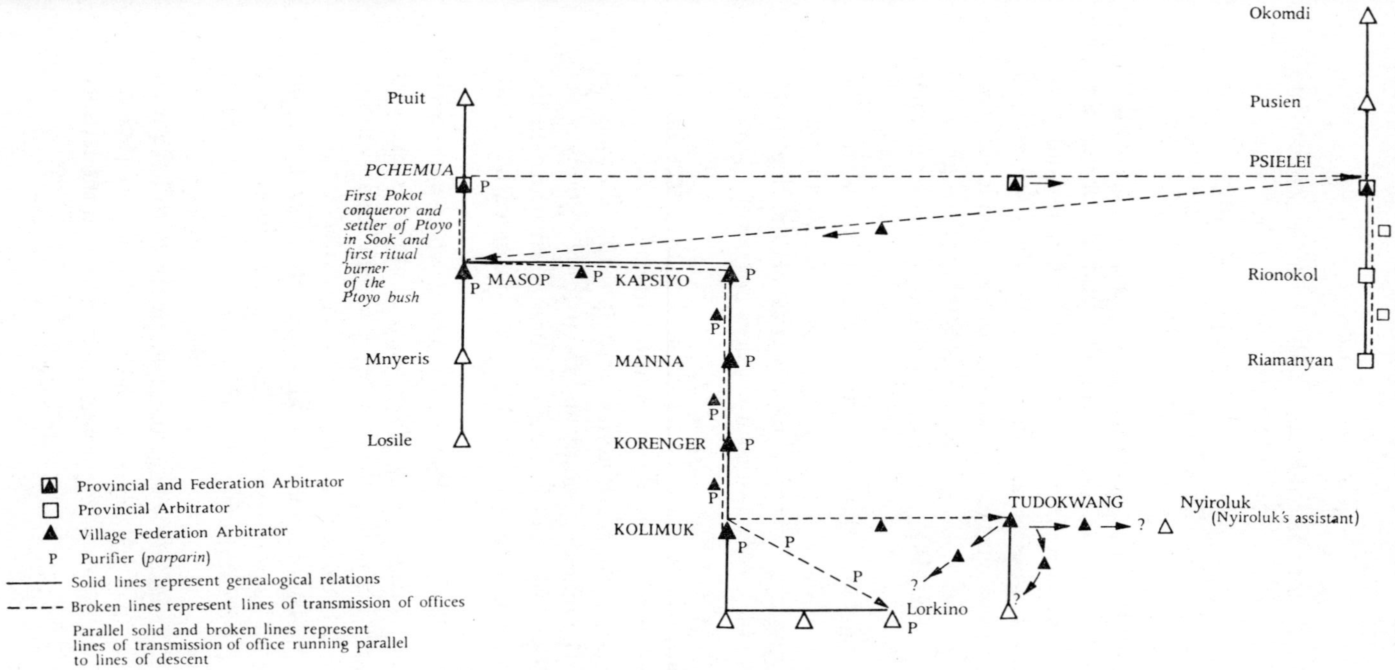

Fig. 10

The diagram illustrates how three offices, originally vested in one man, Pchemua, reputed to be the first colonizer of an area in the vicinity of Ptoyo, became gradually separated so that in the fifth descending generation these three offices were held by three different tenants, each a member of a distinct descent group. (Riamanyan = Provincial Arbitrator, Tudokwang = Village Federation Arbitrator, Lorkino = Purifier).

Only the office of purifier was handed down in an unbroken agnatic line, but even in this case the rule of primogeniture was violated. The future transmission of Village Federation Arbitratorship may be in any direction indicated by the sign →

over the whole province of Sòòk. His decisions concerning litigious matters could not be referred to a higher authority. Psielei was, now, too important a personage to remain simply a federation arbitrator; he kept the promise he had made to Pchemua and handed back this office to his son Masop.

Fig. 10 illustrates ensuing events. Masop and his descendants retained the offices of federation arbitrator and of purifier until the time of my narrative (depicted in Fig. 10), when not only two but three offices were separated, so that 'purification' as well as federation and provincial arbitration became vested in different persons, while Psielei, his son Rionokol, and Psielei's grandson Riamanyan preserved the office of provincial arbitrator in their line.

It is interesting to note (Fig. 11) that Riamanyan, who is the principal elder of his village and of the province, is not one of the three ranking elders of his federation and that the chief elder, the *kiruokin-nio-woo* of the federation, does not occupy a similar status in his own village.

The implications of Riamanyan's claim should be seen in the context of the wider political system of the irrigation hill-Pokot, a system diluted, because of historical development and ecological necessity, by the mixed economy and the pastoral sections of the tribe. As the political and judicial institutions have formed the subject of a previous publication,[23] they are presented here only in brief outline.

The basic, politically significant, segment is what, for reasons of convenience, I call a village. This may comprise as many as fifty or more homesteads, the distance between them varying from a few yards to over a mile. The village is endowed with a territorial, an economic, and a political identity, this last being expressed through the council of elders whose position within it is determined by commonly recognized personality and status considerations.

Within each irrigation village one lineage claims to have been its original occupier. A senior member of this agnatic lineage acts as the ritual leader of ceremonies concerned with the fertility

[23] Peristiany, 1954.

of its soil, with the spirits of its inhabitants and acts as intercessor between its dead and living members, irrespective of lineage affiliation. The purifier, *parparin*, may also act as chief village arbitrator, but the judicial office is not necessarily vested in his person. Indeed, many irrigation Pokot claim that a good *parparin* is not a *kiruokin*, an arbitrator, a court counsellor, as a *parparin* advises his 'children' (i.e. his fellow villagers) rather than takes sides.

A number of neighbouring villages form a common economic and political unit which I call a federation to indicate that the component villages do not merge. Each preserves, internally, its own status, and its own economic, judicial, and political system but in relation to intra-federation disputes, or to federation activities, the members of the component villages recognize a common status and a common office hierarchy. The members of a common federation are said to be *pi po kokwa akongo*, members of the same council, of the same arbitration court, and they are often known, to other federations, by a physical characteristic of this court.

A larger area, covering several federations of villages, may unite for initiation ceremonies and for certain important rituals, as well as for the organization of raids. This area, whose Pokot generic name (usually *kor*) is never as precise as that of 'village' and, in a descending order of precision, of federation, I have termed a province. Its effectiveness, as a unit, is a transient one and is merely due to the authority that great *kiruokin* (advisers, judges), great war leaders, and, most significant of all, great prophets may acquire within it.

We shall see, in the discussion of the political system of the Pokot, that the very essence of the political position of the prophet is his transcendence of minor local bonds; the greater his prophetic gift, the more extensive its territorial recognition and the more tenuous his dependence on local criteria of status. A great prophet is often an alien. Riamanyan's fame was, as yet, localized. His claim to descent from the first settler, in reality to a particular relationship with that person, was devised to ensure his recognition as a legitimate traditional leader. His assumption of the role of protector of the Pokot against a trespassing foreigner, and this,

H

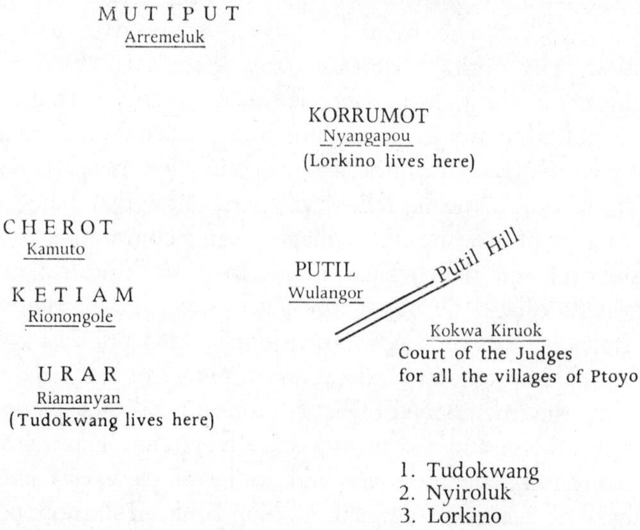

MUTIPUT
Arremeluk

KORRUMOT
Nyangapou
(Lorkino lives here)

CHEROT
Kamuto
          PUTIL
KETIAM
Rionongole

          Wulangor

                    Putil Hill

                    Kokwa Kiruok
                    Court of the Judges
URAR   for all the villages of Ptoyo
Riamanyan
(Tudokwang lives here)

                    1. Tudokwang
                    2. Nyiroluk
                    3. Lorkino

FIG. 11. *Korok po Kokwa Ptoyo* (Villages of the court of Ptoyo). Capital letters indicate the name of a village. This is followed, in smaller type, by the name of the principal elder of each village.

Order of precedence

1. The principal elder of each village is variously called *kariman, kariman na korok, etchotion*, etc.

2. Principal elders of the joint court of the six villages of Ptoyo, *kokwa Kiruok*, the court of the judges.
   First, Tudokwang (*kiruokin-nio-wou*, or *wōoo*, 'arbitrator-who-big').
   Second, Nyiroluk (*kiruokin-nio-mining*, 'arbitrator-who-small').
   Third, Lorkino (*kiruokin-nio-mining* or *weiperi*); *chenokopur* and *weiperi* have the meaning of 'one who follows', e.g. the junior initiation sub-set in relation to the senior one.
   Tudokwang, Nyiroluk, and Lorkino (also Riamanyan) belong to different clans and are not agnatically related.

3. *parparin* (purifier) for all six villages: Lorkino.

4. *kiruokin-do-kor*, judge-of-the-province of Sook, of which Ptoyo is only a section: Riamanyan.

in the first instance, in territory far distant from his province, was devised to establish him as a prophet of the first magnitude at a time when the need to settle *inter alia* the age-set crisis necessitated the arrival of such a person on the Pokot political scene.

We have noticed how various unrelated events which occurred

during marches over extensive areas had been meaningfully strung together so as to establish Riamanyan's claim to uncommon powers and that on my having, quite unwittingly, disregarded the various 'attacks' on my life Riamanyan openly but unsuccessfully attempted to bewitch me. Riamanyan could not rest on these failures. Some months after my journey to Ptoyo he invited me to attend a meeting of elders well beyond the confines of his province. The debate concerned the advisability of admitting members of a certain Kalenjin tribe to settle in the vicinity of the meeting. This, in itself, was astonishing. The matter had already been debated. The qualified leader had publicly opined against it. He was, therefore, committed to this decision. A reversion would have resulted in an irreparable loss of face.

Riamanyan was, nevertheless, approached by influential residents (to whom, I was to learn, promises of generous bride-wealth for their daughters and offers of loans of heifers for themselves had already been made by the strangers), who asked him to work magic so as to change the dissentient elder's mind. Riamanyan accepted the challenge. He declared, with what seemed to me unwarranted confidence, that before so many days had passed the previous decision would be recalled. Knowing the elder's pride, honesty, and stubbornness, I was convinced that Riamanyan would, yet once again, be undone. It was my turn to be discomfited. The elder himself called a meeting within Riamanyan's allotted time limit and, to the fascination of those present, advocated that the strangers be permitted to settle in the area. Here I have to make a personal statement. Whatever explanation there might have been for this volte-face no suspicion of venality or of subversion may be entertained in this case.

The outcome was a personal triumph for Riamanyan, whose victory was immediately broadcast through Pokotland as that of the man who had 'defeated' and 'weakened' an elder of exceptional political consequence. Whatever power the reneging elder's *mukulogh*, heart, had been credited with before this 'defeat' now accrued to Riamanyan whose position as *werkoyon*, as prophet, became unqualified; for who but a *werkoyon* could use magic so potent as to 'defeat' a well-known leader of men?

Riamanyan—this was for me a constant source of wonder—
often treated me as a confederate, or could it be as a witness? He led
me, that same night, to the vicinity of the elder's home pointing
out, on the way, various inconspicuous mounds where he had
buried the appropriately treated heads of oxen so that, when
their target-elder stepped over them, he was rendered pliant, like
an ox, to his master's handling.

Riamanyan returned to Ptoyo on the morrow. I was not to
see him again. Presents of live animals and birds were brought at
his bidding to me and to my wife and small son, to both of whom
he was much attached, and this until the day of our departure.

The Pokot regard the imparting of information concerning
their prophets as dangerous both to themselves and to their
people; the more powerful the prophet the stronger being also
the aversion to refer to him. It is sometimes said that to mention
a prophet is to evoke him, this being hazardous at all times but
particularly so at night, when his 'head' roves freely over the
earth. But for the friendship of Riamanyan I would not have
begun to overcome these difficulties.

VI. *The role of the prophet in the Pokot political and conceptual system*

Rū, amongst the Pokot, means both to sleep and to dream.
Ngor, on the other hand, is to have, mainly during repose and
at night, prophetic visions. *Werkoyon* (pl. *werkoi*), male or female,
is the visionary or prophet. The salient differences between an
ordinary dream and a prophetic vision lie both in the condition
of the patient and in the content of his experience. We all dream,
only prophets have visions. Dreaming itself is a frequent experience, a prophetic vision is not only exceptional but dangerous.
During its occurrence the head departs alone on its journeys.
A sudden awakening may slay the prophet as what in the head is
wōoo (big, powerful) may not return in time to join the body's
visible head. The Pokot belief, then, appears to be that the travelling head is the spiritual counterpart of the physical one, a replica
embodying its vital forces. As regards the content of the vision,
this usually includes a visit to, or evocation of, distant places and
an exploration of the past and of the future, seen in relation to the

present. The Prophet's head, during the vision, travels through time and space in order to discover the most favourable solution to pressing problems. *Ngoria* (or *ngorsetin* in its Nandi form), the prophetic vision, is not an idle but a purposeful exercise as, in a true prophet, it should result in his voicing both a fore-warning of events to come and a prescription of remedies against approaching adversity.

The language of prophecy is a mixture of human and divine speech. It is interspersed with apocalyptic images, with words which, in themselves, appear meaningless or seem unusual in their context, while some resemble animal cries. The utterances of the first humans resembled these cries, this being also the parlance of the elders enacting the role of the primeval beings during male initiation ceremonies. Ilat himself may use this form of speech during his terrestrial visits and the spirits of the dead signify their presence through it to the living. Use of the medium commemor-ates the origin of Pokot man. It serves as proof that its vehicle, through his participation in the various worlds which were once united, also knows how to solve their riddles.

The prophet knows the mind and the will of Ilat, the god nearest to humans. He also communicates with the minds of man, with the spirits of the deceased, and with animals and plants. The Above and the Below are part of his domain. He travels through the air, treads the soil, and explores the bowels of the earth. He thus unites in his person all the worlds known to the Pokot. Time itself presents no obstacle to the prophet as he moves freely in the past, the present, and the future. Standing, as he does, at the point of articulation of all known worlds he is, like the gods, an originator. He decides when a new age-set should be initiated, when war is to be waged, when people and cattle should be moved, the proper time for planting, settling on, or cultivating new lands.

Ilat is at the divine and the *werkoyon* at the human end of the synapsis of the Above and the Below. If Ilat is, to humans, the most accessible of gods, the *werkoyon* is the most exalted of humans. Ilat carries messages, water, and his own divine seed to the earth, while the uppermost part of the *werkoyon*'s body is so endowed as to propel itself in the heavens. The gods give men warning of the effects of their wrongdoing, the *werkoyon* interprets the signs and discovers the means of appeasing divine anger, using as prophylactics or as apotropaics the colours associated with the cycle of Ilat beliefs.

The *werkoyon* himself may stand in a filial relation to Ilat and here the pronounced male character of Ilat and the necessity for him to act through a female principle is clearly revealed. Apart from clouds, thunder, and rain, Ilat is associated with lakes and watercourses which provide water to fertilize the earth and with women who are inseminated by him. The feminine is a complement of Ilat, seen as a god of fertility, and his action upon or through females is consistent with this representation. Endowed with an aggressive virility he shows a predilection for boys (as his emissaries) and for maidens (as intermediaries with other humans and, later, as consorts) as long as neither have ever used their sexual attributes.

Ilat favours men whose mothers' firstborn was a daughter. Again the power of the *werkoyon*'s gift is increased when, in cases of hereditary transmission from grandfather to grandson, a woman prophet (herself the daughter and the mother of a prophet) acts as an intermediary step. One representation of the prophet's power is that of the energy of Ilat, sexually the most clearly defined divinity, being mediated by a human female, the conjunction of the divine/human, especially of the 'divine male'/ 'human female' categories evoking for the Pokot the most potent of ambiguities. For ambiguity is the domain of the *werkoyon* and of all liminal forces.

The sexual character of Tororut and of Asis is not stressed. They are male-oriented rather than male-defined gods in the sense that they are usually spoken of as males, but without a particular stress on their virile attributes or actions. They act through males; the 'pure' persons who invoke them, who intercede on behalf of man and who offer the gods libations and sacrifices, being always male and always powerless, both politically and charismatically. These intermediaries of Tororut and of Asis are moved by, and reflect, an external force but *qua* intercessors they are incapable of self-promotion. On the contrary, the *werkoyon*, from the moment of the revelation and recognition of his gift, appears to be *autarkes*, self-sufficient. To close the cycle of this argument, Ilat is the last, in order of appearance, of the gods, he is, in terms of physical and social distance, the nearest to man, and is the only divinity defined by a sexual attribute, itself an instrument linking him with humanity, preferably female humanity. Here the position of the *werkoyon*, potentially an off-spring of the Above and the Below, and their synapsis, becomes clear. In Pokot cosmogony sexual differentiation follows, temporally, a stage of non-differentiation. The position of Ilat as the most masculine while being the last in order of appearance of the gods tallies well with this belief as does the conception of the *werkoyon* as the nearest, in potency and understanding, both to the powers of the Above and to the earliest of terrestrial beings.

What is the nature of the prophet? Here again we move in a world of ambiguity. Had his father been a prophet, the origin of his gift would be patent. If the charisma were transmitted from a male through females, its source would, once again, be clear, as this mode of transmission is said to enhance its power. When prophecy cannot be traced through human ancestors it is suspected, especially when the prophet is a dominant one, that he is a child of Ilat.

Amongst the Pokot prophecy is an avenue which leads to social effects distinct from those of envy. Envy is a sign that the person against whom it is directed is seen as a competitor in a field in which other men, men with human gifts, are competing. In this case envy is ever watchful and ready to strike and to reduce to the common rank, through accusations of witchcraft and the evil eye, a man whom good fortune has elevated above his fellows. Envy acts as a force of social conformism. Exceptional success coupled with the presumption of prophetic powers breeds awe and fear rather than envy, and this serves to exclude and to differentiate from the world of man. Beliefs concerning the prophet elevate him to an extra-human, or marginally-human, category, thus effectively separating him from the sphere of competitive social activity. The greater the prophet's success, the greater his isolation, an isolation from normal human contact which is shared by his wives and children.

Even when the prophetic gift has not been revealed it may be surmised in cases of unexplained, especially of sudden and rapid, success followed by a commensurate rise in political influence. Although the term *werkoyon* is only applied to persons endowed with the gift of prophetic vision, eminently successful wizards and medicine men (see pp. 177 f.) may be credited with prophetic gifts as that is the apex of extraordinary power. Thus, the dividing line between most of the successful magical practitioners and the humbler prophets may be a tenuous one. In the context of political leadership the degree–kind discontinuity is clearly exemplified in the recognition of the gift of prophecy to women who are denied, because of their sex, the possibility of rising to positions of public leadership. Powerful prophetic gifts and political power are conterminous to the extent that the want of the second in women is a demonstration of the deficiency of the first. It may therefore appear legitimate that I describe only male prophets and that I focus my exposition on those who have attained a certain degree of eminence.

Throughout their history prophets have been intimately connected with Pokot struggles for survival. The earliest tribal traditions contend that the Pokot fought their way from the north-east, harassed and preyed upon, during their long march, by manifold enemies. Their descendants take pride in pointing to the behaviour of the soldier ants as an exemplar of their ancestors' fortitude. The assailants themselves are often portrayed as larger than humans. Thus, the 'Kopembich'[24] have become, in Pokot fantasy, one-eyed ogres who prowl around huts at night kidnapping their children. Other raiders ambushed them by night and abducted their most comely maidens. The Pokot tracked these enemies to the shores of their lake dwelling-places[25] only to discover the captives fettered to large rocks guarded by giant warriors. The Pokot stood fast until the flapping of Ilat's vast

[24] They identify the 'Kopembich' (a play on words to designate their monocularity) with the Marille.
[25] For the majority this is Lake Baringo, while a minority opts for Lake Rudolf.

wings was heard over the waters and the god appeared in a blinding light, his divine effulgence striking terror into the hearts of the enemy. Ilat then consorted with the acquiescing maidens, engendering thereby a breed of men, powerful in mind and limb, which was destined to reunite the scattered remnants of the Pokot and to lead them to their present pastures.

During a period whose events are verifiable through recourse to living memory, here the first decade of this century, the most powerful Pokot prophets were Ptura and Arimot. Ptura was *werkoyon* of Plegit from Baringo up to Mnagei. Also of Sɔ'k, Seker, and Leila. Arimot was *werkoyon* of the pastoral Kasauria, the 'Karasuk', from Riwa and Lokales up to Kopokogh, also of the 'cattle-people' of Baringo. These large areas, including the whole of Pokotland, extend well over 2,000 square miles. The territorial divisions mentioned above are indicative of ecological distinctions. Thus Ptura was *werkoyon* of *Pi-Pa-Pagh*, the people-of-the-grain (largely agricultural—but also mixed-economy—people), living mainly in the central Pokot hills. Arimot was *werkoyon* of *Pi-Pa-Tich*, of the people-of-cattle, the pastoralists living in the western and eastern plains, on either side of the central massif.

The exercise of their gifts by the grain and the cattle prophets places them at the nodal point of relations between large segments of their tribal sections.

The grain prophet advised his people as to the opening of new areas for cultivation and grazing, concerning the relative quantity of new crops and the correct time for planting them. The cattle prophet's gifts pertained mainly to pastures and cattle, to their movements, their health, their protection, and their increase.

Apart from these activities, related to ecological constants, the grain and the cattle prophets were the only advisers, each for his own tribal section, for two activities of supreme importance: the opening and closing of initiation ceremonies and the planning and probable outcome of raids.

One of the politically significant considerations in relation to both these pursuits is that they are co-ordinated on a territorial basis.

The offensive military organization is patterned, especially amongst the hill people, on the territorial organization, each province forming its own regiment and each regiment, in important raids, occupying a position (right, central, or left, in the crescent Pokot battle formation) corresponding to its provincial provenance. Thus, large raids were planned by an extensive territorial area, while this area acting, in this context, as a whole of jointly operating parts had to seek the prophet's advice concerning the combined activity. This was done by delegating elders and regimental leaders to the *werkoyon*'s home, all paying court to him during the day and sleeping at some distance from his hut during the night until he disclosed his vision concerning the raid.[26] If the vision was inauspicious, the visitors returned to their home. When it indicated a favourable outcome the prophet explained in detail the general strategy of the operation, what route the warriors should follow, what encounters they would make on the way, and finally the strength of the enemy, the number of enemy cattle to be captured, their colours and markings, and the safest return route. The secondary tactical decisions were usually left to the regimental leaders.

According both to Riamanyan and to my later Pokot informants the first most valuable advice dispensed by the prophet concerned the omens encountered on the way to combat. Precise details were given as to their propitiousness, the warriors being cautioned to return if they came across adverse signs. The second most valuable intelligence concerned the strength and

[26] During the raid the *lu' po-poyon*, 'the staff of the elder', usually of knobkerry form and marked with red-and-white stripes, arranged in a design particular to each prophet, was carried by a member of an age-set senior to that of the youngest warriors. The most adverse sign is for this staff to split, break, or be chipped during the raid. The war party has, then, to turn back whatever its success. It is commonly believed that the knob section of the staff is representative of the prophet's head and of its gifts.

The *lu' po-poyon* is the prophet's emblem. When he wishes to communicate with an area which acknowledges his form of leadership, he delegates a messenger bearing his emblem and his message either to the most important elder in that area or to a person specially chosen for this function by the local elders. My data point to the fact that he is both chosen by, and is representative of, the local people rather than of the prophet. As this elder is blamed by the prophet for misunderstanding or misinterpreting his instructions when these did not yield the desired result, the method of his choice facilitates his use as a scapegoat.

the strategy of the enemy. I was informed by elders who had participated in these raids that the description of the enemy, of the positions he occupied as well as of the number and colours of his cattle, matched reality so closely that (and this was repeated on various occasions) the prophet had either been vouchsafed a clear vision of the enemy camp or had been the recipient of information concerning it. It is, of course, well known that great prophets had their informers scattered not only over their section but over the entire tribal territory, especially the land close to the borders. The suggestion made here was of a different order. It pointed to the possibility of malignant prophets receiving information directly from the enemy, in this case their Karimojong or Turkana counterpart. The unbelievers, and those whose hatred dominated their fear, claimed, in my presence, that some Pokot *werkoyon* and the prophets of neighbouring tribes both launched the raids and decided their outcome after mutual consultation. Defeats were attributed to the inexact application of the prophet's advice, the outcome of, indifferently, victory or defeat being a share of the spoils. The Marich Pass disaster is blamed to this day on collusion.

Apart from advice based on his vision of the raid the prophet assists his warriors by equipping them against adversity while, by a reversal of his actions, he weakens the resistance of the enemy.

The Pokot warriors, after abstaining for a time from sexual intercourse and heavy eating, undergo a ritual which, when performed by a great prophet, results in their sins being taken from them and then being 'thrown', by the prophet, in the direction of the enemy. This causes the enemy to be 'heavy and bitter', it pollutes him, that is, with the Pokot sins which are thus added to his own so that Ilat will avert his gaze from him and only look with favour upon the 'pure' Pokot. The Pokot warriors then bathe in clear (if possible, running) water, beloved of Ilat, and their body is painted by the prophet with white and red clay, white being the colour favoured by peaceful Ilat, who will thus recognize his own in battle, and red the colour devised to strike terror into the enemy, as this is the colour of the thunderbolt and

of lightning, the visible signs of Ilat's angry presence. Red, the
colour of war and strife, is also the colour of blood. When
smeared by the prophet over the left side, over the heart, red
performs an apotropaic function in relation to enemy weapons.
The warriors are finally blessed by the prophet, who presents
them with amulets, their own or the prophet's, over which the
werkoyon has performed his strongest magic, specific, in each case,
to his particular vision of the raid.

War should not be waged or peace concluded with an enemy
tribe unless the advice of the prophet has been sought. Indeed,
the relations of the Pokot with the non-Pokot belong, to this
day, mainly to the prophet's domain. The Pokot demonstrated
this by saying that prophets tell them when to fight and with
whom to keep the peace and claim that their peaceful attitude
to the Europeans was determined by the cattle-prophet Arimot.

Arimot, when at the height of his power, took his eldest son,
Pkel, to a large boulder, which he moved. Both went deep into
the earth. There Arimot pointed to Pkel clay of various colours
instructing him in the qualities and associations particular to each.
When he came to the white clay he advised Pkel that this was the
'cleanest, lightest, and sweetest' colour of all, as this was the
colour of purity-loving Ilat. Arimot then instructed Pkel that
a people of this white colour were coming from across a large
expanse of water,[27] belching fire and smoke from their mouths
and nostrils. These, as their colour demonstrated, are Ilat people
against whom no one can prevail. They will bring with them tall
cattle and many riches. One day they will depart as suddenly as
they came, abandoning all their possessions to the Pokot.

I shall mention but one other activity of the prophet and that
is the seeking of his permission for the opening of a new circumcision initiation period involving the assumption of the next age-
set name within the cycle. We have already noted the importance
of the rotation of names. The advancing or postponing of a new

[27] Ilat, when on earth, is attracted by water as this, like the heavens, is his
natural element. The Ilat *gesta* are often situated near lakes or watercourses
and relate the adventures of Ilat flying down from the sky or emerging from
the water to rescue beautiful maidens tied to waterside rocks by earthbound
monsters.

named period may influence both the success of the operation[28] and the welfare of the tribe, especially as reflected in the fortunes of war. Only the most respected prophet of the grain people may open—and close—initiation periods. Here again a close association exists between territorial sections and the exercise, on a large scale, of the prophet's gifts. The opening circumcision festival[29] always takes place in the Mwina-Cheptulel hills, which are said to have formed the first bastion of the tribe against foreign marauders; initiations then follow the original route of Pokot colonization. Thus the elders of the large areas concerned, which I have termed provinces, each comprising a number of village federations, have to co-operate concerning the time-sequence and the organization of the initiation festivals and to ask, as an organized whole covering the largest (the circumcising) section of the tribe, the advice of one prophet whose transcendent gifts they thus publicly recognize. In this manner the seeking of advice for extensive raids and for the opening of circumcision festivals establish the undisputed order of precedence of prophets and their relation with defined territorial sections.

We have seen that during the first decade of the century Ptura and Arimot were the recognized major prophets of the Pokot, having carved up, between them, the whole of Pokot territory. On their death, those of their sons whose charisma was acknowledged dispersed over their father's territory, each becoming the prophet of a large area. On the death of these sons their gift was diluted even further so that today unrelated individuals moved by prophetic visions or by ambition vie for recognition. On my arrival amongst the Pokot, Ptura was already dead and his son Longor had also died leaving only insignificant descendants. (See Fig. 12.) Longor had held sway over Pkomo, Mnagei, Sóók, and Seker, the very areas for whose politico-ritual leadership Riamanyan was contending.

[28] It is claimed that initiation wounds do not heal when the prophet's interdict concerning initiations has been disregarded.

[29] All the grain people, people of the hills, are circumcised. The pastoral people's tendency to circumcise is related to the distance and length of their residence from the hills and to the degree of their commitment to become visually indistinguishable from their non-circumcised pastoral neighbours.

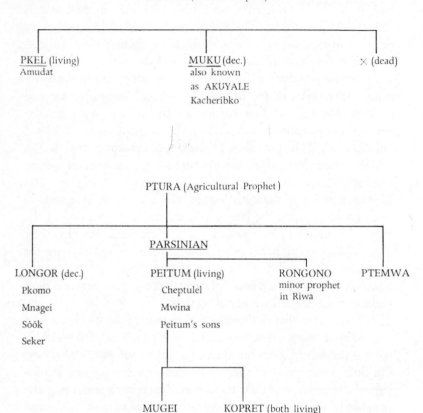

ARIMOT (Pastoral Prophet)

PKEL (living)   MUKU (dec.)   × (dead)
Amudat   also known
                       as AKUYALE
                       Kacheribko

PTURA (Agricultural Prophet)

PARSINIAN

LONGOR (dec.)   PEITUM (living)   RONGONO   PTEMWA
Pkomo   Cheptulel   minor prophet
Mnagei   Mwina   in Riwa
Sóók   Peitum's sons
Seker

MUGEI   KOPRET (both living)
minor prophets in
Cheptulel and Mwina

Fig. 12. The names of the politically important sons of the two great prophets
are underlined. The areas which recognized the gifts of major and minor descendants of Arimot and Ptura appear in small letters.

Pkel, being the only surviving son of Arimot and a gifted man, tended to
assume importance as a prophet in his father's pastoral section. Ptura was, like the
Kipsigis and Nandi prophets, a member of the Talai (Lion) clan. His clan subdivision was Cherelkat and his descent group Cheposait. Arimot's clan was
Soton (Sun), Cheptumegha subdivision. Tumegha resembles an onion and is
edible.

Although a minor prophet is politically significant only in the vicinity of his
residence the belief that the spirits of his deceased kin who had been recognized
as prophets (especially the spirits of his father and grandfather) are eager to advise
him favours the extension of the area of competence of the Prophet, as he visits
their graves and the sites where they buried their medicine.

The Pokot live in a socially fragmented world whose daily political horizons are encompassed by their minor settlements, the villages comprised in the same federation. A Pokot venturing beyond its confines has to use, mainly, his kinship, para-kinship or age-set affiliations in order to graft himself on to the local social fabric, often acting as a client in his own tribal territory. The recognition of a prophet-leader assimilates, jurally and politically, the area of his influence to that of a single federation of villages, for no one within that area will appeal against the prophet's decision. Thus, the territorial extension of the prophet's recognition coincides with the extension of political unity, in the sense of the rapid and final settlement of conflicts within his domain.

At the same time the rise to eminence of great prophetic leaders is exceptional. During their absence admired arbitrators tend to assume (mainly) judicial functions over large areas; the Pokot themselves speaking of their land as forming ten *kor*, ten provinces, each 'led', when a sufficiently eminent person exists, by a *kiruokin do kor*, a provincial arbitrator, whose main jural function is to administer *muma*, the judicial oath, which 'closes' the case through the death or the withdrawal of one of the contestants. An ordinary provincial arbitrator—that is, one who is not credited with prophetic powers—cannot otherwise 'close' a case between members of two federations unless he has succeeded in persuading their elders to accept a compromise. To contravene this rule of political wisdom and to attempt to force through a solution opposed by even a minority of the elders of one federation would almost certainly result in the non-recognition of his advice and be attended by a loss of prestige followed by his tacit demotion. No such doubt may be entertained in the case of the prophet. His advice, even indirectly voiced, has a finality that only the temerarious may disregard.

Here I would like to express an opinion confirmed by many of my encounters with Pokot leaders. If, for the Pokot, the capacity to resolve conflicts rests partly on knowledge of judicial precedents and partly on the correct assessment of the circumstances of the opponents and of their supporters, it is also a function of the arbitrator's personality. Political and jural leadership rests on a knowledge of the past and of the present and assumes the prescience of things to come; it pertains, therefore, amongst the Pokot, to the domain of prophecy. Again, the common arbitrator sways the masses by his knowledge and his rhetoric. The prophet adds to these gifts not only his own exceptional knowledge but the awe that his powers inspire. If only a prophet may be a supremely successful leader, a supremely successful leader cannot escape the assumption of being endowed with prophetic gifts. Thus, an aura of expectation surrounds the successful leader of public opinion, the expectation that he is endowed with latent prophetic gifts. Throughout Pokot cosmogony and history power was exerted by beings at the synapses of all known worlds; today only prophets are the representatives of these powers.

If this is true in the context of a restricted territorial plane it is even more apt when projected against a wider political and territorial canvas. No one may advise—and I am quoting this as an actual example from my experience—even a small group of stock traders concerning exchange of cattle with a neighbouring tribe unless he is credited with prophetic gifts. The prophet is an essential element of the social structure in the context of war, peace, and inter-tribal relations, in the initiation of large-scale economic activities, in ascertaining the cause of and prescribing the cure for wide-ranging afflictions and, finally, for inaugurating, closing, curtailing, or eliminating an age-set, thereby influencing the course of tribal history. If I were to group all these actions under a common denominator I would assert that no action vitally affecting a large tribal section and, through it, the tribe as a whole, may be undertaken without the advice of an influential prophet. If seeking and deferring to the advice of a prophet for these actions is necessary, the use of a prophet's gifts for the settlement of internal conflicts and for advice concerning matters of lesser moment is useful but not essential. At the same time the belief that only a prophet has access to all sources of knowledge and that only a prophet can be an ideal leader tends to affect the evaluation of all successful leaders, their very success being translated into an assumption that their bearer is, actually or potentially, a prophet, and that his powers will become manifest whenever a prophet is needed for the integration, for common action, of the inhabitants of a large territorial segment. The ideal prototype of the leader is ever present as are alive the memories concerning the Pokot past: the times when the prophets led their wandering people. The Pokot live with the expectation (their cyclical age-sets providing the perfect conceptual framework) that similar conditions will be repeated and that similar leaders will arise. When outstanding prophetic leaders have not as yet emerged both the crises that I have described and the normal functioning of the Pokot institutional system provide the necessary conditions for their emergence and for, partially, transmuting the ideal into the actual.

At every turn of the Pokot apprehension of the individual and national identity, we have encountered the themes of fragmentation/fall and unity/salvation. The prophet actualizes the ideal as the model intermediary between various manifestations of life, between humans and the god nearest to man, between life and death, between man and the elements, etc. His power is greatest during times of wide-ranging danger or affliction and most limited during the humdrum periods of everyday existence. Many Pokot, especially those who are most acutely aware of the increasing disaffection of the pastoral sections towards the traditional values of their tribe, are yearning for stress, conflicts, and calamities which will temper the unity of the people while providing the necessary conditions for the rise of great prophetic leaders rendering manifest this ideal in their function and their person.

Thus one main thread, one aspiration, runs through the tales of the Pokot concerning their creation and their early migrations— that of stability and unity. The Pokot consider their present condition as a fall and they yearn for their pristine state when man, animals, and plants were at one, both among themselves and with their creator. The prophet incarnates this ideal. The closer he draws to it, the more clearly he is seen to incarnate it, the readier and the more extensive the recognition of his gifts. When, as in the present, no great prophet prevails, minor practitioners contend for this position supported, in their endeavours, by the expectations of the people. In a fragmented world the prophet embodies the dream of primeval unity. His partial expression of this ideal is the main source of his power. Again, the prophet is human and as such he is riddled with human frailties, often using his power, especially amongst the hill people, to pursue personal ends. It is interesting to note that the Pokot consider this as a betrayal of his mission, which is to lead them to a world of plenty, health, and happiness in which man is at peace and in communion with the gods, and with all animals, plants, and humans, even with the Karimojong and the Turkana raiders.

The *werkoyon*, the prophet, is also the synapsis between the largest politically coherent territorial units. These are, usually, village federations, or, at best, a plurality of neighbouring federations of villages.[30] In political terms a federation of villages possesses both the necessary decision-making machinery and the agents for the settlement of the affairs of its component villages. What is lacking is the machinery for inter-federation conflicts or ventures. Within the federation the qualifications for political leadership are wisdom, knowledge of, and interest in, federation affairs, qualities ideally embodied in a descendant of the man whose agnatic ancestors were the first to occupy the federation land and to render it habitable.

Qualifications for advising and leading a plurality of neighbouring federations are no longer sought in the virtues habilitating a man for federation office, but rather in qualities which tend to be of tribal rather than of local significance, in the sense both of the nature and of the territorial extension of their concern and of their position in the hierarchy of values exemplified in the cosmogony and the conceptual framework of the Pokot. This is even truer of the type of leaders who unite for common action large provinces round their person.

Living Pokot prophets, in my experience, are characterized by fierce individualism. They do not form a class or a corporation. To this observation I should immediately bring two corrections. The first concerns the days of the two great contemporary prophets Ptura and Arimot whose sway over the two ecological

[30] Peristiany (1954).

sections of the Pokot followed the filial agnatic descent line. The second exception *may* concern the Lion clan and, more specifically, the subdivision to which belonged the great agricultural prophet Ptura.[31]

At the time of my field-work, and in the memory of the living, there was no other trace or recollection of prophets being linked by a special structure, or of the operation of existing institutions to form a political network using prophets as its articulations. The evidence points rather to the fact that the emergence of a great prophet cast its shadow on the fame of minor prophets practising in his territory so that the major prophet dealt increasingly with matters of public concern while the minor prophets sank to the role of private practitioners.

The unpredictability of the inheritance of this gift, and the want of coherence amongst those so endowed, are partly responsible for the lack of co-ordination of the activities of recognized prophets, many of whom may coexist in the same area, the hierarchy of recognition being established only during periods of sectional or tribal need for unity.

Structured power both flows through and is limited by its own structure. The limits of as yet unstructured power tend to be, on the one hand, the magnitude and urgency of the exceptional social needs this power is attuned to answering and, on the other, the affinity between the qualities attributed to the exceptional leader and the ideal type of leader of that society. The prophet is a reflection and a reminder of the events that mark, indelibly, the Pokot ethnic identity. The closer the resemblance, the wider and the more fervent the recognition of the charisma. The ideal transcends the actual while the actual appears, especially during moments of crisis, to anticipate the advent of a transcendent leader embodying and enacting the 'timeless' ideals. Thus, when a large section, or the whole, of Pokot society is faced with common needs which cannot be satisfied by the use of their fragmentary administration, charismatic leaders, reflecting the distinctive ideals of the Pokot, tend to arise.

I must add that the need for a prophet/leader and the recognition

[31] See Fig. 12.

of his gifts undergo such extreme variations that the prophet but seldom becomes the permanent focus of tribal interests. The provisional alignments and realignments under the prophet and his waxing and waning powers exercise but a transient influence on the fabric of the political structure. From the enactment of the role of an important political personage, when his services are needed on an extensive territorial scale, the prophet reverts to the role of private practitioner when social needs and the rhythm of life return to the normal, fragmented, everyday reality.

REFERENCES

BEECH, M. W. H., 1911, *The Suk, their language and folklore* (Oxford, Clarendon Press).

PERISTIANY, JOHN G., 1951, *a*, 'The age-set system of the pastoral Pokot. The Sapana initiation ceremony', *Africa*, 21, 188–206.

—— 1951, *b*, 'The age-set system of the pastoral Pokot. Mechanism, function and post-sapana ceremonies', *Africa*, 21, 279–302.

—— 1954, 'Pokot sanctions and structure', *Africa*, 24, 17–25.

9

Getting Your Own Back: Themes in Nilotic Myth[1]

GODFREY LIENHARDT

THIS essay touches on three of Professor Sir Edward Evans-Pritchard's major interests: the Nilotic peoples of Africa, African philosophies and oral traditions, and the anthropological study of reciprocity in human relations. With regard to the last, his appreciation of the moral bonds created by gift and exchange is warmly expressed in his introduction to the translation of Marcel Mauss's *Essai sur le don*, a translation which he himself did much to encourage.[2] That introduction, in the spirit of Mauss's own work, is about reciprocal affection and esteem. But in his many studies of witchcraft and vengeance, Sir Edward has also recognized the other side of that coin, the reciprocity of enmity and aggression; and this contribution connects with his understanding of both reciprocal affection and enmity, as with that also of some of the Nilotes who have occupied so much of his thought.

A few words first about the nature of the narratives which follow. An indigenous Nilotic literature has started to develop sporadically only in the last twenty years or so, and the myths and traditions here recorded have certainly until now been handed down for the most part by word of mouth. Since they explain, among other things, religious practice at the present day, I have called them 'myths', but in that their substance is

[1] This is an entirely rewritten, reworked, and somewhat expanded version of a paper first read at a conference on mythology sponsored by Clare Hall, Cambridge, in 1971. The information comes from the Nilotic peoples of the Southern Sudan, Uganda, Zaire, and Ethiopia. I had thought to find more comparable material from other parts of Africa, but an admittedly rapid and unsystematic search produced only the references given in a note at the end of the article.

[2] *The Gift: Forms and Functions of Exchange in Archaic Societies*, by Marcel Mauss (1925), trans. Ian Cunnison, London, 1954.

held to be historical by those who tell them, they might as correctly be called 'legends', and it will be interesting to see what may happen when Nilotic scholars and others are able to compare a wide range of such legends systematically collected in writing. Father Crazzolara and Professor B. A. Ogot, to mention only two pioneers in this field, have already indicated something of that confrontation between Nilotic legends from which, if slowly, all that can be known about earlier Nilotic history might emerge. In the course of that study too, more detailed accounts than we now have of the close ethnic connections between all the Nilotes, and of the diffusion of their ideas between themselves and to their non-Nilotic neighbours, might be worked out. There is undoubtedly a historical factor behind the distribution of the versions of the myths here discussed; but in what follows I consider only the different conjugations, as it were, of a myth in different cultural contexts of the present day.[3]

This paper discusses for the most part two myths, which may be called 'The Myth of the Bead' and 'The Myth of the Spear', and I begin with a Nuer version of the former, quoted from Sir Edward Evans-Pritchard's *Nuer Religion*:

Some Nuer lineages respect cattle with certain markings. The Kwock lineage of Western Nuerland and their kinsmen among the Atwot people (a section of the Nuer who have to a large extent adopted Dinka culture) will not keep in their herds an animal with *ma reng* markings, that is an animal which has a coloured back but is otherwise white. [As will be seen, the emphasis may be upon the light belly]. It is related—the theme of the story is widely distributed among the Nilotic peoples—that a man of the lineage went to bathe in a stream and placed his bead-strung girdle on the bank where a *ma reng* cow came and looked at it while he was bathing. The man saw the cow near his girdle, but he did not see a kite swoop down and carry the girdle away in its claws; so when he discovered that it had disappeared he thought the cow had eaten it, and he killed the animal and examined

---

[3] The myths do not have a fixed form of words, and those who tell them are more concerned with the matter than the manner of presentation. They are not publicly recited nor used as vehicles for eloquence, are not taught systematically to the young, nor directly re-enacted in any ritual. Yet the forms and situations of the rituals and the understanding of them presuppose knowledge of the myths, which also furnish images and allusions for hymns and songs.

the contents of its stomach in vain. Later someone found the girdle a long way off, where a kite had dropped it, and brought it back to its owner, who was then sorry that he had killed the cow. Moreover the owner of the cow uttered a conditional curse against him, saying that the spirit of cattle with *ma reng* colouring would kill him and his descendants were they ever again to drink the milk of cattle with *ma reng* markings, use their dung for fires, or clean their teeth with the ashes of the burnt dung.[4]

Among the Dinka of the Western Bahr-al-Ghazal there is also a clan which has the *reng* configuration in cattle as its clan-divinity, or totem, and is called after it:

A child of Pareng (the House (clan) of *reng*) was accused of swallowing the beads of a member of another family while he was bathing. The family whose member had lost the beads insisted upon having the Pareng child cut open to retrieve the beads, which were later found in the dung of a *reng* cow, which had swallowed them. Pareng then left the village of its unreasonable neighbours and thereafter 'respected' —here with the main sense of 'avoided'—the *reng* configuration.[5]

The main purpose of these myths, for the peoples themselves, is to explain why particular clans respect and avoid *reng*-marked cattle, and they are in this respect functionally the same as other myths quite different in content, which explain how other clans acquired their different divinities. As moral tales (in the Dinka case at least, as a moral tale the story is known quite widely beyond the clan in question) their teaching is explicit: that from over-reaction and vengeful anger, bitter consequences follow. The emphasis on searching the dung of the *reng* cow, or examining its stomach, clearly establishes that the victim of rage and selfishness was entirely innocent, and public sympathy is with the owner of the cow or the parents of the eviscerated child. And that would seem initially to be an adequate brief gloss on the Nuer version. The Dinka version, however, with its theme of the separation of peoples following the cutting open of the child, connects as later discussed with myths among other Nilotic peoples, among whom

---

[4] E. E. Evans-Pritchard, *Nuer Religion* (1956), pp. 74–5.
[5] From Godfrey Lienhardt, *Divinity and Experience: the Religion of the Dinka* (Oxford, 1961), p. 166.

also it is combined in a single narrative with a version of a further Dinka myth, the Myth of the Spear. This explains how the clan Pajieng, the House of Ajang, came to have the black cobra as its clan divinity:

A black cobra bit a cow belonging to Ajang, the ancestor of the Pajieng clan. He speared it with a spear belonging to Akol Adiangbar, founder of the Padiangbar clan, but it escaped with the spear still in its body. Ajang offered to replace the spear by another, but Adiangbar insisted on the return of his very own spear and no other. Ajang therefore went after the snake, and followed it down through an ant-hill to the land of the snakes. There he found the cow which the cobra had bitten and the wounded cobra. He offered the cow in compensation for wounding the cobra, and asked to have the spear back. The snakes returned the spear and offered him one of their daughters as a wife. (Here there are accounts of his indecision as between different kinds of snake some being more beautiful and harmless than the black cobra.) He was persuaded to choose the black cobra, and returned home with his wife and the spear, which he returned to Adiangbar its owner. Adiangbar's son had meanwhile died, and had been buried in a skin belonging to Ajang. Ajang then demanded to have his very own skin back, and Adiangbar therefore had to dig up the grave, from which he took the skin and stuck his spear through it. Since then Pajieng, the House of Ajang, has had the black cobra as its clan-divinity, and Pajieng and Padiangbar cannot live happily together.[6]

Among the Dinka, this myth and the Myth of the Beads, with their totally different narrative content,[7] are told by two quite different clans to explain why they have their particular clan divinities and why they are socially incompatible for ever with certain other clans. Their common moral theme is obviously that getting your very own back, a kind of reciprocation without exchange, leads to the permanent alienation of neighbours so that they can never again live together as members of the same community. In its simplest form, of course, some such moral is familiar far beyond the Nilotic world. Like the Dinka themselves,

6 Lienhardt, op. cit., pp. 117–18.

7 On some folklore systems of classification, they might rightly appear under quite different headings, the Myth of the Spear for example being obviously connected with other myths involving dangerous quests, or the presence of snake-wives or snake-husbands.

we can see that the self-assertiveness represented in the myths goes far beyond any that might be tolerated on grounds of reason or justice. But in that Nilotic world, the meaning of the myths is to be construed in relation to other factors also—ecological, economic, political, legal, and religious—which are not so apparent outside it, and to which I now turn.

Amongst these Nilotes, personal adornments, and spears,[8] are among the few possessions which are clearly owned outright by individuals, and even for these the Nilotes' profound sense of an obligation to share is still usually uppermost. Thus to refuse to lend a friend one's spear in a moment of crisis, or one's beads for some particular occasion, would amount to the repudiation of friendship. Nevertheless, if a person had borrowed another's beads or spears—let alone taken them without permission—the owner would be justified in asking for his very own back and being reluctant to accept a substitute.[9] In such a situation, the extent to which this reluctance could be overcome would depend upon the relationship between those concerned. The myths clearly imply it was then at breaking-point, if the taking of such small liberties between close neighbours provoked a reaction which endangered or took life itself.

Even without going to those extremes, in contemporary Dinka custom to want one's very own back in a relationship of exchange is a sign that the relationship is broken. In Dinka marriage custom, the bridegroom's people hand over an agreed number of cattle to the people of the bride, who make a smaller return gift of cattle. In this transaction, where an on-going relationship involving further gifts is being formed, it is essential that cattle handed over by the bridegroom's people should *not* be included in the counter-prestation made by the bride's.

But in divorce people tend to want their very own back, and

[8] This is an ordinary hunting- and fighting-spear, not the sacred spears of the Dinka, though there is some suggestion that Pajieng thus acquired a sacred spear irregularly.

[9] Those who have ever borrowed and then lost something unique, in whatever small respect and of however small material value, will know the feeling that no substitute, even of something objectively more valuable, quite replaces the lost original. There remains a debt which can never be repaid, and which makes for some permanent, if trivial, sense of distance.

attempts will be made to demand the return of the beasts originally exchanged or their progeny. Since cattle (unlike beads,
spears, and some other personal possessions) constantly circulate
through the community in other marriages and exchanges, this
is a very arduous task. Though exactly the same cattle may never
in fact be returned, they are sought through much travelling
with all its hazards, recalling the quest for the spear in the land
of snakes.

The Dinka set great store by living together in harmony with
their neighbours, even if they do not always achieve it, and
neighbourliness involves a willingness to share, give, loan, and
accept compensations for wrongs. The activities of the most
respected men in any community, be they priests or others, are
largely directed to promoting a spirit of generosity and magna-
nimity which makes peace through their mediation possible. And
although it would be untrue to say baldly that cattle are collectively
owned, rights in them are shared in various ways, unlike the
ownership of spears and beads. The individual possessiveness
about the latter shown in the myths would, if applied to cattle-
ownership, undermine the whole Dinka ethic and social order,
and would, as in the myth, set people apart for ever. While people
remain basically friendly and reasonable, the individual ownership of some small personal items does not conflict with the ethic
of shared rights in the herd. When they cease to share, however,
individual aggressiveness and assertiveness threaten to destroy
communal harmony, and the selfish individualism which private ownership could logically imply contradicts the unselfish
communalism, based upon their pastoral values, which Dinka
ideally aspire to. In the myths the contradiction is resolved
practically by the separation of neighbours, and morally (since
that separation is shown to be both bad in itself and based upon
insufficient cause) in favour of the communalistic ethic of cattle-
ownership and against the individualistic ethic of owning weapons
and trinkets.

And there is another, related theme in the myths so far recounted. In them, very usual incidents (in such circumstances
a man might well pick up the nearest spear, or a child swallow

a bead) set in motion a chain of violent reactions ending in total severance of relations. It can be thus also today, that a small incident, especially where there is a history of bitterness, or aggressive hot temper, between the parties, starts the recriminative exchanges which end in feud, and can end in the total withdrawal of angered factions from their original political community.[10] In feud itself, while there is hope of eventual settlement by the acceptance of compensation and religious reconciliation, a positive relationship of sorts is preserved; but groups of feuding kin are required to keep apart by religious prohibition, according to which it would be death for individuals from feuding groups to eat together. Consistent with this is the lesson of the myths: 'if you will not accept compensation,' it might be phrased, 'you must separate.'

And before we turn to similar myths with rather different implications, there is another point connected with that theme. For the Dinka and Nuer, the clan divinity or totem symbolizes the power and moral demands of agnatic kinship. Since these myths explain primarily how clans acquired their divinities, it would seem to be implied that before the bead was swallowed or the spear was thrown, with all the consequences of those acts, agnatic differentiation within the local communities involved, though present, was latent. The basic composition of those communities is seen as one of intermarried neighbours,[11] and in the ordinary course of village life today it is as such that villagers appear to one another. A man speaks, for example, of his 'mother's brother' or 'wife's brother' far more frequently by those kinship terms, assimilating them to him and his, than by reference to their membership of agnatic descent groups different from his own. But if a major quarrel arises, agnatic loyalties begin to polarize opinion in the community and divide it into opposed segments. If the quarrel results in a death, then either it must be speedily compounded by the acceptance of compensation, or one group must leave the

---

[10] Cf. 'Nuer say that feuds and quarrels between lineages chiefly led to their dispersal, and they can cite many examples' (E. E. Evans-Pritchard, *The Nuer* (Oxford, 1940), p. 209).

[11] Though this is not explicitly stated in the myth, a Dinka or Nuer local community could not be otherwise.

village, feud at such close quarters being impossible,[12] since death would at once follow death up to mutual extermination.

So, as the Dinka proverb says, 'The second hit is much greater than the first' when you prefer your strict rights to the life and safety of your neighbours.[13] For the Dinka and Nuer, moral community is more important than the theoretical rights of individuals,[14] and insistence on getting your own back may destroy that very community which gives you those theoretical rights. It is a serious deprivation for a Dinka or a Nuer to be banned from keeping even one particular kind of cow or consorting with even one particular clan; the religious prohibition against the former, which the bead myths explain, follows from a selfish indifference to the values of cattle, children, and communal peace and co-operation.

In neither the Myth of the Bead nor the Myth of the Spear is the missing object really lost, though in the Dinka story it would have been had it not been for the highly unreasonable reaction of the owner. This might suggest that the spear and the bead were, in themselves, important for the owners. But for the Dinka and Nuer, such relatively worthless possessions could not possible justify the vengeful anger with which their owners pressed their rights, and for them the bead and the spear are no longer significant after they have pointed this moral. It is the cow which becomes the clan-divinity and lives on in modern religious thought and practice. The Nuer and Dinka myths do not in themselves explain why, particularly, the myths involve *beads* and *spears*; but clearly comparable myths are found among other Nilotic peoples with whom the Dinka and Nuer have undoubted ethnic connections, with some of whom they are only in more or less peripheral

---

[12] It may be—I do not press the point—that there are suggestions of being *too* close together (of incest and adultery) in the myths. There is the cutting open of the child, which recalls the Dinka ceremony for counteracting incest in which a living beast is cut open down the belly and the unauthorized use of the spear (? a phallic symbol) and of another's sleeping-skin, which implies adulterous or incestuous intercourse.

[13] I thank my friend Mr. Isaiah Majok Akoc for this proverb and many other helpful comments, including: 'This heartless pursuit of rights can be exercised with foreigners but not members of the same clan or family, or friends.'

[14] An analogous theme appears in *The Merchant of Venice* and research would probably identify it more widely.

contact, and with some of whom (the Alur later mentioned) they have had no contact in the knowable past, and whose royal emblems include beads and spears. A historian might indeed reasonably suppose that the presence of beads and spears in the myths considered so far is accounted for by a historical connection between those Nilotes and other Nilotic peoples for whom those objects *are* of central social importance, but that is not the line of inquiry of this particular paper.

The following comes from the Luo of the Bahr-al-Ghazal Province of the Southern Sudan, a small (perhaps 16,000) group of the Shilluk-Luo speakers where kingship, if it can so be called, appears only in a relatively humble form, but where memories of it persist:

Dimo is the father of the Jo Luo. He is the brother of Nyikang, the first Shilluk and culture hero. The two brothers were living together and their sons were playing with beads. Dimo's son swallowed Nyikang's son's bead. Nyikang's son cried and ran to his father. He told him that his brother's son had swallowed the bead. Nyikang was very angry. He went to Dimo and said: 'Your son has swallowed my son's bead. I want it back immediately.' Dimo said: 'My brother, the children are playing together and we do not know how my son came to swallow your son's bead. I will look when my son defecates and I will bring the bead back to you immediately.' Nyikang was not satisfied. He said: 'I must cut open your son's stomach.' Dimo said: 'Do you really want to cut open my son's stomach to find the bead?' Nyikang answered 'Yes'. Nyikang called Dimo's son who had swallowed the bead and cut open his stomach in the presence of Dimo and gave the bead back to his son. Dimo called his wife and his other children and said he wanted to leave his brother. So the Jo Luo went to the south. Nyikang and his descendants remained in the north.[15]

[15] Andreas Kronenberg, 'Jo Luo Tales', *KUSH* (1960), 250–1. In another version it is Dimo himself who cuts open his own child—now a daughter—to retrieve for Okangi (Nyikang) a cowrie shell belonging to Nyikang's daughter. The spirit in which it appears to have been told is of some interest: 'Dimo, with feelings of sorrow and revenge opened up his daughter's belly, he looked for his brother Okangi's daughter's cowrie and gave it to Okangi saying: "Now that my daughter has died because of your daughter's cowrie we shall separate, it is not possible to live together any more, we shall never meet again on this earth." ' (Trans. from P. F. S. Magagnotto, F.S.C., *Dal fiume delle gazelle: il sentimento religioso tra i Giur* (Padua, 1926).)

Here then the bead becomes a central property in a drama of dynastic conflict, as is seen still more clearly in a Shilluk version of the myth which (consonantly with the more highly elaborated royal institutions of the Shilluk) is fuller and more circumstantial.[16] Coming from the Nyireth (prince) Othwon Dak Padiet, son of the past King (*reth*) Dak Padiet of the Shilluk, it is itself a significant addition to the published ethnography of that people:

The separation of Dimo and Nyikango came about as a result of a series of quarrels, one of them being over the inability of Dimo to accept the right of Nyikango to rule over their dissident group. But the most quoted reason is the fact that the followers of Dimo and Nyikango could not live at peace as occasioned by the famous search for the spear and the killing of a child to get a bead out of its stomach . . .

A man who is identified with Nyikango had borrowed a spear from another man who is identified with Dimo. The man with the spear went hunting. But later when he reported back home, the spear was missing. He confessed that the spear was taken by an elephant which he had tried to kill.

The owner of the spear quarrelled and refused compensation of any kind. He wanted his very spear.

The man who had lost the spear had no alternative but to try and look for the spear. He spent months until one day he came to a village completely unknown to Nyikango's people. He explained his case to the people he found there. They told him to see an old woman who in turn told him to wait for her husband. When the latter came, he brought a spear which the seeker recognized as the one he had lost.

The man explained that he was speared with the very spear, showed the wound which he had received and gave the spear back. (These people commuted their lives between human beings and elephants when it suited them.)

The seeker took the spear back to its owner. But at the same time

'The Shilluk version is very poorly represented in the published literature, and the Anuak version, as far as I could find, not at all. In any case the story would not appear to be as important to the Anuak as to others. I had completed a draft of this article with minimal reference to these peoples, and concentrated on the Alur versions, when through Mr. Natale Olwak Akolawin I received further information from the Shilluk and Anuak. The Nyireth Othwon Dak Padiet, Mr. Michael Bann Ajang, and Mr. Philip Obang, as well as Mr. Akolawin, all furnished information for which I thank them warmly—the more so in that they confirm some details of interpretation which in the earlier draft I had admitted to be speculative.

the mother of the owner of the spear had died during his absence and his (the seeker's) skin was used to bury her. So he demanded that the very skin be given back to him. The body had to be dug up to produce the skin.

The quarrel now deepened and polarized between Nyikango and his followers on one side and Dimo and his people on the other. And there was a spirit of vengeance in the air harboured by both sides. It was the people of Nyikango who got the opportunity again. While one of the followers of Nyikango sat stringing beads, a child from Dimo's group (sometimes believed to be Dimo's child) swallowed his bead. The owner asked that he should be given back the very bead. Everything was done to make the child disgorge the bead, but everything failed, so eventually the child's stomach had to be slit open to get the bead. This was the last straw. Dimo and his followers packed, and after a mutual pledge between him and Nyikango that their followers would not see each other again, the former led his people away. Hence proverbially 'the separation of Dimo and Nyikango'—separating not to see each other again. Dimo and Nyikango had a last exchange of words however. After Dimo had moved a few yards, he persuaded Nyikango to look back towards him—a thing Nyikango was not supposed to do following their earlier pledge. But Nyikango did look back, and Dimo without looking back threw to him a *Kwer dikok* (the hoe with the hooked handle) saying: 'Take that, Nyikango; you will need it for burying your people.' 'What does it matter?' replied Nyikango, 'death will take from among my people, but they will not finish. But your people even without death will remain few.'[17] This is where the *Kwer dikok* derived its death symbolism from in dreams among the Shilluk.

This version is essentially the same as one given by Mr. Michael Bann Ajang, who also allows for another version which appears in fragmentary form in other sources,[18] in which it is Dimo who insists upon having Nyikango's child cut open. The same point is made—that of the irreconcilable differences between the brothers—but among the Shilluk there may be some ambivalence about attributing the cruel treatment of the child to the king himself. As is seen above, this prince's version attributes it to a

[17] As they have, as against the Shilluk, who number over 120,000.
[18] Especially M. E. C. Pumphrey, 'The Shilluk Tribe', *Sudan Notes and Records*, 24 (1941).

follower, not the king, but even so the king identifies his interests with his follower's. In the main version given by Mr. Michael Bann Ajang, it is Nyikango himself who insists upon the evisceration. In the letters I have received from both, the bead of the myth is associated with important royal beads of the present day, and Othwon Dak Padiet further associates the spear and the skin as royal symbols. In his comments on a short comparable Anuak version, Mr. Philip Obang also connects the bead of the myth with the Anuak royal beads.

Leaving further commentary until later, I now turn to the myths of the Alur and Acholi of Zaire and Uganda, using for the most part Fr. Crazzolara's work.[19] There is some variation in the names of the principal characters from one group to another. Here they are Nyipiir, as the character parallel to Nyikango, and Tifool as the character parallel to Dimo.

The story is as follows: Nyipiir speared an elephant with a spear belonging to his brother Tifool. The elephant escaped with the spear in its flesh, and Tifool refused any substitute for it. Nyipiir then had to make a long and dangerous journey to the land of the elephants to find the spear. The mother of the elephants received him kindly, telling him that after all the elephant had not been killed and that he had a right to protect his field. She then gave Nyipiir food for the journey home, in which, unbeknown to him, she had mixed a special kind of bead (now the perquisite of royalty). He returned the spear to his brother. His brother's wife visited him with her child when Nyipiir was stringing the beads he had found in the food, and the child swallowed a bead. Nyipiir demanded that very bead back. For

[19] The full story has much fascinating detail, some of which, since Fr. Crazzolara was making specifically historical investigations, gives the story a much more apparently historical setting than that of any other version. This précis comes from J. P. Crazzolara, *The Lwoo, Part I, Lwoo Migrations* (Verona, 1950), pp. 62–5. The Myth of the Bead is also told to account for the divisions of other Lwoo groups, as recounted in J. P. Crazzolara, *The Lwoo, Part 2, Lwoo Traditions* (Verona, 1951), pp. 113–14. Other versions which do not differ from those given enough to affect this discussion may be found for example in Wilhelm Hofmayr, *Die Schilluk, Geschichte, Religion und Leben eines Niloten-Stammes* (Anthropos, Vienna, 1925), pp. 12–13; R. M. Bere, 'An Outline of Acholi History', *Uganda Journal*, 11 (1947); J. P. Crazzolara, 'The Lwoo People', *Uganda Journal*, 5 (1937); and Fr. Vanneste's collection of Alur texts later cited.

several days the child's stools were examined but it did not pass the bead. Then, to quote directly from Fr. Crazzolara:

Tifool said: 'If you refuse any substitute, you may cut open the belly of the babe.' Nyipiir said: 'All right, I will do it.' So Nyipiir took a *wer* [a royal wooden dish, of the kind his beads had been placed in when the child swallowed one], spread a leopard-skin over it, as the royal dignity of the babe demanded, and laid the babe on it. He first washed the baby with fresh milk, so that the bead could be distinguished in the belly.[20] Then Nyipiir took a knife, slit the belly open and recovered his precious bead which he showed around that everybody be convinced that he had not told a lie. Lastly he washed the corpse and returned it to Tifool, who buried it. *Nyipiir took great satisfaction at having recovered his bead . . .* [My italics.]

Tifool declared to his brothers that he would have nothing more to do with Nyipiir; he would separate from them in order that he should never set his eyes on him.

Finally to complete the textual material here discussed, there is a story published in a collection of Acholi texts with Dutch translation by Fr. Vanneste,[21] and translated privately into English for the Institute of Social Anthropology, Oxford, by Dr. Pieter Koornhof.[22] This accounts for the separation of Nyipir (*sic*) and Nyivongo, the former regarded here as the leader of an Alur group, the latter of the Banyoro, where he appears in another version as 'Nyabongo'. The Alur text, clearly retaining some of the drama of its original telling, also conveys the attitude of its narrator. It records how Nyipir, required to return the spear, offered to substitute two spears, then two bundles of spears, but Nyivongo insisted on his own. So: 'Nyipir said: "So is it, my brother, if you are so antagonistic towards me, what shall I do? Now I shall go on an aimless journey to look for your spear."' Nyipir then went with his men, found the spear in the land of elephants, where he was directed to it by an old woman to whom

---

[20] Recalling the light belly of the *reng* cow in the Dinka and Nuer versions.

[21] M. Vanneste, *Legenden Geschiedenis en Gebruiken van een Nilotisch Volk: Alur Texten* (Brussels, 1949), pp. 30–4.

[22] Suitably enough, in this context, at the behest of Professor Sir Edward Evans-Pritchard.

he gave tobacco. (Here exchange and gift appear as themes.) Nyipir returned the spear, but he 'kept this event in his heart'; and one day, seeing his brother's twin children playing, he placed a cowskin on the ground, and set his beads upon it. He then put his own children to the left of the skin, and his brother's children to the right, nearer to the beads.[23] A child of Nyivongo swallowed a bead. Nyivongo offered whole baskets of beads to replace it:

This also Nyipir refused. He said: 'That thing, even if you give me many others, the trouble you take is futile. My bead only, which you produce, that I want! . . .'
Nyivongo spoke: 'O, my brother do you speak thus?' His brother said 'Yes, I do indeed speak like this!' Nyivongo summoned his servants, they came. He said 'Take the child, bring him!' They took the child and brought him. They jabbed a knife into his stomach, they cut it open. They examined all the entrails; they found the bead in it. They took the bead, they washed it. They gave it to Nyipir. Nyipir said: 'I, I looked for this!' (that is what I wanted).[24]

So Nyivongo and Nyipir turned their backs to one another and separated for ever, placing an axe between them.[25]
In this version, it will be seen, Nyipir is deliberately contriving his revenge, and, in part of the text not quoted, tells his brother that he is demanding his very own bead back because his brother had refused to be 'lenient' towards him over the spears. It is all but explicitly stated here (and *is* explicitly stated in Othwon Dak's comment on the Shilluk myth) that the bead represents an independent kingship, and the quarrel over beads and spears is thus a dynastic quarrel over what are now royal emblems.
For the Shilluk, it would appear that the actual beads and spears of the myths are not directly associated with the actual beads and spears of modern kingship. So, describing the installation of the *reth* (king) Anei Kur in 1943, P. P. Howell says that the royal beads, *ocoro*, are regarded as having been part of the bridewealth

[23] Here, perhaps, since 'right' normally equals 'legitimate', proving against the rule that his own children were the effective heirs. Cf. Esau and Jacob, etc.
[24] Vanneste, op. cit., pp. 30–4.
[25] Recalling the *Kwer dikok* of the Shilluk myth (p. 223 above).

of one of Nyikango's daughters.[26] At an important stage in the installation, he writes,

> The *reth* then appeared at the door of the homestead, and, stepping over a white sheep which had been pegged down in front of him, he stood with his back to the fence facing the multitude. The spears, wrapped in a white cloth, *and which together with the beads of ocoro are collectively known as 'Nyikang'* [my italics] was brought and held beside him.[27]

Othwon Dak writes: 'By sheer coincidence the symbols—spear, skin and bead—that brought about the separation between Dimo and Nyikango are connected with power and authority. So it could be said that the separation between Dimo and Nyikango resulted from disagreement over power and authority.'[28] But with Alur legends, the coincidence noted and association spontaneously made by a member of the Shilluk royal house himself appear less coincidental.

For with the Alur the association between the beads of kingship and the beads of the myths is direct. Aidan Southall writes of the death and succession of an Alur king:

> The old chief would express his wishes as to who should succeed him, and would interview the son of his choice. Whether this son actually succeeded depended on the council. He validated his ritual title by putting a bead in the mouth of a dead chief, and then went into hiding. This is a symbolic re-enactment of the myth in which Nyabongo's son swallowed the bead of Thiful.[29]

Also with regard to the bead and present kingships, Southall relates[30] that when kings die a royal bead is placed in their mouths, and in one account the royal successor is chosen by placing a bead in porridge which the king's sons share, the one who finds the bead in his portion being chosen to succeed. The knife used in cutting open the child is said to have been preserved at one time

[26] P. P. Howell and W. P. G. Thomson, 'The Death of a Reth of the Shilluk and the Installation of his Successor', *Sudan Notes and Records*, 27 (1946), p. 47.
[27] Ibid., p. 51.   [28] Private communication.
[29] Aidan Southall, *Alur Society, A Study in Processes and Types of Domination* (Cambridge, n.d.), p. 359.
[30] Ibid. The variants of the names are considered below.

among the regalia, and the special royal dishes of today recall those dishes in myth which held first the beads, then the child's excrement while the bead was being sought.

I noted earlier—and given more fully the Alur and Acholi information would show this with some detail—that the names of the principal characters and their roles vary from version to version. Above, for example, it is Thiful's (Tifool's) bead that is swallowed. I suspect that informants may differ in the extent to which they are prepared to associate the act of evisceration with their own kings personally; but more importantly, the names of the main characters and parts they play vary with the geographical and political context, and in a different, more 'historical', study it would be possible to relate these variations to their particular contexts, showing how in each local situation it provides a 'mythical charter' for contemporary political relations.

But the rituals of Alur kingship point to an interpretation which allows for but transcends these local differences of detail. What those rituals plainly represent—and what appears in the myths themselves—is that to *retain* the bead, to incorporate it (as in the mouths of the dead king and his rightful successor) is to be a king. Hence the bead itself has an intrinsic significance for those Nilotes who have a royal legitimacy to validate, whereas to the Nuer and Dinka myths, and their political lives, the beads and the spears are ultimately extrinsic. It is the theme of *ingesting* the bead, I shall suggest, which has a comparable meaning, analytically, in all these myths. With this in mind I now turn to a consideration of the similarities and dissimilarities in the myths and the different but related cultures from which they come.

The Dinka Myths of the Bead and the Spear are for the Dinka quite distinct, and in introducing them earlier I therefore deliberately quoted the Myth of the Bead before the Myth of the Spear. If the Dinka myths alone were known, there would be no justification for placing them in any sequence, though I do not doubt that any Dinka would readily see in both of them the theme of 'getting your own back'. But in the Alur and Shilluk versions, where the actions connected with the spear and those connected with the bead are related episodes in a single narrative, the episode of the spear always comes first, followed by a logic of escalation entirely consistent with the sense of each separate myth among the Dinka: that is, one unreasonable demand leads to a more unreasonable counter-demand—'the second hit is much greater than the first' as in the Dinka proverb quoted—until quarrelling people must separate for ever. In the Alur and Shilluk versions, the episode of the bead is the climax of the whole narrative, and it is this episode, in one context or another, that all the stories have in common.

The Nuer version concerns a Nuer's beads. It is the simplest in structure and is in some respects eccentric in relation to all the rest. There are initially only three, and individual, characters: a Nuer, a cow, and the cow's owner. The Nuer acts on impulse in killing the cow, then regrets it and must in future avoid contact with its kind. The killing of this cow, however, must be understood in relation to Nuer values. Neither the Nuer nor the Dinka kill cattle outside the situation of sacrifice, and sacrifice involves, as is amply attested in the Nilotic literature, an affirmation of the community of interests—the communion it might rightly be called—of the sacrificing group. The individual and spiteful killing of a cow is thus a hasty, uncalculated repudiation of the ideal of community, but analogous in wickedness to the more deliberate killing of a child in the Dinka version. The Nuer and his descendants must henceforward then avoid the type of cow which calls to mind this sinful act, as the Dinka must avoid the type of cow which calls to mind the even more extreme act of the murder of the child.

This Nuer version, simple as it is, nevertheless places some emphasis upon a detail which is common to all myths—the examination of the stomach (or in other cases the stools) of the suspected swallower of the beads. This common theme seems to call for some explanation.

Among all these Nilotic peoples, beads and spears, intimately bound up with proper self-esteem and personal power and prowess, are strongly representative of the owners themselves. Thus in the Nuer version of the Myth of the Bead, what the angry Nuer tries to establish by killing the cow and searching its stomach is that the beast, belonging to and representing somebody else, has tried to assimilate, by ingestion and digestion, an important part of himself. But he is proved wrong in his suspicions, and the consequence of the whole action is the permanent separation of the Nuer and his descent group from the type of cow he has suspected, by the religious force of a curse which, in Nuer terms, is more lasting and serious than the impulsive self-assertion which gave rise to it.

The Dinka version of the Myth of the Bead has some different implications. There two *families* are living side by side, and one insists upon killing the other's child to retrieve its bead. The killers, in this case, fear assimilation of part of themselves by a member of the group whose child they kill. Again they are proved wrong by the *reng* cow, which does not retain the bead in its stomach, while the child never had the bead in its stomach at all. The cow, calling to mind the wrong they have suffered, is henceforward avoided as a 'totem', and in addition the two groups involved are permanently separated.

One implication common to both Nuer and Dinka versions is that if the bead *had* been swallowed and *retained*, the extreme reaction of the owner, though still reprehensible, would have had a semblance of justification, and here the political systems of the Dinka and Nuer have some bearing on an anthropological interpretation of these myths. Dinka and Nuer political communities, from the smallest to the largest, are based upon agnatic-descent groups, which while always retaining their distinct identities for themselves are assimilated to one another in relation to opposing groups of the same kind. Thus those who regard themselves as members of different lineages at one level of political action are united as a single lineage at a higher genealogical level and in different political situations. Similarly, in any local community, groups of different agnatic descent appear as undifferentiated friends, allies, and neighbours from some points of view, and as members of their own distinct groups from others.

Only between the extremes of total assimilation of one group by another, and total separation of different groups, is the working Nuer and Dinka political process of fusion and fission possible.

Total assimilation of one descent group by another (as with the swallowing and retention of the bead, had that occurred) or total separation (as it follows in the myth) would destroy the political form of the society and the moral basis upon which it is founded. The myths then represent, between the resented (but only suspected) ingestion of one group by another, and the total separation which becomes its consequence, the logical extremes between which the Dinka and Nuer political process moves; but which also, should either be actually realized, would make their forms of society impossible. Those who must have their very own regardless of compromise, who will not accept substitutes or compensation, cannot live together in that kind of society, as both the myths and Nilotic political history show. In the Nuer version, this theme of separation from and avoidance of those from whom you have wished to get your very own back appears only in the permanent separation of the *reng*-marked beast from the descent group of the man who killed it. In the Dinka version, there is the further total separation of the families involved, as well as the religious avoidance of the *reng* beasts which symbolize the original suspected assimilation.

The dialectical themes of total assimilation and total avoidance[31] appear in the Shilluk-Luo versions with different implications congruent with their different political systems and values. Though the Shilluk-Luo peoples are still partly pastoral and their vocabularies retain strong evidence of pastoral origins, they have far fewer cattle than the Dinka and Nuer, and set less store by them morally and religiously. In their versions of the Myth of the Bead, the cow plays no part, while for the Nuer and Dinka the ostensible reason for telling the myth is to explain the relations between certain clans and a certain type of cow. Without the Shilluk-Luo versions, the Dinka and Nuer versions might well be interpreted as simply validating 'totemic' practices, in stories incorporating also a wider moral principle about the tolerable limits of asserting individual rights. And such, as far as that goes, they are.

---

[31] Even in one English usage 'avoidance' (excretion) is in a sense the opposite of 'assimilation', absorption into the system.

But the Shilluk-Luo versions show that neither cows nor 'totemism' are necessary for the explanation of these myths, and in those versions too the moral is differently slanted. Certainly, a tone of moral outrage at the unreasonableness and cruelty of the characters comes through even in the Shilluk-Luo accounts I have quoted. It is no small thing to cut open a child for a bead, for the Shilluk-Luo as for the Dinka and Nuer. But whereas for the latter that evisceration is specifically shown to be unjustified by the facts, in the Shilluk-Luo versions the child actually *has* swallowed the bead, and the bead, representing the kingship, is no small thing either. For the Dinka and Nuer, the evisceration of the cow or the child is an extreme form of other reprehensible acts destroying communal life. For them, egalitarian and democratic, 'give and take' (or more correctly 'give and ask for', since just taking, as the myths show, seems a threat of assimilation) is politically and morally essential. The evisceration of a living being to get one's own small private possession is there ultimately wrong.

Among the Shilluk-Luo, royal rank modifies this ideal of equity. That very bead alone carries with it the kingship, and no substitute will replace it. So the child's life must be taken (though with royal ceremony, it will be noted). In parts of the texts, including some I have not quoted, the king who takes the bead at the cost of the child's life shows clearly that he wishes to be publicly acknowledged to be in the right in having taken that extreme action. One can feel, even in translation, the triumph of the king in the Alur version (p. 226) as he takes his bead and the kingship: 'I, I looked for this!'

If then the bead of kingship can be retrieved only through the death of a dynastic rival's child which, indeed, has challenged the king and unconsciously shown that very rivalry by swallowing it, the killing is politically justified. And in Shilluk-Luo political history, dynastic rivalries have in fact accounted for many deaths. The occasional wilfulness and caprice, even cruelty, of kings and princes asserting their rightful leadership is well attested in the Nilotic literature, is politically accepted while it may be morally deplored, and in an ambivalent way may sometimes be admired. The second Shilluk king, Dak, for example, is famous for his

headstrong and aggressive self-assertiveness, and that these aspects
of kingship are valued is shown by the importance of his effigy
in the installation rites. Exact reciprocity, some form of natural
justice, an ideally balanced system of exchanges—these are not
expected in relations with kings and princes, though kings may
be revered for showing regard for them.

In the Nilotic kingships, the political process depends finally
not on a balanced equivalence of descent groups but on the
practical hostility of dynastic rivals. If for the Dinka and Nuer the
taking of a spear or swallowing of a bead without permission
seem to threaten (though, as it turns out, only in the imagination)
the independence and integrity of different agnatic groups, for
the royal Nilotes it really threatens the ambitious prince and his
followers. Ingestion (the 'swallowing' of the kingship) would be
followed by digestion and assimilation, the absorption of the
kingship into another branch of the royal house. The metaphor
taken (and taken in these myths) from the digestive process itself
is exact, and is followed through in the myths with their emphasis
on the disgorging or excreting of the royal bead. Only when it
is not disgorged or excreted is the ultimate (and by ordinary
Nilotic moral standards wicked) evisceration performed, and
justifies itself. In a realistic metaphor, a very prominent Anuak
noble, when asked by a District Commissioner to co-operate in
forming an electoral college of nobles which would circulate the
royal emblems by agreement and without bloodshed, said: 'Do
you not realize we nobles are like fish, we eat each other?'

And again, for the royal Nilotes, the separation of the opponents'
people, the religious prohibition to see ever one another again,
has a different significance from that which it has among the
Dinka and Nuer. For the Nuer this theme of total avoidance after
threatened total assimilation is expressed only in the avoidance of
reng-marked cattle. That totemic avoidance though, it may be
noted, involves most importantly not eating the flesh of the
totemic beast. Since the totem represents the principles of segmentary agnation, which requires a balance between the assimilation of descent groups to one another and the preservation of
their separate integrity, the prohibition against the ingestion and

absorption of the totemic animal symbolically preserves that balance. To eat one's totem would be to assimilate all the descent groups which respect it to one's own part of the clan. So also with the Dinka, for whom, however, with the evisceration of a child, unjustified malice has gone so far that the community also breaks apart into groups which avoid one another. In both cases, the myths represent the situation as deplorable.

Not so among the royal Nilotes. There the death of a child is the price of an independent kingdom, and the episodes of the spear and the skin, lack of fellow-feeling for the living followed by lack of reverence for the dead, unreasonable and unjustified, chart the progress of a dynastic quarrel to the final separation of the rivals which, in their terms, *is* justified. Their own independent kingdoms are what rival princes and their followers seek, and historically have obtained. The princes of Shilluk, for example (here by custom and not by religious prescription), are brought up and live away from the court of the king, their one-time rival, unless he happens to be their own father, to whom in a sense they are also rivals. There is only one king. In the myth, the avoidance imposed between Dimo and Nyikango has the same religious force as that imposed upon the Dinka and Nuer in their avoidance of *reng* cattle. It reminds them of a killing for which compensation has not and never will be obtained, and from which therefore, short of total separation, there would be an unending sequence of deaths.[32] In Nilotic terms, the penalty for disregarding the prohibition against ever meeting again, is thus quite realistically, death. Here again total assimilation and total avoidance are dialectically opposed, but in the Shilluk-Luo myths total assimilation of the kingship actually has been attempted by one dynastic group.

The popular moral of these myths may well be the same for all the Nilotes who have versions of them: that is, that life, human or bovine, is more important than inert possessions. The danger to life involved in getting back the spear does not finally justify the demand for it in any version. And here the Shilluk-Luo versions, like the Dinka version, imply that to have accepted compensatory

[32] As death, in the myths, is the penalty imposed for ever seeing one another again.

substitutes ought to have been enough. All the myths show a recognition of the importance of respecting life as against material possessions, and the need for compromise and forbearance. The Shilluk-Luo versions, like the Dinka version, imply that, normally, compensatory substitutes should be accepted from those who have wronged one, that to refuse reconciliation and forgiveness is to face alienation and death.[33] Up to this point all the Nilotes share common notions of equity and morality. In the Myth of the Spear, both the Dinka and Shilluk-Luo myths seem to stress that the dangerous beasts from which the spear was retrieved, snakes, or elephants, whether or not anthropomorphic beasts or zoo-morphic humans, were more reasonable and kindly in their deal-ings with the man who had wronged them than were human neighbours and brothers. Here the sense of equity, and the gener-osity, of the beasts are contrasted with the selfish and uncontrolled aggression of the human actors. In the episode of the spears, it is from the land of the snakes that the clan-divinity, the ultimate support, of the wronged Dinka comes, and from the land of the elephants that the Shilluk and Alur obtain the beads of kingship, the symbols of their own political order.

But the myths also show the conflicts inherent in these different political systems, and which also turn on a common moral, though differently applied in different political contexts. They all dramatize a logical contradiction (when people invoke logic alone) between altruism and self-preservation. They show that people cannot live together if they do not respect one another's independence and integrity, but nor can they live together if any of them is over-jealous of his own independence. In the Dinka and Nuer versions of the Myth of the Bead, the threat of assimila-tion of one party by another is merely imagined. The process of digestion has never started in the Nuer cow or the Dinka child, and the Dinka cow, by excreting the bead, shows that there was

---

[33] Mr. Natale Olwak Akolawin tells me that the force of the prohibition of any future meetings between the children of Dimo (the Luo of the Bahr-al-Ghazal) and the children of Nyikango (the Shilluk) was such that they still felt some constraint when meeting in much more recent, and politically very differ-ent, circumstances. Here again *eating* together, as between those who have an un-settled feud between them, initially caused some feeling of discomfort.

no attempt to retain it. In the Alur and Shilluk versions on the other hand, the usurper, innocent though he may be, will not disgorge or excrete naturally the bead of kingship. Then the claimant to kingship gets back his own (not now merely a personal possession nor even personal and family integrity, but public office and the power of a dynasty) by stopping, if forcefully and unnaturally, the process of its assimilation in the infant descendant of his rivals.

NOTE

The theme of demanding a child in lieu of a material object, with dynastic reference, occurs among the Lunda:

> Kaponto came from the country of Matanda . . . He and Matanda both belonged to the Clay Clan. Their daughters were playing by the water and Kaponto's daughter threw a doll belonging to Matanda's daughter into the water and lost it. Matanda demanded Kaponto's daughter in repayment. Kaponto refused, and to save trouble went away.[34]

The theme of getting one's very own spear back is reported by C. W. Hobley[35] as a Kikuyu legend about the origin of fire. Here a man borrows a neighbour's spear to kill a porcupine which is damaging his garden. The porcupine disappears into its burrow with the spear, and the owner refuses compensation. The borrower makes a hazardous journey to the land of porcupines, who treat him well and return the spear, but also give him fire to take back to the upper world. He tells the owner of the spear that if he wants some fire he must climb up the smoke and get it, which the owner attempts. Then the elders intervene, say that fire shall be for the use of all, and make the bringer of fire their chief. Here as in the Shilluk-Luo stories, the man who survives the dangerous quest to meet an unreasonable demand receives political office.

More distantly related in actual narrative content, but still representing explicitly and, it would appear, simply for entertainment, the taking of life to get one's own back is a story from the Ila-speaking peoples of Zambia[36] about two fools. They go hunting with a dog and a pot. When they have eaten the game they have killed and cooked, the dog licks the pot and gets its head stuck fast. The owner of the pot insists that the dog's head shall be cut off in order to preserve his pot. They return to the village, where

> . . . the owner of the dog found his child sick, and he thought: 'You person who has the pot, his child took my brass bracelet . . .' he said, 'My friend, give me my bracelet.' They called the girl, but the bracelet refused to come off her arm, for it

[34] Ian Cunnison, *The Luapula Peoples of Northern Rhodesia* (Manchester, 1959), p. 34.
[35] C. W. Hobley, *Bantu Beliefs and Magic* (London, 1922), p. 34.
[36] E. W. Smith and A. M. Dale, *The Ila-speaking peoples of Northern Rhodesia*, vol. ii (London, 1920), p. 410.

had been put on long ago while she was yet a child, and now she was grown into a maiden. Said he: 'As it refused to come off let us cut off her hand.' Said he: 'My friend, don't cut off the hand, let us rather give you another bracelet.' That man said: 'I don't want another, this is my bracelet.' 'Which is of more consequence, the bracelet or the hand of the child?'

The owner of the bracelet refuses any substitute, and cuts off the arm of the girl: 'He took his bracelet, saying: "This is the hand of your child, join it up and let us see how you will join it. You cut my dog's head off."' Here there is a happy ending for the owner of the dog (and the bracelet) who takes the bracelet to a diviner, who gives advice which enables him to restore his sick child.

The 'what is of more consequence?' theme is of course familiar in much literature and folk-lore. I include this Ila version of it here because it explicitly states a dilemma which is latent, if near the surface, in the Nilotic myths discussed in the essay.

10

Bundela Genealogy and Legends: The Past of an Indigenous Ruling Group of Central India

R. K. JAIN

Introduction

UNTIL a year after the independence of India in August 1947, the northern districts of Madhya Pradesh formed the territories of Native States ruled over by the scions of Rajput (literally 'Kingly sons' from the Sanskrit *Raja-putra*) families. From the beginning of the nineteenth century the British had established their paramountcy over the Native States. This paper deals with the traditional history of these native kingdoms (*rajya* or *raj*) as rendered in the oral narratives and indigenously written sources of this area. More specifically I am concerned here to demonstrate the value of these sources in defining the region of dominance and salient social institutions of a ruling group known as the Bundela. The area of former Bundela kingdoms is still known by its indigenous name 'Bundelkhand' (literally, 'the domain of the Bundelas'). It might also be mentioned that besides designating the territory of former Bundela rule, Bundelkhand is the name of a linguistic region of India. The great majority of the people of four southern districts of Uttar Pradesh and eight northern districts of Madhya Pradesh speak Bundeli, a dialect of Western Hindi. The Bundeli linguistic region is much larger (27,000 square miles) than the area of former Bundela kingdoms and domains (8,564 square miles).

The data were collected in the course of intermittent anthropological field-work from 1969 to 1971 in several villages and

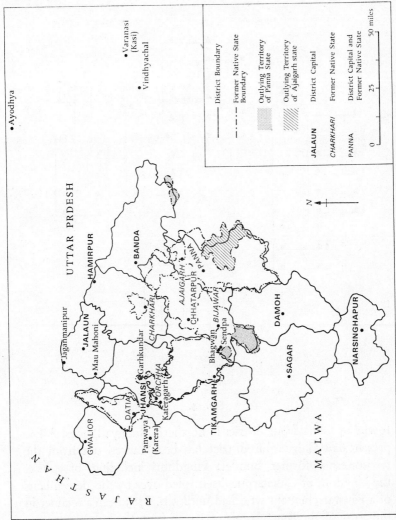

FIG. 13. Map of Bundelkhand.

THE BUNDELA AND THEIR MARITAL ALLIES, FROM PANCHAM TO SOHANPAL

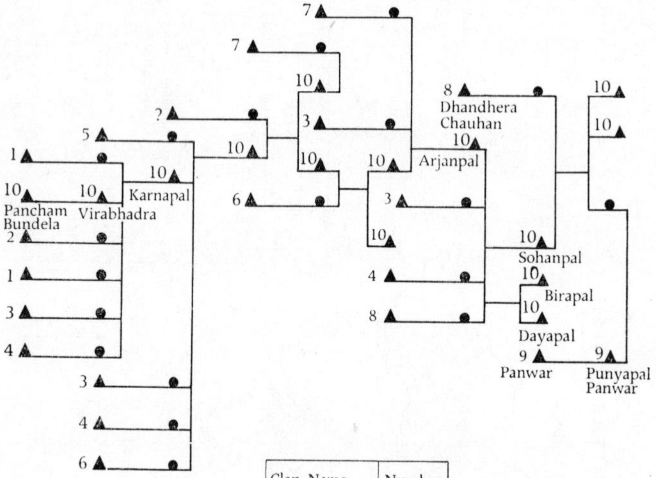

Clan Name	Number
Bais	1
Baghela	2
Chauhan	3
Tonwar	4
Parihar	5
Rathor	6
Gaur	7
Dhandhera } Chauhan	8
Panwar	9
Bundela	10

FIG. 14.

towns of Chhatarpur district in northern Madhya Pradesh.[1] The present-day Chhatarpur district has been carved out from the territories of former Bundela kingdoms including, of course, the kingdom of Chhatarpur, itself ruled over by the descendants of a Panwar chieftain who had until A.D. 1785 been a retainer in the army of the Bundela raja of Panna (thus the hybrid 'Panwar Bundela' as the 'caste' of Chhatarpur dynasty in official records). Besides Panna, the other Bundela kingdoms surrounding Chha-

[1] I wish to express my thanks to the Indian Institute of Advanced Study for the grant of a Fellowship towards carrying out the field-work and to the Wenner-Gren Foundation for Anthropological Research for a grant-in-aid to collect the documentary evidence.

tarpur were Orchha, Datia, Charkhari, Bijawar, and Ajaigarh. Orchha was the parent Bundela kingdom founded *c.* A.D. 1501. The kingdoms of Datia and Panna separated from Orchha in A.D. 1626 and 1675 respectively. Charkhari, Bijawar, and Ajaigarh were formed from Panna territory in the second half of the eighteenth century, following dissensions amongst the descendants of Maharaja Chhatrasal (1649–1731), the founder of Panna.

The Bundela Genealogy

The most comprehensive charter for the Bundela past is their genealogy (*vamsa-vali*). It is the record of a strictly exogamous patriline. When it is rendered in the form of a diagram, it shows only males descending from males. The women are not represented.

Histories compiled from primary or secondary sources—in Hindi and English—take the form of succession lists of the ruling dynasties. The ruling line is the main or the senior line, besides which these sources also contain lists of subsidiary or junior lines, since all descendants of the ruling stock (*rajya vamsa*) were normatively included among the right-holders (*haqdar*) in the kingdom. Since these lists might become unwieldy, only those agnates from junior lines are selected who possessed large hereditary appanages (*jagir*) in the kingdom. Those marital allies who held appanages in the kingdom are also listed. A typical example is the compilations in the series *Rulers, Leading Families and Officials in the States of Central India* (Calcutta and Delhi, 1911–41).

At present the most senior living member of a Bundela patrilineage in one village or a group of near-by villages usually possesses an up-to-date genealogical extract of his own residential unit (*patti*). This local group corresponds to a minimal segment of the Bundela patriline. The apical ancestor for this segment would be the Bundela founder of the *patti*. Nevertheless, the term *patti* denotes a share. It implies division from a larger entity and segmentation of the group from a higher level. The definition and scale of customary rights to a share are validated at this higher pre-*patti* level of segmentation which involves reference to those areas of the genealogy where a local Bundela patrilineage is linked by descent to a particular ruling house. This indigenous procedure of tracing rights among the rural Bundela landholders was imperfectly understood by the British authorities who intervened in their land-disputes throughout the nineteenth century. The discrepancy between Bundela custom and an alien juridical framework which the British attempted to enforce on the local Bundela dominants (*thakur*) is epitomized in the repeated assertions by the latter that they were co-sharers (*hissedar*), and not merely right-holders (*haqdar*), in particular Bundela kingdoms. This is not to deny the existence of customary law, regulating the distribution of rights, offices, and titles over territory in the indigenous kingdoms. What I wish to note is the strong linkage of Bundela customary law with Bundelas' rules of descent, succession, and inheritance—the sphere of 'family law' as Maine saw it—and the problems arising in attempts to align it with substantive law through a 'double institutionalisation of custom' (Bohannan, 1965, pp. 34–7).

In the context of our present discussion of the Bundela genealogy we simply note that the Bundelas had a vested interest in emphasizing their common descent from the rulers. This is reflected in the rural Bundelas' ability to trace, beyond the *patti* level, their patrilineal links with the ruling dynasty of the kingdom where they are located. Furthermore, since all Bundela kingdoms grew by a process of political fission in the patriline, the links between various ruling dynasties are also contained in the Bundela genealogy. As mentioned earlier, historically the Bundela dynasty of Orchha was the parent ruling house from which the other Bundela kingdoms subsequently separated. The last Bundela kingdom thus formed was Charkhari. The *patti* level of Bundela patrilineal segmentation, which I designate as the dominance level of Bundela genealogy, is thus subsumed by the dynastic level which spans, socially and politically, the time and space of kingdom formation in Bundela history.

However, in the genealogy itself the origin of the Bundelas and their kingship (as distinct from historical kingdoms) belong to a legendary and mythical past. The legendary and mythical levels of the genealogy are an invaluable repository for the anthropologist to explore the unconscious structure of Bundela ideology of descent-based rule. The view of their past depicted at these levels exercises a powerful hold on the popular imagination of the people of this area. It is expressed in a variety of media—stories, songs, poems, and anecdotes. The Bundelas themselves enact their legendary origin in the annual ritual worship of Devi (the female principle in divine creation) while the categories of Bundela rule—the boundaries of socially legitimate exercise of power by the ruling group—are constituted by the formal and sensory properties of symbolic statements and enactments associated with the legendary and mythological past. Through an analysis of Bundela myth and legends of origin and kingship in the next section of this paper, I wish to demonstrate that these levels of the Bundela genealogy, like the dominance and dynastic levels, do not stand in isolation. They form an integral part of a hierarchical series of encapsulated history of the ruling group. Before proceeding to that analysis, however, I should like to make two further clarifications.

The Bundela myth and legends of origin have a double aspect. The legends trace Bundela descent from their eponymous apical ancestor at the same time as they describe the origin of Bundela kingship in the present territory, the region of the Vindhya mountain. In regard to the specificity of geographical information the identification in the legends of Bundela territory with the Vindhya mountains lies in between the much clearer geopolitical boundaries of kingdoms given in the dynastic histories and the elemental and transitive sacred geography described in mythology. The association of the group with a more or less specific territory is one criterion for distinguishing a legendary level from the mythological one. The latter, in the absence of an unequivocal territorial specification, should be viewed as the standard 'great tradition' prolegomena to Hindu royal genealogies.

The second clarification concerns the analytical vocabulary to be adopted in discerning patterns of descent at various levels of Bundela genealogy. I have so far used the concepts 'patriline' for the genealogy as a whole, and 'local patrilineage' and 'royal house' for territorially identifiable groups corresponding to the dominance and dynastic levels of Bundela genealogy. The term 'patriline' is a translation of the indigenous *vamsa*. Owing to the segmentary structure of Bundela unilineal descent groups, however, the same terms *vamsa* may occasionally be used to denote a smaller unit, e.g. a 'local patrilineage' and a 'royal house'. But in a context where the smaller units need to be distinguished from more inclusive descent constructs, for example, the patriline as a whole, the terms *kula* and *khandan* are used interchangeably to denote them. Among terms denoting a more inclusive descent construct for the Bundelas, the indigenous *kuri* and *bans* belong to the same semantic set as *vamsa*. Lexically, *bans* is a corruption of the Sanskrit *vamsa*. In the written genealogies of Bundelkhand, the Sanskrit *vamsa* is invariably employed to designate the record as a whole (genealogy = *vamsavali*), and in the mythological portion of the genealogy, for example, to designate the two main branches—solar (*surya vamsa*) and lunar (*chandra vamsa*)—of the ruling (*kshatriya*) clans. However, from the legendary level downwards the unilineal descent segments, not only of the Bundelas but of their 'Rajput' marital allies as well, are designated as *bans*. In spoken Bundeli, moreover, the term *bans* is uniformly employed to designate the genealogy as a whole (*bansavali*), the mythological branches, and the 'Rajput' clans (e.g. Bundela *bans*). As the commonest designation for Bundela corporate identity the last of these meanings is already given in the speech behaviour of the Bundelas, viz., in the expression 'The Bundela clan is not a friend of brothers' (*Bundela bans bhaiyya ka mit nahin hota*). I locate the meaning of *bans* as clan at the legendary level of Bundela genealogy. In my definition, the Bundela *bans* is a clan in that all Bundelas trace their mythical descent, through males, from an eponymous ancestor; through him they identify themselves with a more or less specific territory; and they practise *bans* exogamy. It corresponds to the maximal level of segmentation of the Bundela patriline.

Closely allied to the ideas of *vamsa* and *bans* but much more complex in connotation is the term *kuri*. The most frequent local usage of this term is in expressions implying the classification of Rajput *bans* into two categories along an East–West territorial axis. Each category is indigenously known by the number of clans composing it; thus there are the 'three-kuri Rajput' (*tin kuri ke Rajput*) and the 'thirty-six-kuri Rajput' (*chattis kuri ke Rajput*), belonging to the eastern or Bundelkhand region and the western or Malwa and Rajasthan region, respectively. In designating the two categories of Rajput clans the term *kuri* is being used in its meaning of 'kind', 'type', or 'variety' (Hindi *prakara*). This translation is offered by the informants themselves. But the concept 'kuri' in the above formula does not by itself suggest the basis for classifying Rajput clans into these two categories. Nor does an ancillary formulation where individual Rajput men or families are sorted out as belonging 'either to the three or the thirty-six' (*tin me ke, ya chattis me ke*) tell us any more than that besides being different from one another each category represents a unity of some kind.[2]

A second meaning of the term *kuri* and the sentences generated by it is more explicit. A Hindi Lexicon (*Nalanda Visal Sabdasagar*) gives the following meanings: '[noun, masculine gender] (In Sanskrit), 1. a grain, 1. bean sprout. (In poetry), *vamsa*, *gharana*, *khandan*. (In Desaja), a plough. [noun, feminine gender] (in Hindi), "a subdivision", "a part", "a portion".'

Undoubtedly the term *kuri* is a derivative from the Sanskrit *ankura* which means 'a sprout', 'shoot', 'blade', 'hair', 'water', 'blood' (Monier Williams, 1964, p. 7). In this semantic set the term *kuri* is a metaphor for the segmentary ideology of Bundela descent. The Bundelas themselves express the idea of fission and fusion of their patriline in this statement about the process of the formation of segments (e.g. a local patrilineage): 'formerly all were one, subsequently different *kuri* sprouted' (*pahle sab ek the;*

---

[2] Had each category comprised an equal number of clans, and the two categories as a whole been exhaustive for all Rajput clans of central India, we might have regarded the categories 'three-kuri' and 'thirty-six-kuri' as moieties. In the case at hand the clans comprising each category constitute distinct clusters, practising 'territorial endogamy'. Moreover, there is a third category of inter-marrying Rajput clans, the 'thirteen-kuri' (*terah kuri ke Rajput*), with a mixed territorial distribution, which I do not discuss in this paper.

bad me alag alag kuri phut gayin). *Kuri* in this statement, and in many similar statements, is associated with 'sprouting'. Similarly, with reference to a particular apical ancestor or brothers, it is said that from him or them 'the branching-out commenced' (*phutan chali*). Here the apical ancestor—always male—is likened to a seed. An apt graph of the collective representation of the Bundela patriline in the metaphor of sowing and sprouting is the genealogical extract characteristically drawn in the form of a creeper or a plant, with the male descendants only being shown as leaves on several veins and the leaves again sprouting more leaves on more veins. The orientation is always from the bottom upwards.

As handled in speech by my Bundela informants, the concept *kuri* connotes both fission and fusion aspects of their patrilineal descent ideology. Yet the principle of *patrilineal* segmentation cannot be extended to the classification of Rajput clans, including the Bundela clan, into the 'three-kuri' and 'thirty-six-kuri' categories without further exploration of the internal structure of each category. I hope that in this exploration our identification of the exogamous 'clan' segment at the legendary level of Bundela genealogy will prove serviceable. The grounds for setting up an experiment in Bundelkhand ethnology are provided by the fact that the eastern or Bundelkhandi category (the 'three-kuri Rajput') can be identified with three exogamous clans, viz. the Bundela, the Panwar, and the Dhandera. Intermarriage among the three follows a rule of non-hypergamous circulating connubium. However, in a legend of Bundela kingship the Bundela conquerors are depicted as having consciously formed a league of intermarriage with the other two groups, following help rendered by them in their victory against an out-group, the non-Kshatriya Khangar. Thus martial alliance preceded marital alliance. Here then is a perfect case of two structures which, as comparative social anthropology tells us, interpenetrate each other—on the one hand, political and, on the other, 'descent and alliance'. My limited purpose in the paper is to clarify the terms of this juxtaposition on the basis of the Bundelas' view of their past.

The Myth of Royal Origin

The mythical beginning of the royal Bundelas has a typical Hindu character. The account starts with Lord Visnu (Narayan, reclining on the serpent, Sesa who holds the universe). From Visnu's placenta, in the form of the stem of the lotus flower, issues Brahma. From Brahma issues Marichi. From Marichi is brought forth Kasyapa. By Kasyapa's wife, Aditi, are born the eldest son, Surya (the Sun), and the gods (*devta*); of his twelve other wives, by Diti are born the demons (*daitya*): the descendants of Surya (*suryavamsi*) are Iksvaku, Dilip, Raghu, Aja, Dasaratha, Ramachandra, and the two brothers Lava and Kusa. Lava becomes the ruler of Punjab. Kusa succeeds to the throne (*gaddi*) of Ayodhya. The descendants of Kusa are Haribrahma and Vihagaraja. In the seventh generation from Vihagaraja his named descendant is Kiratdeva. A few generations after Kiratdeava, Virabhadra, the Raja of Kasi (Benaras), is descended. The Bundelas, in this version, are the descendants of Virabhadra through the line of his *younger son*, Hem Karan, alias Pancham, alias Jagdas.

This mythical prologue contains elements which carry a symbolic significance at all levels of royal-descent ideology and for the Bundela genealogy as a whole. The origin of the rulers from the stem of the lotus flower is one such element. In Hindu ideas, on account of its free-floating roots, the lotus flower is a persistent cosmological motif for depicting the exalted origins of royalty (Bosch, 1960). It symbolizes the special creation and inherent legitimacy of kingship, investing royal descendants with the spiritual authority which they must possess as lords and protectors of 'land-cum-people'.

Secondly, in the oral tradition, Bundela kings are descended from the Sun (Surya) and belong to the solar pedigree (*surya-vamsa*). The conjunction of the sun and the lotus is auspicious in Hindu ideas; both these and their related attributes occupied a significant place in Bundela symbolism of kingship, e.g. in royal architecture. Third, demons and gods are brothers as Kasyapa's sons. While the idea of brothers as potential enemies permeates

Bundela royal agnation, the principle of succession by primogeniture is clearly expressed in specifying that Rama's elder son,
Kusa, succeeds to the throne of Ayodhya. Finally, at this level,
kingship is associated with sacred geography. Only two capitals,
Ayodhya and Kasi, are identifiable places. Both have multiple
associations with the Hindu sacred tradition. Along with three
other pilgrim centres they belong to a quintet of sacred locales
of the Hindus. As a 'great tradition' mode of classification this
quintet, rather like the fourfold *varna* scheme, serves to legiti-
mize kingship in the idiom of descent.

The flexibility inherent in associating royalty with sacred
locales has been exploited by genealogists to insert fictions of
glorious antecedents for their Bundela patrons and by priests and
poets to align the royal pedigree with their own priestly pedigree.
A good example of the latter is an early seventeenth-century
poetic biography of the Bundela ruler of Orchha composed by
his Brahman priest and poet Kesava Das.[3] Kesava Das, whose
own ancestors came from Kasi, constantly refers to his Bundela
royal patron by the honorific 'Kasiraja' (the Ruler of Kasi). The
title did not conform to the historically known boundaries of the
kingdom of Orchha, which never included Kasi (Benaras or
Varanasi in modern Uttar Pradesh). The point here is *not* that
Kesava Das was fabricating Bundela history; rather, on account
of its sacredness in Hindu ideas Kasi, like Ayodhya, is a good
place to think about as the seat of royalty.

The Legend of Bundela Origin

The legend of Bundela origin narrated to me in Sendpa village
is as follows: Virabhadra, the king of Kasi, had two queens. From

---

[3] Kesava Das Misra, an eastern (Sanadhya) Brahman, was a noted Hindi poet.
His family held the hereditary offices of royal mythographer (pauranic) and
councillor in the court of Bundela kings of Orchha. Maharaja Bir Singh Deva
Bundela, the patron-king of Kesava Das, ruled at Orchha from *c.* A.D. 1606 to
1630. Bir Singh Deva, a junior son, had usurped the kingdom of Orchha from
his elder brother under the protection of his ally and patron, the Moghul emperor
Jahangir. Yet, as a native historian puts it, Bir Singh Deva was 'mindful of the
sin he had committed . . . and feeling great remorse, in penitence made nine
pilgrimages and offered innumerable sacrifices'. (Mazboot Singh translated by
Silberrad, op. cit., p. 114.) Kesava Das officiated at the coronation ceremony
one year before he composed the poetic biography, *Birsingh Caritra.*

the senior queen (*patrani*) there were four sons; Rajsingh, Hanasraj, Mohan, and Man. The son of the second queen (*lahuri rani*; literally, junior queen) was Jagdas alias Hemkaran. Following Virabhadra's death, the half-brothers of Jagdas refused to give him a portion (*hissa*) in the kingdom of Kasi and banished him. Jagdas wandered away to the shrine of Vindhyavasini Devi (literally, 'the Devi who dwells in the Vindhya ranges'. 'Devi' is the manifestation of the female principle in divine creation; when not regarded as a deity localized in the Vindhyan mountain ranges she is known by her generalized name 'Devi', or by any of her other manifestations as 'Bhawani', 'Durga', 'Kali', etc.) to do penance under her protection. Despite the most arduous penances, he received no signs of blessing from the Devi. Dejected by this Jagdas decided to offer his life in sacrifice to the Devi by beheading himself with his sword. No sooner had a drop (*bund*) of blood dripped on to the floor from a cut in his throat, than the Devi appeared and held the hand of her devotee. She blessed him with the boon that from the drop of his blood a brave son would be born who would conquer large territories to be known the world over as Bundelkhand.

With a few variations and additions of detail the same legend appears in an eighteenth-century poetic biography of Maharaja Chhatrasal, the Bundela ruler of Panna, composed in his lifetime by the poet (*bhat*) named Lal Kavi or Gorelal. In this text (Lal Kavi, *c.* A.D. 1700) the name of Virabhadra's son from the second queen alone is mentioned. He is called Pancham or Devadasa. Both these names are formulaic in the sense that they refer to the attributes of the person being designated; Pancham means 'the Fifth' (his place in the sibling birth-order) and Devadasa, 'the deity's servant' (his disposition for acquiring a boon from the goddess). Although the text is far from explicit, it seems to indicate that Virabhadra in his own lifetime partitioned his estate (*puhumi* meaning 'land'; it might also stand for 'kingdom') among his sons. Pancham being a minor, Virabhadra as father and king became the trustee of his share of inheritance. Following Virabhadra's death, the older four brothers of Pancham grew covetous, took advantage of his minority and appropriated his

250 *Bundela Genealogy and Legends*

portion of the estate 'partitioning it among themselves in four shares'. There is no mention of Virabhadra's successor to the seat of Kasi which makes sense if we bear in mind the mythical character of this 'seat', and my view that the story of Pancham marks the point of transition from a mythological to a legendary level of Bundela past.[4]

The forward-looking facet of the legend which enables us to view Pancham as the founder of the Bundela clan is his gaining a kingdom and a patriline of royal descent following the gift of a heroic son by the Vindhyavasini Devi created from a drop of Pancham's own blood and appropriately called 'Bundela' (*bund* = drop). Details of the boon in the form of the gift (*varadan*) of a son to Pancham and the son's 'special creation' by divine inter-position are vividly portrayed in the poem. The mental process by which Pancham, the unhappy prince, is drawn towards Vindhyavasini Devi is known as 'yoga-nidra' (which Pogson renders as 'Jog Nidruh'), 'the tranquil repose of the mind from an abstraction of ideas' (Pogson, ibid., p. 6). Pancham practises penances and austerities at her shrine in Vindhyachal, the hills near Mirzapur in Uttar Pradesh, and a neighbouring town of re-ligious resort on the Ganges. The episode is thus narrated in text:

After the first seven days Pancham heard a voice from the sky say to him, 'Your land will be restored to you.' He replied, 'I have practised these austerities to win your (Devi's) favour.' Whereupon the voice returned to the sky. Somewhat heartened by this he devoted the next seven days to even stricter penances and gradually lost all hopes of gratifying his wish. He took out his sword and poised it to behead

---

[4] My inference that Pancham's exile was caused by a dispute over inheritance is supported by the following observations: (*a*) The partition of heritage amongst sons within the ruler's lifetime is known historically to have been a Bundela custom as indicated, for example, by Chhatrasal's letters regarding the partition of Panna heritage (cf. Gupta, 1958, pp. 151–3); (*b*) The phrase 'bala bahikrama' (from Sanskrit, *bala vayahakrama*, meaning 'young age') in the text shows Pancham to be a minor at the time of his father's death. Although the Dharmasastra enjoined upon kings the duty of protecting the minor heirs' interests (Kane (1946), iii. 574), the expropriation of Pancham's share by his brothers appears to signify weak royal authority in a principality (kingdom or domain) of that period.

Because of insufficient evidence I am unable to pursue Professor Derrett's suggestion (in a personal communication) that Pancham was the son of a lady whose status was open to doubt.

himself in sacrifice to the Devi. By now his perseverance, piety, and devotion had won her affection. She appeared in person and wrested the sword from his hand. In the process his head received a few gashes and drops of blood oozed out 'like stars shooting from the sky'. The sight filled her heart with pity. She immediately conveyed to the wound a portion of the *amrita* or water of immortality inherent in every *devta*. At the same time *amrita* rained from the sky. One drop of Pancham's blood on the ground became animated and assumed the form of a child, the exact resemblance of Pancham. On beholding the infant she yearned with maternal affection and put it to her breast, which supplied a copious flood of nourishment. Then blessing Pancham and the babe, she, with prophetic spirit, revealed that the sword should always help him in war, and be the prop of his prosperity, to which the sovereignty should continue from one generation to another . . . 'Thou, O favoured mortal,' she added, 'shalt repossess thy estate, increase them to the full extent of thy wishes and conquer all against whom thou wagest war.' Then placing her hand on his head, she said, in commemoration of the drop of blood (*bund*), 'Thy descendants shall be called Bundelas.'

In this version the conjunction between the principle of descent and territory in Bundela ideology of kingship is expressed in the metaphor of divine intervention in human affairs (the *pauranic* device). In reality the Vindhyas are a mountain range which give the name to a territory and to the female principle dwelling in that territory. In the metaphorical structure of the legend Vindhyavasini Devi represents 'territory-for-kingdom'. (She is actually designated *puhumi* or 'Land' (fem.) in the course of the poem.) Bundela, the son from a drop of Pancham's blood on the earth, is nourished by Vindhyavasini Devi as the divine female principle, blessed by her with a line of brave royal descendants; and is gifted away to Pancham. This Son Incarnate is to be distinguished from Pancham's other, 'real', son Bir Bundela. The former never again makes an appearance in the book. What remains of him is only the name 'Bundela' assumed by Pancham himself after the incident, and passed on to his descendants. The Son Incarnate is, therefore, a ritual apotheosis of the principle of clanship at the legendary level of Bundela genealogy. All Bundela royal houses worshipped Vindhyavasini Devi as their clan goddess (*kula devi*), although the members of Bundela lineal segments localized in rural areas worship their clan goddess in her generalized form, Devi. What is significant about the legend of Bundela origin is its representation of territory in the form of Vindhyavasini Devi endowed with multi-vocal symbolic significance as the female principle, the territory, and the giver and nourisher of princes. Through her divine intervention unilineal descent (blood) and territory (milk) complete the picture of Bundela royal agnation in the idiom of clanship (*bans*).

A Legend of Bundela Expansion

The expansion of the Bundela clan following the boon to Pancham is closely associated with the legendary martial exploits of his royal descendants in the Vindhya region. One particular event, again the founding, by conquest, of a separate kingdom by one of the royal siblings, is repeated extensively in all oral narratives and does not escape significant mention in the literary works as well. The following summary is based mainly on the latter set of sources: Arjanpal, ruler of Mahoni had three sons: Birpal, Sohanpal, and Dayapal. Sohanpal was a most capable warrior. He reduced the forts of Garhkundar and Kateragarh.[5] Sohanpal undertook the successful expedition to Kateragarh on behalf of his father. His victory at Garhkundar followed the death of his father and his elder brother's succession to the throne of Mahoni. The cause of this expedition was Sohanpal's dissatisfaction with his share of inheritance. With forty-five sepoys and thirteen sowars, Sohanpal went to Naga (alias Hurmat Singh), the Khangar raja of Kundar, seeking his help in taking his share from his brother.

This Naga promised to do on condition that he would eat, drink and intermarry with him. Sohanpal was very much enraged at this suggestion, and was about to leave Kurar [Kundar], but hearing of his

[5] Mahoni is recorded by the name Mau-Mahoni in Bundela chronicles. Mau (26° N. 79′ E.) is a village on the eastern bank of River Pahuj in Jalaun District while Mahoni itself lies a short distance across the river in Gwalior territory. Kundar (25° 29′ N. and 78° 57′ E.) is located in Tikamgarh District. Kateragarh is 'better known as Katera, the seat of a Jagirdar and Titular Raja in pargana Mau (Jhansi District) 26 miles S.-E. of Jhansi' (Silberrad, p. 105).

intention, Naga formed a plot to forcibly detain him and compel him to accede to these proposals. Sohanpal, hearing thereof, fled from the court, and went to Mukatman Chahan, who was a descendant of Dhandhera Deva and commanded 4,000 men on behalf of Naga. Him he requested to assist him against his brother, but Mukatman refused, saying that he would remain neutral. After this, Sohanpal, leaving his small force behind, went alone successively to the Salingars, Chauhans and Kachwahas, and told his story to them. But none of them offered to assist him. However, a Panwar Thakur named Panpal [Pun yapal], Jagindar of Karhara, offered assistance, and the two conspired to remove Raja Naga by stratagem from his kingdom, which was worth 13 lakhs. It was agreed that Sohanpal should go to Kurar and pretend to accept Raja Naga's conditions of intermarriage, etc., and invite the raja and his relations to his house. Sohanpal went to Kurar and did as agreed on. After a time Raja Naga with his brothers and ministers, came to Sohanpal's house, whereupon Panpal arrived with 300 Kshatris, and as soon as Raja Naga and his followers had sat down to eat, Panpal Panwar and Sohanpal Bundela fell upon and slaughtered all the Khangar chiefs, and immediately seized the fort of Kurar. In this way, on Wednesday the 2nd of Kartik Sambat 1345 (1288 A.D.) Sohanpal became Raja of Kurar and appointed Panpal and Mukatman as ministers. He said to them, 'As no Kshatri in time of my distress gave me help except you, no other save yourselves shall marry into my family.' Accordingly he gave his daughter in marriage to Panpal and as dowry a village named Itaura, and to his younger brother a jagir of one lakh. From this time the Kshatris were divided into three different classes of Bundelas, Panwar and Dhandheras. The total revenue of the whole Bundela territory was 26 lakhs of which half was possessed by Birpal and the rest by Sohanpal. (Silberrad, op. cit., pp. 105–6.)

This is the most secular of early Bundela legends. It depicts two social processes which must be kept conceptually distinct in order to understand the political process of the expansion of Bundela rule in the Vindhya region. The first is a process of caste segmentation. Luard (1909, p. 15), Tiwari (1933, pp. 118–22), and Archival Records (B. A. R., 1905, 48/51) contain information about the natal clans of the wives of Bundela rulers from Bir Bundela to Sohanpal (Fig. 14, p. 240) which confirms that before the capture of Garh Kundar, the Bundela intermarried exogamously with a large number of Rajput clans. The marriages of Sohanpal's immediate descendants, on the other hand, take place with the Panwar and Dhandhera clans only. Tiwari further hints that the narrowing of the Bundela endogamous circle involved their exclusion from commensal relations with the other Rajput clans. Similarly there is evidence that the Panwar and the Dhandhera had also experienced exclusion from a more inclusive Rajput category. The views of nineteenth-century amateur historians (Elliot, 1869, i. 45; Smith, 1881, pp. 1–52; Franklin, 1827, pp. 259–81), attributing inferior or impure Rajput status to the Bundela, on account of miscegenation with the non-Aryan Khangar, could also be seen to describe a process of caste segmentation by exclusion.[6] Whatever the specific terms under which this process is perceived, the concept of caste segmentation emphasizes the relative hierarchy of statuses among the Rajput. In this particular case an endogamous segment of the main body of Rajput caste, formed by a process of exclusion, had a definitely lower ritual status *vis-à-vis* the rest.

What is excluded from the main body of Rajputs constitutes the inclusive category, the 'three-kuri Rajput'. The constituent units of this category are three intermarrying exogamous clans. The discrete groups belonging to the three clans are localized lineage segments. The principle of inclusion, I submit, cannot be elucidated by the process of caste segmentation, but only through the complementary processes of dispersed clanship and merging lineage segmentation (Fox, 1967, pp. 122–31).[7]

[6] Elliot, basing himself on the testimony of a Mohammedan historian, advanced the 'racialist' view that the legend of the capture of Garhkundar is a Bundela myth fabricated to conceal the fact of their being the progeny of a Gaharwar Rajput from a Khangar concubine. In a similar vein Tod constantly reduces the Rajput value of 'honour' in matters of bride-giving to a notion of racial purity. The fact of the matter is that giving away a woman was, for the royal clans, tantamount to capitulating territory. Purity of blood, on the other hand, was preserved by preventing indiscriminate mixing, in the first place by the strict observances of patrilineal exogamy and the incest taboo.

[7] This is a structural imperative because the series of hierarchically graded statuses cannot be extended either to the 'three-kuri Rajput' category amongst whose constituent clans there is non-hypergamous connubium or below it where another opposition, that between the Kshatriya (e.g. the 'three-' and 'thirty-six-kuri Rajput'-clans) and the non-Kshatriya (e.g. the Khangar) becomes operative, leading to a qualitatively different basis for 'exclusion'.

In our exploration of these processes we encounter the Bundela legend of expansion not in its function as a cover for social and ritual exclusion, but as a charter of social and political inclusion. The contextual information in our sources elucidates this function.

Rajput territorial organization in much of insular central India during the pre-Bundela period was based on dispersed clanship. Each named clan (*bans*) was an exogamous unit and its constituent patrilineages at various levels of segmentation were designated, in addition to the clan name, by the locality (a village or cluster of villages) where the relevant apical ancestor is supposed to have created rights in land and its produce either by conquest or political alliance. These rights tended to become presumptive. Thus even when they were overlaid by superior rights, say through conquest by another clan or by a foreign power, or during the protracted absence from the locality of the members of the original descent-group, they could still be revived if the occasion warranted. Their non-recognition by the authorities became a frequent cause of rebellion (cf. Malcolm (1824, i. 508–11) on the rights of the Grassia chiefs; Sleeman (1915, pp. 245–52) on the 'bhumia' of Bundelkhand; also, Irfan Habib (1963, ch. v) for central India during the Moghul rule). This customary claim (whatever be its historical character) by deep patrilineages to particular territories formed the basis of their local identification. Legends of former rule by the clans concerned which still abound in these localities are probably not without some historical foundation, so long as we take care to distinguish alleged dynastic succession from agnatic inheritance of presumptive rights in land and its produce and a fully fledged state political system from a combination of feudal and acephalous political systems.

The various localized patrilineal segments of Rajput clans referred to in the legend of Bundela expansion may reasonably be set against the background of social and political organization delineated above. They were located in the Gwalior–Jalaun–Jhansi region, roughly the same area as Arjunpal's seat of Mahoni. The various chiefs who exchanged women in marriage appear to have been *primi inter pares* as dominants (*thakur*) in their localities. The diversity of titles assumed by them either emanated from their position in the segmentary lineage structure stratified into senior and junior branches (e.g. *rao*, *diman*, and *sawai diman*) or they referred to offices currently held or held in the past in a local patrilineage as feudatories to a superior power (e.g. *raja*, *rai*, and *diwan*).

The power equality of chiefs or dominants in the regional political system on the eve of Bundela conquest of Garhkundar at the end of the thirteenth-century A.D. is vividly portrayed in a historical novel (Verma, 1956). Hurmat Singh the Khangar ruler of Garhkundar was descended from Khet Singh, appointed Governor of this region after Prithviraja Chauhan's victory over a former Chandela ruler (*c*. A.D. 1182). After only a decade of overlordship Prithviraja himself lost to the Muslim invader, Shahabuddin Ghori. For the next 100 years or so the line of Khangar governors, even though divested of representative authority derived from a superior power, maintained some kind of suzerainty over the regional Rajput dominants.[8]

By the time of Hurmat Singh repeated Muslim invasions spelt utter chaos in the wider political arena and rendered the regional political sytem completely acephalous. In order to gain political advantage through territorial expansion local lineage segments of Rajput clans arranged and rearranged themselves in patterns of marital and martial alliance.

In interpreting the formation of the category 'three-kuri Rajput' from the legend of Bundela expansion one must carefully distinguish between the facts of martial-cum-marital alliance in the context of regional, social, and political structure and the message concerning the superiority of Kshatriya rulers *vis-à-vis* that of the non-Kshatriya Khangar. The former cannot be wholly understood in terms of merging lineage segmentation, nor the

---

[8] Luard (1909, p. 10), basing himself on the Khangar annals, mentions the names 'Bucha' for Khet Singh and 'Bhup Singh' for Hurmat Singh of Bundela chronicles whom Verma seems to have followed. According to Luard's sources Bucha, appointed Governor at Garhkundar, had eight sons whom he assigned the eight forts of Tehrauli, Bamora, Kachra, Malhara, Chhoti-Parasin, Kanta-Kamta, and Sikri Sunta. These sons were known as the *Ath-garhiyaval* (Keepers of Eight Forts) a name which clung to their descendants. He also appends a list of twenty-nine Khangar clans (*gotra*), each identified with a place of domicile (*khairo*). The clans are totemistic and exogamous.

latter wholly as caste segmentation in the idiom of ritual hierarchy. What is the middle ground left, in historical fact and conceptualization, between these dominant modes of interpretation? The answer suggested by a contextual interpretation of this Bundela legend has, as I shall point out in conclusion, wider implications.

The lineage organization of ruling clans at this time had an important political function. The Khangar ruled over the wild tracts of south-eastern Bundelkhand by allocating political authority to localized lineage segments, where each segment was identified with a fortress serving as a military garrison. Fortresses assigned to the rulers' sons as secondary capitals continually figure in Bundela legends and traditional history also. Conflict between half-siblings in the Bundela ruling lineage of Mahoni is presaged by a military expedition commanded by Sohanpal to capture the fort of Kateragarh. According to Bundela annals (Silberrad, op. cit., p. 105) Sohanpal was disinherited of this fort, besides being overlooked in the succession. It is conceivable that this disinheritance was the main cause of the quarrel between him and Birpal. In later Bundela history it became a standard tactic for a ruler to assign a fort far away from the capital to a turbulent junior brother. As later researches (Drake-Brockman, 1909, p. 188) have shown, Kateragarh is not the southern fort of Silberrad's account. It was located uncomfortably close to Mahoni for Birpal to assign to Sohanpal.

However, the agnatic factionalism in the ruling lineage which is the efficient cause of Sohanpal's expedition against the Khangar does not, even according to the legend, lead to a permanent fission. The fate of the senior branch (Birpal-Dayapal) after Sohanpal's capture of Garhkundar is not passed over in silence. The breach between the half-siblings is healed on terms dictated by Sohanpal. There is an equal division of territory between him and Birpal, while Dayapal is assigned an appanage (*jagir*) of one *lakh*. This is an early example of the process of merging lineage segmentation in the Bundela ruling group. The idiom in which this merger is expressed is that of kingdom (*rajya* or *raj*) but we have no need to assume that it refers in this case to a centralized state political system.

The legend tells us that a connubial league between the Bundela, Panwar, and the Dhandhera was formed following their martial alliance in defeating the Khangar. Why, we may ask, does this inclusive category (the 'three-kuri Rajput') cover all Bundela and not merely Sohanpal and his descendants? There is no indication whatever either in Bundela history or in present-day practice that some Bundela, viz. the descendants of Birpal and Dayapal against whom partly the martial league was formed, were excluded from the marital league. Conversely, no section of the Bundelas has shown consistent normative preference for marriage with the Rajput of thirty-six kuri and a corresponding disinclination to intermarry with the Panwar and the Dhandhera. It would be easy to 'explain' the exhaustive inclusion of the Bundela into the 'three-kuri' category by evoking the superior and contagious efficacy of ritual exclusion over political alliance: the well-known phenomenon of sub-caste formation. To the extent, however, that there are in the Bundelkhand region deep localized patrilineages of Bundela Rajput, a long history of kingdom formation and rule by Rajput branches from the mid fifteenth century to the mid twentieth century, and the lack of a consistent hypergamous pattern of marriages in the three-kuri Rajput 'caste', the framework of intra-caste ritual hierarchy is by no means self-evident. Correspondingly, explanations of socio-political organization in terms of ritual hierarchy, inclusion/exclusion (to wit, caste-segmentation), do not work automatically, i.e. outside time. These social facts urge that analysis be pressed in a different direction. The internal dynamics of lineage organization bears a structural relation to its external political function. In the case of Bundela lineages during the period of their expansion the organizational framework of their external political functioning is dispersed clanship.

To examine the political implications of Bundela dispersed clanship we may begin by specifying the internal and external functioning of patrilineages in clans allied to them by marital and martial bonds during the episode of the capture of Garhkundar. The clans directly involved are the Panwar and the Dhandera, but the Chauhan, the Tonwar, and other clans belonging to the category 'thirty-six-kuri Rajput' also enter the picture. Punyapal to whom Sohanpal gave his daughter in marriage belonged to a Panwar patrilineage in Gwalior state. The Panwar of Gwalior enjoyed high rank among the regional Rajput, taking brides from eastern Chauhan dominants (Sherring, 1872, p. 165) and Tonwar rulers (Luard, 1907, p. 16). Thus, Punyapal's father had received the appanage of Panwaya in dowry from the Tonwar ruler of Gwalior, whose daughter he had married. We have no comparable data for appanages and offices held by the affines of Bundela rulers at Mahoni. From the fact that the Bundela during this period are constantly shifting their capitals southwards, we may speculate that the quest of Bundela heroes, 'territory for kingdom', pervades the entire legendary phase culminating only in the founding of their first dynastic capital at Orchha in *c*. A.D. 1531. With their victory at Garhkundar, however, we begin to hear about appanages and offices granted by Bundela rulers to their affines. In developmental terms, Bundela at this juncture enter the cycle of kingdom formation in which the Tonwar of Gwalior have attained maturity.

The case of Punyapal Panwar reveals in a striking manner the link between marital and political alliance in the Rajput cycle of kingdom formation. At the same time it throws up certain geo-politically conditioned contrasts[9] between the social organization of dominance between the 'three-kuri Rajput' (the eastern division) and the 'thirty-six-kuri Rajput' (the western division). According to a legend,

Punyapal Panwar possessed a horse which his uncle [Mother's Brother] coveted. This horse he agreed to exchange for a beautiful dancing-girl of his uncle's. On the appointed day he went to his uncle's residence mounted on the horse. As he rode up he saw the dancing-girl standing among the people surrounding his uncle. Without waiting to make a salutation even, Punyapal rode up to the girl, swung her onto his saddle and, followed by his people, galloped home. For this insult his uncle, it is said, persuaded all the Rajputs to have nothing to do with Punyapal's family. (Luard, 1907, p. 16.)

9 It is not possible to discuss the geo-political factors fully within the scope of this essay. I allude to the over-all pattern in note 12.

The broken exchange between the mother's brother (the Tonwar ruler) and the sister's son (the Panwar 'vassal') expresses a political conflict in the kin-feudated Rajput polity of Gwalior. In Rajput legends of Bundelkhand the gift of a concubine's daughter frequently symbolized the value given in exchange by the ruler to a political ally. Translated into quasi-jural terms, she represented some kind of subordinate territorial rights granted to an ally by the ruler (cf. Kanhaiyaju, 1928, pp. 169–208, for Chhatrasal and the Peshwa). The horse, on the other hand, represented the oath of martial fealty by a Rajput 'vassal' (*jagir-dar*), to his politically superior kinsman. An exchange that involved a Rajput's parting with his favourite horse might seal a political alliance between kinsmen or ritual kinsmen; such transaction did not extend to non-kin, even though the party proposing the transaction was paramount ruler himself (Sleeman, 1915, p. 182).

The consequence of the broken exchange, as given in this legend, is that not only the Tonwar but also the other Rajput clans having marital and political links with the Panwar stopped inter-dining and intermarrying with the 'family' of Punyapal Panwar. Nevertheless, in the case of the Panwar, unlike the Bundela, the exclusion applies only to the Panwar patrilineage of Panwaya; the western Panwar patrilineages (e.g. of Malwa) continued to intermarry with the 'thirty-six-kuri Rajput'. Punyapal Panwar of Panwaya, the head of the excluded family, marries the daughter of Sohanpal Bundela, who gives him the appanage of Karera in dowry. Being thus included among the eastern or Bundelkhandi 'three-kuri Rajput', Punyapal Panwar becomes the apical ancestor for localized segments of Panwar patrilineage of Bundelkhand.[10] In political terms Punyapal replicates the career of his father; he establishes the same kind of political-cum-affinal link with Sohanpal Bundela as his father did with the Tonwar ruler of Gwalior.

In relation to the exogamous Panwar, then, the process of

[10] Panwar sublineages intermarrying with the Bundela and the Dhandhera are descended from the four sons of Punyapal: from Ratansah, the Panwar of Karera; from Jetsah, the Panwar of Kairuwan; from Shankarsah, the Panwar of Barechha; from Chandrasena (illegitimate son of a prostitute named Chandrabhaga), the Panwar of Ghati Mayapur.

exclusion (of a section from the 'thirty-six-kuri') is marked by asymmetry of ritual status,[11] but that of inclusion (of a section into the 'three-kuri') is characterized by the symmetry of political forms. The former process lends itself to conceptualization, both by the observer and the observed, as an occurrence in mythical time. The latter process is remembered in legends of territorial expansion and political incorporation which represent to the people themselves events in historical time.

Just as Panwar and Tonwar constituted a special alliance in the regional set of intermarrying Rajput before the Bundela capture of Garhkundar, so also the Dhandhera and Chauhan are depicted as special allies. All Dhandhera claim to be the descendants of one Dhandhu, an officer in the army of Prithviraja Chauhan (Drake-Brockman, 1909, p. 92). This is the martial link. The marital link with the Chauhan is indicated in the description of one Mukutman Chauhan, master of an appanage of the Khangar of Garh Kundar, as 'a descendant of Dhandhera deva . . . which probably means that he was Dhandhera on his mother's side' (Drake-Brockman, ibid., pp. 92–3). The same Mukutman Chauhan has been depicted as *matul* (classificatory mother's brother) of Sohanpal Bundela (Verma, op. cit., p. 25). He chose to remain neutral in the quarrel between the Bundela brothers. It is likely that Sohanpal's avuncular relationship with Mukutman derived from 'linked affinity' between the regional Bundela, Dhandhera, and Chauhan patrilineages. Our information is deficient on the local identification of intermarrying lineages, but it is sufficient to indicate the fact that the Dhandhera only *gave* their daughters to the Chauhan and Bundela.

Does this suggest the ranking of these intermarrying patrilineages in a hypergamous pattern? Sherring, writing about the Chauhan of the Benaras region (the eastern Chauhan), speaks of a pattern of directional hypergamy. The western Panwar are included among the wife-takers of the Chauhan, but the Bundela and the Dhandhera are not mentioned either as givers or takers. Bundela sources, on the other hand, suggest that the Bundela

[11] The Panwar outside Bundelkhand are segmented into sub-castes. For the Waiganga valley see Russell and Hiralal (1916), iv. 340.

rulers of Mahoni and Jaganmanipur were the Chauhans' wife-takers, which contradicts the supposed rule of exclusively northern (and western) hypergamy among eastern Chauhan. The Chauhan of the Sagar region (southern Chauhan) are discussed by Russell and Hiralal, who report the breakdown of clan exogamy and the formation of Chauhan sections into territorially endogamous sub-castes. As a system of sub-castes the Chauhan developed a ritual hierarchy of marital unions, the products of unequal unions being assigned to an appropriate status-gradation. The offspring of unequal Chauhan unions would perpetuate the status inferiority of their birth. The matrifilial identification of Mukutman Chauhan with the Dhandhera would seem to belong to this system. It is in terms of the operation of this system that we may explain also the identification of the Dhandhera of Sagar region (southern Dhandhera) as an offshoot or branch of Panwar clan (Russell and Hiralal (1916), iv. 418, 439). Since the Panwar and the Dhandhera of Bundelkhand region intermarry, it is obvious that the southern Dhandhera had branched off from the western Panwar. Thus there is a structural homology between the Chauhan and the Panwar. In both cases the clan is subdivided into localized branches (thirty-five in each case), some of which cluster in territorially endogamous and hypergamous sections or sub-castes. The Bundelkhandi Panwar and Dhandhera branches fall outside the framework of clan transformed as caste, and the lack of internal status gradations regulated by hypergamy in these branches indicates the strength of clanship among them.

The clanship of the Bundela of Mahoni, who provided the leadership for the capture of Garhkundar, clearly constitutes the pivot for the political incorporation of their martial and marital allies into the 'three-kuri Rajput' division. Unlike their Panwar and Dhandhera allies, the principle of clanship of the Bundela emerges untrammelled by any claims to a previous connection with the clan-caste configuration of the 'thirty-six-kuri Rajput' division. As constituted in the ideology and traditional history of Bundelkhand, the 'three-kuri Rajput' division has shown no tendency for internal hierarchical segmentation. The western Rajput tendency for the exogamous clan to be transformed into caste has in the east been checked and converted into territorial expansion and political consolidation by kin-feudated kingdom formation.[12]

It is vital to distinguish between the political function of clanship and the ritual function of caste (*jati*) as an idiom of hierarchical status distinctions. The typification of hypergamy as a characteristically 'Rajput' phenomenon in the Indian sociological literature (Rivers, 1921; Dumont, 1966, pp. 116–23) rests on a confusion between these two functions. It will not do to say simply that the ritual function of *jati* subsumes the political function of clan. What I am contending for Bundelkhand is the absence of a necessary *and* sufficient interdependence between the attribution of ritual status by *jati* segmentation and the processes of political power which in the case of the 'three-kuri Rajput' category developed, changed, and atrophied by the principle of clanship. The reason why a distinction has not been maintained between the two functions and why, in discussions of Rajput hypergamy, the political functions of descent have been reduced to manifestations of ritual status hierarchy is not far to seek. The cultural premiss 'Rajput hypergamy *par excellence*' is based on one variant of the conscious model, that provided by the western-Rajput division, which has so far been studied to the exclusion of other regional modalities. A few indigenous Rajput scholars complained against this bias in the work, for example, of Tod (cf. Sengar, 1927, p. 1049).

A more serious deficiency in the Indian sociological literature emanates from the elaboration of an 'unconscious' model from one variant of the conscious model. The 'truth' of this partly observer, partly observed model of hypergamy as an entailment of hierarchy is beyond doubt, but the model takes account only of mythical time. To the extent that historical time (even in the limited sense, as defined on p. 242) is excluded from it, a simplified equation between hierarchy, caste segmentation, and hypergamy

[12] The regional political system never formed an effective part of a higher-level power (cf. Cohn, 1962, pp. 313–14, for levels of the political system in eighteenth-century India). Moreover, the ecological frontier for south-eastern expansion with ravines, forests, and plateau was particularly favourable for swift guerrilla action by local battalions such as the Bundela commanded.

of the indigenous ruling groups hinders rather than helps the perception of key variables in the social organization of domin-ance. This in any case holds good for the Bundelkhand region during the pre-British period. But my plea is more than merely one of putting the historical record straight. It would seem that the residue of institutionalized conflict in nineteenth-century central India leading up to the currently publicized menace of 'dacoity' (brigandage) in Gwalior and Bundelkhand at the present time cannot be understood without restoring to their legitimate place in our analysis the ideology and processes of clanship in the traditional ruling groups.

The Clanship of the Ruling Group

We can see how the regional Rajput ideology of kingship contributes to kingdom formation by transforming the Bundela martial alliance with the Panwar and Dhandhera into a marital alliance. The symbolic equivalence of 'territory for kingdom' with the female principle as contained in the Bundela legend of origin is conducive to the formation of a territorial state based on a confederation of three Rajput clans who exchange women. For the dynastic and dominance phases of Bundela past there is much evidence to suggest that the form of their polity was defined by processes of kin (including affinal) dispersal and merger. The legendary phase enables us to view these processes delimited by the symbolic constraints of exogamy and alliance as aspects of the ideology of clanship in the ruling group.

Clearly the principle of clan exogamy alone is insufficient to explain all the available facts of political and affinal incorporation involved in Bundela expansion and kingdom formation. Why should the connubial league of the ruling group be confined to three 'Rajput' clans? What prevented the Bundela from inter-marrying with the non-Rajput Khangar, as amateur anthropolo-gist-historians speculated they actually did? The answer would seem to lie in the operation of the ideology of legitimate rule derived from the attributional category (*varna*), *Kshatriya*. Indigenous sources consistently oppose the Kshatriya Bundela and other 'Rajput' clans to the Khangar as non-Kshatriya. As the myth of royal origin specifies, the appurtenances of legitimate rule belong only to those who are born Kshatriya. Nevertheless, as we noted earlier, the same myth also sacralizes territory. It serves as a cover for the uncertain possession of actual territory by the 'kingly-sons' (see p. 238). Now, the insertion of the territorial equation into the attributional category Kshatriya is manipulated by the notion of royal clanship. In accordance with the rule of royal-clan exogamy, a Kshatriya clan might give and take daughters (or have political agreements over territory) with the other Kshatriya clans, but not with the non-Kshatriya. Hence the absolute refusal of Sohanpal Bundela to have connubial and commensal relations with the Khangar.

In relation to the vanquished Khangar, the Bundelas' Kshatriya role, as rulers protecting 'territory-cum-people', is narrated in an oral version of the legend of Garhkundar;

Maharaja Sohanpal led an expedition to Garh Kundar and he killed all the Khangar men who had gathered in the fort. He spared their women since it is forbidden for the Kshatriya to kill women. One Khangar woman hurled her new-born son at Sohanpal's feet and begged for mercy. Her wish was granted and the baby was spared. But from then on it became the bounden duty of the Khangar to be the 'shoe-bearing servants' (*naquib*) to Bundela rulers. (Narrative from village Sendpa.)

The descendants of the Khangar boy were incorporated into Bundela polity under the general title *khasbardar* (aides-de-camp) of Bundela rulers. The Khangar tradition recorded by Luard (1909, pp. 10–11) corroborates the story of their political incorporation as *khasbardar*: Luard notes that it became a hereditary title for the Khangar of *Athgarhiyawal* families (see note 8, p. 256) employed by Bundela royals in their service as petty officials. Furthermore, the nature of this conflict as between the Kshatriya and non-Kshatriya is underscored by the symbolic significance of a set of restrictions imposed on the Khangar by the Bundela victors: 1. they were not to wear red turbans; 2. never to touch *kathris* (swords); 3. never to drink liquor; 4. never to allow widows to remain unmarried; 5. their females were never to put red lead on their hair-parting; 6. never to eat *rotis* (baked bread) sold in public; 7. to eat no *kachchi* (boiled food) touched by a Kshatriya, Vaishya, or Shudra (Luard, op. cit., p. 11). These restrictions cannot be understood simply as defining a low ritual status for the Khangar in the caste hierarchy; they are precise ritual diacritics confirming the loss of political power and pretensions to royal prerogatives which are now legitimately wrested from the Khangar by the victorious Bundela as Kshatriya. Again the system of social stratification of ruling groups of the 'three-kuri Rajput' category seems supported by rituals which do not fit neatly a theory of caste-segmentation operating in mythical time. They appear rather as creations conjoint with political developments in historical time.

Finally we broach a question which has evoked considerable controversy among scholars, namely, Rushton Coulborn's contention (Coulborn, 1968, pp. 371–2) that the kinship idiom as recorded by Tod in Rajput polities of nineteenth-century Rajasthan is a cover for weakened feudal relationships of medieval India. Richard Fox has correctly reversed the terms of Coulborn's contention (Fox, 1971, pp. 135–8). By delineating the full developmental cycle of Rajput lineage in North India, Fox attempts to show that the political role of kinship might appear weak in later stages of the lineage cycle, but among regional communities of Rajput dominants throughout pre-industrial North India there always existed a potential for kinship solidarity to re-emerge and initiate a new cycle of lineage-based dominance. 'Genealogical categories', says Fox, 'are like phosphorized halloween costumes. The sun may set on the interactional political fortunes of local corporate kin bodies, but the largely attributional categories of lineage, clan, caste, and varna would continue to glow eerily as luminiscent reminders of what once had been.' (Fox, op. cit., p. 171.) Fox regards 'lineage, clan, caste, and varna' as attributional categories of the same order, manifestations equally of 'superstratification'. In so far as he lumps together the various denotata of 'Rajput' ideological unity, Fox's case, like that of many previous scholars, rests on positing a functional equivalence between hypergamy among the unilineal-descent-based Rajput groups and the processes of caste-segmentation in the non-Rajput *jati*. The case of the 'three-kuri Rajput' category of Bundelkhand, supported perhaps by Mayer's discovery of a lack of conscious ideology of hypergamy and weakly developed unconscious practice of 'directional hypergamy' among the Rajput of Malwa (Mayer, 1965, pp. 29, 210–11) raises serious questions on the applicability of Fox's generalization for the Rajput of central India.

Fox admits that his understanding of Rajput clanship, in the crucial issue of defining the boundaries of exogamy and endogamy, is inadequate; thus, for example, his data for North India are inconclusive as regards the endogamy of various 'lineages of recognition' claiming to be related by Chauhan clanship (Fox, op. cit., p. 41). As I have shown above, our sources for the Rajput of central (Malwa and Bundelkhand) and eastern (Benaras) regions suggest a distribution pattern, along a broadly West–East axis,[13] which fits with the indigenous classification of Rajput clans into bunches of thirty-six and three. Both these patterns are constituted by the complementary principles of caste and clan. According to the relative dominance in each of one or the other principle, they may be written down as caste-clan (western) and clan-caste (eastern) patterns. Chauhan or Panwar 'branches' in the first pattern belong to an endogamous or hypergamous system, while those of the second retain an emphasis on clan exogamy. Indigenous political development in pre-industrial northern and central India would also seem to be governed by the varying modalities of these two patterns.

As our final example, we note that the expanding Bundela rulers received constant military support from the Ahir cattle-keepers. The Ahir groups of Bundelkhand, like their namesakes in other parts of north and central India, belong to a well-known caste-category which ranks lower than the Rajput. Similar to

---

[13] The East–West axis is a 'template', a standard unit of classification in areas of Rajput dominance. In its various applications, with or without accessory classifiers (e.g. elements of the terrain, viz. river, plateau, valley, etc.), it may refer to indigenous regions and sub-regions. On account of its relative application, geographical or administrative areas cannot be fixed absolutely by means of this classifier. In this sense Fox's choice of the solar metaphor (minus the phosphorized Hallowe'en costumes) is appropriate for translating Rajput representations.

their affinal alliance with Rajput clans and political incorporation
of the Khangar, the Bundela rulers forged a link of pseudo-
agnation with the Yadu-bansi Ahir in the ritual idiom of clanship
through 'the line of milk'. The 'milk brotherhood' between
the three Bundelkhandi Rajput clans and a regional section of
the Ahir, called the 'Dauwa', has frequently been noted in the
nineteenth- and early twentieth-century literature. In all the
historical accounts and legends collected by me in villages of
Chhatarpur and Tikamgarh districts this special relationship of
Bundela rulers with the Dauwa is connected with their conquest
and settlement in the Vindhya region. While the Ahir men, who
came to be designated '*dau*' (father's elder brother) by the Bundela
princes, provided the fighting militia, their wives as wet-nurses
(addressed and referred to as *day-ma* or *dudh-ma*; literally, 'milk
mothers') nourished the princes by their own milk. It would take
me far outside the scope of the present paper were I to link this
practice up with the royal-clan exogamy of the 'three-kuri
Rajput'. Suffice it to note that the pseudo-agnatic incorporation
of the Dauwa, not only with the Bundela but with the Panwar
and Dhandhera as well, furnished an ideological solution for
the problem of the breach of incest taboo created by restricted
exogamy and repeated affinity of the 'three-kuri Rajput'.[14] As to
the ideological rationalization of the special relationship there
are two versions; one relates the Dauwa as 'brothers' generally
to royalty and the other applies particularly to the Bundela–
Dauwa alliance.

The first version was given to me in the form of a legend by
the Bundela residents of Bhagwan village.

Once the daughter-in-law of Indra (the King of Gods) prayed to Lord
Visnu. The Lord appeared in the garb of a beggar and demanded her
amputated breast in alms, which she offered without a moment's
hesitation. The Lord was pleased and asked her to name a boon. She
wished Him to be born as her son. This the Lord granted, saying that
she would be born as Nandini and her husband as Nanda. He would
then be incarnated as Krishna in Gokul and suckle at her breast. The
Dauwa are the progeny of Nanda and Nandini.

[14] I have developed this theme in an unpublished paper, 'Rajput kinship and
the social organization of dominance in central India'.

Veena Das, in a paper on the caste *purana* of Gujarat (Das, 1968) has shown the miraculous appeal of Krishna as the epitome of Kshatriya ideals in validating the claims of a wrestler-Brahman caste to a confirmed Brahman status in *Kaliyuga*. Here too, Krishna, the reincarnation of Lord Visnu, is the divine prince but unlike the Brahman of Gujarat, the Dauwas' special relationship with rulers is not mediated by Brahman priests but by the symbolism of breast and its metonym, milk, Furthermore, the myth is enacted in the ritual practice of Dauwa women suckling royal princes, and the foster relationship is institutionalized by the elaboration of an appropriate kinship terminology.

The second version is derived from *Chhatraprakasa* (see p. 249). It pertains to the mythical origin of Vindhyavasini Devi, the tutelary deity of the Bundela. It will be recalled that in recounting the legend of Bundela origin Lal Kavi, the author of *Chhatraprakasa*, refers to a mental process known as *yoga nidra* by which Pancham is drawn to the shrine of Vindhyavasini Devi. In the text of the poem the same mental process appears deified as the prior aspect of Vindhyavasini Devi identified with the uterine daughter of Krishna's foster-mother Nandini or Yasoda (Pogson, op. cit., pp. 6–7). According to the *Devi Bhagwat Purana* Kansa, the ruler of Mathura, had decided to kill his sister Devaki's son, Krishna, as soon as he was born. The Devi, as *yoganidra* or *yogamaya*, decided to be born as Yasoda's daughter who would be exchanged for Devaki's son (Krishna) in order to protect him from Kansa. Krishna and Yoganidra are born at the same time from the wombs of Devaki and Yasoda respectively. The exchange having been successfully accomplished, Krishna survives as the foster-son of Yasoda while Kansa prepares to kill Yoganidra, Yasoda's daughter in Devaki's possession. As soon as she is hurled on a rock to be killed, Yoganidra assumes her real form as Devi and rising to the sky utters the curse of Kansa's eventual death at Krishna's hands. Then she retires to dwell in the Vindhya hills as Vindhyavasini Devi.

The Ahir as Yadubansi trace their descent from Nanda and Yasoda. On account of the myth of their fosterage by the couple, they regard Krishna and his brother Baladeva to be Yadubansi as

well. The myth of the Devi is shared by all Hindus of Bundelkhand, including the Ahir and Rajput groups. For these groups
however, the Krishna episode in the mythical cycle of Devi
(*Devi Bhagwat Purana*) provides an excellent rationalization for
claiming a special solidary relationship in the idiom of descent.
Thus Vindhyavasini Devi as the Bundelas' tutelary deity represents 'the line of milk' and is symbolically identified with the
female principle and territory for rule; for the Ahir, though un-
connected with territory, she is the uterine daughter of their
progenetrix, Yasoda. The insertion of the territorial equation in
their descent ideology of clanship enables the Bundela at once to
retain a premium on kingship and yet to exploit the allegiance of
the Dauwa as foster-brothers. The ritual suckling of Bundela
princes by Dauwa women is in conformity with this symbolic
conjunction.

Conclusion

An unfortunate consequence of using caste as a blanket term
for all hierarchical status distinctions has been to obliterate the
perception of other contextually meaningful schemes of classifying political and social relations. Thus if we do not freeze the ruling
groups' descent in a caste framework but examine it in the context
of the expansion of indigenous rule, we can discern at least three
bases of political relations between the ruling groups and their
allies in Bundelkhand: intermarriage (Bundela–Panwar–Dhandhera), pseudo-agnation (Bundela–Dauwa), and dispensation
(Bundela–Khangar).

At a more general level, I have to reverse the hypothesis of
sanskritization to understand the dynamics of political processes
in pre-industrial middle India as exemplified by the case at hand.
Far from political power being converted into *jati* status to become
legitimate and meaningful, the expansion of Bundela rule shows
that under certain geo-political conditions throughout middle
India, exclusion from a confirmed *jati* status was the means of
gaining power and creating a new framework of statuses and
offices.

REFERENCES

BOHANNAN, P., 1965, 'The Differing Realms of the Law', in L. Nader (ed.), *The Ethnography of Law* (American Anthropologist Special Publication), pp. 33–42.

BOSCH, F. D. K., 1960, *The Golden Germ: An Introduction to Indian Symbolism* (The Hague).

COHN, B. S., 'Political Systems in Eighteenth Century India: the Benaras Region', *Journal of the American Oriental Society*, 82, pp. 312–19.

COULBORN, R., 1968, 'Feudalism, Brahmanism, and the intrusion of Islam upon Indian history', *Comparative Studies in Society and History*, 10, pp. 357–74.

DAS, V., 1968, 'A Sociological Approach to the Caste Puranas: A Case Study', *Sociological Bulletin (Journal of the Indian Sociological Society)*, 17, pp. 141–64.

DRAKE-BROCKMAN, D. L., 1909, *District Gazetteers of U.P., Vol. XXIV, Jhansi* (Allahabad).

DUMONT, L., 1970, *Homo Hierarchicus: the caste system and its implications* (London).

ELLIOT, H. M., 1869, *Memoir on the History, Folk-lore, and Distribution of the Races of the N.W.P. Being an Amplified Edition of the Original Supplemental Glossary of Indian Terms by the late Sir H. M. Elliot*, ed. and revised by J. Beames (London).

FOX, R., 1967, *Kinship and Marriage, an anthropological perspective* (Penguin).

FOX, R. G., 1971, *Kin, Clan, Raja, and Rule* (Berkeley).

FRANKLIN, J., 1827, *Memoir of Bundelkhand* (Transaction of the Royal Asiatic Society of G.B. and Ireland, i. 259–81).

HABIB, I., 1963, *The Agrarian System of Mughal India (1556–1707)* (London).

KANE, P. V., 1946, *History of Dharmasastra (Ancient and Mediaeval, Religious and Civil Law)* vol. iii (Poona).

LUARD, C. E., 1907, *Central India State Gazetteer Series, Eastern States (Bundelkhand), Vol. VI-A, Text* (Lucknow).

—— , 1909, *Bundelkhand Castes* (Lucknow).

MALCOLM, J., 1824, *A Memoir of Central India*, vol. i (London).

MAYER, A. C., 1965, *Caste and Kinship in Central India* (London).

MONIER-WILLIAMS, M., 1964. *A Sanskrit-English Dictionary* (New Edn., Oxford).

POGSON, W. R., 1828, *A History of the Boondelas* (Calcutta).

RIVERS, W. H. R., 1921, 'The Origin of Hypergamy', *Journal of the Bihar and Orissa Research Society*, 8, pp. 9–24.

RUSSELL, R. V., and HIRALAL, 1916, *The Tribes and Castes of the Central Provinces*, vol. iv (London).

SHERRING, M. A., 1872, *Hindu Tribes and Castes as represented in Benaras* (London).

SILBERRAD, C. A., 1902, 'A Contribution to the History of W. Bundelkhand', *Journal of the Asiatic Society of Bengal*, 71, pp. 99–135.

SLEEMAN, W. H., 1915, *Rambles and Recollections of an Indian Official*, revised and annotated by V. A. Smith (Oxford).

SMITH, V. A., 1881, 'Contributions to the History of Bundelkhand', *Journal of the Asiatic Society of Bengal*, 60, pp. 1–52.

Vernacular Sources

BUNDELKHAND AGENCY RECORDS (B.A.R.) Vernacular Files, 1880–1915, *Series II, National Archives* (Delhi).

GUPTA, B. D., 1958, *Bundelkhand Kesari Maharaja Chhatrasal Bundela* (Agra).

KANHAIYAJU, KUNWAR, 1928, 'Eka aitihasika bhramasansodhana', *Nagari Pracarini Patrika*, 9, pp. 169–208.

KESAVA DAS MISRA, 1904, *Birsingh Caritra (1607 A.D.)* (Kasi).

LAL KAVI, c. 1700, *Chhatraprakasa* (MSS. Hindi), India Office Library (London).

SENGAR, SHIVNATH SINGH, 1927, 'Kannanj ke Gaharwaron aur Jodhpur ke Rathoron ki sajatiyata', *Saraswati*, 28, pp. 1045–53.

TIWARI, GORELAL, 1933, *Bundelkhanda ka sanksipta itihasa* (Allahabad).

VERMA, VRINDAVAN LAL, 1957, *Garhkundar* (Jhansi).

11

North and South in the Book of Genesis

D. F. POCOCK

WHAT has struck the western imagination in the book of Genesis or rather that section of the creation myth known as 'The Fall' is the interaction of Adam and Eve, as though the whole point of the story lay there. Certainly for Christian theology Adam's *felix culpa* has been an important element in the doctrine of redemption.

But for the anthropologist there is nothing very striking in the story of the disobedience of Adam and Eve and the general misfortunes which result from it. In the mythologies of the world the first man and the first woman are well known and their story is often only one of many basic world-shaping myths. As a result of the violation of some arbitrary and for the most part trivial ban, life and death begin, disease, misfortune, and labour for subsistence come into the world.

What is distinctive in the story of the Fall, if indeed it is not unique, is the introduction of the territorial element. To the common inventory of human ills is added the separation from the land given by Yahweh. Once outside the garden, life as human beings know it begins, but for the Hebrews in particular, the fact of their alienation is an additional human sorrow which is somehow and some day to be put right.

Obviously this alienation element in the myth has not been ignored. It has shaped the belief in heaven, the kingdom of God—*post hoc exilium*, and the various secular political derivatives of this. For the early Jews themselves the promise of the land of Canaan, the promised land 'where milk and honey flow' (Exod. 13:5) must itself have seemed, as it is often represented, a satisfactory redemption of Adam's sin.

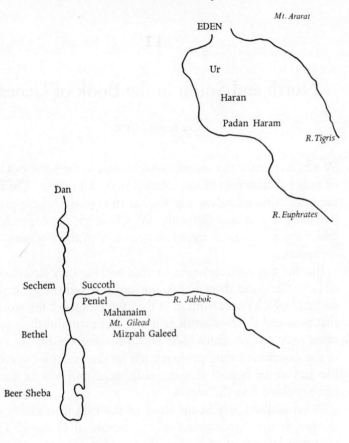

FIG. 15. Schematic map showing places named.

Although the relation between an original exile and the territorial ambition of the Jews is no doubt significant it does not satisfactorily explain the exile element. I would suggest that the myth relates to an altogether more profound intellectual problem which the ancient Hebrews had to face, the problem posed by the lack of an immemorial territorial base such as almost all other recorded peoples have enjoyed. This problem was not to be solved by the mere occupation of another's territory by force of arms, for such an occupation, however supported and blessed by Yahweh, could not constitute that territory as their own sacred autochthony. In the Yahwistic creation myth the Hebrews represent themselves as literally *déracinés*, as a people *created* alien. This, were we to cast the net more widely, would lead us on to consider the implications of the equally non-territorial Yahweh for the history of the growth of monotheism.

In this paper, however, I concern myself with the symbolic geography of the Hebrews and I shall suggest also that the question of marriage takes on for them a peculiar significance in the context of their alienation. This seems worth while stressing at the present time when some anthropologists run the risk of losing sight of the historical specific which is the Jewish people in what they conceive to be a 'structuralist' perspective.

What does one mean by 'symbolic geography'? There is an immediate danger in the term in so far as it implies a distinction between the *real* or *scientific* on the one hand and the *symbolic* on the other. Here one can only alert the attention to this danger and disclaim any such intention without entering into the wide-ranging argument which such a disclaimer might provoke. By symbolic geography here is intended the presentation by a people of moral values by geographic references, a kind of moral geodesy.

The number of geographic references in the book of Genesis is striking. The patriarchs are, so to speak, constantly on the move and the axis of their motion is a line between north and south. It is the direction of movement rather than stopping-places which seem initially significant. Various place-names are mentioned or even created in the course of these travels—Sechem, Lahai Roi, Bethel, and so on, but these appear to be seeds sown for later development in other stories. This is a characteristic of the recensionists' art which establishes the Pentateuch as a masterpiece. The moral qualities of the North are alluded to first in the Yahwistic version of the creation which, unlike the Priestly version, locates paradise as 'a garden in Eden which is in the east' (Gen. 2: 8) and this garden is further located by a reference to the rivers which flow out from it of which two, the Tigris and

Euphrates, have their sources in the Armenian mountains. North-east is the good direction from which the first patriarch originated. Mount Ararat, in the same region, is the point of dispersion for the sons of Noah after the flood. The third patriarch, Abraham, also emerges out of the north-east: Terah, his father, leaves Ur and travels south-west 'to go to the land of Canaan' but settles in Haran, from which place Yahweh calls Abraham to leave his country for a land which will be shown to him (Gen. 11: 27–32; 12: 1–2).

The characterization of the south is more diffuse. Obviously it is the direction of promise and prosperity for Abraham and his descendants but an uncorrected movement southwards has negative moral associations. The known terminus of such a movement, Egypt, is populated by the descendants of Ham, the son cursed by Noah (Gen. 9: 18–29), whose son, Canaan, is the eponymous settler of the promised land before it is taken over by the Israelites. The southern lands in which Abraham's nephew Lot chooses to settle are described as 'irrigated everywhere... like the garden of Yahweh or the land of Egypt' (Gen. 13) but they are also the land of Sodom and Gomorrah. As we shall see, marriage contracted in a southerly direction is a bar to the inheritance of Yahweh. This summary account will be amplified in what follows.

It is a commonplace that lineal purity establishes 'rights' in the promised land. What has not been noted is that the pure or good marriage is associated with geographic direction. This emerges from the story of the marriage of Isaac, the first of the patriarchs to be born in the south. His father Abraham calls a servant and tells him to fetch a wife for his son from Haran, his place of origin (Gen. 24). The servant asks whether he should take Isaac with him in the event that the woman refuses to come. Abraham says that he must on no account do so and goes on to repeat the promise of Yahweh that he and his descendants would be given Canaan. On the face of it there is no connection between the two statements. We are left with the implication that there is something incompatible between the inheritance and a journey northwards for marriage. At the same time marriage with the

Canaanites is barred and the north as a place for good marriage is emphasized. In fact the servant wins the approval of Abraham's kinsmen and brings Rebekah, Isaac's future wife, down south with him. Isaac makes a northerly gesture, so to speak, for he is facing towards the north as the caravan approaches. Isaac's marriage contrasts with that of his elder brother Ishmael, whose mother chose for him as a wife the bondswoman from the land of Egypt (Gen. 21: 21).

The south is certainly the place of bad marriage or sterility, for all that it is the source of material good. This opposition seems to be the point of a trick played twice by Abraham and once by Isaac upon southern neighbours, the Pharaoh first and on the following two occasions Philistine kings. Both patriarchs at different times of famine travel south and pass off their wives as their sisters. They acquire considerable wealth but their unwitting hosts fall for the trick and are punished by Yahweh for an actual or potential sexual relationship with Sarah and with Rebekah. The stories seem absurd. The reason for the trick is said to be that the patriarchs are afraid that they will be killed for their wives' sake and therefore pass off the women as their sisters. The point of the trick seems to be rather that if a beautiful woman is married the only way to possess her is by making her a widow whereas if she is unmarried there always remains the hope of an alliance. But the underlying point which appears to be established is that the southerly movement for material increase is somehow at odds with good marriage and lineal fertility. It is perhaps significant that for Abraham at least prosperity lies only in the south. The fact is underlined in the story of the War of the Four Kings, another Yahwistic narrative, where Abraham makes his only recorded journey north in pursuit of his defeated enemies—as far as Dan. On his return the king of Sodom offers him an unlimited reward but Abraham swears by Yahweh that he will accept nothing: 'You shall not say, "I enriched Abram" ' (Gen. 14). This, if we were dealing with a personality and a narrative, would be an astonishing display of self-righteousness only two chapters after the tricking of Pharaoh!

It is in the pattern set by the opposition of north and south, of lineal purity over against prosperity that the story of Jacob is to be understood. His relations with his brother Esau and with his father-in-law Laban seem to be the culmination of all that has gone before. His genealogy is of a type commonly found in other societies in that his name is preceded by a brief list of single names; either there are no collaterals or they have for one reason or another been disinherited. Through Noah the Hebrews are connected with all mankind, through Abraham they are connected with all the circumcised, but through Jacob they are a united and exclusive people. Unlike Noah, Abraham, or Isaac, all his sons in their different degrees inherit a birthright. He is renamed Israel and is what we call a 'culture hero'.

It might be more precise to call Jacob a heroic trickster. Like the trickster in so many other cultures he seems exempt from the regulations and sanctions which govern others. But, unlike the classic trickster, he is also the father of a people and, if not a warrior, a strategist and a politician.

Jacob is born the younger of twins. His elder brother Esau is a hirsute man of the open country and a hunter, Jacob is a smooth-skinned tent-dweller. Jacob is a cook and tempts his brother with a dish of lentils into giving up his birthright. Isaac, the blind father, tells Esau to go hunting and to bring venison for him preparatory to giving him his blessing. Guided by his mother, Rebekah, Jacob kills domesticated kids from the herd, disguises his smooth skin with animal hair, lies to his father and deceives him, and so tricks Esau out of his blessing.[1] Esau returns and asks for a blessing also but receives what amounts to a curse in that he must live 'Far from the richness of the earth . . . far from the dew that falls from heaven' (Gen. 27: 40)[2].

The story so far presents in general the opposition of settled pastoralists and hunter nomads but the point of the trickery, I suggest, relates to the specifically Hebrew theme which is the

[1] Jacob uses the name of Yahweh to further his deception (Gen. 27: 20). The Jerusalem Bible footnotes the blasphemy but suggests that 'the oriental mentality would see no wrong in it'. I would suggest rather that Jacob's freedom with the sacred name marks him out as peculiarly privileged.

[2] It is important to note here that both Vulgate and Authorized Versions err in giving both sons similar blessings. This is rectified in the Jerusalem Bible.

acquisition of rights to which one is not entitled by birth. In the person of Esau the natural rights of other peoples are set aside by the sanctified trickery of Jacob.

In their marriages also the two brothers are contrasted. Esau marries first two Hittite women, descendants of Heth, son of Canaan son of Ham whose inheritance was taken away. Later Esau marries an Ishmaelite, a descendant of Abraham's disinherited elder son—an appropriate partner. Both Hittites and Ishmaelites are people of the south.

After tricking Esau, Jacob leaves home. Interestingly there are two motives for this, one, simple fear of Esau's anger, and the other a directive from his father Isaac to go north, to Haran, where he can contract better marriages than his brother Esau (Gen. 27: 11, 41–5; 28: 1–5). The parallel with Isaac and Ishmael is almost exact. The younger brother marries in the north, in the homeland of Abraham, and inherits. The elder brother marries in the south and is disinherited. But there is a difference: whereas Isaac was not allowed to move northwards himself to fetch his wife, Jacob is ordered to do so. Jacob is the only patriarch to go right back to the land of origin and, if Abraham's injunction against any such move by Isaac is significant, this marks out Jacob's special power. It is perhaps worth noting in this connection that Jacob's dependence in Haran upon his mother's brother Laban is the sole reference to such a dependence in the Old Testament.[3]

The story of Jacob's life in Haran covers his marriage with Leah and Rachel, the birth of the ancestors of the different tribes of Israel, his acquisition by magic and husbandry of a large flock of goats, and finally his departure for the south. An important feature of the tale is the deception practised by his father-in-law Laban which appears to serve a useful purpose in legitimizing the tribes. Jacob initially desires the younger daughter, Rachel, and Laban allows him to believe that he will marry her. On the marriage night Laban smuggles Leah into the marriage tent and next morning excuses himself with the plea 'that it is not the custom in our country to give the younger before the elder'

[3] See J. Pedersen, *Israel, Its Life and Culture* (Oxford, 1926), vol. i, pp. 74–5.

(Gen. 29: 26). Jacob is only subsequently allowed to marry Rachel. The parallel between this assertion of the rights of the elder and its earlier subversion in the case of Jacob and Esau is too obvious to be ignored. What seems to be done here is that while Jacob, and consequently his descendants, continue to enjoy the fruits of his trickery, the principle of seniority is re-established. By a trick it was violated and therefore it seems that it must be reinstated by a trick. A somewhat similar device may be seen in the fact that contrary to Leviticus 18:18 Jacob marries two sisters but the younger remains barren until the elder has borne children to Jacob directly and by her slave. Again there is a paired reversal that indicates a significant movement in the myth. Leah has children of her own first and then by the slave woman, Rachel has children by her slave woman first and only then, and after Leah's full score is complete, does Rachel bear a son to Jacob—Joseph.

When Jacob claims his wages Laban attempts once more to trick him and is tricked in his turn. This time Jacob's trickery (Gen. 30: 25–43) is the trickery of cunning in the old sense of the word. He leaves with his wives, children, and flocks and sets off for the south-west and Canaan. He has by this point achieved precisely what neither Abraham nor Isaac could achieve—wives, legitimate progeny, and wealth in the north.

This singular achievement is underlined by the curious story variously known as Jacob's wrestle with the angel or with God (Gen. 32: 23–32). Here, once more, Pedersen's interpretation throws light. It is absurd, he argues, to suggest that any Israelite would accept that even Jacob could wrestle with Yahweh.[4] Why moreover should Yahweh attack Jacob on the border of the land which he has promised to him and his ancestors? Pedersen points to the spirit's fear of the coming dawn as further evidence that, if Jacob is dealing with a god here, he is not dealing with Yahweh or a messenger of Yahweh. He concludes that Jacob is in his own person taking on the god of the territory which he is about to enter. The god wrestles with Jacob all night and cannot beat him but finally dislocates his hip. Jacob still holds

---

4 Pedersen, op. cit., vols. iii–iv, pp. 503 ff.

him and only allows him to go in return for a blessing. The god gives him the name Israel and blesses him. Jacob names the place Peniel and goes off limping as the sun rises.[5] This story is only a problem for the rather simple-minded twentieth-century mono-theist who has lost even the Devil from the divine complex. In the Pentateuch, at least, Yahweh exists with other gods whom he overcomes, gods to whom the children of Israel may voluntarily turn, even if they are ultimately punished for it. What is signifi-cant about the story of Jacob's wrestle and what justifies us in calling him a hero, despite all his cunning, is the fact that here he seems to take on one of these other gods as a man and defeats him by his own physical strength. The story is set in a scene where for the first time Jacob is set as a father and protector. From Genesis 31 onwards the emphasis is no longer upon Jacob the lonely refugee pitting his wits against Laban but upon Jacob the head of a large household, having substantial flocks and servants. The heroism is prepared in the verses which immediately precede the wrestling-match. He sends his wives and all his possessions across the river Jabbok by night, 'And Jacob was left alone. And there was one that wrestled with him until daybreak' (Gen. 32: 24).

The wrestling-match and the crossing of the Jabbok divide in half another story which relates the final meeting between Jacob and Esau and concludes this section of the book of Genesis. Thereafter we have the story of Dinah, and the long story of Joseph culminating in the death of Jacob, which closes the book. In terms of western geography the meeting with Esau makes little sense and, indeed, from the point of view of common sense there seems little point to it unless it serves to reaffirm Jacob's capacity for deception.

Jacob has moved south-west from Paddan Aram, the homeland

[5] 'The sun rose as he left Peniel, limping because of his hip. That is the reason why to this day the Israelites do not eat of the sciatic nerve which is in the socket of the hip; because he had struck Jacob in the socket of hip on the sciatic nerve' (Jerusalem Bible, Gen. 32: 31–2). The translators add the footnote that there is no mention of this ancient food law elsewhere in the Bible. In fact, taken in con-junction with Lévi-Strauss's suggestions about the lameness of the chthonic heroes, this isolated reference to Jacob's lameness at this particular point jibes with Pedersen's account of the wrestling-match. See C. Lévi-Strauss, *Anthro-pologie structurale* (Paris, 1958), pp. 238–9.

of Laban. Laban pursues him and catches up with him at Mount Gilead. They conclude a treaty[6] at a place to be known as Mizpah Galeed. After concluding the treaty Jacob journeys onward, names a place Mahanaim and is presumably on his way to the Jabbok when, we are told, he 'sent messengers *ahead* of him to his brother Esau in the land of Seir, the country side of Edom' (Gen. 32:3). His messengers return saying that they have met Esau who is already on his way with 400 men. Jacob sends gifts ahead to placate Esau and at this point there intervenes the section concerning the crossing of the Jabbok and the wrestling-match. Immediately afterwards Jacob encounters Esau, bows down before him, and makes his slaves, children, and wives do likewise. Despite Esau's refusals Jacob forces gifts upon him and Esau says that they should travel together down to Seir. Jacob pleads fatigue and says that he will follow at a slower pace. Jacob in fact travels west to Succoth, just east of the Jordan, and finally settles at Sechem, over the Jordan in Canaanite territory, Abraham's first stopping-place after he left Haran.

The geographic detail here is so specific that it cannot be ignored. Nevertheless, if it is to be taken at its face value it presents contradictions and problems.

If we try to order the facts so that they are consistent with the encounter with Esau we must assume a consistent southwards movement. This would locate Mizpah Galeed, Mahanaim, and Peniel to the north of the Jabbok. Jacob and his company cross the river from north to south where they meet Esau. There are two objections to this interpretation: it negates the immediately preceding emphasis upon Jacob's extreme solicitude for his family (Gen. 32: 8–10) by exposing them to the anticipated attack, and it would also involve a second crossing of the Jabbok, to which the text makes no reference, to enable Jacob to reach Succoth and so Sechem. If alternatively we follow those authorities that situate Mizpah Galeed, Mahanaim, and Peniel south of the Jabbok we have to face the difficulty that Jacob, after leaving Laban and having turned north towards Mahanaim and Peniel is nevertheless described as sending messengers *ahead* of him to Edom.

---

[6] See the Jerusalem Bible, p. 53, footnote to verses 43–54.

We are not, however, dealing with a simple itinerary. Apart from all else, whatever localities might be uncertain, the Jabbok is a fixed point in Hebrew geography and it is no less certain that Edom lay well over 100 miles to the south of it. Nor are we dealing with a human narrative in which we can assess motive and likelihood. The encounter with Esau is to be seen rather as a final confrontation, a juxtaposition serving several purposes. It dramatically emphasizes Jacob's achievement in the north. He is now in a position to give gifts to his elder brother and pay him the respect due to him. As Pedersen points out[7] the gifts represent Jacob as the slave of Esau, but Esau's acceptance of them binds him to peace with Jacob and lulls him into a condition in which he can be tricked once more.

There is perhaps even more in this confrontation if, as we suppose, there is moral significance in movements northward and southward, and if we also accept the location of the whole drama south of the Jabbok. As Jacob journeys southward he is on the run from Laban. It is only after the treaty of Mizpah Galeed and when he has turned north that he takes on stature as head of a substantial household, The culmination of this northward movement is the nocturnal struggle at Peniel which converts Jacob the individual into Israel—a nation. This is the right moment for a final affirmation of the northward over the southward direction.

The book of Genesis forms a remarkable whole. Man is banished from his autochthony. The elder brother Cain kills the younger Abel and is banished. The descendants of the subsequently born Seth repopulate the world after the flood. Noah's youngest son, Ham, disgraces him and is cursed, in the name of his son Canaan, to lose his inheritance. Abraham, the descendant of Noah's eldest son Shem, moves down through the land of Canaan with a barren wife. He achieves wealth in the south and moves north again, where his wife gives birth. His son, Isaac, receives a bride out of the north who is barren but gives birth before Isaac moves south to acquire wealth. Isaac's sons parallel Cain and Abel in several ways but in particular, whereas Cain

---

[7] Pedersen, op. cit., vols. i–ii, pp. 209 ff.

killed Abel, it is Jacob who legally kills Esau. The parallel is important because as the descendants of Seth the Israelites conceive of themselves as a junior line having no rights by seniority of birth. Jacob finally completes and repairs the acts of the former patriarchs: both by rejecting the call of the south and by crossing to the north bank of the Jabbok he leads to the repossession of Eden.

The story makes sense when we look at it from the point of view of the migration from Egypt. The story that links Genesis and Exodus is the story which brings Jacob/Israel, for material benefit, south, to Egypt, where the children of Israel finally suffer. It is perhaps significant that as opposed to the famous flesh-pots of Egypt (Exod. 16: 3) the land of Canaan is only referred to as a land 'where milk and honey flow' (Exod. 13: 5) *after* the people of Israel are on the move north. And even so the theme of southern, material wealth recurs when Reuben and Gad are tempted to stay in the rich pasture lands of Transjordania rather than press on north to Canaan (Num. 32). For the recensionists the movement from south to north was certainly a redemptive movement.

12

Birth Customs of the Akawaio

AUDREY BUTT COLSON

FEW field studies have been made of birth customs of peoples reported to have the *couvade*, or male child-bed, observance. In the Guiana region of South America, a classic area for this type of institution, the most important investigation has been made by Niels Fock for the Waiwai.[1] My own study, which produced similar data, was made among the Akawaio, another Carib-speaking people to the north of the Waiwai, who live in the Guiana Highlands on the borders of Guyana, Venezuela, and Brazil.[2]

This account of Akawaio birth customs is presented to Professor Evans-Pritchard in full and grateful acknowledgement of the debt I owe him personally for my social anthropological education. I hope it may also express the great appreciation which all Americanist scholars have for the inspiration of his outstanding work in social anthropology. His African studies have been carried over and have illuminated those in the New World.

Pre-natal Observances

Observances which I recorded for Akawaio women during pregnancy fall mainly into three categories: those which have the object of avoiding the birth of twins; those affecting the appearance of the child; those ensuring quick and easy delivery.

Akawaio dislike plural births and experience shame when they

[1] Fock (1960). Lack of space prevents me from making a detailed comparative study of Waiwai and Akawaio birth customs.

[2] Acknowledgements and thanks are accorded to the American Association of University Women, the Commonwealth Development and Welfare Corporation, London University Central Research Fund, Oxford University, the Calouste Gulbenkian Foundation—all of whom generously financed my three research expeditions to the Guianas, 1951–2, 1957, and 1963.

occur. Although nowadays, under foreign influence, twins are reared, formerly one of the babies might be killed.[3] It was said that there would not be sufficient milk to rear them. No instances of other multiple births are recalled and when told of these the information was received with incredulity followed by a combined horror and amused disgust. One old woman remarked that 'she would die if she had triplets'. It is sometimes said that twins may occasionally result from intercourse with two different men. It is also asserted that twins may be born if the pregnant woman eats a banana which is partially split or is ridged, so appearing like two fruits joined together. Care is taken to avoid these.

The appearance and attributes of a child also cause concern. If deer were to be eaten by the mother during pregnancy the baby would be born with a long neck. Dumbness is attributed to the mother having drunk from a bottle, or having put a knife in her mouth when eating. To divine whether the unborn child is a male or female a particular bee, *chiligali*,[4] is employed. Its legs are put on the fire and if they go 'pop' the child will be a boy: if they go 'shish' it will be a girl.

Certain measures, of a magical, symbolic type, are taken to ensure an easy birth. For this purpose *körekö* is obtained. This is the root of the *kamai'ing* tree (*Cecropia angulata*) and pregnant women may bathe in an infusion of it every day. This root may also be scraped into cold water and drunk. The slimy property of the sap is thought to cause the baby to slip out quickly.[5] In some instances dietary observances also assist birth. According to an Ataro River informant, when a woman realizes she is pregnant she bathes with her husband early every morning in the creek and begins to observe certain food restrictions. She cannot

---

[3] Very few instances of twin births occur among the Akawaio and since infanticide of this type had stopped it was difficult to get consistent information on which twin would be killed. There may have been no general rule concerning destruction by sex or order of birth.

[4] It is also believed that when this bee (unidentified) is seen guests will arrive.

[5] This root is also used for stopping up cracks in woodskin canoes to make them watertight. For this purpose, the root is chewed, the fibres parted and stuffed into the holes, while the slimy sap is quickly washed off by the water. Thus the Akawaio have selectively used one property for symbolic use in birth rites and another property is ignored which would counteract the effect desired.

eat *okla* (Greater Blue Guan), *powik* (Crested Curassow), *aguti*, peccary, or tapir. If she were to eat these she would suffer a slow birth.[6] She may eat *maru* (Guiana Great Tinamou), a swiftly flying bird which perhaps symbolizes a quick birth. Fish can be eaten with the exception of yarrow, which is a bull-headed, long fish and among the largest in the Guiana Highland area. Garden products can be eaten, cassava bread (*Manihot utilissima*), and pepper pot stew;[7] *paiawalu*, a fermented cassava drink, may also be taken.

It is generally asserted that only the mother-to-be observes the various food restrictions and takes medicines (*debik*) before birth: the prospective father is free to live as usual. However, an informant will occasionally mention some related restrictions. For example, if a man kills a snake or tiger[8] while his wife is pregnant then the baby will fall ill after birth, for these fierce and harmful creatures have powerful and harmful spirits when roused. Referring to the period immediately before birth one informant also remarked that if a prospective father went hunting or working in the forest he would get many chigoes (*Pulex penetrans*) in his toes. The father's role after the birth of his child was also foreshadowed in an incident which took place in Jawalla village in June 1957. King George's wife Ethel was expecting, and when the baby turned round in the womb she experienced some discomfort which she explained by saying that her husband had been working too hard. He had been sawing wood and this had made the baby in the womb sick and had caused her to feel pain.[9] For several days after this incident King George kept quiet: he did not join in the Hallelujah dancing in the village:[10] he did not go hunting: he kept to his hammock for long periods and rested

[6] *Okla* may (as among the Waiwai) be thought to cause blood or be categorized, with the powis bird, as of slow flight. Large animals, peccary and tapir, are forbidden because of their size and powerful spirits.

[7] Pepper pot is a hot, pepper stew containing boiled meat, fish, or spinach-type leaves. It may contain gravy from the boiled juice of the bitter cassava. It is the basis of daily meals, accompanied by cassava bread and lightly fermented drinks.

[8] 'Tiger' refers to members of the cat family, such as jaguar, puma, panther, ocelot.

[9] See p. 290 for post-natal prohibition on sawing.

[10] Hallelujah is the semi-Christian, syncretic religion of the majority of present-day Akawaio.

until his wife recovered and the pregnancy proceeded without more ill effect. Ethel herself presented bowls of *kassiri*, a fermented cassava drink, to those who had been on bad terms with her husband at that time.

Akawaio pre-natal observances mostly affect the mother-to-be. They are mainly dietary regulations which embrace magical aids of a symbolic character which have the object of procuring a satisfactory delivery of one, normal, healthy child. Specifically, the mother seeks to avoid plural birth, physical peculiarities, and a long and painful delivery. Her husband is not totally un-affected and when the birth is imminent or the pregnancy becomes difficult his behaviour begins to foreshadow the post-natal observances which will shortly be incumbent on him; that is, he starts resting and avoids antagonizing the spirit world, especially powerful animal spirits in the hunt. As the time of birth approaches both husband and wife aim to live quietly and unobtrusively.

Birth

Several women said that they would feel ashamed to have a baby in front of people. Nor did they wish to have babies in a hospital because they did not like to be seen naked, especially in front of strangers.[11] Thus, provided there are few people present birth normally occurs in the home, otherwise it takes place in the forest near by, where a shelter is erected and the mother's hammock slung.

The actual birth occurs on the ground, the woman kneeling whilst she is clasped round the breast from behind. This task is often performed by her husband but if he is absent then a mother or sister takes his place. Usually, only the husband and close female relatives are present and assisting at a birth. As the Akawaio follow matrilocal residence a birth normally occurs at the mother's parental home.

---

[11] In 1957 there was a widespread belief that if a woman went to hospital for the birth she would be given medicine which would give her more than one baby at a time. Since no twins had been born in Kamarang hospital it is difficult to account for this fear and the boycott of the hospital. A medical aide thought it might have originated in something said to an Akawaio during a stay in George-town hospital.

After birth the umbilical cord (*pone*) is tied with cotton string and a splinter from the shaft of an arrow is used to cut it.[12] The same method and the same cutting implement is used whether it is a boy or a girl. A knife is never used.

Then the woman puts her finger in a little of the blood and places it on her tongue: this causes her to vomit violently and the afterbirth (*mumböpö*)[13] comes away. The afterbirth and cord are thrown into the forest without any further ceremony. The baby is held upside down at birth to encourage it to cry. It is then bathed in warm water. (Joseph Grant's wife: Ataro River.)

After the bathing of the mother and child by sponging down with water from a pot,[14] the period of intensive restrictions starts.

Post-natal Observances (until the fall of the umbilical cord)

Immediately after the birth husband and wife together undergo a strict regime which is referred to as *jeruma*. This word has two connotations: resting and going hungry or dieting.[15]

Resting. Both the parents must keep to their hammocks for about nine days. Mostly the mother holds the child and she can be seen gazing intently at it for long periods of time. She may occasionally straighten the limbs by gently pressing and extending them and may also sponge the child in a little warm water. During this period neither parent must go outside the house—except to relieve themselves: there must be a fire in the house all night: neither parent must talk a lot: they must both 'stay quiet' and secluded. People may greet them and converse a few moments but long conversations and discussions are avoided.

No work can be done during the nine days and relatives therefore help out. A sister, for example, will do the necessary

[12] This is the arrow cane *Gynerium sagittatum*. The dried shaft is similar to thin bamboo.
[13] *Mumbö* = womb. The suffix *-pö* (or *-bö*) signifies 'past' or 'former'. Thus *mumböpö* = former womb, or afterbirth.
[14] Bathing in a river never occurs after a birth, nor at time of puberty, during menstruation, nor when a person is ill or indisposed. It is considered dangerous, as the water spirit (*Lato*) might attack a person in these conditions.
[15] The closest translation into one single English word is possibly 'retreat', but this has such strong and specific religious connotations that I hesitate to use it.

household work and children may be ordered by the nursing
mother to bring her water, carry firewood, and be generally
useful. It is recognized that 'a woman must rest because she feels
weak', but Akawaio also say that 'if she works it will hurt the
child'. The items of work which she may not do are not elaborated as they are, however, in the case of the father. He must not
use an axe, or a knife, or cut wood. Nor may he use a saw, a gun,
or go into the forest.

These various prohibitions are explained in terms of spirit beliefs. The general assumption is that both parents have to act in
such a way as to avoid the attention of spirits which are all about
and likely to exert a power to cause illness or even death to the
new-born. These spirits may also make the parents ill, but it is
the baby that is mainly exposed. The baby's own spirit is not yet
strong; it is but weakly attached to the body and is still very much
affected by the acts of its parents, having been so recently a
physical part of them and still linked to them spiritually.

The categories of spirits which may attack the child are ghost
spirits (*akwalupö*) and nature spirits (*akwalu*). The spirit of an evil
human who is a sorcerer (*edodo*) is extremely dangerous. To keep
away sorcery a fire must be maintained in the house all night.
The mother has to stay awake for the night after the birth, otherwise an evil spirit may come and enter the baby and kill it. The
father may sleep. Great care has to be taken as regards ghost
spirits and the parents should not go outside the house because
'If you go outside you may see a spirit (*akwalu*) or a family spirit
(*akwalupö*) and go mad. If you go out for a short while you
must put a fire fan (*oli-oli*) on your head.' This cover is perhaps
a measure designed to avoid recognition.

The father's behaviour is regarded as especially important
because the child's spirit is thought to follow him about, to
participate in his actions and be damaged by them. On these
occasions the various nature spirits may be roused. The spirits of
working tools are particularly likely to attack the child. Thus, if
the father chops wood the baby's spirit might get chopped: if he
uses a saw the saw spirit might come and cut the child: if a gun
is used the child's spirit might get shot: if the father goes into the

forest the child's spirit might get lost there. When his child was born Basil's father told him he must not work for a period of two weeks for if he were to do so the child's spirit would be following him and would be doing the work too and so would fall sick and die.

If the father goes away and works the spirit of the child might be right behind him and working too—which would harm it. Therefore the father must stay near the baby until its spirit is firmly fixed, which will occur when the child grows stronger—on the umbilical cord falling off. (Basil: Kamarang River.)

The prohibition on work for both parents is interlinked, for it is asserted that 'he [the father] does not work for one or two weeks: when his wife starts working a little he does too'.

Dieting. An elderly woman at Paruima village, Kamarang River, described the post-natal dieting regime as follows:

After birth of a child the father and mother should go one or two weeks without eating fish or meat, bananas, salt or sugar. Cassava bread (*eki*) and water only may be taken. Old-time people used to do this. My grandfather and grandmother told us not to eat salt or sweet things, meat or fish.[16] Before birth the parents can eat what they like. After the umbilical cord has fallen they begin to eat fish but no meat. About a month after that they start eating everything. The husband does the same as his wife and when she starts eating he starts.

Let us analyse this statement in detail.

Meat and fish are forbidden foods for it is feared that the spirits of animals and fish may interfere with and harm the child. 'Spirits of meat and fish might humbug the child' said one informant; another remarked that 'if the father eats the animal spirits might get cross and make the child ill'. The concern with angry nature spirits and their effect on the spiritually weak and vulnerable baby is therefore as pronounced for food restrictions as for work restrictions.

The prohibition on garden produce of certain kinds, as on wild fruits, is explained by the classification of the essential

---

[16] A second informant added that 'these might block up the body'.

qualities of substances into opposing, but complementary, categories such as bitter and sweet, hot and cold.[17] Bananas and salt,[18] for example, are classified as sweet. Sweet foods 'cause blood', which is itself classified as sweet. Since bleeding must be reduced at the time of, and after, birth, sweet foods which encourage bleeding have to be avoided. Blood is also classified as cold. Cold liquids and foods must be avoided too and it is said that 'the stomach must not have cold things'. According to one informant, 'all food must be warm: cold food would kill the mother'.

These same principles of classification explain other assertions about what should be eaten or drunk in the post-natal period. A little pepper pot with either leaves of the bitter cassava or *arosa* (*Phytolacca icosandra*)[19] may be taken. Pepper pot with but one pepper and *karta*, the boiled juice of the bitter cassava root which makes a gravy, is an alternative.[20] Although a small fish (*korak*) is allowed no other flesh food may be eaten. *Paiawalu*, a lightly fermented drink made from toasted cassava bread, can be drunk by the mother. *Kassiri*, made from the pulp of the bitter cassava, can be drunk by the father. Otherwise, in the unanimous opinion of informants, only cassava bread and water could be taken.

During the nine days or so before the fall of the navel-cord the only safe diet for man and wife is that of cassava and water. Cassava is said not to hurt the child 'as long time people were accustomed to it'. It is eaten in two forms: either as *eki totsa*, a gruel made by crumbling cassava bread into hot or warm water, or just cassava bread toasted and eaten dry accompanied by a drink of warm water. This is the standard diet of the resting period (*jeruma*), as also for all periods of illness and ritual change.

It is often asserted that 'there are no food restrictions before the birth of a child for either the man or woman, but afterwards both must keep to the hammock and not eat' (Basil: Kamarang River). Nevertheless, the regime of dieting does sometimes

---

[17] Butt (1961).

[18] It is said that salt eaten at this time by the parents might cause the teeth of the child to drop out when it grows older.

[19] Known in Guyana as 'calaloo'.

[20] The root of the bitter cassava (*Manihot utilissima*) is made into a bread after processing which includes extraction of hydrocyanic acid. When boiled the poison is converted and is safe to eat as a gravy with preservative qualities.

begin a few days before birth for the expectant mother. Some are said to begin this diet a week before birth. Basil's own sister in 1951 ate only cassava gruel and toasted cassava bread for three days before giving birth and for seven days afterwards.

A non-dietary observance which seems to be related to the Akawaio system of classification concerns scratching. If either parent scratches, their hair will fall out or permanent marks be left on the skin. Akawaio sometimes speak of a 'sweet itch'[21] so that the prohibition may, in effect, be a means of avoiding a sensation of sweetness and cooling on a warm and irritated spot.

The Attainment of Ghost Protection

Both parents, then, after the birth, stay in the house resting and dieting (*jeruma*) for a period of about nine days, and caring for their child together. This is the time required for the umbilical stump to dry and fall off. The mother then washes and rubs herself with the leaves of the bitter cassava plant, so emphasizing the bitter principle which safeguards her health as opposed to the sweet which endangers it by generating excess of blood.

It is said that when the navel-cord falls the child gains strength and the parents are free to return to normal, everyday life. It is at this stage that a ghost spirit (*akwalupö*) may enter the child, staying inside for some years, strengthening and protecting it during the crucial years of growth. If it is a boy the ghost of a deceased relative of the father's family enters the baby; if a girl, a ghost of the mother's family enters in. The ghost stays for a few years. Some informants said for perhaps three or four years, that is, until weaning; others mentioned eleven or twelve, until puberty.

A dramatic instance of ghost activity of this sort was revealed during a shaman's seance. The patient was a young boy, son of Josephine and her deceased husband Morgan. The child had been crying a lot, had a bad cold, and was not eating. During the course of the inquiry Morgan's ghost was summoned to the seance.

---

[21] Itching feet (often a symptom of hookworm infection) may be treated by rubbing in hot ashes and then bathing them with the juice of bitter cassava leaves which have been squeezed into hot water, so opposing sweet (itching) and cold with bitter and hot. These complexities of thought require further investigation.

He confessed that he was inside his sick son: he had had a longing for some strong drink but as he had not obtained it through his son, as hoped for, the child was ill. The next time the women brewed they determined to make some especially strong fermented drink to give to the child, through whom it would reach the thirsty ghost. *Imawali*, the forest spirit, who also possessed the shaman as a helping spirit, admonished Morgan's ghost saying that he must stay in the child and be a protector.

Akawaio say that they know of the fact of possession through the shaman, who discovers it when he is consulting the spirits and himself enters the spirit world. Then he can see the protecting spirit inside the child. Nevertheless, possession is often suspected previously, either because the child suddenly gains strength on the fall of the navel-cord, or later when it displays unusual and adult-type behaviour. For example, it wants to start eating fish and meat or drink strong brews before it has finished drinking the mother's milk.[22] This sets people thinking of ghost intrusion so that when the shaman next conducts a seance he may confirm what has already been suspected. After this the people start calling the child by the term they used for the ghost when he or she was alive. It often appears as if the child is being addressed by the most inappropriate kinship terms whereas in fact they are addressing the ghost within. By possession of a living child the ghost spirit is believed to be getting what it is longing for in the way of human companionship, food, and drink; the child's relatives are happy because they believe that a friendly and affectionate ghost relative within the child will help to strengthen, protect, and care for it. The ghost will keep out antagonistic ghosts and nature spirits. This is particularly welcomed when a family has lost several children, for it is believed that the deceased relative has come to the rescue of the other children still living.[23]

The Length and Intensity of Post-natal Observances

Although the formal resting and dieting period is said to end after about nine days, when people see that the baby is stronger

[22] Since the child is not weaned until three or four years of age the desire for solid food is not surprising unless it is especially pronounced or precocious.

[23] Wavell, Butt, and Epton (1966), pp. 85–6.

and may already be possessed and protected by a ghost, the prohibitions are relaxed only gradually. The mother first performs a
few light household tasks, leaving the baby for a few minutes at
a time with her mother, sister, or husband. She may even leave
it alone, cradled in the hammock, for short periods. She and her
husband may go and visit other households, those near by and
then more distant houses in the same settlement. They will look on
quietly at the communal meals and dance feasts but it will be many
weeks before they eventually join in. One stage merges imper-
ceptibly into another. For example, Alice, daughter-in-law of
Danny, Kamarang River, did not join in family meals or eat
from the communal pepper pots until about a month after giving
birth, although the settlement consisted of just one house occupied
by a number of very closely related nuclear families. She did not
visit her garden near by until after a month had elapsed and then
she left the baby at home in charge of a female relative. The
father similarly takes care not to engage in hard work immediately
after the resting period.

As with work so with diet. Food prohibitions do not cease
abruptly. A man can eat only fish, *powik* (Crested Curassow),
maru (Guiana Great Tinamu), together with cassava bread and
with *kassiri* to drink, between the time the cord falls until three
months after birth. He is not allowed to eat deer or the larger
animals until after three months.

Modification of the length and severity of the resting period
also depends on the sex of the child. If the baby is a girl then the
father will observe only about one week of strict diet and rest.
If it is a boy he will observe about nine days to two weeks. If the
birth was difficult, or the baby falls ill, is sickly or weak, then the
restrictions are extended until the child is strong.

In Kataima village, Mazaruni River, December 1951, two
births occurred almost simultaneously. The sex of the babies
differed and so did their health. The resulting contrast between
the behaviour of the two sets of parents shows how the resting
and diet period will vary. During the night of 20–21 December
Bengie and his wife Akwa had a daughter. The birth was quick
and easy. On the night of 22–23 December John David and his

wife had a son. Whereas Bengie was deciding to stay in his
hammock for just over a week John David planned to stay longer
and to eat nothing but cassava gruel and water for four days. The
initial decisions seem to have been determined entirely by the sex
of the babies.

Both sets of parents spent all their time in their hammocks for
the following few days. On 25 December Bengie stood for a
time leaning against his house-post looking at the Hallelujah
dancing in process in the village church. John David went and
stood in the church for a while but did not dance or converse.
On 27 December, seven days after birth, Bengie forsook his
hammock for a longer period and his wife deposited her baby in
the hammock and began peeling cassava roots. John David
remained in his hammock still, his baby having developed leg
sores. On 29 December Bengie visited me and on the following
day went to other households and was seen about the village.
Meanwhile, it was reported that John David would have to rest
longer for his child was sick. He continued in his hammock
consistently, merely relieving the monotony by singing Hallelujah chants from time to time. On 30 December he was nibbling
cassava toast and complaining that he was very hungry.[24] The
child's condition improved but it was not until 3 January, twelve
days after birth, that the formal observances ended. The family
then left the village for their garden place, from which they
intended to poison a creek for fish.[25] Hard work was still avoided
and on 26 January, when John David was asked to do some sawing, he refused because 'the child's legs would in some way be
cut off'.

Some birth restrictions continue for three months or longer.
They have the object of avoiding spirit wrath which will harm
the newly arrived small and fragile human. The main danger is
from the spirits of slain animals, especially from those large ones

[24] Similarly, during puberty seclusion, girls are instructed not to bite cassava
toast but to nibble it.

[25] This is permissible activity. The parents can now start eating fish (which are
all very small in the Upper Mazaruni District). Poison, used to stupefy the fish,
is bitter and, being the opposite of sweetness, is not dangerous to the mother of
the child. See p. 298.

with powerful spirits, size and power often being equated. This danger is latent throughout babyhood and formerly measures were taken to relieve the parents of such severe restrictions entailed.

Years ago an old axe or stone might be put in the fire and all the bones of animals eaten were put on it when it was hot. Then water was poured on and steam rose. The baby was held in the steam for a few minutes. This is because fire burns the animals' spirits and takes these spirits away from the baby. This might be done every so often. The axe never gets sick or ill—thus the baby will stay so. Similarly, a stone might be used.[26] (Basil: Kamarang River.)

Some precautions relate to the avoidance of harmful ghosts. For example, a parent, through sharing food with people in mourning, may convey sickness to a baby.

People are soft.[27] If someone dies they bury him and afterwards all eat together; then the child of a parent taking part may get sick and die—so the people know from this that the ghost spirit of the deceased may have entered the child. For this reason the father of a baby may not eat with relatives of the deceased. (Austin: Chinawieng Village.)

For this same reason shaman Joe of Chinawieng would not eat yams cooked by Leonard, whose mother had died shortly before Joe's baby was born. It is said that a woman should take her baby away from a dying person, avoid the corpse, and not stay in the same house, on pain of the ghost troubling the child. A woman with a baby should not go near the grave, or even use the path over which the corpse was carried to be buried.

Breaking the Birth Regulations

The prohibition against eating flesh foods is a particularly lengthy and rigorous one so that ritual means are sometimes used to evade or lighten it. A small caladium with a red centre to the leaf was grown at Walbaima as a woman's charm. Its juice,

---

[26] Compare Fock (1960), p. 58. This information unconsciously recalls the time when Akawaio used stone tools. Stones and stone tools are hard and strong and therefore not vulnerable to sickness. Where cremation occurs among Carib-speakers it is said that fire helps to release the spirit which ascends in the smoke.

[27] Categories of hard and soft sometimes enter into myths of the culture heroes.

squeezed from the root into the skin, enabled a mother to eat prohibited foods during the nine- to ten-day post-natal period. Ritual blowing (*taling*)[28] is done to food to make it safe when the parents eat it again for the first time.

By 1951 Akawaio who had been most in contact with Western ways were in the process of severely modifying the birth observances. For example, Thelma, whose husband was working at the Government Station, took her baby on an expedition to poison a forest pool for fish only four days after its birth. Ten days later the child fell ill and the father had to be summoned from work. It was suffering from thrush, caused by dirty breast-feeding, but the general opinion was that the rainbow (*ögoima*) had seen the baby during the fishing excursion and had eaten up the child's spirit.[29] Eric Reed of Waramadong, who had spent much time outside the tribal territory, confessed that he had fasted one day and then felt so hungry on the next that he opened a tin of sardines and ate them with his cassava bread.[30] He maintained that the mother should not do this!

District Officers, missionaries, visiting officials, and others, have, in the past, had to give way before a father's determination not to work during the immediate post-natal period of extreme vulnerability. By 1957 foreign influences, which included scorn and cajolement, had noticeably begun to have effect. Anxious discussions were taking place as worried fathers tried to decide whether to continue working or not, being afraid lest by doing so they would make their babies ill and even endanger their lives. Ignorance seemed to be no advantage, for as one man explained, even if he were away working and unknowingly continued to do so when his wife had given birth, the baby would still fall sick and die.

Even the most sophisticated Akawaio compromised. Providing the baby was healthy many of the restrictions were only partially

[28] Butt (1956 and 1961).

[29] *Ögoima* is thought of as a large snake. In particular it may cause boils. In this instance the baby's mouth and tongue were coated with small white pimples.

[30] Small, tinned fish would be the least harmful food which a father could eat. Foreign foods are sometimes regarded as different and outside the usual observances.

and briefly observed. Fathers would take a day or two off from work and be careful to avoid eating meat. Many parents resorted to traditional methods for relaxing the diet prohibitions, hoping to safeguard the child ritually. Inevitably there was a reversion to ideal practice as soon as any sign of ill health appeared in the child. An excellent example of this trend occurred in Chinawieng village in July 1957, and was subject to a shaman's inquiry.[31] A month-old baby boy had a severe cold: the father, Leonard, was suffering from swollen joints. Spirits possessing the shaman announced that the child's sickness was due to the mother having eaten too much at birth. The spirits of the meat eaten[32] had entered the child and were troubling it. The spirits of the charms she had taken to enable her to eat the meat safely had rebounded on the child and captured its spirit. The father too, by using ant frames[33] to treat his swellings, had caused the spirit of the ant to take the child's spirit. Finally, instead of resting, the parents had been 'walking all about' with the baby and a lizard spirit seeing this had captured the child's spirit.[34] Imawali, the forest spirit, had declared that the child's father's mother's ghost had been angry at all this bad treatment and evasion of responsibility but she had now got inside and would protect the baby. If the parents did not take good care this ghost spirit would come out and the child would fall ill again. Moreover, the ghost might then take the child's spirit away with it.

In this one case all the major facets of birth observations can be seen, but all the rules had been broken. The mother had been taking charms in order to break the prohibition on eating meat. The father had used charms on himself. This superabundance of charms (*murang*) had rebounded on the child. Both parents had ignored the rest period. Thus they had endangered the child's

[31] Butt (1965–6), pp. 161–9.
[32] Akawaio use one word, *ok*, for 'animal' and 'meat', so making a closer identification between a living creature and its consumer than where a different word is used for what is eaten.
[33] Ant frames consist of lattices of palm splinters with ants sandwiched between them. They are made to bite parts of the body where aches and pains are felt.
[34] Akawaio conceive of spirit fractions (*ewang*) making up a total body spirit (*akwalu*). The fractions can be taken away individually so that the shaman has to restore all of them to restore full health.

life, exposing it to dangerous spirit forces which the shaman had had to counteract. With the possession of the baby by a protective ghost and reversion to traditional practice—the parents were to 'stay quiet'—the baby would recover. In fact, when the baby did recover the father agreed to risk walking by trail to the next village, carrying a load for a day and a half.

In this case sickness caused only a temporary reversion to former customs. Before foreign influences were pronounced parents certainly had ritual ways of relaxing the severity of the birth period, utilizing charms and ritual blowing. However, they probably used these circumspectly and in moderation, carefully observing most of the birth customs for the requisite period of time.

Weaning

A period of sexual abstention is supposed to follow birth and to be broken only after three to four years when the child is weaned. The reason given is that the parents do not want another baby until the previous one is independent of the mother's milk. The fear is that when two babies are taking milk at the same time there will not be sufficient for both and the elder child will deprive the younger of its sustenance and perhaps cause it to die. It is also asserted that if a man were to lie with his wife while she was suckling a child the baby would be continually crying and would not grow well. By 1957 this custom was being increasingly disregarded. An elderly woman at the Seventh Day Adventist Mission of Paruima, Kamarang River, remarked that 'Children don't grow good here because women sleep with their husbands and may get another baby quickly'. As imported milk foods and foreign contact increased so, it seemed, this particular observance was lapsing.

Birth Ritual

Parents are constrained to rest and diet whenever their child falls ill, between the time of birth until it is eleven or twelve years old, that is, until puberty or near puberty. A strict observance of this occurs when the child is very young but may also be followed when the child is older on the occasion of severe and dangerous sickness. This modification of parental behaviour seems to be based on the assumption that the younger the child the more tenuous is its connection between body and spirit. No doubt this relates to the high rate of child mortality in the past.[35]

Nevertheless, Akawaio birth observances are not isolated phenomena, peculiar to the time of birth only. The term *jeruma* is used to describe identical behaviour on the following occasions:

1. *Illness.* Resting and fasting occurs until the individual feels better, whether in a few hours or weeks later.

2. *Charm-taking.* Usually only about a day is passed resting and dieting, except at puberty when boys take many hunting-charms and undertake longer periods.

3. *Girls' puberty.*[36] Several days of resting and fasting are enjoined at this time and also during succeeding menstruations.

4. *Shaman practice.* During the learning period a shaman pupil undergoes successive periods of resting and fasting. A mature shaman will do the same on the day he is due to conduct a seance.

5. *Mourning.* Seclusion and dieting by the relatives of the deceased occur for several days after burial.

Including birth, there are thus six main types of occasions which share the same ritual injunctions. Indisposition, depression, frustration are also marked in the same way, though perhaps only for a few hours. Ordinary resting, sleepiness, or tiredness are not described as *jeruma*. The crises of life, conditions of stress, change, and spiritual danger, give rise to the same behaviour. Birth ritual has therefore to be classified in a wider context than just the occasion of birth,[37] but to discover the social significance of the birth period and its observances it is necessary to look

[35] Akawaio are noticeably sensitive about their children under eleven or twelve years, even when they are healthy. They do not like them to tell their personal names and are averse to photography in case their spirits are 'taken out'. Adults have the same fears, but to a lesser extent.

[36] Many of the detailed observances at time of puberty are identical to those observed by parents after birth, e.g. the cassava gruel diet; nibbling and not biting toast; prohibition on scratching; avoiding meats and sweet foods; washing in water and juice from bitter cassava leaves.

[37] I hope to compare the various ritual observances referred to as *jeruma* in subsequent publications.

beyond details of ritual and to consider social roles and inter-relationships.

The *couvade* was first considered to be an imitation by the husband of his wife's labour in childbirth: a physical re-enactment of the total event. This does not occur among the Akawaio. *Tu-seruma-sang*[38] is a phrase which refers to both parents submitting to post-natal restrictions on work and diet. In general, the parents observe the injunctions equally. Nobody else is affected, not even classificatory fathers and mothers of the baby, or its siblings, whether real or classificatory. On the contrary, these are the ones who keep the household going by performing all necessary tasks while the parents are resting. Immediately following birth there is thus an isolation from others, imposed on the parents nursing their new baby. The birth rites mark this.

The timing of the birth observances also coincide. The parents should do the same things at approximately the same time. When the one begins to rest and diet then the other has to do so: when the one relaxes than the other will relax similarly. Although the mother may begin to diet before the birth this is not recognized as the ritual rest period which, although foreshadowed, starts only after birth when both parents act in concert.

The post-natal behaviour of both parents is deliberately linked and made identical, but identity of outward signs masks an essential complementarity of roles which is explicable only in terms of concepts relating to male and female roles in general. It is noticeable that the major concern of the father is to avoid the anger of the nature spirits, particularly of animal spirits and of powerful tools such as axes, saws, and knives, which could damage the vulnerable, new-born spirit. This concern relates to the men's province of work, hunting, fishing, entering the forest to cut gardens and utilize wood. Birth prohibitions for the man aim at the spiritual ambience of his labour sphere. Sympathetically, the mother will not eat flesh foods which would arouse the animal spirits, nor engage in gardening and household work which is the woman's province and has its own spiritual connotations.

[38] This is the reflexive and group plural of *jeruma*.

The primary concern of the mother relates to her own health; thereby the physical stress of giving birth is emphasized. Birth observances for the woman are of a magical, medical type whereby she avoids eating foods which are cold and sweet and cause blood. She may begin these observances before birth as precautions which help to bring about a safe, easy delivery of one normal, healthy child without physical deformity. Sympathetically, the father will not, after birth, partake of foods which encourage bleeding.

Thus, starting from somewhat different concepts and roles, husband and wife arrive, after the birth of their child, at approximately the same pattern of behaviour.

The Akawaio View of Conception

The nature of the complementary role of the sexes in the 'making of a baby' also shows up in the Akawaio view of conception. The first cause is spiritual and is uniformly attributed to God (*Papa kapo*—Grandfather in the sky). All informants asserted that God makes a child. One added: 'The spirit of the child is made by God. God makes the eyes, limbs, and everything of the child while it is in the belly of the mother.' This ultimate origin could be derived from Christian teaching, through the Christian-inspired, syncretic religion of Hallelujah, but it also harmonizes with the traditional belief that all life and spirit strength derive from a source in the sky (*akwa*, light, brightness).[39]

Akawaio fully realize that sexual intercourse may lead to pregnancy and that when her menstrual periods stop a woman is normally pregnant. However, it is believed that pregnancy does not necessarily result from one act of intercourse but that a baby is built up gradually after successive acts during the month before the menstrual period ceases, each act adding something to the child.[40] It is asserted that, after God, both man and woman

[39] Butt (1954).
[40] If a woman has consorted with more than one man then each is believed to have had a share in making the child. Whilst participation is acknowledged the child is regarded as 'made' by the man she has been with most frequently, 'by whoever she gets most from'. The role of genitor is therefore shared and the main genitor is the one who had most frequent access.

'make their child together'. This mutual sharing of creation is always firmly emphasized. The role of the male is to put the baby inside the woman: he is often said to 'make' the baby. For example, one informant asserted that 'the man makes the baby inside the woman and the woman looks after the baby inside'. According to another: 'something in the woman makes the hands and feet and parts of the child to come.' In effect, the Akawaio concept is that the male is the genitor and the female fosters and develops his child inside herself until the time of birth. For this reason it is said that a baby belongs to its father 'because he put the child in and it is his own'.[41]

An explanation of how a posthumously born child is regarded by the man who inherits a widow who is pregnant sums up the general attitudes. In it a pregnant woman is compared to a money box: on a second occasion the comparison was to a garden with plantains.

If someone—a relative—leaves you money in a box when he dies, then it is yours to draw out, and as it is yours you will want it. The woman is like the box. What is inside belongs to the first husband. When this first child is born then you are taking out the child left to you, but which is your brother's child.[42] (Henry: Kataima Village.)

Concerning the spirit link between father and child, Austin of Chinawieng thought that, at the time of intercourse, the man's spirit goes into the child and so 'the father makes the spirit of the child'. Basil, Kamarang River, remarked that he thought that the father gave some of his spirit to the child when it was born and that before the navel-cord falls this spirit is not too firmly fixed. 'Having derived from the father it may return to him, leaving the child if he is not careful in his behaviour.'

Logically, Akawaio birth rites suggest that the male role is dominant in the spiritual sphere: that the new spirit embodied in the baby is very close to the father: that the falling of the cord is

[41] If the principal genitor is not also the husband of the mother, and no divorce is being considered, his rights are overridden. The husband's rights over his wife's fertility take precedence and he will be the social father of the baby.

[42] A widow is expected to take as her second husband a brother or appropriate close relative of her deceased husband. Similarly, a widower should take his deceased wife's sister or appropriate close relative as his succeeding wife.

a material sign of a further stage of separation, spiritually as well as physically, which frees the father from the most exacting of the post-natal observances. However, investigation along this line of thought, separating the spiritual role of the father from the more physical one of the mother simply yielded firm assertions, first that 'God makes the child', secondly, that 'both father and mother make it too'.[43] We should recall that even in the spiritual sphere the mother has a supporting role. What she eats of animal food may open the baby's spirit to attack as the result of breaking the diet restrictions, as was shown during the shaman's inquiry at Chinawieng.[44] It is also believed that:

If it is a girl baby the spirit will stay with the mother and the father observes only about one week of restrictions on work and diet (*jeruma*). If a boy is born then the father has to stay at home longer—nine days to two weeks, because a boy's spirit will go with his father, because it is a boy.

We may recall that John David intended to stay longer in his hammock because his wife bore him a son, while Bengie anticipated a shorter period, having had a daughter.[45]

With regard to the physical links of the baby to its parents it is sometimes asserted that, after God, a girl gets her body from the mother and a boy from his father.

A number of important points can now be emphasized:

1. There is a different period of restrictions for the father during the post-natal period, which is dependent on the sex of the child.

2. There is the belief that the girl's spirit stays near the mother so that the father is restricted severely for only a week. A boy's spirit stays near the father, on the other hand, so that the birth observances are longer.

3. When a ghost protector enters a child after the fall of the navel-cord a baby girl is possessed by a ghost spirit of the mother's family: a boy is possessed by a ghost spirit of his father's family.

---

[43] The Akawaio also saw this logic but they always rounded off assertions concerning the man making a child physically and spiritually by adding that the woman does so too.

[44] See pp. 299.   [45] See pp. 295–6.

4. A girl gets her body from her mother: a boy derives his from his father.[46]

The pattern which emerges shows a complementary relationship between the sexes and the respective family groups. It divides husband and wife, in their roles of father and mother, at the parental level. It also continues the division to the sibling level, for sons are associated more closely with their father, physically and spiritually, against daughters who are associated more closely with their mother. Thus brothers are grouped in a complementary opposition to sisters. An analysis of birth ritual suggests the following divisions within the nuclear family structure:

Husband — Father $\quad\Big|\quad$ Mother — Wife
Brother — Son $\quad\downarrow\quad$ Daughter — Sister.

This separation between siblings of different sex is consistent with the pattern of marriage which prescribes union between the children of a brother and sister (whether real or classificatory), and prohibits it between the children of two brothers or two sisters (real or classificatory); that is, it is consistent with cross-cousin marriage and the classification of parallel cousins as siblings. It also allows for the rarer avuncular marriage, whereby a man marries his sister's daughter, as well as aunt-and-nephew marriage, whereby a woman marries her brother's son. In addition, this pattern harmonizes with the inheritance of possessions by sex, whereby a woman's belongings are usually left to daughters or sisters and a man's to his sons, or brothers. There is also a well-defined division of labour between the sexes.[47] Finally, the spirit links through ghost possession come from the father's or mother's family according to the sex of the child. These are not traced backwards through any particular line of ascent, as might be the case in an organized lineage system. Relatives of the first ascending generation from the appropriate

[46] Fock (1960), p. 56, records a Waiwai statement that the spirit of a male child comes from its father and that of a female from its mother.

[47] See ibid., p. 53. The Akawaio are fully matrilocal: a man takes up permanent residence with his in-laws although he returns to visit his parental home from time to time, taking his wife and family with him.

side of the family can possess the child and protect it, but afterwards there can be no real distinction of lineage. This is because, with the assumption of symmetrical cross-cousin marriage, a couple will have grandparents in common.[48] At the level of the second ascending generation it is indifferent from which side the possessing ghost spirit is reckoned. Thus Leonard's male child (see p. 299) was possessed by its father's mother who could also be its mother's father's sister. Whichever the line of relationship utilized the child would speak of 'my grandmother', *urö nok.*

Fock describes the Waiwai rule concerning bilateral descent as 'constituting the background for an equally close link between the child and the father and mother respectively, which results in natal restrictions for both parents'.[49] This is true for the Akawaio in that they consider a child as being made by both parents together and as belonging to both, as well as to their respective sets of kin. Nevertheless, within this complementary frame there is a strong recognition of differentiation by sex at the parental and sibling levels which the birth rites and accompanying concepts also stress.

Is there a Couvade?

If the word *couvade* is to be retained as a convenient description of Akawaio birth customs then the essence of its meaning must reside in the strict complementarity of marital and parental relationships and the ritual expression of these.[50]

In structural terms the Akawaio *couvade* is the application of certain observances, *jeruma*, at the time of birth which is the primary occasion for the nuclear family. By primary occasion I mean the time of the creation of the nuclear family, or its re-creation, when the first descending generation comes into being, or is being added to. Although the same rites are observed on other occasions those who are involved are either the individual

[48] This applies whether real or classificatory cousins marry, so having real or classificatory grandparents accordingly.

[49] Fock (1960), p. 63.

[50] I agree with Coelho (1949), p. 51, on the Black Caribs: 'The couvade is but a part of a unified world-view as it regards the interaction of the spiritual realm and the everyday life of man, and of the relations between husband and wife, between father, mother and child.'

(in charm-taking, puberty, shamanist activity, and adult illness), or close kin (in mourning). Only at the birth of a child, or at the time of any serious illness, is the nuclear family involved as a distinct unit, when the ritual observances define the relationship of husband and wife as father and mother, and together as parents to their new-born child. The enlargement of the child's kinship ties occurs, according to its sex, only after the immediate post-natal period when a ghost spirit of the extended family unit possesses it. Thus the fall of the navel-cord not only symbolizes a further degree of separation from the parents but also signals the possession taken of the child by a larger community of kin. At each birth the interrelationships of the nuclear family are confirmed by the expression of them in the rites of the immediate post-natal period, for each successive offspring individually creates its ties between itself and its parents, as well as again confirming the relationships of man and wife. At the same time the general interrelationships of male and female are emphasized, when the child becomes associated primarily with the parent of its own sex. This combination of the divisive and complementary nature of sex differences shows not only in the form of ritual interplay of the post-natal period but is also expressed in the ideology of conception.

Akawaio birth customs thus emphasize two structural features. First, they distinguish and separate the sexes at the parental and sibling levels; since these are crucial ones for the control of procreation it is not surprising that this form of distinction harmonizes with marital customs (predominantly cross-cousin marriage), and with the recognition of bilateral kinship. Secondly, Akawaio birth customs emphasize the nuclear family and its nature within a form of organization in which the extended family (a number of closely related nuclear families of various degrees of kinship and affinity) is the primary unit of exploitation, co-operation, sharing, and survival, which usually occupies one house, hamlet, or village segment. At the time of birth the nuclear family emerges as unique in creativity, in mutual care, and in complementary behaviour between its members according to sex distinction. Whether the ritual demonstration of these features and associated concepts in the complex of birth observances is an adequate basis for the identification of a *couvade* institution is a problem which can only be answered when studies of more birth customs allow for a wider, comparative analysis of the essential elements.

BIBLIOGRAPHY

BUTT, A. J., 1953, 'A Study of Beliefs of the Carib-speaking Akawaio of British Guiana', *Social and Economic Studies*, 2, no. 1 (University College of the West Indies).
—— 1956, 'Ritual Blowing. *Taling*—A Causation and Cure of Illness among the Akawaio', *Man*, 56, p. 48.
—— 1961, 'Symbolism and Ritual among the Akawaio of British Guiana', *Nieuwe West-Indische Gids*, 2.
—— 1965–6, 'The Shaman's Legal Role', *Revista do Museu Paulista*, N.S. (São Paulo).
COELHO, R., 1949, 'The Significance of the Couvade among the Black Caribs', *Man*, 49, p. 64.
FOCK, N., 1960, 'South American Birth Customs in Theory and Practice', *Folk*, 2 (Copenhagen).
WAVELL, S. (ed.), BUTT, A., and EPTON, N., 1966, 'Trances' (Allen & Unwin).

13

Initiation and Bead-sets in Western Mandari

J. C. BUXTON

I

In this account of initiation and bead-sets in Mandari I hope to
show how a system of youth *mores* and preoccupations is founded
on these institutions, which mark a distinct phase in the life cycle
of a man—the years between childhood and marriage. Though
the Mandari example has certain individualities, I believe that the
main elements exist in similar institutions throughout the Nilotic
peoples and that evidence for this can be found by careful reading
of the literature.

Nilotic initiation and the frequently associated age-sets have
not, however, received a great deal of attention, partly because,
as Evans-Pritchard has pointed out and the work of other writers
confirms, they are unimportant in comparison with their counterpart among the Nilo-Hamitic people to the south, whose societies
can scarcely be described, certainly not understood, without
reference to age-stratification.[1]

The lack of emphasis given to this area of Nilotic life may also
be due to the direction of interest of the writers concerned.
Nilotic age-sets have little political and no ritual significance,
their influence is diffuse and difficult to assess since they often
appear to duplicate the functions of more prominent institutions.
Their effects appear to be most pronounced in the sphere of young
people's activities, codes of behaviour, and values, and this area
has not in general been isolated as a field of inquiry in the Nilotic
context although Evans-Pritchard has dealt with some aspects of
it in his analysis of Nuer initiation.[2]

[1] E. E. Evans-Pritchard, 'The Political Structure of the Nandi-speaking Peoples
of Kenya', *Africa*, 13 (1940).
[2] E. E. Evans-Pritchard. 'The Nuer: Age-sets', *Sudan Notes and Records*, 19. 2
(1936).

Initiation and age-sets are most developed among the Nuer.[3] Though important in some tribes the Dinka form lacks homogeneity and often shows Nuer influence.[4] Both institutions have been dismissed as generally unimportant among Shilluk-Luo-speaking Nilotics and they never existed among the Luo of Uganda or the Jo Luo of Sudan, while some doubt exists in the Acholi case.[5] Nalder claimed to find evidence for them; Girling categorically states the contrary.[6]

II

The Mandari had, in the past, no tradition of initiation and lacked age-sets, but during the last few decades they have systematically acquired both, in the form practised by the Atwot, a Nuer people separated territorially from the main Nuer tribes by the Western Dinka. The Mandari borrowing is curious in that it is generally assumed that age-sets, because of their political or military significance, tend to die out on contact with colonial administrations: those of Mandari have, on the contrary, recently developed. Further, though the Atwot are north-westerly neighbours, Mandari have more regular and enduring contacts with the Aliab Dinka in the north-east. Since the explanation they give for the borrowing was to avoid Aliab Dinka ridicule (an excuse similar to the one given by Dinka who have borrowed from Nuer, according to Evans-Pritchard), the more natural solution might have been to take from the Aliab. If not from the Aliab, the Tsera and Kobora might appear to be a more logical source from which to borrow. Age-sets, which I observed to be similar to those of the Bari, are indigenous among these neighbours,

[3] Ibid., p. 234, and *The Nuer* (1940), pp. 249–61.

[4] Godfrey Lienhardt, 'The Western Dinka', *Tribes without Rulers* (ed. Middleton, 1959), pp. 118, 131–2; P. P. Howell, 'Notes on the Ngork Dinka of Western Kordofan', *SNR*, 32 (1951), 239–55.

[5] E. E. Evans-Pritchard, 'Nilotic Studies', *Journal of the Royal Anthropological Institute*, 80 (1950); P. P. Howell, 'The Shilluk Settlement', *SNR* (1946), 56–67; Evans-Pritchard, 'The Luo Tribes and Clans', *Rhodes–Livingstone Journal* (1949). Audrey Butt, 'The Nilotes of the Anglo-Egyptian Sudan and Uganda', *Ethnographic Survey of Africa*, part 4 (1952).

[6] L. F. Nalder (ed.), *A Tribal Survey of Mongalla Province* (1951), p. 145; F. K. Girling, *The Acholi of Uganda* (1960), p. 67.

culturally close to Mandari and living to the east of them on the Nile banks.[7] They have a migrant Mandari group living among them (and are, in fact, referred to as 'Mandari'). The choice of the Atwot model suggests that Mandari were interested in something more than mere acceptance in adult Nilotic society, though this motive would undoubtedly have been present. A clue is given by the Mandari themselves when they explain that they chose the Atwot form 'because it is the better of the two', meaning the more elaborate and therefore the more worth while. The simple Aliab alternative is openly and disparagingly dismissed.

Mandari began to initiate about the second decade of this century, as government forces gradually subdued the Dinka tribes with whom Mandari had a tradition of continuous hostilities.[8] The creation of a more settled climate allowed a form of inter-tribal co-operation to develop, whereby Mandari and their Nilotic neighbours began to share grazing lands.[9] Mandari herding groups, composed mainly of young men, penetrated Nilotic grasslands where they witnessed initiation; eventually they developed their own ceremonies. Thus in 1950 I found that men of about forty had been initiated, but those of older generations had not.

Before the development of initiation and formal sets, the notion of the age-mate, *ber*, had always been of considerable importance. The Mandari *ber* was, and for many purposes still is, someone of the same sex, born in the same year—in a dry season and following rains. Birth coevals are linked in an enduring relationship of mutual help and comradeship, culminating in the attendance at an age-mate's mortuary rite. For a man the notion of the coeval has now been extended to include those sharing a single initiation course but the new concept lacks some of the ritual importance of the original age-mate link.

[7] Accounts of Bari age-sets are given by A. C. Beaton, 'The Bari: Clan and Age-class systems', *SNR*, 19 (1935), 131–45.

[8] Military pacification patrols were sent against Atwot in 1907 and against Aliab Dinka in 1918, 1919, 1920, and 1923. Cf. Mohamed Omer Beshir, *The Southern Sudan: Background to Conflict* (1968), p. 19.

[9] For details of Mandari/Aliab/Atwot grazing exchanges see Buxton (1964), pp. 13 and 133–45.

Mandari have also always performed pre-teenage transformations. The most important, the extraction of the six lower front teeth, takes place around the age of eight or nine and is carried out jointly for a group of coevals of both sexes. Tooth extraction was never initiation to adult status—although a person with a full tooth complement is not acceptable as an adult and will not find a mate. It must now be completed before initiation and a new word, *adwek*, is used to describe boys after the operation and before initiation. Head-scarring, optional for both sexes, may be done at any time. Boys who wish it will be scarred before initiation, but it is never a part of initiation itself. Biological adulthood in both sexes has always been formally recognized, in the case of girls, by a minor puberty rite at the first menses which confirms maturity but not readiness for marriage. Youths used to be regarded as mature on the criteria of bodily development, at about fourteen. A bow and arrows, spear, and, ideally, the personal ox were then given by the father or mother's brother; marriage followed much later. Adulthood for both sexes allowed full participation in dancing and courting activities centred round girls' courting-huts.[10]

Initiation, with less emphasis on actual biological maturity, now determines male adulthood, and because of the spacing of initiation, some boys reach it sooner than they would have done in the past. Initiation is now absolutely essential for all those who follow the traditional cattle-camp life, and this includes about 97 per cent of males. The age-mate relationship had presupposed knowing when a person was born and this had restricted the size of the traditional age-mate group and its territorial range, but since initiation courses are carried out by land-owning and dominant clans and include the members of their attached client lineages, the age-mate group may now cover all the coevals of a single chiefdom.[11] Its members are drawn from a wider area than those of the former *ber* group, but the ties between some of the members are weaker.

[10] Girls' courting-huts are described in my article 'Girls' courting huts in Western Mandari', *Man* (April 1963).

[11] Administrative divisions, which may include several formerly independent chiefdoms, are not the basis of initiation courses.

Each chiefdom carries out initiation individually but, when one group of boys goes forward, those of neighbouring chiefdoms try to follow suit because to fall far behind places youths at a disadvantage in the competition for girls. Strong rivalry exists between the young men of different chiefdoms, despite the fact that the bead-sets into which they are grouped have never had political functions.

Initiation courses are held every four years if there are enough boys to make this worth while. A single initiation phase may be carried over to a second year if large numbers are waiting. The system is flexible and adapts to actual requirements. Youths go forward two or three years after tooth extraction and the average initiation group comprises fifteen to thirty boys, who show an age difference of up to three years. The initiands of Mokido, whose lodge I visited, included one boy who looked about eleven and others who might have been thirteen. Age discrepancy is due to 'missing out' for various reasons—being just too young, being an orphan, observing mourning. Inability to acquire the beads worn after initiation makes it pointless to go forward and, as putting a son through the bead-sets is a heavy expense, the sons of client retainers are assisted by their patrons.

Initiations are held during or following the late rains, when food is plentiful. The boys themselves decide when they are ready, and will be joined by others, of whom some will have missed the course in their own chiefdom and will choose the mother's brother's chiefdom, or, failing this, a neighbouring chiefdom where community links are established.

The boys approach a young but influential married man who runs a good homestead with a shade-tree—often the father of one of their number—and persuade him to lend his homestead as a seclusion lodge.[12] His wife acts as lodge-mother. She and her daughters vacate the hut at night but spend the day there, cooking the initiand's food. She is responsible for feeding any boys from far afield and later, in return, the course will eat at their homes

---

[12] I use the word 'lodge' as a convenient term, and not as implying a special hut isolated in the bush. For contrast see the Konzo lodge. Kirsten Alnaes, 'Nyamayingi's song. An analysis of a Konzo circumcision song', *Africa*, 37 (1967).

while touring. Mothers of boys who live close by cook for the rest and sisters carry the food to the lodge. A young man of about twenty-five—often one prominent in his own course, and related to some of the boys—acts as instructor. He receives no reward but, should an ox be killed by an initiand's father when the course disperses, he is given the hide.

Initiation Sequence: Cutting-off

The instructor collects the boys together and drives them with cuffs and slaps to the meeting-tree of the chiefdom. Those joining from outside assemble at the tree. In front of members of the community the boys are made to sit in the dust, and any little necklaces they are wearing are ripped off and thrown down for younger children. Their faces and hands are then washed, and their heads shaved by the wife of a notable. This ceremony, followed by a short seclusion, completes the Aliab Dinka initiation, which Mandari dismiss as poorly developed.

Mandari initiands enter the lodge for a closed period of seclusion and instruction, followed by an open period of touring. The length of the two phases varies: Dari and Mokido chiefdoms in central and western Mandari have a ten-day seclusion and a month's open touring; Mijiki to the east have a month's seclusion with two to three months' touring.

Initiands are referred to as *achatni* and the course as *pita na achatni*.[13] While detachment from the community is implied, radical separation is not. Villagers are not forbidden to pass the lodge or see the boys. Only girls from other areas, from whom forfeits will be claimed during touring, and who will later be courted, keep away. The emphasis is on the separation from childhood, not on separation from the community. The partial nature of the isolation is in keeping with the whole tenor of the Mandari institution as they have chosen to develop it. Radical severance, so often characteristic of initiation, is also perhaps not enforced because domestic arrangements have already to some

---

[13] It seems clear that *achatni* is a derivation from the Nuer word *cöt* ('initiand') and *cötni* ('initiand during a form of open period'). E. E. Evans-Pritchard, 'The Nuer: Age-sets', pp. 241 and 244.

extent separated children from close parental supervision at an earlier age.

III

Closed-period Seclusion

The most striking features of the seclusion are the use of routine activities and bodily functions as a source of punishments, and the stress placed on the notion of linked identity. Initiands are forced to act as a corporate body, individual action is forbidden, and the whole course is punished for the misdemeanours of a single member.

Confinement to the lodge and shade-tree is enforced and punishment, a deliberate feature, described as 'they are corrected', '*kok ririna*', begins. Emphasis is laid on faults common to childhood, and on the known failings of individual initiands. Correction is seen to expunge faults, and instil adult virtues. The following are some examples of the way in which transformation is effected. Control of bodily functions is imparted: initiands are only allowed to urinate twice daily, as a group, and when taken out for this purpose. A morning urination follows the dawn rising, the second follows the evening meal. Should a boy need to relieve himself in between, the whole course must go with him; attempts to slip off unobtrusively lead to the cuffing and switching of the offender and any other initiand within reach of the instructor. After the morning meal the course is taken to defecate. Learning to control thirst, an essential part of adult training, restricts drinking. Initiands drink once a day, in the morning. Pots of water brought by local children are handed round by the instructor, who allows only a few sips and cuffs those who attempt to take large gulps. Apart from the disciplinary associations, Mandari consider that drinking a lot of water is 'thinning', and one object of the lavish food is to develop the adolescent physique.

The two large meals eaten morning and evening are a further excuse for punishment. The food, though good and varied, is soft and cooked; raw food, or food requiring slow chewing, is excluded. It must be eaten quickly and with both hands, sitting cross-legged round the steaming food-pots. The scalding food cooked in the lodge must be eaten as swiftly as the cooler food brought from elsewhere. Slow or dainty eating, or trying to avoid burnt hands and mouths, brings punishment. The instructor wanders round, switching indiscriminately, to the accompaniment of a monologue: 'You there; you were always greedy and dirty: stubborn, a messy eater . . . lazy and rude . . . Now hurry up and eat: Let all obstinacy and slovenliness come out of your head!' Roasted ground-nuts, the only solid food included, feature in a separate test. The ground-nuts are heaped in the yard, and, at a command, the boys rush to grab as many as possible and put them in individual heaps until the pile is finished, when each boy eats his own nuts. When I watched this test, the larger boys first made the headway, then the quick-witted ones began to run around outside collecting up the bigger boys' heaps and taking them away. The purpose of the tests is to teach control of childish behaviour by restriction, or by enforcement of excessive and uncomfortable indulgence.

Much of the time is spent under the shade-tree learning and practising the ten or more initiation songs in the Atwot language, later sung during touring.[14] The small ebony sticks, known as *chuar*, and carried during touring and later at dances, are carved and decorated with brass and copper wire. Ox-names are also taken and initiands compose ox-poems. The ox-name is either that of the animal now received from the father or mother's brother, or of one already acquired from a sister's marriage. Those without an ox take any name they like; the name and poem, which are shouted out at dances, in this context being of greater importance than a real ox. Ox-names taken at initiation are Nilotic ones; the traditional Mandari versions have virtually disappeared.

Pleasurable things, like pipe-smoking, a habit often acquired before initiation, and bathing, are forbidden, although water is

[14] I am told that in Dinka the songs extol the age-mate, the initiation activities, and the head-cutting, in Nilotic areas a central feature of initiation, and that the songs are actually composed by the initiands themselves during the seclusion.

brought daily for washing face and hands. At night initiands sleep crammed in the lodge with the instructor, who may deliberately wake them up or prevent them from sleeping until the early hours.

Having a foreign source, initiation does not give instruction in Mandari traditions or values, but it features continuous moralizings on correct male behaviour from the instructor and young notables who visit the lodge. Especially emphasized is the fact that the indulgence accorded to childhood is finished, and that initiands must now equip themselves as men. Faults openly condemned and disciplined in the tests which aim to teach self-control by the enforcement of uncomfortable and excessive indulgence, or by restriction, are laziness, slovenly personal habits, and lack of adult control. Rudeness is also condemned, particularly rudeness to strangers and the old, and the ridiculing of the ugly, deformed, or sick.

Special trials, which are often painful and known as 'punishments', *rinisi*, are also devised by the instructor and given whenever he chooses. I give some examples from the Dari course. Initiands may be told to place thorny twigs under the armpits, hold the arms to the sides, then pull the stems out, leaving the thorns embedded in the flesh (endurance of pain). A cattle-peg is hammered into the ground and must be punched—perhaps for two days running—until the knuckles are raw. During this test the instructor denounces 'childish fighting and quarrelling', and strikes those who punch half-heartedly. The instructor may also deliberately mislead, for instance by walking away and then whistling; when the boys dash after him he rounds on them accusing them of running away, and laying about him with his switch: denials bring punishment 'for lying' (be prepared to be deceived and falsely accused). On another occasion a boy is made to sing solo (poise). Tests aim at instilling a sense of achievement, and initiands try to excel and to gain a good reputation.

Ex-initiands with whom I discussed the course, while agreeing that the discipline was tiring and painful, did not consider it over-severe, and the good spirits of the initiands I visited seemed to confirm this.

Open-period Touring

The period of seclusion is brought to an end when the initiands are taken to a pool or river and made to bathe. This removes the physical dirt accumulated during the course, and also demonstrates that childhood has been washed away. From then on they bathe every day and oil their bodies 'like men'. Thereafter they continue to act in unison under the instructor's orders but abuse and trials cease and initiands eat slowly, with shell spoons. Daily wrestling-contests at the waterside, after bathing, become very important. The aim is to prepare to challenge rival bands of initiands. The instructor demonstrates techniques, and the wrestling is bound by rules and must not be excessively rough, but injuries are not compensated. The boys wrestle against opponents of roughly equivalent size; once thrown a boy is eliminated and regular winners become informal leaders.

Tours alternate with rest periods at the lodge during which light tasks, such as picking beans, are undertaken and rewarded with food by the owner of the field. For the touring an additional escort joins the instructor. Both are fully armed, mainly as a precaution, since safe conduct is an essential condition of wide-range touring. Initiands travel swiftly in single file, the shortest leading; each carries his *chuar* stick in the right hand. A number of chiefdoms are visited, and the initiands stay overnight with mothers' brothers, the families of initiands from outside the sponsoring chiefdom, or with the local chief, who provides a hut and an old woman to cook. An ox may be killed to feast the visitors. Evenings are spent in singing initiation songs and in dancing. Girls' huts may not be visited and should the initiands attend a local dance they dance as a group and are not selected as partners. During the dancing, local girls armed with grain shafts make mock attacks on them. Wrestling-contests take place with other bands of touring initiands encountered *en route*, with the aim of gaining renown for the set, and in order to have the prowess of individual youths remarked on by girls.

The main objective of the touring, however, is to spy out the land for girls' huts and to collect forfeits. When a girl is sighted, the initiands quickly close in and circle round and round her singing initiation songs and shouting out ox-names. Necklaces, bracelets, or small change are then demanded. A girl is never stripped of all her beads, but one who refuses or is thought mean with forfeits will continue to be tormented. Some girls are said to be reduced to tears, but no attempt is made to help them, since the teasing is conventional. Planned attacks are also made on girls' huts; the inmates, on the alert, scatter and hide. Once seen, a girl must stand and pay, and if an initiand finds a girl cowering in the grass, he begins to sing and his age-mates run up and encircle her.[15] All forfeits are divided out by the instructor at the end of the course, beads and trinkets are handed on to sisters, and money is kept for buying set-beads.

During touring, an initiand may order the instructor to kill any ox found grazing unattended. This animal, which is thereafter referred to as 'the ox of so and so', is roasted and eaten by the set; as the owner must be compensated with a calf, such a killing confers prestige since it implies that the youth has property. Mandari suggest this practice is more typically Nilotic.[16]

The object of wide-range touring is to broaden experience by providing the opportunity of visiting remote parts of the country. It is also the means by which a new batch of young males can be seen and appraised by the country at large, and as an institution for publicizing personal attributes perhaps serves the same purpose as the girls' courting-hut.

The end of the open period is marked by head-shaving; the hair is cut away around the edges leaving a central tuft. Initiands disperse to homes or camps, but continue to meet in groups of five or six, similar to the traditional *ber*, depending on the location of homesteads. Periodically the whole set reassembles or forms a hunting-party: it also gives its members the traditional assistance with the formalities of betrothal and marriage. As far as the work of camps and cultivations permits, energies are now geared to the

[15] Although these boisterous attacks are alarming, they are mild compared with the licence described for Nuer by Evans-Pritchard, 'The Nuer: Age-sets', p. 244.

[16] It is possible that such killing has been derived from the Nuer institution of *Nak*. Cf. Howell, 'The Age-set System and the Institution of "*Nak*" among the Nuer' (with a note by E. E. Evans-Pritchard), *SNR* (1948).

pursuit of girls, to dancing, and to the collection of beads, which leads me to describe the groups into which ex-initiands form as 'bead-sets'. The wearing of beads features importantly in the rivalry which exists between age-mates of different chiefdoms for the favours of girls and for acquiring a good name. While ideally competition should be peaceful, partisan loyalties may be expressed in clashes and skirmishes when several groups of ex-initiands meet, as for instance at an important dance.

IV

The Bead-Sets: toteton: rem[17]

Ex-initiands are known as Roti. Beads are worn, but only on the neck, as large collars. It may take six months or more for all to accumulate Roti beads, then the whole set puts them on together. The exact length of time for which they are worn is the affair of the set; the average is about eighteen months. As Roti is a transition stage between initiation and full maturity, during which courting-huts are visited but marriage does not take place, it is unlikely to be extended beyond three years. The set then strips off these beads and spends perhaps a year accumulating adult set-beads, which are worn as a wire-framed 'corselet' covering waist and hips and sometimes extended up the chest. After some years the set may become bored with their beads and change them, or they may decide to retain them.

After Roti, it is again entirely a matter for the group concerned to decide for how long a bead is worn, the colour of the bead chosen, and whether it is later changed for another coloured bead or not. Bead-sets are not fixed, structural divisions with a continuing reality over time: a particular bead is not inevitably associated with a particular age-span or a particular group of

---

[17] 'toteton' 'pertaining to young males'; 'rem', 'to spear'. Spearing in this context is putting on set-beads; the association is partly based on the 'spearing' of the bead in the threading, and partly on the idea of impaling something for one's self, as with a spear. Both are Mandari words. *teton*, from which *toteton* is derived, means 'young man', usually with the additional sense of 'unmarried'.

wearers. The only essential feature is that if and when a set—as defined in terms of the members of a specific initiation course—decides to change, the change is made by all its members simultaneously.

Set-beads are seldom worn for long after marriage. With a young family, a man is drawn into the orbit of responsibilities and interests which are centred in the village rather than the cattle-camp and he loses interest in beads, which begin to have a juvenile association. He has less time to spend with age-mates, many of whom are also married. He removes his corselet, and either hands it on, broken up or complete, to younger relatives, or stores it away for special occasions. Should he have substantial possessions and be able to marry a second time while still young, he will wear it again to visit courting-huts. Since the more fortunate set members begin to marry fairly soon—probably only a few years after acquiring their adult beads—a set often retains its initial bead because, after four or five years when the wearers might begin to tire of it, many are married and the remainder do not wish to make a costly change. The very fact that they are still unmarried implies that they are the least well off. Changing beads, or the reverse, also depends very largely on the success of a bead. A bead that catches on may have a very long run and be taken up by following sets while a bead that fails is dropped. Set-beads are mostly trade-beads, and bush shops know the right kind to stock. Fashions are entirely promoted by the young people and a bead which is not liked will simply not be bought. In the past, sets have used traditional beads made from the eggs of the ostrich and widow bird or from wood, but those are not really suitable because a corselet requires anything from fifty to one hundred strings—and the making of a corselet from traditional bead materials would involve hours of arduous labour, whereas mass-produced trade-beads, on the other hand, are easy to manipulate. They are, however, expensive, and to acquire them an ox or small stock must be sold.

A bead-set, in the sense of a group some of whose members still habitually wear the bead, lasts a maximum of fifteen years—usually less, its members all having married. Although the bead is still known, no one wears it as a set-bead, so the set is, in effect, obsolete. A few individuals always linger on, wearing the beads which mark their unmarried state after their bead-mates have given up, and with them will be those who have donned them again to court second wives.

In practice the observer will only see one well-defined bead-set in existence in any one chiefdom at any one time. All its members are unmarried and their bead stands out prominently as the bead-mates go about their activities. From earlier sets, smaller groups of bead-mates are distinguishable, but only one or two individuals wear the beads of a set whose initiation course took place further back in time. Those initiated when the system was first introduced never wear set-beads. These are men of about forty who put on traditional decorations when seeking new wives—a single heirloom bead on a neckband, an ivory armband, mounted leopard tooth, or other significant *objet trouvé*.

Not only is continuity through time lacking, but also any widespread uniformity over Mandari-land—though there is borrowing and copying from rivals, which 'spreads' a bead. It is possible to indicate for any one chiefdom what is currently worn, and has been worn in the past, and to give an age connotation to these beads, but the same order may never be repeated and it may not hold good for neighbouring chiefdoms, whose young people may be wearing different beads, or the same beads in a different order.

Thus, in Dari in 1950 and 1952, set-beads were worn as follows:

Eyor, the bead of the current Dari set at the time of my fieldwork, had already been worn for five years and a new group of ex-Roti aged about 15–17 was also busy collecting it to wear again. Its extraordinary popularity had led two consecutive initiation courses to choose it. I found that by 1968 its popularity had waned: the girls had taken it over, and were wearing the beads as large shawl-like collars. (Although girls do not initiate or form sets, they operate their own lavish bead fashions, often based on styles worn by the men. Unmarried daughters may be as costly to 'dress' as sons.) An ex-*eyor* I had known in 1952 summed it up: 'We were bored with *eyor* and gave them to our sisters.' The current ex-*roti* were wearing the orange-red *aketch*.

Average age of wearers (approximate)	Name of bead[18] and set	Colour of bead
38+	*rem rear*	Bead now never worn. Obsolete, difficult to obtain. One of the first groups
33-5	*rem magok*	Yellow. Seen occasionally; also for second marriages
28-30	*rem alek*	Pale green
23-6	*rem aketch*	Orange-red
19-21	*rem eyor* (one)	Pale pink. Had a fantastic run. Very popular
15-17	*rem eyor* (two)	Pale pink
11-13	*roti*	Red bead, alternating with black bead. Or a small version of the pink *eyor* bead, all worn as large neck-collars

V

Bead-sets are not associated with the acquisition of power and status within the mature community, and there is no competition between ranked sets, no pushing out of senior sets and holding down of junior ones; indeed, the Mandari system is, in many ways, a contradiction of the conventional age-set pattern. Bead-sets are of such short duration that they cannot even have the minimal function—as have Nuer sets—of providing appropriate terms of address amenable to extension through the society, and allowing any male at any time to place himself in relation to any other.[19] There is no prohibition on marriage with an age-mate's daughter, and a very popular pastime is courting the age-mate's sister, although from my observation these affairs usually end long before marriage is achieved. Initiation does not establish a sexual division of labour as it does for Nuer; girls, and not uninitiated youths, do the milking and there is no specific status consideration which debars an adult man from doing so should this be necessary.

[18] The word which follows *rem* is the name of the bead of a particular colour, but it cannot be directly translated as meaning 'pink' bead or 'yellow' bead. All are Nilotic words.   [19] *The Nuer*, pp. 257-60.

Bead-mate behaviour often seems to involve little more than a duplication of traditional behaviour patterns. For example Adwek (pre-initiates), and Roti (most recent initiates), are expected to 'fag' for bead-set members, but the service required of them accords with the sort of demands always made by adults on small boys and youths. The latter also perform the more menial cattle-camp tasks. The fact that set coevals may eat together in certain circumstances, while their set is operative, is much like the sharing of food by members of the traditional *ber* groups or by girls in their courting-huts.

It is consistent with the interests of the age generation which evolved the system and continues to operate it, that initiation conspicuously lacks religious emphasis, is free of ritual prohibitions, and is not symbol-loaded: the activities are run by younger people for younger people and religion and ritual are the preoccupation of mature generations. The songs, having been borrowed piecemeal from the Nilotics, do not embody ideological themes of cultural relevance to Mandari.[20] Older Mandari, however, see some analogies with traditional ceremonial. I have heard the cutting-off ceremony compared with installation to chiefship through the common elements of ceremonial bathing and seclusion. Stripping and shaving are also said 'to leave the boys black and nude as at birth'—demonstrating the new beginning by analogy with the birth situation.[21]

Although these organizations are of negligible importance for the structure of the society as a whole, they are of vital interest to young people themselves. For them initiation spells out clearly, in a form they approve, acceptable values and, in particular, the ideal image of young manhood. Having a good personality and admired virtues is as important as having good looks, or even more so, and the young of both sexes are extremely exacting in

---

[20] The ideological importance of initiation songs is stressed by Eileen Jensen Krige, 'Girls' puberty songs and their health, morality, and religion among the Zulu', *Africa*, 38 (1968).

[21] Shaving itself represents a cutting off from a former state or condition which has become inappropriate or dangerous. It follows killing a human being or a marked predator; dying or being a closely related mourner, bearing a child or being born.

applying their own standards.[22] It is significant, however, that these standards conform to the standards of the wider society and, in this sense, initiation can be seen as a preparation for mature living.

As a channel for harmless competition, initiation and bead-set activities may, to some extent, compensate for the excitements of the past—the skirmishes and cattle raids—in the present state of relative security. Pre-eminently they satisfy the Mandari pre-occupation with display, permitting the creation of distinctive dress, and allowing for the rapid changes in styles and fashions, which are based on unstable and unaccountable enthusiasms and equally unaccountable loss of interest. The preoccupation with personal appearance, perhaps a characteristic of all young people, is here fully catered for. An element of narcissism is even present, together with an intense interest in the opposite sex, who, in turn, mirror changing male fashions. Young Mandari set great store by organizing their own activities, and a sharp contrast is always drawn with the activities of the older generation, who in turn accept this fact. The development of the exclusive self-image representing an age-phase is sought through identification with the age-mate, but this image and identification loses much of its intensity after marriage when emotional attachments and interests of other kinds are formed.

Mandari youth activities are not based on inter-generation hostilities. Relations between older and younger age-groups are good and their roles are seen as complementary, not conflicting. Bead-set activities are accepted as belonging to a passing phase, and as correct in this context. In spite of heavy demands on older kin for help with dress, I have never heard resentful or disapproving comment. Neither are attempts to reform traditional values an objective of the youth activities.

It would not be true to assume that this new Mandari preoccupation reflects social disintegration. Traditional institutions function vigorously and there is no evidence yet that youth has become disillusioned with traditional modes of life. On the

[22] Similar values from the girls' standpoint were discussed in my article on courting-huts (*Man*, April 1963).

contrary, they have enriched these with their own imaginative contributions.

Accounts of other Nilotic societies indicate that many of the features, developed perhaps in a more extreme form in Mandari, exist within the traditional Nilotic framework. Youth activities with an emphasis on dress, dancing, courtship, and rivalry are widespread in Nuer and Dinka within the framework of more formal age structuring: they are also found among the Shilluk.[23] Mandari have deliberately acquired, from outside, the rich content of institutions which appealed to them while ruthlessly discarding their formal structures.

[23] The wearing of ornaments is important in the coming of age of Shilluk youths, and a period of 'travel' also features. Howell, 'The Shilluk Settlement' (1946), pp. 61-5.

14

Preface by Louis Dumont to the French edition of *The Nuer**

TRANSLATED BY MARY AND JAMES DOUGLAS

FRENCH publishing has taken a happy turn. Only yesterday the translation of foreign work in the human sciences was sparse and haphazard; now there is suddenly an entirely new interest and healthy competition in the field of translation. For example, we have Panofsky revealed at last to the French reading public, thanks to two translations which appeared just before his death. In a different field of study we have in the present volume Evans-Pritchard with his *Nuer*; soon we shall have his *Azande*. And we are also to have the great Max Weber, after a delay of half a century. Whether the trend will last depends, apart from technical questions, upon sound selection. Due allowance being made for the viewpoints of different editors, the principle upon which outstanding works should be chosen for translation seems clear. In practice the specialists of any given discipline must and do read in the original language. The translation is destined for a wider public—nowadays mainly readers whose speciality is other than the one the book represents. Here is a basic social need which must be fulfilled if translations are to be sufficiently widely read. Consequently priority must be given to works which are not only important in themselves, but are also representative of their field.

Apart from articles often reprinted or summarized in later books, Evans-Pritchard has devoted three volumes to the Nuer, of which this is the first. The second, a shorter one, is on kinship, the third on religion. This present volume is the most renowned.

* © Éditions Gallimard, 1968.

Through its own content, and even more, perhaps, through the influence it has exerted, it is able on its own to give the French reader a fair idea of a whole literature, one might say of a whole school. Indeed, *The Nuer*, published in 1940, and before it *The Azande* (1937), inaugurated a sociological approach to tribal society which has flourished for over a quarter of a century, mostly across the Channel, and which covers a large part of what is included under the term social anthropology. *The Nuer* provides the archetype for the theory of descent groups and of political groups; it is also, more widely, the model, long revered and still viable, for any English anthropologist from the moment he seeks to give definitive form to his research. What is more, even though Evans-Pritchard's thought is rooted mainly in the British tradition, it has been nourished by French sociology, and it was under his aegis that in the last two decades, thanks to Rodney Needham and others, a whole series of translations of the works of Mauss, Durkheim, and Hertz have seen the light of day. Knowing, too, that Evans-Pritchard writes with the elegance born of precision and clarity, one would surely think that such a book needs no preface to introduce it to the French reader.

However, an introduction has been requested from one who, having taught for four years at Oxford and having acquired a large part of his scientific training there, feels a deep admiration for the author of *The Nuer* and is honoured by his friendship. Impossible in such a case to evade the perilous honour. So without, if possible, wandering too far from the reader's general interests, we must face the problem of placing the present volume in the context of English anthropology.

The sub-title announces the book's twofold aim: on the one hand to describe the environment and the way of life it imposes, on the other to present a system of concepts and mechanisms which owe nothing to the environment, but on which is founded the 'ordered anarchy' which the author sees as the 'political system' of the Nuer. The contrast between the two approaches is so marked that at first sight one might be tempted to say that the book has two sides, the materialistic and the idealistic. Perhaps, since the reader is free to stress one side or the other, this accounts for the book's popularity among the professionals. One might even go so far as to ask whether this heterogeneity does not mark a turning-point, a conversion, in the author's intellectual journey. Indeed, it is clear that he did not begin and end the book in exactly the same state of mind. To see this, it is enough to compare the end of the Introduction and the last paragraph of the conclusion. Actually these passages are of merely technical import. The author, aware of the limitations of an investigation whose difficulties he has related, has wished to restrict his ambition by offering a 'contribution to ethnology' rather than a 'detailed sociological study'. But, by an obvious paradox, the poverty—entirely relative—of his material has led him to develop the analysis of the system of territorial and other groups, so that the conclusion first admits to 'a short incursion into sociological theory' and a little later confesses to his having tried to advance a theory that goes beyond the analysis of 'social masses and a supposed relation between these masses', an expression the precise meaning of which we shall see later.

Questioned, the author denies that his ideas evolved while he was writing *The Nuer*; he explains that his aim was to set these people squarely within their mode of subsistence, and within the framework of natural factors, before abstracting the political and 'lineage' aspects of their life. This is indeed the ethnographer's task; and it is what Mauss taught us when he insisted upon the importance of the material elements of social life, of everything that can be listed, numbered, measured, drawn. Only a naïve over-confidence—common enough today—in the methods of analysis could lead anyone to sacrifice, to one particular angle, that general framework, those strong and visible guide-ropes, which provide the analyst with a firm hold for his clumsy hands, and at the same time serve to control his wandering imagination.

It remains to draw attention to the book's admirable composition, and its internal movement. There is certainly duality in its heart, but it is very natural that the author, anxious from the first to include and then to follow up exhaustively all the natural determining factors of Nuer life, sees another sort of determining factor appearing and increasingly imposing itself. What we call the physical environment on the one hand, and human relationship on the other, in their pure state dominate respectively the beginning and the end of the book. The book is a sort of *continuum* in which the first variable fades out as the second emerges, in an intricate mesh of mutual dependence. The chapter on time and space provides the hinge. There we see juxtaposed an ecological time, dominated by the rhythm of the seasons and the 'double morphology'—to use Mauss's phrase—which results (dispersal to villages in the wet season, increasing concentration by the water-holes in the dry season), and a structural time that is (purely) social. The political system, being a system of territorial groups, is in close relation with the environment, while the lineage system has only an indirect connection with it. What weight should be given, then, to the criticism that the 'social structure' has been arbitrarily detached, as something existing in its own right, from the material aspects of social life?[1] It seems on the contrary that Evans-Pritchard has traced with great subtlety the manifold complementarity between the internal and external faces of society; relations between people, and relations between people and their surroundings.

To help us assess the place of *The Nuer* in English anthropology we are fortunate in being able to draw on a privileged witness. We shall do so as much as possible. David Pocock touches on this question in a little book, *Social Anthropology*, which appeared in 1961, and his testimony is all the more valuable in that the book was written at Oxford and that the passage that interests us certainly, in its outline, had the approval of Evans-Pritchard himself. We may recall that English social anthropology was formed under the auspices of Radcliffe-Brown, whom Evans-Pritchard was to succeed at Oxford in 1950. David Pocock has accurately summed up Radcliffe-Brown's style of anthropology, and the reader will pardon a long but indispensable quotation.

[1] E. R. Leach, *Pul Eliya, a village in Ceylon* (Cambridge University Press, 1961), p. 305: 'in practice each half of the book is autonomous and can be understood independently of the rest.'

For a generation of social anthropologists—mostly in England—the end of field-work seems to have been the search for the integrating factors in society, and this led them into circular arguments. Society is an adaptive mechanism and maintains its internal harmony as a natural organism is supposed to do. This harmony is demonstrated in the relationships between institutions and between these institutions and the general beliefs of the society; the function of the part is, then, its role in maintaining these relationships. As far as formal organisation was concerned this function was given in the description of relationships—kinship maintained the solidarity of the clan, the chief became 'a symbol of the solidarity of the tribe', the function of assemblies was to re-affirm the solidarity of those assembled. The problem came over those aspects of social life which were not immediately reducible to 'groups and relations between groups' as Durkheim had noted. But the conception of society was not widened, as it had been by Durkheim. Instead, these phenomena were explained to the extent that they could be understood as integrative factors making for the integration of groups. Religion, various forms of art, including story-telling, dances and myths, the cosmologies of primitive peoples, could be shown to express, symbolize and stress certain values which were important to the continuance of the family or tribe, and beyond that there was little to say about them. There was little to say about them because there was no language in which to say it. The business of social anthropology was the study of social structure and that was contained in the description of groups and relations between groups. Radcliffe-Brown's sociology provided no concepts, as Durkheim's had done, for the sociological consideration of these phenomena in their own right.[2]

Against the background of this functionalism *The Nuer* stands out in strong relief: there is nothing here about 'social integration'. On the contrary, in the conclusion there is a challenge to 'groups and relations between groups', short and discreet certainly, but quite categorical. We have already mentioned this, but to quote again from Evans-Pritchard: 'Social anthropology deals at present in crude concepts: tribe, clan, age-set, etc., representing social masses and a supposed relation between these masses. The science will make little progress on this low level of abstraction, if it be considered abstraction at all, and it is necessary for further

---

[2] D. F. Pocock, *Social Anthropology* (Sheed and Ward, London and New York, 1961), Newman History and Philosophy of Science Series, vol. 7, pp. 62–3.

advance to use the concepts to denote relations, defined in terms of social situations, and relations between these relations.' (Quoted in Pocock, p. 74.)

Next our guide insists on the relativities of Nuer language (Pocock, p. 74). The word *cieng*, 'house', *chez soi* ('home', in English), or 'residence', takes on a different sense *according to the context* in which it is said. So for us, if someone asks 'Where do you come from?' the answer can refer according to the context to France, Paris, the 9th *arrondissement*, the Rue Lafayette, etc. Evans-Pritchard has generalized still more widely from the perception of an element of experience as embedded in its context, whether synchronic or not, and this dates back to his earlier monograph on witchcraft among the Azande. This is perhaps his most essential contribution, and certainly the least questioned. The words used and the things or behaviour to which they refer are to be understood in their relatedness as constituting meaningful systems (Pocock, op. cit., p. 75). Thus, in passing from Radcliffe-Brown to Evans-Pritchard, we find a movement from 'function to meaning' (ibid., p. 76), and here our source stresses Evans-Pritchard's convergence with Lévi-Strauss. It might be rash to identify the two positions, and we shall have to return to this point, but that there was some sort of convergence, Pocock shows by citing a passage where it is clear that structure is not the 'social structure' of Radcliffe-Brown, but something very different, a mental reality. 'I emphasize this character of structural distance at an early stage because an understanding of it is necessary to follow the account of various social groups which we are about to describe. Once it is understood the apparent contradictions in our account will be seen to be contradictions in the structure itself, being in fact a quality of it.'

This shift 'from function to meaning', on which, as I have said, we have Evans-Pritchard's assurance that it represents at least in retrospect what he thought he had achieved, constitutes a real revolution, and it is astonishing that it was so discreetly presented. The discretion was apparently intentional, and throws light on the modesty we noted in the Introduction. What Pocock adds is important for the history of the subject in England: 'The author's refusal to make explicit the shift in emphasis had certain tactical advantages' (p. 79): no storm, no dust raised, but, with outward continuity maintained, the successful infiltration—proved by the book's influence—of the meaning that the actors give to what they do. On the other hand, there was a disadvantage: Radcliffe-Brown's organic theory was not directly challenged and ideas of equilibrium and social harmony were to continue to hold sway as explanatory principles. It was only in 1950, in his Marett Lecture, that Evans-Pritchard exploded the bomb whose fuse had been burning for at least ten years: he rejected the pretensions of social anthropology to be one of the natural sciences, he challenged positivism, and drew the logical conclusions, this time in an extreme form, of the transition from laws to structure.[3] His colleagues, who had applauded *The Nuer*, were for the most part scandalized. The rift with Radcliffe-Brown was complete.

The controversy which broke out after the Marett Lecture, in contrast with the prestige that *The Nuer* has never ceased to enjoy and the influence it has never ceased to exert in the same circles, raises a more general question concerning the book: can we identify in it a collective element and a personal one—that is to say, an element corresponding to the predominant trends of English anthropology and another which, in contrast, is the author's own, even opposed to current thought? One might then go on to attribute direct social determinants or concomitants to the 'collective' element.

It is not difficult to answer this question in general terms. Indeed, in its essence, the theory of unilineal groups and the political system was adopted, developed, and continued; in fact for twenty years this research became the central hub of English anthropology, while, in contrast, what is properly and strictly the structural aspect of *The Nuer* has never really taken root in England. This does not of course mean that there has been no borrowing at all, nor that Evans-Pritchard has had no followers.

[3] 'Social Anthropology, Past and Present' (Marett Lecture, 1950), in E. E. Evans-Pritchard, *Essays in Social Anthropology* (Faber and Faber, London, 1962), pp. 3–28.

Plausibly to distinguish between these two aspects, one should logically begin with the progeny of *The Nuer*; the non-collective aspect would thus appear as a residue. For convenience I shall proceed the other way round. It is the aspect of 'structure' that represents Evans-Pritchard's fully personal and original contribution. Taking account of what the French reader is acquainted with in this respect, there is need for a sharper focus. We saw above, following Pocock, the 'relativities of language', and more generally of meaning, in relation to the situation or context. What is characteristic of *The Nuer* is the application of the method to social groups, territorial or 'political' groups, patrilineal descent groups: I am a member of group *A* in a situation which opposes it to group *B*, but in another situation in which two first-order segments of *A* are opposed, say *A1* and *A2*, I am a member not of *A* but of *A1*, and so on for the lower-order segments. The groupings at different levels coexist all the time, but they are manifest only alternately, according to the circumstances. The permanent reality is the tendency towards fission and fusion. In particular there is no unilineal group which could properly be called 'corporate', through existing permanently as a *persona moralis* holding goods in common.

The insight is structural, but a problem is implied in the term 'opposition' which I have just used: in concrete situations the 'opposition' is usually a matter of fact, a conflict, as in the blood feud. Evans-Pritchard starts from 'groups and relations between groups' to relativize the groups and show that their very existence arises out of their relations. But it is clear that underlying these factual oppositions the author sees conceptual oppositions, oppositions in the structuralist's sense. A Nuer 'identifies himself with a local community and, in doing so, separates himself from other communities of the same kind'. Referring to the quotation above, where it is said that 'contradiction' has to be seen as a quality of the structure itself, we see that the author has well and truly discovered structuralism on his own account without direct borrowing—as was the case in other quarters—from contemporary developments in neighbouring disciplines (phonology, Gestalt theory). It is all the more remarkable that the successors of *The Nuer* show that here Evans-Pritchard was not expressing the main current of British social anthropology. On the contrary, his profound insight remained largely uncomprehended, 'structures' for him being contrasted very precisely with the 'laws' of social life, the discovery of which continued to attract most of his colleagues. However, we shall see later that it is possible to detect in our author, at a submerged level, an orientation similar to that of his future opponents.

Compared with what Mauss taught us in Paris until 1939, *The Nuer* presents a whole series of differentiations. Where Mauss was still speaking of 'politico-domestic organization', Evans-Pritchard distinguishes between distinct 'systems' and in particular between territorial and political groups on the one hand, and descent groups (clans and lineages) on the other. It is in the political sphere that the author of *The Nuer* has most clearly expressed his school and period. In this field, the work seeks to extend the category of politics to societies which have no differentiated political institutions (not even a king): in a given territory there is order without rule; there is, so to speak, 'ordered anarchy'. In retrospect *The Nuer* appears as the starting-point of a vast literature on the political aspect of tribal societies. This literature extends far beyond its source, and it does so in two streams: on the one hand political analysis is extended further and further by means of a widening definition of 'the political'; on the other, this particular analysis tends to achieve an increasingly autonomous status in relation to the general framework of social anthropology. What Evans-Pritchard treated as no more than one sub-system among others of the global social system now seems, among certain recent authors, to have become a specialization on its own, a 'political anthropology' which tends to dispense with the global society. Though no doubt it would be wrong to see in *The Nuer* all these developments in embryo, yet it is fair, having regard to the historical significance of *The Nuer*, to inquire into the meaning and value of this movement as a whole.

Here as elsewhere, there is room for studies of a fundamental kind and also for more superficial ones. To assess the ultimate value of a particular approach in social anthropology, we can ask how far it works towards transcending the obvious differences between the so-called 'primitive' societies, and those more complex ones which can be called 'traditional', on the one hand, and the modern type of society on the other. This would be very much in the spirit of our author himself[4] and of Mauss's emphasis in 1897:[5] it is not enough to adopt modern or western categories, even with modifications; rather the modes of thought of the two universes must be subsumed under categories that fit them both. In this instance, the problem appears indirectly in the difficulty of defining the theoretical field, in the impossibility (to this day) of finding agreement among specialists on the definition of political phenomena in general. The advocates of this approach postulate that since *we* have politics, all societies must have them. It might be better to seek equivalences between what we place in certain categories and what elsewhere is either placed in different categories or has only an uncategorized form. This is what is done, to a large extent, in *The Nuer*, where the political system is defined as the system of territorial groups, that is, of groups named by the Nuer whose territorial character the author has chosen to emphasize. In other words, there is no guarantee that, just because modern societies clearly distinguish the political dimension, it makes a good comparative dimension. On the face of it, it would even seem unlikely that it could do so, since many types of society do not make this distinction. I myself would go as far as to maintain that this approach has already been falsified in experience, but that is an extreme view which many would reject.

How then are we to explain the success of the political approach with so many anthropologists? I would risk the hypothesis that it is grounded in the mentality of the anthropologist as a modern man. This should not be taken too much amiss, because in this discipline this kind of collective subjectivity cannot and should not be left out. It is not a matter of the psychology of good intentions, even if these do play some part, in so far as one chooses

---

[4] See his *Essays in Social Anthropology*, p. 22; *Social Anthropology* (Cohen and West, London, 1951).

[5] 'La religion et les origines du droit pénal' in *Revue de l'histoire des religions*, 34 (1896), 269–95 and 35 (1897), 31–60 (for example p. 37: 'He does not define…, he classes according to the common notions . . .').

to emphasize what reduces the distance between us and the societies and peoples that we most often study, rather than to concentrate on what, at first sight at least, seems to accentuate the distance—magic, for example. It is rather the fact that we moderns have a certain idea of man deeply entrenched in us, which we tend to preserve and apply on all occasions. The political approach fits into this habit of thought, while other approaches would challenge its validity. This is the explanation that I propose, at my own risk and peril.

In brief: the comparison of modern with non-modern societies turns on two contrary configurations of value. For us, man is an individual, the individual subject as an end in himself; for non-modern societies, it is to a large extent the society, the collective man, to which the individual is referred. I call the first way of thinking individualism, the second 'holism'. The movement, the transition, which the anthropologists must make from one to the other is not easy. Just as the Anglo-Saxons in particular have reproached Durkheim for having reified the social life of individuals in speaking of 'collective consciousness', so they may be reproached in return for treating this profound difference in values as if it did not exist, and for seeing everywhere individuals in the modern sense of the term, people imbued with the values of liberty and equality and ignoring or devaluing those of order, interdependence, subordination, and hierarchy, or, as is predominantly our way, valuing tradition less than 'rationality'.

Now in considering modern political philosophy or political science, one is struck by a feature which is not usually noticed because it is so completely taken for granted. Certainly, the political field is defined by specific features. Thus Max Weber's definition of the State (monopoly of *legitimate power* in a defined *territory*) is readily taken as a base in English anthropology, at the outset at least. But the political point of view corresponds as well to something different, that is, to considering not just the social facts that present distinctive political features, but the *total society from the point of view of the individual*. This is very clear in Hobbes, Rousseau, and Hegel.[6] On a closer view the latter

[6] Cf. 'The modern conception of the Individual' in *Contributions to Indian Sociology*, 8 (1965), 13–61, especially pp. 38 ff., 57 ff.

approach is usually implicit when the former is acknowledged, and it becomes explicit in the most recent anthropology. It is as if for the modern individual the total social field were no longer conceivable except within the category of politics. (Of course this holds true only if one excludes sociology, or rather a certain kind of sociology, but it largely holds good for everyday thinking.)

If this is so, then politics will naturally attract the modern, and especially the Anglo-Saxon, anthropologist, unless he is prepared to take up the challenge that non-modern societies offer to his own consciousness and to his cherished individualism. In the political or even the economic dimension, whatever other difficulties you may encounter, you will have before you, no matter where you look, individuals 'maximizing' their advantages and 'manipulating' situations within the latitude permitted by traditional institutions. Even if you live in great physical discomfort in the Antipodes, you need not give up your intellectual comfort. Once intensive field-work had become the established technique, the anthropologists of the preceding period were mocked for being satisfied with armchair research. One might say of our colleagues that the more they emphasize the political dimension, the less they stir out of their metaphysical armchair, the more comfortably they remain encased within the fallacy that dominated the nineteenth century, once moral and political individualism had come to be confused with a description of social life.

This is a far cry from the work of Evans-Pritchard, who would himself probably reject a large part of the work that ensued, and of course it would be wrong to lay responsibility on him for what has followed. But it is still true that *The Nuer* opened the way for a trend in contemporary anthropology, a trend which has moved far from its model, and which has proved to be in my view, inadequate, influential as it is. This raises another question: how did *The Nuer* come to be exploited in this way? Retrospectively, it is the very differentiation of a 'political system' that seems to have given impetus to the trend. What was for Evans-Pritchard the beginning of a more precise and systematic analysis than could be provided by the approach through 'groups and

relations between groups' afforded by its very character an
opportunity for modern researchers to leave their own pre-
suppositions unquestioned. To venture another opinion which,
this time, I think I can justify elsewhere (*Introduction à deux théories
d'anthropologie sociale*, Paris, 1971, pp. 70–3) there is certainly
room for distinguishing a territorial dimension or a territorial
attribute in the case of certain groups, but one could, I believe,
without taking anything essential away from the real content of
The Nuer, avoid treating this attribute as a substance, the principle
of a sub-system in its own right. In this case, there would be only
one system instead of two: a system of unilineal descent groups
without a territorial dimension.[7]

   As far as descent groups are concerned, the literary progeny of
The Nuer seem to have taken a different turn. We saw our author
occupied, in effect, in relativizing these groups. Now, immediately
afterwards, the opposite tendency to reify or solidify, in the
manner of Radcliffe-Brown, was vigorously asserted by Meyer
Fortes. This is not all; one sees in Meyer Fortes's work another, and
original, development in the analysis of the relation between
kinship on the one hand, and unilineal descent groups on the other.
To return to Radcliffe-Brown. He knows of course that there are
unilineal descent groups, clans or lineages. For him these groups
form an integral part of the kinship system. With Evans-Pritchard
the lineage system is emancipated from the more inclusive
system of kinship, and organizes itself independently: this
follows the ideas of the Nuer themselves, who distinguish
kinship in the family (*gol*), cognatic kinship (*mar*), which they use
to refer to all of an individual's close relations of kinship external
to the family, and finally distant agnation (*buth*) which applies
only between persons of different lineages. Does this justify
making the system of descent groups appear not as a sub-system
within the global system of kinship, but as a distinct system from

   [7] The reverse solution reducing unilineality and segmentation to an expression
of the political order has been proposed, it seems, by M. G. Smith ('On Segmentary Lineage Systems'), *Journal of the Royal Anthropological Institute*, 86. 2 (1956),
39–80, particularly pp. 64 ff.). Smith writes, for example: 'The lineage is *govern-
mental* and ideological *kinship*' (p. 71, my italics).

that of individual kinship relationships, which appear as centred upon a hypothetical and abstract subject, or, as we say, upon an Ego? At the next stage, Meyer Fortes makes the system of descent groups superordinate to that of individual kinship relations. We are told that descent 'links' the external, that is political and legal, aspect . . . and the internal or domestic aspect [in which] kinship carries maximum weight'.[8] In short, the system of descent groups, which began by being emancipated from the over-all system of kinship, is now presented as hierarchically superior to the network of individual kinship relationships. This is not the place to discuss this methodologically peculiar thesis. But its metaphysical implication (so to speak) is worth indicating: where there was at the outset a universe of relationships (individual relationships centred on a subject—for Evans-Pritchard, group relations which brought successively into existence groups of one level of segmentation or another), now there are collective entities, solid and 'corporate' unilineal groups, which have superseded the relationships. The relativistic and relational features of *The Nuer* analysis are dismissed. Radcliffe-Brown's point of view of 'groups and relations between groups' reasserts itself, even succeeds, I would say, in reducing to a minor position the domain in which relationship (at least after Morgan's time) traditionally reigned, that of kinship in the ordinary sense of the term. Moreover, since the 'corporate groups' of which this is the apotheosis are conceived basically as collective individuals, we are led back to the same trend that we encountered on the level of politics: the anthropologist develops every possible refinement, but he does not leave his personal metaphysical moorings, nor does he abandon his own society's conception of mankind.

We have seen that where descent groups are concerned, even if he has opened a path industriously exploited by others, Evans-Pritchard's own inspiration, his structural and relational analysis has in England met with remarkable opposition or misunderstanding. It remains for me to justify briefly the statement that

[8] Meyer Fortes, 'The Structure of Unilineal Descent Groups', *American Anthropologist*, 55 (1953), 30.

this collective trend, opposed to the author's own original achievement, is also to be found at a submerged level in *The Nuer* itself. Let us examine his starting-point. What is a system? It is a set of relationships between groups (p. 264). Structure, defined at first minimally as what is enduring in society, is in effect little different from system: it is said that a whole set of personal relations is not a structure, because since no groups intervene, it has no permanence. We are bound to see a paradox in this double accent on groups and on relationships. Kinship relations, which also transcend the ephemeral individual, are not accorded the same dignity as the relations between groups seen as a system of groups. It is true that in some sense this takes us back to the beginning again, and that the author's whole effort has been to destroy the substantive character of these groups and to show their 'structural relativity'. It may well have been natural to start from what was central to Radcliffe-Brown, but despite the tactical advantages mentioned by David Pocock, this will hardly do. For the decision itself to isolate the political (or territorial) dimension too evidently corresponds to Radcliffe-Brown's substantivist *a priori*. Yet if there is on this point a radical ambiguity in *The Nuer*, its progeny have removed it, as we have seen. Henceforth it is clear, for me at least, that the truly structural perspective is antithetical to the over-valuation of the political. Inversely, the pride of place usually granted to politics is due to the reintroduction, whether surreptitious or blatant, but always naïve, of the modern individual into a subject where this very book, like our other master-books, has shown us the opposite path, that of relationships.

15

Language, Ethnicity, and Population

EDWIN ARDENER

I

IT may seem difficult at first sight to understand exactly the relationship between the three terms 'language', 'ethnicity', and 'population' in a conference of the African Studies Association[1] at which the focus is primarily on the third. We are, of course, used to some doubts about the precise application of the first two in African circumstances. For example, as far as 'language' is concerned, even a simple list (let alone a classification) of linguistic units leads to hoary problems of 'language' versus 'dialect', 'cluster', 'family', and the like, or to discussions of criteria of 'genetic' or 'typological' or other sorts. With 'tribe' or 'ethnicity', discussion turns on the overlap with 'race', 'culture', or 'language' itself (however ultimately delineated). We are less used to doubts about the third term—'population'. As is common in human studies, we confuse different ideas. Thus we imagine that population is a reality, 'infrastructural' to the other two. Population measures have all the earmarks of objectivity and, for many, the reality of the term 'population' is itself an expression of the various indices used by demographers: birth, death, fertility, and nuptiality rates, and enumerations and samplings of various kinds.

Yet what is a population? What is, in each case, the unit to which the demographic measures relate? In a study of the Bakweri of Cameroon, some years ago, for example, a central

[1] This was the introductory paper to the Session on 'Language, Ethnicity and Population' (Co-Chairman, Dr. D. Dalby) at the Birmingham Conference on 'The Population Factor in African Studies' of the African Studies Association, 11–14 September 1972. It was first published in the *Journal of the Anthropological Society of Oxford*, 3. 3 (1972), 125–32.

question began to emerge. Were the Bakweri a declining population? Now the Bakweri tend to think that those of their number
who live in modern centres are not quite 'real' Bakweri. The
Bakweri picture of themselves made a clear distinction between
those inside their village fences (leading a 'Bakweri way of life'
as it were) and those outside them. The modern centres (*par
excellence* outside the fence) were ethnically mixed, cosmopolitan,
un-Bakweri. There was a sense then in which if the rural heartland was losing population the Bakweri were also declining *in
toto*. The definition of the target population as rural, in an area
notorious for a vast 'multitribal' migration to an adjacent planta-
tion industry, moved the question of Bakweri 'decline' out of
the realm of demography into that of ideas. For the rural population was not, as it stood, a self-perpetuating population. Demographically it was marked by 'distorted' age-structures and sex
ratios—and probably fertility patterns too.[2]

   This did not prevent us from usefully wearing out a demographic armoury on the mensurational aspects of the problem,
and learning a great deal of value thereby. The most valuable
lesson was that in the discussion of the dynamics of a population,
your unit—'the population'—is not merely subject to a statistical
determination on the part of the observer, it is dependent on the
subjective definition of that population by the human beings
concerned. Over time, therefore, population series are continually
affected by changing definitions on the part of both the measurers
and the measured. This factor has received less general emphasis
than it deserves, in part because of the dogmatic, even ideological,
definitions of populations that accompanied the development of
the nineteeth- and twentieth-century nation states.

II

In Africa, the assumption that ethnicities were entities of the type
that would yield a 'population' has always been too easily made,
in both linguistic and biological studies. For that reason the figures
for 'tribal' membership and for language-speakers are really even

----

[2] See Ardener (1962, 1972*a*).

more difficult to evaluate than we usually suspect them to be. The extreme north-west corner of the Bantu-speaking area (I adhere for the present to the boundary according to Guthrie, 1948) illustrates this problem with remarkable clarity. We are presented with some two dozen entities, usually called 'tribes', but which also form the elements of the linguistic classification of the area. These entitites are marked by very small individual populations—from 300 or less to about 30,000, with 6,000 or so being the mode. They are surrounded by 'groups' of quite another scale—Efik, Ekoi, Bamileke, and so on. What are we to make of discrepancies of this sort? We are in a difficult area of analysis, which belongs to a field of wider interest than our more limited regional concerns. The classification of human groups will exhibit features common to the classifying of all phenomena. Some part of the question of the particular scale of the north-west Bantu ethnicities lies in the criteria of the Bantu classification itself—determined, if you like, in armchairs in Europe.

First, then, the scholars. It is easy to start with the recognition that the tribal and linguistic classifications were not independently arrived at. Even so, in what sense is it true that the speakers of Nigerian 'Ekoid' languages are more linguistically homogeneous than the West Cameroon group of Bantu speakers? We may answer this in different ways, but we should note that any scholarly or scientific classification occupies a specific taxonomic space. Its confines are to some extent coercive and they must be taken into account when problems of relationship within the space are being examined.

The conventional units which make up the taxonomy of the Bantu languages are defined, on the face of it, by fairly clearly determinable criteria (e.g. Guthrie, 1948). The north-west Bantu entitites belong, of course, to this taxonomy. If these criteria are strictly applied we shall not be surprised that the taxonomic space of the Bantu classification does not correspond with that independently set up for the West African languages, since the latter notoriously depends on a much less rigorous set (even a mixture) of criteria, and belongs on a different plane of analysis from that which is feasible in Bantu studies (Ardener, 1971, pp. 218–19).

Secondly, the 'people'. We have to consider here the nature of self-classification or self-identification. For the 'people' themselves play the part of theoreticians in this field. Here we touch on the close match of the classifying process with the workings of language itself. It has frequently been noted that the Bantu languages have 'overdetermined', as it were, precisely along the axis of classification. The smallest differentiation of humanity can immediately be linguistically labelled, with a *ba*-form, homologous with that used for the largest ethnic entities. The Bantu taxonomy is continuously self-amending.

In the interaction between insider and outsider, the Bantuizing tendency has aided the differentiation and discrimination of units. The multiplication of 'separate' Bantu languages was even an overt aim of nineteenth-century scholars. For the north-west Bantu area, it is a fact that many of the divisions now in existence lean on classifications in which the scholar-turned-administrator or the administrator-turned-scholar (German, British, and French) played a not insignificant part. There was a feedback to the people, so easily achieved from interpreters and others, to confuse the matter further. After all, one of the more inaccessible 'populations' of the zone is quite content to be called, and to call itself, 'Ngolo-Batanga', a hyphenated form which owes its existence to classifying for the convenience of scholars and foreigners[3]—thus joining the select but expanding company in which are found 'Anglo-Saxon', 'Serbo-Croat', and some others.

The Bantuizing tendency itself belongs to that well-documented domain of structure in which language and reality are intermingled. It is also something of a special case of the more complex phenomenon of 'taxonomic scale'. This is underlined when we consider the neighbouring Ekoi case. The intervention of British-style, ethnically minded, Native Administrations had given by the 1930s a local reality to general classifications whose autochthonous basis was originally limited and contradictory. The search for one Ekoi ethnicity, rather than a series of ethnicities, must be brought into relation with the particular scale of the main elements of the southern-Nigerian ethnic space. Dominated as

---

[3] To distinguish them from the distant Batanga of the South Cameroon coast.

it was by the entities labelled Yoruba, Edo, Ibo, and Ibibio, it became virtually determined that 'Ekoi' would be set up homologously with these—despite the possibility of establishing several Ekoi 'tribes' (Talbot, 1926; Crabb, 1965).

The effect of two essentially different taxonomic spaces in this zone upon tribal divisions can be seen in the usage of the German and British administrations. The former, 'Bantuizing' in tendency, used three 'ethnic' names to divide up the relatively small Ekoi-speaking area which overlapped into its territory. On the other hand, when West Cameroon came under British administrators, some of the latter (e.g. Talbot), being more at home on the Nigerian scale, classified the whole 'Bantu' group together, for population purposes. This did not become general, but the ethnic 'diversity' of the area always remained a source of classifying malaise to them.

In the colonial period, then, the scale of the units in the prevailing ethnic taxonomies was far from uniform. The accepted scale was, in a sense, a result of arbitration between the foreigners and the politically important groups. The Yoruba and Bini kingdoms set the scale for southern Nigeria, but this was itself set in some ways by the imperial scale of the Fulani-conquered north. It should not be forgotten that the still unsuccessful search for Ekoi unity was preceded by the Ibo case, the successful outcome of whose progress from label to population was not self-evident. It is by continuous series of such contracts and oppositions (to which, I repeat, both foreigners and Africans contributed) that many (and in principle all) populations have defined themselves.

Much of the discomfort of West Cameroonians in the Federation of Nigeria derived from the discrepancy between their 'Bantuizing' taxonomic scale and that of the Federation as a whole. This led to the paradox, noted at the time, of the growth of a new 'Kamerun' ethnicity of Nigerian scale, covering this 'artificial' political unit—which actually, despite its internal diversity, was, while the taxonomic constraints existed, one of the most homogeneous-looking of the units of the Federation. The Bantuizing scale of the new Cameroon state clearly suits

West Cameroon better at present. The West Cameroon area nevertheless still preserves elements of the newer and broader 'ethnicity' generated by the Nigerian phase of their experience (Ardener, 1967, pp. 293–9).

The position of minority peoples in a zone of 'large populations' is thus more complicated than it seems. I wish to bring out of the discussion so far these points, as they relate to the African situation. I think they have more general validity.

(1) The ethnic classification is a reflex of self-identification.

(2) Onomastic (or naming) propensities are closely involved in this, and thus have more than a purely linguistic interest.

(3) Identification by others is an important feature in the establishment of self-identification.

(4) The taxonomic space in which self-identification occurs is of overriding importance.

(5) The effect of foreign classification, 'scientific' and lay, is far from nautral in the establishment of such a space.

III

'Tribes are not permanent crystalline structures, belonging to one "stage" of historical or social development . . . the process of self-classification never ceases.'[4] There is a true sense in which the human populations ascribed to some of these entities do not therefore represent demographic units with purely demographic pasts or futures.

Take an entity such as the Kole, one of the labelled units on the border of the Bantu and Efik linguistic domains. This was ascribed a population in 1953 of hundreds. The Kole, or some of them, speak a dialect of Duala, and are traditionally offshoots of the latter people, who live some 100 miles down the coast. Something corresponding to the Kole entity has been attested for 130 years, and on some interpretations of the evidence it could be 200, even 300 years old.[5] This small population always seems to be on the brink of extinction. What is meant by the demo-

---

4 Ardener (1967), p. 298.
5 Under the name of 'Romby'—Ardener (1968, 1972*b*).

graphic continuity of populations of this sort? Do we assume they are all the rump remnants of larger groups in the past? For various reasons, the evidence for ethno-linguistic continuity on this coast tends to suggest the opposite—that we are dealing with populations bumping along in exiguous numbers over fifty or a hundred or even several hundred years. With populations of millions, extrapolations back and forward in time using demographic indices may not generate truth, but they contain plausibility. With small hunting and gathering bands an ecological balance is at least a hypothesis (although Douglas, 1966, has called it into question). The populations of the type to which I refer are not at this elementary technological level. In the Kole case, it may well be that the whole dynamic of the 'population' is linguistic or socio-linguistic.

The Kole environmental interest is a border interest—between the Efik and Duala trading zones. The 'Kole' coast probably always had a mixed population. Kole may have always used a trading dialect, whose structure may reflect several neighbouring Bantu languages. Kole as identifiable people under that label were probably those members of the commercial group who maintained some connections with the Duala and perhaps with the intervening Isubu. The category Kole may have been filled according to different criteria at different times. Perhaps sometimes, the Kole were mostly Efik. Perhaps sometimes the Kole speech was learnt by all in the zone. Perhaps sometimes it was spoken by nobody of social importance. In all these coastal areas the expansion and contraction of slave or client communities, and their relationship to their masters and hosts, must also be borne in mind. In a case like this the dynamics of a 'population' with a certain label over the centuries are not the dynamics of cohorts, and of fertility or mortality rates. They are the dynamics of an economic, social, and linguistic situation.

Who, or what, however, determines the preservation of the classification itself? We can easily hypothesize a situation in which everyone can point to a Kole, but no one calls himself Kole. Labels of this sort are fixed to what may be termed 'hollow categories'. In the actual case, the Efik no doubt maintained the category of 'border coastal Bantu people' without much concern for the exact constituents of the category. The Bantu-speaking Duala, Isubu, and others might equally maintain the category of 'those like us, nearest the Efik'. I suspect that the Kole were in part a hollow category, like this. They were fixed as an 'ethnic group' in the British administrative system. No wonder many were puzzled by the tiny number of 'linguistic' Kole, among a welter of Efik and other migrants. No wonder too that linguistic Kole itself was so hard to pin down, a language of aberrant idiolects. Perhaps it had never been any different?

In order to summarize the population characteristics of a hollow category we may express the matter so: since the category is filled according to non-demographic criteria the population's survival or extinction, growth or decline, age-structure or fertility, are not determined in demographic space.

A close congener of the hollow category is the entity maintained by continuous replenishment from a home area. Thus the ethnic map of Cameroon contains stable, growing, or declining concentrations of Ibo, Bamileke, Hausa (and the like), which are demographically not necessarily self-perpetuating. This type of unit is familiar now in Africa, as well as in most of the urbanized world. Such concentrations were, however, also known in the past. Nomadic groups such as the Fulani, or economically defined groups such as the Aro among the Ibo, and others elsewhere shared some of the features of such continuously concentrated but demographically unstable groups.

Their close connection with hollow categories lies in their tendency to *become* hollow. Thus the supposed Bali settlers on the Cameroon Plateau are now, in their main settlement, an entity which under close examination turns out to look like a representative sample of all of their neighbours. Their present dominant language is a kind of average Cameroon Bantoid. In northern Cameroon the category 'Fulbe' has become 'hollow' in this way. In various places and times the categories 'Norman', 'Pict', 'Jew', 'Gipsy', 'Irishman', and many others may have become, or be becoming hollow—a mere smile surviving from the vanished Cheshire cat. Thus not only can a hollow category become a 'population'; a population can become a hollow category. Indeed, this process need never stop: the category may become a population again. Certain peculiar features in the supposed continuity of certain ethnic, even 'national', groups may well be elucidated in this way.

It is essential to make this effort to separate the concept of 'population' from those of language and ethnicity. In the past the separation has been urged in biological terms. A biological population, it has been pointed out, may not coincide in its history with the affiliations of its language or of its culture. I am not repeating this truth, or truism. For we are not able to be so confident about the concept of a biological population. We are concerned with continuities whose processes are only in part biological. Fulbe, Jews, and (as we know) Britons are created by definition as much as by procreation. We are dealing with 'structures' of a clearly recognized type whose transformations may be documented in statistics, but whose dynamics lie outside the field of statistical extrapolation. I have made this assertion of principle without the important modifications and qualifications in order to highlight its importance in African studies. We may, in the West or in the global context, avert our eyes from these contradictions. Our largest units of human classification have reached such a scale that population dynamics now form the tail that violently wags the human dog. This is not so even with smaller Western units or sub-units. It was rarely so with African ethnicities.

IV

I have kept these remarks brief. I have not alluded more than sketchily to the topographical, ecological, economic, and political elements which enter into identification and self-identification. Ultimately, among the things that society 'is' or 'is like', it 'is' or 'is like' identification. The entities set up may be based upon divisions in empirical reality, or may be set up on reality by the structuring processes of the human mind in society. In such statements 'reality' is, however, frequently only a compendium of 'positivistic' measures and approximations. We experience the structures themselves as reality: they generate events, not merely our experience of events.[6] Anthropologists would argue, I think, that this process is analogous to language, possibly subsuming language, rather than a process *of* language. But all agree that language acquires a position of critical empirical importance in its study.

For population studies, the most impressive advances have occurred in the study of entities of a macrodemographic scale to which statistical and mensurational indices are central. Nevertheless, *changes* in these indices come back to the differentiation of entities ('minorities', 'classes', 'sects', 'ideologies') within the mass population which redefine, or restructure population 'behaviour' and thus, the population. This differentiating process is of exactly the kind which in our more parochial field of interest is associated with the waxing and waning of 'ethnicities' and the like. I have used only two or three elementary formulations ('the taxonomic space', 'taxonomic scale', and 'hollow category'), but the basic approach is a small part of recent movements which restore scientific validity to the mentalistic framework within which human societies shape and create events. Thereby, population studies themselves may be given back some of the intuitive life and colour that their subject matter deserves.

REFERENCES

ARDENER, E., 1962, *Divorce and Fertility: an African Study* (Oxford University Press, London).

—— 1967, 'The Nature of the Reunification of Cameroon', in A. Hazlewood (ed.), *African Integration and Disintegration* (Oxford University Press and Chatham House, London).

—— 1968, 'Documentary and Linguistic Evidence for the Rise of the Trading Polities between Rio del Rey and Cameroon 1500–1650', in I. M. Lewis (ed.), *History and Social Anthropology* (Tavistock, London).

—— 1971, 'Social Anthropology and the Historicity of Historical Linguistics', in *ASA* 10 (Tavistock, London).

—— 1972a, 'Belief and the Problem of Women', in J. La Fontaine (ed.), *The Interpretation of Ritual* (Tavistock, London).

[6] For a full-scale treatment of this problem see Ardener (1974).

—— 1972*b*, Introduction and Commentary to J. Clarke, *Specimens of Dialects* (Berwick-on-Tweed, 1848, reprinted, Gregg Press).

—— 1974, 'Population and "Tribal Communities"', Wolfson Lecture delivered at Oxford on 6 Feb. 1973, to be published 1974.

CRABB, D. W., 1965, *Ekoid Bantu Languages of Ogoja* (Cambridge University Press, Cambridge).

DOUGLAS, M., 1966, 'Population Control in Primitive Groups', *BJS*, 17, p. 3.

GUTHRIE, M., 1948, *The Classification of the Bantu Languages* (London).

TALBOT, P. A., 1926, *The Peoples of Southern Nigeria* (Oxford University Press, Oxford).

16

Charles Staniland Wake, 1835–1910
A Biographical Record

RODNEY NEEDHAM

> The iniquity of oblivion blindely scattereth her poppy,
> and deals with the memory of men without distinction
> to merit of perpetuity.
>
> SIR THOMAS BROWNE

I

THE subject of these notes has two immediate connections with Professor Sir Edward Evans-Pritchard, to whom the paper is dedicated.

The first is circumstantial, but points to something more constant and characteristic. Some fifteen or more years ago I happened to find in a second-hand bookshop in the Turl, at Oxford, a copy of Wake's *The Development of Marriage and Kinship* (1889). Much impressed by its analytical tenor, and concordantly put out that I had never heard of the author in my anthropological education, I searched in the usual places for information on Wake himself, and also for published assessments of the value of his monograph, but came upon nothing. Imagining therefore that I had made something of a discovery, I reported my find to Evans-Pritchard. He knew the book (had bought it years earlier in the same bookshop), and had long forestalled me in my opinion of it.[1]

The other connection resides in the historical nature of the investigation that is reported here, namely in the intention to

[1] It was this coincidence of judgement which led eventually, with Professor Evans-Pritchard's encouragement, to the production of a new edition (Wake (1967)).

establish—with no care in the first place other than to discover simply what had happened in the past—the facts of Wake's life. Evans-Pritchard had his undergraduate training in history, he has made distinguished contributions to the history of the Sanusiya order among the Bedouin tribes of Cyrenaica (1949) and of the Zande kingdom (1971), and he has constantly adjured his colleagues to take due advantage of the examples and general practice of historians (1962, ch. 3). It is appropriate, therefore, that the present article—minor and inconclusive though it is— should respond to so dominant an interest on his part.

Wake's own claim to this much attention is, to begin with, that history has not so far accorded it to him, in spite of the quality of the monograph that occasioned his professional revival, and in spite of the talents that he amply displayed in some seventy-five other publications (bibliography in Wake, 1967, pp. xliii–xlvii).[2] Indeed, a prime occasion for compiling some record of his life is that during his lifetime he was so much neglected by those who, on scholarly grounds at any rate, might well have granted him their respect (Needham, in Hocart, 1970, pp. xciv–xcv).[3] Moreover, his intrinsic merits aside, he was closely implicated with many better-known persons in the establishment of anthropology, during the latter decades of the nineteenth century, and their renown reflects some historical importance on him also.[4]

The only biographical account of Wake so far published consists of the four pages that form part of the editor's introduction to the reissue of *The Development of Marriage and Kinship* (Wake, 1967, pp. xviii–xxii). The present record includes what is published in that place, adds numerous particulars, and specifies in greater detail the sources of the information. It comprises, for

[2] See also below, Appendix A, for other titles and particulars since collected.

[3] Although Wake was a member of the legal profession, as were such other anthropological predecessors as Bachofen, Maine, McLennan, Morgan, and Kohler, he was not a gentlemanly lawyer: he was a solicitor. It may be that this social factor was one reason that he was not better recognized by his contemporaries. One can quite easily imagine that snobbery had something to do with Lord Avebury's glaring failure, in an 'Answer to Critics' ,to make any response to Wake's telling criticisms of his arguments about the evolution of marriage (see Needham, in Wake (1967), p. vi).

[4] See, in this connection, Burrow's excellent studies of Victorian social theory (1963; 1966).

whatever value may eventually be found therein, every significant fact that I have so far[5] been able to discover about Wake's life.

This is a biographical record in two senses: it is a record of a biographical investigation, and also a record of the biographical facts thus uncovered. The course of the investigation will itself be instructive, I think, in showing how many obstacles and dead ends are to be met with in reconstructing the life of a man who published so much over a period of forty-seven years, was active at a time when the doings of the intellectual class in Britain were in general so abundantly documented, and died so recently as the end of the first decade of this century. The account should also be helpful in providing some practical hints, to those who (like myself) are not much experienced in such ventures, about how to undertake an inquiry of this kind.

Since the sources of information are so various, and those who helped me are so numerous, references and acknowledgements are for the most part inserted directly at the pertinent places in the text. I wish to express my special indebtedness, however, to the following individuals who have contributed most signally to our knowledge of Wake's life: Mr. George H. Davis, Chicago; Mr. R. F. Drewery, D.P.A., F.L.A., Chief Librarian, Reference and Local History Library, Kingston upon Hull; Mr. Maurice English, formerly of The University of Chicago Press; Mrs. Norah K. M. Gurney, Archivist, Borthwick Institute of Historical Research, University of York; Miss Margaret E. Kenna; the Revd. Michael D. B. Long, Elloughton, Brough, Yorkshire; the late Mr. Charles Sanderson, Elloughton, Yorkshire; and Mr. E. Leland Webber, Director, Chicago Natural History Museum.

II

Charles Staniland Wake is not listed in any volume of the *Dictionary of National Biography* or in British, American, and Continental encyclopedias or other standard works of reference. So far as has been discovered, only the *American Anthropologist* (12 (1910), 343–4) published an obituary notice. This estimation,

[5] November 1971.

evidently written by Frederick Starr (editor of the *American Antiquarian*, to which Wake had made many contributions), reported that Wake, although 'well known and greatly respected by a large circle of neighbors and friends', had been 'a man of unusually retiring and unassuming character' who 'rarely figured conspicuously in public'. Certainly, he has since then proved an exceedingly elusive character.

In attempting to find out something about him, I began by placing a request in the 'Information, Please' columns of *The Times Literary Supplement* (11 June 1964, p. 516), asking for any information about Wake's life. This brought no response, but in Chicago Mr. George H. Davis found for me (at the kind instance of Mr. Maurice English) a list of Wake's addresses, as given in the annual issues of the *Lakeside Directory*, and also an entry on Wake in *Who's Who in America* (Chicago: A. N. Marquis & Co., 1910), vi. 1992.[6] This entry ran as follows:

Wake, Charles Staniland, anthropologist; *b.* Kingston-upon-Hull, Eng., Mar. 22, 1835; ed. Hull Coll., Eng. With Field Mus. of Natural History, Chicago, since 1895. Ex-dir. Anthrop. Inst. of Great Britain and Ireland; mem. gen. com. British Assn. Adv. Sci.; corr. mem. Brooklyn Ethical Soc.; asso. Soc. for Psychical Research, Eng. *Author*: Chapters on Man, 1862; The Evolution of Morality (2 vols.), 1878; The Origin and Significance of the Great Pyramid, 1882; Serpent Worship, and other Essays, 1888; The Development of Marriage and Kinship, 1889; Vortex Philosophy, or the Geometry of Science, 1907; also System of Color and Musical-Tone Relations. Editor of Memoirs of the Congress of Anthropology, Chicago, 1893-4. Contr. on anthrop., sociol. and philos. subjects. *Address*: 5603 Washington Av., Chicago.

These details corroborated the date of Wake's birth, as given in the *American Anthropologist* obituary, but otherwise were not very helpful. Notably, the entry included no information on the subject's parentage (though this was standard in other entries) or on any marriage that he might have contracted.

The Chicago Natural History Museum, formerly the Field Museum of Natural History, confirmed that Wake had been employed there (though there was a discrepancy, as will be seen,

[6] Reprinted in *Who was Who in America* (Chicago, 1960), vol. i (1897-1942).

about the year of his appointment), and said the only further information they had was that Wake had been a 'widower with a daughter in England' (Mr. E. Leland Webber; 29 Oct. 1965). The Royal Anthropological Institute, with which Wake had been prominently associated and which had published a number of his articles, reported that it had nothing at all on him in either the archives or the manuscript collections (Miss B. J. Kirkpatrick; 27 July 1965). The Society for Physical Research supplied dates of Wake's associate membership and a Chicago address, but had no further information (Sir George Joy; 3 Aug. 1965). It subsequently turned out that Wake had been an associate member of the American branch of the Society, not of that in London, but in any case there was still no information to be had other than two of his addresses in Chicago (Mrs. Pauline Osborn; 6 Jan. 1966). The Brooklyn Ethical Association, of which Wake had been a corresponding member, issued publications between 1889 and 1895, but had apparently long been defunct (Miss Margaret Currier, Peabody Museum Library, Harvard University; 9 Feb. 1966), possibly after 1900, when references to it cease (Mr. Kenneth L. Fahlberg, Brooklyn Public Library, N.Y.; 28 Feb. 1966). The Association's publications listed 'Mr. C. Staniland Wake, Chicago, Illinois' among its corresponding members in the years 1891–2 and 1895–6 (Mrs. Judith W. Young, Long Island Historical Society, Brooklyn, N.Y.; 18 Mar. 1966), but no further information was to be had by this route. The U.S. consular offices in London made no reply to a letter (23 Oct. 1965) asking whether the Immigration and Naturalization Service might have any record of Wake's immigration into the United States. An advertisement in the personal columns of *The Times* (17 Sept. 1965) yielded nothing. A request in *Victorian Studies* (March 1966, p. 317) for information on Wake, a portrait, or the whereabouts of descendants, was similarly unsuccessful.

Evidence began to come in, however, with a detailed letter from the chief librarian of the Reference and Local History Library at Kingston upon Hull. This reported a number of addresses in and near Hull at which Wake had lived, and also the firms of solicitors there in which he had been a partner, together

with particulars on Hull College, where he had been at school;
but a check of the local newspapers had not produced any report
of Wake's emigration or any notice of his death (Mr. R. F.
Drewery; 24 Aug. 1965). The Law Society, London, subsequently reported that its own records department had not been
opened until 1907, but it did provide from the annual Law Lists
the date of Wake's admission as a solicitor and a dated record of
the firms in which he had been a partner and the addresses at
which he had practised (Mr. H. A. R. Langford; 3 Nov. 1965).
The Hull Law Society was unable to find any record of Wake,
since its records did not cover the period when he practised in
Hull: the honorary secretary thought that 'these earlier records
must have been lost or destroyed' (Mr. A. W. Bowes; 12 May
1966).

Armed, at any rate, with the date and place of Wake's birth,
I turned to the register office of Kingston upon Hull, but their records of births dated back only so far as 1837, two years after Wake
had been born. At the suggestion of the superintendent registrar
(Mr. H. L. Sleight), I wrote to the Precentor of Holy Trinity
parish church, Hull, to ask whether Wake's parentage could be
found from the baptismal registers; but a search of the registers
from 1835 to 1837 found no record of his baptism there (Revd.
Martin H. Hunt; 19 Oct. 1965). From Holy Trinity, I was
directed to the vicar of All Saints, Hull, for the records pertaining
to Sculcoates parish: these registers turned out to have been
deposited in the Borthwick Institute of Historical Research at the
University of York, but the archivist of the Institute could find
no trace of Wake in them (Mrs. Norah K. M. Gurney; 27 Oct.
1965). An alternative source, suggested also by the vicar of Holy
Trinity, was St. Mark's, Hull, for the Lowgate parish register;
but the sexton there found no entry of a Wake baptism in the
period 1835–40, nor any marriage entry from 1829 to March
1835 (Mr. Gerald D. Burton; 1 Dec. 1965).

The Record Keeper at the Principal Probate Registry, Somerset
House, London, reported that a search for the will or letters of
administration of the estate of Wake, for the years 1910 to 1912,
had discovered no entry (20 Oct. 1965).

From Mr. Drewery I learned that Wake had been an active member of the Hull Literary and Philosophical Society, and a past President of the Hull Subscription Library, as well as the Library's first honorary solicitor. But Mr. W. Foot Walker reported that although Wake had been a member of the Hull Literary Club during the 1880s, and in 1885 had delivered a paper to it, there was nothing further to add: 'He does not appear to have taken an active part in the social life of the town' (23 Feb. 1967). From the Hull Subscription Library the Librarian wrote that the Library's building had been bombed in an air raid in 1944 and that most of its records had thus been destroyed (Miss L. Hogg; 23 Feb. 1967).

The Oxford University records showed that Wake had not been at Oxford (*Alumni Oxoniensis: The Members of the University of Oxford, 1715–1886* (Oxford, 1888), vol. iv); and the University Registry at Cambridge stated that there was no trace of him in their registers of matriculations and degrees for the period 1851–1900 (2 Jan. 1966).

The Director of the Chicago Natural History Museum recalled a possible link with the staff of the Field Museum in Wake's time: Dr. Fay-Cooper Cole's appointment had coincided by a couple of years with Wake's employment there, and his widow was still alive. Mrs. Mabel Fay-Cooper Cole replied, however, that she and her husband had been in the Far East for years and only briefly in the Museum after 1910. She had a faint recollection of having heard Wake's name, but thought she had never met him (4 Mar. 1966). Miss Rose Watson, who for many years had been secretary of the Department of Anthropology at the Museum, and who could certainly have recalled Wake (see Appendix C below), died about 1964. There was no person currently on the staff who had joined the Museum prior to 1918 (Mr. Donald Collier; 8 Feb. 1966).

Since it was known that Wake and Sir Richard Burton had together been elected vice-presidents of the London Anthropological Society (*Anthropologia*, 1 (1873–5), 1), it was reasonable to expect that some reference to Wake might be discovered in the biographies of Burton; but the standard sources (Burton, 1893;

Hitchman, 1887; Stisted, 1896; Wright, 1906) make no mention of Burton's official partner in the Society.

Parallel to these lines of inquiry, I was also trying to find a portrait or photograph of Wake, or any representation or description from which might be learned at least what he looked like. The portrait collection of the Royal Anthropological Institute contained nothing of Wake (Miss B. J. Kirkpatrick; 29 July 1965); the Chicago Natural History Museum had no picture or portrait of him, and patiently explained that it had no further material on Wake (10 Aug. 1965); Miss Margaret Kenna, who was compiling a catalogue of portraits of anthropologists, had been unable to discover any picture of Wake (22 Aug. 1965); and the *Radio Times* Hulton Picture Library, in the possession of the B.B.C., had nothing of the kind (16 Sept. 1965).

It occurred to me, nevertheless, that a member of the professional class in nineteenth-century Hull would surely have had a portrait photograph made, and that a firm in that town might still have a print or even the original plate.[7] Mr. Drewery again supplied detailed advice. He had checked the Hull directories but without being able to find any photographic firm that had been in existence in the nineteenth century and still existed. There was one firm, however, namely Messrs. Turner & Drinkwater, which had begun (so he thought) about 1876 and continued at various addresses up till 1960, when it closed down at the retirement of its owner, whose current address he supplied (Mr. R. F. Drewery; 3 Feb. 1966). I wrote to this gentleman, and he kindly replied that when the firm was closed, in the hundredth year of its existence, all of its 100,000 negatives were either dispersed or destroyed (Mr. Eric Turner; 12 Feb. 1966). Mr. Turner suggested that certain long-established law firms in Hull might have a photograph including one of their nineteenth-century colleagues, but inquiries of these firms led also to a dead end (Messrs. Andrew Maxwell Jackson & Co., 16 Feb. 1966; Messrs. Hearfield & Lambert, 16 Feb. 1966; Messrs. Gosschalk, Austin, & Wheldon,

[7] Later, in 1968, when writing the biography of A. M. Hocart, I managed to trace the plate of a portrait photograph that had been made in 1930 and had been stored since that date. Not so long a span as that involved in Wake's case, but an encouragement in other investigations all the same.

21 Feb. 1966). Mr. M. V. Gosschalk, one of the founders of his firm, was at the time nearly ninety years old but had never heard of Wake.

Another possibility that seemed worth exploring was that the publishers of Wake's last major work, *The Development of Marriage and Kinship* (1889), might have in their records some papers relating to Wake. The book had been published by a firm under the name of George Redway, at York Street, Covent Garden, London. These publishers no longer existed, and the National Book League informed me that the firm had closed down as a separate publishing house between 1901 and 1905, but that a reference in the publisher's list of Sonnenschein's 'Best Books', edition of 1935, stated that George Redway were amalgamated with Kegan Paul (National Book League; 3 Aug. 1965). Messrs. Routledge & Kegan Paul reported, however, that most of the George Redway records had disappeared and that no reference at all could be found to Wake (Mr. Norman Franklin; 9 Aug. 1965).

Another approach was through the printers of the *Development*. These had been Messrs. Turnbull & Spears, of Edinburgh (Wake, 1889, p. 484), and it was just possible that this firm might have kept the manuscript or related letters. The Edinburgh directories listed no printing firm under these names, but the postal superintendent of the Head Post Office found out for me that Turnbull & Spears were incorporated in the firm of Morrison & Gibb (Mr. T. G. Fraser; 6 Aug. 1965). The latter replied that although the incorporation had taken place some time before, their own records dated back only so far as 1911 and contained no trace of the book or its author (Mr. J. C. Keppie; 9 Aug. 1965).

Other attempts to get somewhere had even less success than the foregoing ventures, but it was difficult at the time to know what else to do. Mr. Drewery had supplied me with a list of Wake's private addresses, so I wrote to the residents at these places. From Welton, near Brough, Yorkshire, the postmaster, with admirable initiative, reported that he had found out that Wake had been a solicitor in Hull in 1872: he gave the name of the firm in which Wake had then been a partner, told me that Wake was said to have lived in Westbourne Avenue, Hull, and advised me to try the Law Society (Mr. H. W. Wady; 13 Sept. 1965). No. 74, Wright Street, Hull, had been taken over by Messrs. Brumby & Clarke, a printing firm: they agreeably passed my letter to Mr. Drewery (26 Oct. 1965). A letter addressed to the occupants of 2 Westbourne Avenue, Hull, was not answered.

After these fruitless beginnings the obvious recourse was to seek any surviving members of Wake's family. The Wakes are an ancient line descended from Hugh Wac or Wake, baron by tenure of Bourne and Deeping, who lived in the time of King Stephen (*c.* 1097–1154) and from whom the first baronet (created 1621) was fifteenth in male descent (*Debrett*, 1964, p. 877). Charles Staniland Wake, however, had no known connection with this ancestral stock. Sir Hereward Wake, the present baronet's father, knew nothing of him; and Miss Joan Wake, C.B.E., although very interested in family history, had never heard his name mentioned. My inquiries did bring out, though, that Wake was a very common name in the north of England. There have been Wakes in Northumberland and Northampton since the Middle Ages, so it was not surprising that towns such as Newcastle were full of them. This fact made it the more understandable, too, that Mr. Hereward B. L. Wake (Chichester, Sussex), who had a genealogy of the Wake family, could not find C. S. Wake on it. Similarly, it appeared less unexpected that H. T. Wake's memoir of a branch of the family, covering the period from 1666 to 1860, should also lead nowhere.[8]

In January 1966, therefore, I wrote to all the Wakes listed in the telephone directories of Hull and London, and also to those in the directories to Oxford, Southampton (where there happened to be quite a number), and parts of Berkshire and

[8] The number of Wakes discovered dashed also the hope, born from this memoir, of finding that Wake might have been a descendant of an illegitimate line. This line itself, however, is worth a note as a sinister comment on a past morality. Elizabeth Wake (baptized 16 July 1711), daughter of Robert Wake, a clergyman, and granddaughter of Sir William Wake, Bt., never married but at the age of seventeen gave birth to a male child. He took her surname and was called John after his father, of whom nothing is known except that he was a clergyman in poor circumstances. John Wake was given no education and was left a farm labourer all his life.

Hampshire. Forty-seven letters were sent out, each enclosing a stamped and addressed envelope for reply, asking whether anything was known of C. S. Wake. Thirty answers came back,[9] each one stating an entire ignorance of him.

The name Staniland was unusual and worth looking into, especially since a Charles Joseph Staniland was listed in *Who's Who* for 1897 as having been born in Kingston upon Hull in June 1838; but the usual searches in current directories drew blank. A firm of engineering contractors at Hull, carrying on business under the similar name of Stanland, said that none of its members had any knowledge of Wake (January 1966).

On 28 January 1966, when I had given up much hope of getting any further reply, I had a letter from Mr. John Newbigin Wake in which he wrote: 'I cannot help you very much, as Charles Staniland Wake died when I was very young. He was a family connection of my father, and held in some regard by both my parents. My late brother was named after him.' Mr. Wake wrote from his private address, in Oxford. He worked in offices in the Banbury Road, only a few hundred yards north of the Institute of Social Anthropology (51 Banbury Road) from which I had sent out my inquiries.

Mr. Wake (b. 1908) was descended from a line of farmers traceable, so far as he could recall, back to his great-great-grandfather Joseph Wake, of The Moor Leazes, near Lanchester, Co. Durham; but from no point in this genealogy could he make any connection with Charles Staniland Wake. His younger brother, named Charles Staniland (1911–40) had, by an apt coincidence, been admitted a solicitor in 1939 and was killed flying with the R.A.F. over Europe. Mr. Wake recollected that he had heard C. S. Wake spoken of when he was a small boy, and that Wake had died in America. His younger brother had been named Charles Staniland for sentimental reasons, but he could not be sure what these had been. More generally, he reported that some of the

---

[9] This seemed an unimpressive return at the time, especially since each person addressed had only to scribble a note 'Sorry, never heard of him', or something of the sort, and pop the envelope into a post box; but others more versed in postal inquiries have told me that actually this proportion of answers is rather good.

3. Mrs. Hilda Gregory, *née* Wake (*c.* 1914)

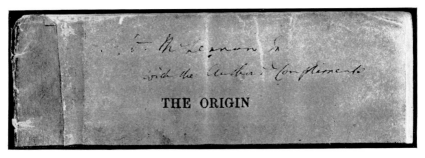

4. Inscription by C. S. Wake to J. F. McLennan (1879)

Wakes had been Dissenters (which would explain, as Mrs. Gurney
had already suggested, Wake's absence from the Hull baptismal
registers) and that in general they were staunch opponents of the
established order of things. In the end, though, my interview
with Mr. Wake proved as uninformative about Wake himself as
any of the previous sources had been. Later, Mr. Wake mentioned
that C. S. Wake had been associated in some way with his own
mother's cousin, Sir Joseph Cowen, though he did not know
if the connection was social or political. Cowen was a radical
politician, Mr. Wake told me, with a very wide circle of friends
and associates; but a search in two substantial biographies of
Cowen (Duncan, 1904; Jones, 1886) unearthed no reference to
Wake.

A week afterwards, however, Mr. Wake called me to say that
he had spoken on the telephone (2 Feb. 1966) with his mother's
sister, who lived in Rome. According to this conversation,
Wake's father had come from Sunderland[10] and his mother from
a Hull shipping family. The lady said that Wake had been a very
handsome man. She had a poor opinion of him, I was told,
because he had abandoned his young daughter when he emigrated
to the United States. For more information she suggested that
I write to Mr. H. W. Wake, of Sunderland; but he replied that
he could not help (9 Feb. 1966).

The investigation had thus at last got tantalizingly close to
Wake, but yet once more it had come to a dead end. I deplored
especially the fact that I had not after all been able to discover
the married name of Wake's daughter, through which information I might have hoped to trace surviving descendants. In
January 1966, however, I had again pestered the Director of the
Chicago Natural History Museum, asking specifically whether
the name might somehow be found; and now, just after the
latest setback, Mr. Webber unexpectedly wrote (3 February 1966)

[10] In *Kelly's Directory of Sunderland and Suburbs* for 1886 there are twenty-two
Wakes. As a final attempt to learn more of this origin, I wrote on 3 Dec. 1971 to
the fourteen Wakes (excluding Mr. H. W. Wake, with whom I had already
corresponded) in the 1970 telephone directory to Sunderland, enclosing with
each query a stamped and addressed envelope for reply. Five responses came back,
all negative.

to say that the name of Wake's daughter was Hilda Gregory, and that Museum correspondence—copies of which were to follow—gave her address in June 1910 (when Wake died) as Elloughton, Brough, Yorkshire.

This was a great encouragement, and it initiated a series of fresh inquiries and led to some discoveries. The main thing was to find Mrs. Gregory or, if she were dead, some descendant. Telephone inquiries of the post office at Brough, Yorkshire, and then at that of Newport, Yorks., disclosed (10 Feb. 1966) that a Mr. W. Gregory had lived at Manchester House, Newport, near Hull.[11] He was said to have left that address in 1965 and to have moved to York, but the York telephone directory did not list his name. The occupant of the house helpfully confirmed that Mr. Gregory had lived there, and got the post office to forward my letter to him. He also named a firm of solicitors that might be able to help, and these gave me the full name of the gentleman in question and also the name of the solicitor who had acted for him in selling the house (Messrs. Taylor, Broomer, & Co.; 21 Mar. 1966). The latter gave me an address in York (Mr. H. W. Rennison; 23 Mar. 1966), at which I wrote by recorded delivery to Mr. Gregory (24 Mar. 1966); but neither on this occasion nor subsequently was there any reply, and in the end I had no idea whether this Gregory was really Wake's grandson.

The superintendent registrar at Kingston upon Hull, to whom I was now able to give the name of Wake's daughter and (from the Museum papers) that of her husband, produced a set of interconnected dates. The entry of death of Mrs. Wake was traced, thus giving her age and consequently some idea of the period to be searched in for an entry of marriage. It was then necessary to search a fifteen-year period, from 1870 to 1885, for an entry of marriage, though this was without success. A search for the entry of birth of Wake's daughter, Hilda, in the period from 1880 to 1885 revealed this date, but a search for her marriage in the period 1898 to 1908, and then 1908–23, was unsuccessful (Mr. H. L. Sleight; 22 and 23 Feb. 1966). Next, I myself searched the

[11] Another Mr. W. Gregory, of Bridlington, Yorks., knew nothing of Wake; and a Mrs. Hilda Gregory, of Hull, proved not to be the latter's daughter.

registers at the General Register Office (Somerset House, London) and found in them the date of birth of Wake's wife, that of Wake's marriage, and also that of the marriage of his daughter. Certified copies of all these entries then supplied such related particulars as places of residence, occupations, names of witnesses, etc. From the date of Hilda Wake's marriage, the Holderness register office estimated and found an entry for the birth in 1908 of Phyllis Mary Gregory, Wake's granddaughter (Mr. D. G. Jackson; 19 Apr. 1966). There was thus an excellent chance that at least one direct descendant of Wake, his granddaughter if not his daughter, would be still alive and might possess papers and pictures.

Almost at the same time, moreover, there came a greater stroke of fortune. After ascertaining the marriage of Hilda Wake to Frank Gregory, I had written to Mrs. Gurney, at the Borthwick Institute of Historical Research, to ask whether she could find the births of any children of that marriage in the registers of Sculcoates parish. She replied that there were no such entries in the period 1907–22, but advised me to write to the incumbent at Elloughton (18 Apr. 1966). I did so at once, and the Revd. Michael D. B. Long replied from there that a Mr. Charles Sanderson had been a friend of Mrs. Gregory and might be able to help.[12]

Mr. Sanderson could indeed help. In a series of patient and interesting letters (22 Apr. 1966, et seq.) he brought together a number of decisive details about Wake's descendants. After Wake had emigrated, his daughter was brought up in the family of a solicitor, Maxwell Jackson, who was distantly related. She was especially close to the daughter of the family, some ten or twelve years older than Hilda Wake, who later married and, as Mrs. Johnson, became a close friend of Mr. Sanderson. Mrs. Gregory had died, I learned, some five or six years before the latter's correspondence with me (actually in 1960, as I found from a copy of the death certificate), and Mrs. Johnson a few years before that. Mr. Sanderson knew nothing directly of Wake, though he was able to tell me that Mrs. Gregory had been extremely good-

[12] It will occasion no surprise, by this point, to report that the Elloughton parish church had earlier burned down.

looking, from which recollection he conjectured that perhaps Wake had been also.

Mrs. Gregory's daughter, Mrs. Phyllis Wade, was still alive, however, and residing in London. Since she was too ill to receive a strange inquirer, or to carry on a detailed correspondence, Mr. Sanderson wrote to her on my behalf and later paid her a visit, only to find that she knew nothing of her late grandfather and possessed neither papers nor photographs relating to him. She did have a photograph of her mother, which she very kindly offered to lend me, and this amply bore out Mr. Sanderson's assessment of Mrs. Gregory's looks (see Plate 1). I wrote of course to the present owners of the photographic firm named on the print (Messrs. Albert E. Parkin, 58 King Edward Street, Hull), to ask about any other photographs in connection with Wake himself; but the letter was returned by the post office, which had not been able to find any such firm or its successors.

When Mrs. Gregory's husband died, Mrs. Wade helped her in the destruction of a great many family papers. These had included letters to Mrs. Gregory from her father, as well as anything else that had to do with Charles Staniland Wake.

III

Here follow in chronological order the particulars relating to Wake's life that were eventually ascertained in the investigation reported above.[13]

1835

22 March: Born, Kingston upon Hull, Yorkshire, England (*Who's Who in America* (Chicago, 1910), vi. 1992; *American Anthropologist*, 12 (1910), 343); son of Robert Wake, merchant (C. S. Wake's marriage certificate; register of marriages in the district of Sculcoates, Yorks., 1876, entry no. 183).

[13] The list of publications in my 'Bibliography of Charles Staniland Wake' (Wake (1967), pp. xliii–vii), which also is chronological, may be consulted together with the account given here.

c. 1842

Educated at Hull College, a proprietary school at Spring Bank, Hull (founded *c.* 1836, closed 1852).

The *Hull Collegiate Gazette* records three pupils named Wake at the school in this period, one in the preparatory school and one in the senior school; an S. Wake is listed in one of the school cricket teams, but no other details of forenames are given (Mr. R. F. Drewery; 24 Aug. 1965).

1858

Easter Term: Admitted a solicitor (Law Society, London; 3 Nov. 1965).

1859–60

Partner in Robertson, Atkinson, & Wake, solicitors, 89 Chancery Lane, London, W.C. (Law Society).

1861

Practising alone at 9 Gray's Inn Square, London, W.C. (Law Society).

1862

Partner in Wake & Farnfield, 11 Crooked Lane, London, E.C.; until 1864 (Law Society).

1863

Member, Anthropological Society of London. Publication of first paper, 'The Relation of Man to the Inferior Forms of Animal Life', in the *Anthropological Review*, the organ of the Society.

1865

Practising alone at 27 Lincoln's Inn Fields, London, W.C. (Law Society).

1866

Practising alone at 8 Gray's Inn Square, London, W.C.; until 1867 (Law Society).

1868

Partner in Skeet and Wake, 3 Raymond Buildings, Gray's Inn, London, W.C.; until 1869 (Law Society).

1870–1

Not in the Law Lists (Law Society, London; 3 Nov. 1965); publication of papers in the *Journal of Anthropology*.

1871

Delegate from the Anthropological Society of London to the annual meeting of the British Association for the Advancement of Science; co-signatory to the report of amalgamation between the Anthropological Society of London and the Ethnological Society of London in the formation of the Anthropological Institute of Great Britain and Ireland, 14 February 1871; appointed first Director of the Anthropological Institute (*Journal of the Anthropological Institute*, 1 (1872), Appendix, p. xxxvi).

In a letter to Sir John Lubbock, asking him to be first President of the Institute, T. H. Huxley writes: 'We have taken the Council of the new body, half from one society and half from the other—and altogether I think that the arrangement is a very fair one . . . We have retained the Anthropological [*sc.* from the Anthropological Society of London] Director' (Hutchinson, 1914, i. 117–18). The director in question is Wake.[14]

1872

Partner in Owst-Atkinson & Wake, Quay Street Chambers, 1 Quay Street, Hull; senior partner in firm, Anthony Atkinson, formerly practising at 3 Parliament Street (1861–4) and then at 1 Quay Street from 1867 on (Mr. R. F. Drewery; 24 Aug. 1965; Law Society, 3 Nov. 1965).

Replaced as Director of the Anthropological Institute in favour of E. W. Brabrook (*Journal of the Anthropological Institute*, 2 (1873), 442), in a manœuvre by which nearly all the officers of the Institute who had been members of the Anthropological Society alone (some were members of both this and the Ethnological Society) were ousted and supplanted by former members of the Ethnological Society (cf.

---

[14] But the source does not mention his name, any more than Huxley did.

Journal of the Anthropological Institute, 1 (1872), xxxvi–vii), a move to which Sir Richard Burton was to allude as 'sharp practice' (*Anthropologia*, 1 (1873–5), 2; cf. Stocking, 1971, p. 384).

1873

March: Vice-president (until December 1875), London Anthropological Society, founded by a group of members who in this year break away from the Anthropological Institute; the other vice-president is Sir Richard Burton (*Anthropologia*, 1).

1875

Member, Anthropological Institute ('List of Members', Anthropological Institute of Great Britain and Ireland (London, July 1875), p. 15). Address: 74 Wright Street, Hull ('List of Members'; Mr. R. F. Drewery, 24 Aug. 1965).

1876

17 August: Marriage to Fanny Laetitia Morley, daughter of Thomas William Morley, merchant, of Welton, Yorkshire; at the parish church, Welton, in the presence of James Nutter (?), Mary A. E. Jackson, Kate Jackson, E. G. Wake, and John Morley (register of marriages, district of Sculcoates, 1876, entry no. 183).

Fanny Morley was born on 10 August 1852 at 7 Carlton Terrace, Myton, near Kingston upon Hull; her father's occupation was merchant; her mother was Mary Morley, *née* Morley (register of births, district of Kingston upon Hull, 1852, entry no. 340). The Jacksons are presumably the distant relatives and friends of the family mentioned above (§ II); nothing has been discovered concerning E. G. Wake.

1877

Meeting with J. F. McLennan, author of *Primitive Marriage* (1865); discussion of 'the Australian marriage system', followed by correspondence (Wake, 1889, p. v; 1967, pp. xliv–l; cf. Rivière, in McLennan, 1970, pp. xxi–ii).

1878

Member of Council, Anthropological Institute; until 1882 (Miss B. J. Kirkpatrick; 27 July 1965).

1879

Offprint of 'The Origin of the Classificatory System of Relationships used among Primitive Peoples' (*Journal of the Anthropological Institute*, vol. 8, pp. 144–79) inscribed to J. F. McLennan (see Plate II; ultraviolet photograph kindly supplied by Dr. H. W. Ratcliffe, Librarian, University of Manchester).

1881

23 August: birth of Hilda Mary Wake, at 2 Westbourne Avenue, Saint John's Wood, Cottingham, East Riding, Yorkshire (register of births, district of Sculcoates, 1881, entry no. 184).

Residence: Clevedon House, 2 Westbourne Avenue, Hull; until 1885 (Mr. R. F. Drewery; 24 Aug. 1965).

1882

Partner in Atkinson, Wake, & Daly (until 1887); commissioner for oaths, and solicitor for the Whitby Gas Co. and the Thirsk Gas Co. (Mr. R. F. Drewery; 24 Aug. 1965).

The third partner in this firm of solicitors was Henry Percy Daly (Law Society).

1885

Member of Council, Anthropological Institute (Miss B. J. Kirkpatrick; 27 July 1965).

Paper 'Early Land Tenures' delivered to the Hull Literary Club (Mr. W. Foot Walker; 23 Feb. 1967).

Address: Clevedon House, 2 Westbourne Avenue, Hull (*Kelly's Directory of Lincolnshire with the Port of Hull and Neighbourhood* (London, 1885), p. 94; see also pp. 191, 251).

20 April: death of Fanny Wake, at Westbourne Avenue, Saint John's Wood, Cottingham; of pleuritis and consolidation of the right lung, followed by whooping-cough and pneumonia of the left lung; certified by Dr. Kilburn King, M.D.; reported on 22 April by Annie E. Rimes (of Westbourne Avenue, Saint John's Wood, Newland), present at the death (register book of deaths no. 8, sub-district of Cottingham, in the district of Sculcoates, 1885, entry no. 72).

1887

President, Hull Subscription Library; until 1888 (Miss L. Hogg; 23 Feb. 1967).

1889

Member of Council, Anthropological Institute; Foreign Member, Anthropological Institute of New York.[15] Address: Welton, near Brough, East Yorkshire (*Journal of the Anthropological Institute*, vol. 18 p. 93).

Partner in Wake and Daly; last appearance in the Law Lists, although Daly continued the practice until adjudicated bankrupt in April 1902 (Law Society; 3 Nov. 1965).

Annual report of the Hull Subscription Library, December 1889, states the appointment of a successor to Wake as honorary solicitor, but no reason for the change is given (Mr. R. F. Drewery; 24 Aug. 1965).

Article in the *American Antiquarian* ('The Distribution of American Totems'; vol. 2, pp. 354–8), published in Chicago; first printed evidence of American connections.

Emigration to the United States of America, probably in the latter part of this year. Frederick Starr, the only source to mention the matter, says merely: 'Removing to the United States Mr. Wake located in Chicago' (*American Anthropologist*, 12 (1910), 343). Contemporary issues of the Hull newspapers appear to make no mention of Wake's emigration (Mr. R. F. Drewery; 24 Aug. 1965). Leaves daughter, aged eight, in care of Maxwell Jackson, a solicitor and distant relative (Mr. Charles Sanderson; 22 April 1966).

It is recalled that Wake left England when someone close to him died, perhaps his wife (though she had died in fact four years earlier), and this was the reason for his move (Mr. John Wake; 3 Feb. 1966).

1890

Publication of 'Growth of the Marriage Relation' in *Sociology: Popular Lectures and Discussions before the Brooklyn Ethical Association* (Boston: James H. West, 1890), pp. 69–87; a printed version of a lecture delivered in New York. Wake refers at one point to 'your President' signifying that he himself was not yet a member.

[15] The Anthropological Institute of New York published one issue of its *Journal* (1, no. 1 (1871–2)), but no more ever appeared. The Institute is not mentioned in historical accounts of anthropology in the United States. (Miss Margaret Currier, Peabody Museum Library, Harvard University; 9 Feb. 1966.) The solitary issue of the *Journal* contained no paper by Wake (Mr. K. L. Fahlberg, Brooklyn Public Library, N.Y.; 28 Feb. 1966).

The volume comprises a series of seventeen such addresses: the first and second are dated 1889; the third is dated 1890 and Wake's contribution, which is the fourth, is also dated 1890. There is no other indication of the date of the original lecture, but the inference is that it was delivered in the early part of this year.

1891

March: elected an Associate of the American Society for Psychical Research (Mrs. P. Osborn; 6 Jan. 1966). Address: 349 North Clark Street, Chicago (Sir George Joy; 3 Aug. 1965).

Corresponding member, Brooklyn Ethical Association, a society connected with the Second Unitarian Church of Brooklyn and devoted to the study of sociology and evolution in science and art. Address: Chicago, Illinois. (Mrs. Judith W. Young, Long Island Historical Society; 18 Mar. 1968).

1893

Secretary to the local committee of organization, and to the publications committee, International Congress of Anthropology, held at Chicago (Wake (1894), p. vi).[16]

1894

Editor, *Memoirs of the International Congress of Anthropology, Chicago* (Wake, 1894), a report of the proceedings held at Chicago in 1893. Address: 4401 State Street, Chicago.

1895

'With' the Field Museum of Natural History (*Who's Who in America*, vi (1901), 1992); 'added to the staff' of the Department of Anthropology at the Museum, in the capacity of 'recorder' (Starr, 1910, p. 343).[17]

1896

Address: 411 45th Street, Chicago (*Lakeside Directory*; Mr. George H. Davis; 16 Oct. 1964).

[16] Frederick Starr was also a member of the organizing committee; Franz Boas was secretary to the executive committee of the Congress, and Otis Mason was a member of this committee (Wake (1894), p. vi).

[17] Cf. particulars under 1898.

1897

Listed as 'journalist' in the *Lakeside Directory* (Mr. G. H. Davis; 16 Oct. 1964). Address: 411 45th Street, Chicago.

1898

1 February: appointed 'preparator and clerk' in the Department of Anthropology, Field Museum of Natural History, Chicago (Mr. E. Leland Webber, Director, Chicago Natural History Museum; 29 Oct. 1964). Address: 392 Chicago Avenue, Chicago (*Lakeside Directory*; Mr. G. H. Davis, 16 Oct. 1964).

1898–9

Last year listed as Associate of the American Society for Psychical Research (Mrs. P. Osborn; 6 Jan. 1966).

1899

Listed as 'clerk' at the Field Museum in the *Lakeside Directory* (Mr. G. H. Davis; 16 Oct. 1964). Address: 5745 Rosalie Court, Chicago.

1901–5

Address: 'The Rosalie', 248 East 57th Street, Chicago. At some time most probably in this period Wake's 600-page manuscript on 'vortex philosophy', embodying ten years' work on his philosophical system,[18] is lost by fire, together with all of his other papers (Wake, 1907, p. 3).

1906–7

Address: 5468 Ridgewood, Chicago (*Who's Who in America*, 1907; Mr. G. H. Davis, 16 Oct. 1964).

1907

8 October: marriage of Hilda Wake, of Welton, to Frank Gregory, wine merchant, at St. Helen's church in the parish of Welton, Yorkshire, in the presence of Clive Wilson and Geraldine England (register of marriages, district of Sculcoates, 1907, entry no. 305).

Frank Gregory was the son of George Gregory, a corn merchant. Wake was evidently not present at his daughter's wedding.

[18] 'For many years he was interested in working out diagrammatic representations of the principles operative in nature and man' (Starr (1910)); see Wake (1904), and cf. Needham, in Wake (1967), p. xii.

1908

Address: 5603 Washington Avenue, Chicago (*Who's Who in America*; Mr. G. H. Davis, 16 Oct. 1964).

27 July: birth of Phyllis Mary Gregory, Wake's granddaughter, at Elloughton, Yorkshire (register of births, sub-district of South Cave in the district of Beverley, county of York, 1908, entry no. 471).

1910

Listed as 'anthropologist' in *Who's Who in America* (vi (1910), 1992).

21 June: death, at the age of seventy-five, at 'The Rosalie', 248 East 57th Street, Chicago (Mr. G. H. Davis; 2 Mar. 1966).

23 June: buried in the Chestnut Lawn section of Oak Woods cemetery, 1035 East 57th Street, Chicago (Mr. G. H. Davis, 2 Mar. 1966; Mr. Michael M. Moffatt, 24 Jan. 1970): Section R, Division 2, Lot no. 56–7N.

Mr. D. C. Davies, Recorder to the Field Museum, later (4 Aug. 1910) writes to the Director, Mr. Frederick J. V. Skiff, to report Wake's death (Museum papers, courtesy Mr. E. Leland Webber; 3 Feb. 1966):

I beg to report that C. S. Wake, Preparator and Clerk in the Department of Anthropology, died Tuesday evening, June 21. Mr. Wake had been compelled to absent himself from the Museum for the previous five days. At midnight, June 21, I was called up on the telephone at my residence by the people with whom he boarded, and was asked for instructions as to the disposal of his body. I suggested that an undertaker be called in and said that I would take up the matter of his burial the following morning. I cabled his daughter, who lives in England, and asked her for instructions. She replied that she had none to give but that she was writing. As he seemed to have absolutely no friends in Chicago, I undertook to order an undertaker to prepare his body for burial and arranged for a grave at Oakwoods. The total cost of his burial and the payment of the nurse who attended him in his sickness and sundry small items amounted to $138·36. Bills have been sent to the Museum by two doctors and by his landlady amounting to $77·40. There was found in his clothes the sum of $22·00 and his bank deposit book shows $11·00 to his credit. This with salary due him from the Museum, $50·00, shows all his assets to be, outside of books and personal property which have little or no value, $83·00.

In a memorandum which Mr. Wake left he asks a man named J. J. Van Nostrand to act as his executor, but Mr. Van Nostrand refuses to act or to have anything to do with his affairs. All his personal property is at the Museum and I have his bank book and the money that was found in his clothes.

I wrote to his sister [*sc.* daughter] as per copy of letter attached, and I received a letter from her thanking the Museum authorities for what they have done and intimating that she cannot pay his obligations. I attach her letter herewith.

I suppose that an Executor should be appointed by the Court to wind up his affairs.

The letter from Mrs. Gregory, which was probably transferred to another file, has not survived among the papers on Wake held by the Museum.

Wake left a brief informal will (see below, Appendix C). The law required certain information on Wake's relatives before an administrator of Wake's estate could be appointed. Messrs. Isham, Lincoln, & Beale, counsellors at law, of 115 Adam Street, Chicago, wrote to ask the Recorder of the Field Museum to ascertain the names of Wake's wife or wives, his children or other descendants, and any brothers or sisters and their children (30 Aug. 1910). Mr. Davies sent a letter to Mrs. Gregory, putting these questions to her (31 Aug. 1910). There was apparently no reply, and on 10 October 1910 he repeated his request for this information, explaining that the funeral bills could not be paid until the Probate Court had the desired particulars of Wake's relatives and had appointed an administrator. There is no record that he received any reply. A Mr. Stephen C. Simms was eventually appointed administrator of the estate, at the charge of the Field Museum, and drew up an account of Wake's possessions that was signed, with Mr. D. C. Davies as auditor on behalf of the Museum, on 1 May 1911 (see below, Appendix D).

In a note to Wake's last published article, 'Unity or Plurality of Mankind?' in the *American Antiquarian* (32 (1910), 65–76),[19] the editor, Frederick Starr, wrote (p. 65):

A notice of the death of Mr. C. Staniland Wake has reached the editor of this journal. It has awakened many memories of the past. Mr. Wake was known to a large number of archaeologists of Great Britain, and his articles have been appreciated by the readers of the *American Antiquarian* through many years.

Starr also wrote, over the initials 'F. S.', a formal obituary of Wake for the *American Anthropologist* (12 (1910), 343–4).

The Oak Woods cemetery has no record of a headstone having ever been placed on Wake's grave, and at the site there is nothing to show where his remains lie (Mr. Michael M. Moffatt; 24 Jan. 1970). [*Postscriptum*: a granite marker bearing the inscription 'Charles Staniland Wake 1835–1910' was placed on the grave in the autumn of 1972.]

[19] I had overlooked this title when I wrote (in Wake (1967), p. xii) that *Vortex Philosophy* appeared to be Wake's last publication.

1912

The Royal Anthropological Institute, of which Wake had been first Director, which he had served also as a member of its Council, and with which he had been constantly associated over a period of some twenty years, mis-spells his name as 'R. S. Wake'[20] in a list of deceased members and reports, as its sole epitome of his life, merely that he had been 'a member of the Anthropological Institute since its commencement, having joined the Anthropological Society [sc. of London] in 1863' (Report of Council for the year 1911, *Journal of the Royal Anthropological Institute*, 42 (1912), 3–4).

IV

This has been in many respects a melancholy and frustrating relation. Of Wake himself we know not much more than that, late in his life, he was a man of unusually retiring and unassuming character who rarely figured conspicuously in public. We do not even know what he looked like, and the nearest we can get is to look at the portrait photograph of his daughter (Plate 1) and to try to guess what features she may have inherited from him.

The most striking aspect of the investigation is the thorough-going extent to which Wake's life has been made obscure. He was born two years before civil registers were kept, and professional records often do not reach back so far as his time; the institutions for which he worked, and the societies of which he was a member, can tell nothing of him; his descendants are dead or cannot help; his manuscripts have not been preserved by publishers or libraries; all of his own papers were destroyed by fire; his daughter destroyed what letters and family documents remained; photographic negatives by the tens of thousands were discarded; a parish church burned down; a library and its records were bombed.

Wake's past has indeed been so much obliterated by circumstance and by all manner of disaster that he could scarcely have

[20] Perhaps by confusion with R. S. Charnock, a former member, with Wake, of the Anthropological Society of London and vice-president of the Anthropological Institute in the year of its foundation under Wake's directorship (*Journal of the Anthropological Institute*, 1 (1872), xxxvi–vii).

done worse if he had actually contrived that the course of his life should never be traced. It certainly turns out, at any rate, that we know practically nothing about him otherwise than through his published writings. The more we consider these, moreover, the deeper the puzzle becomes; for he wrote so extensively, on so many topics, and with such competence that the literary neglect he suffered is unaccountable. Also, he held office in the anthropological societies of his day, took a part in the foundation of the subject, even became first Director of the Anthropological Institute, and in all these activities came into touch with some of the greatest names of the period (Huxley, Lane Fox, Lubbock, Burton, Boas, and others); yet we still have no report, from all these communications, or from the subsequent histories and biographies, of what sort of a man he was. It is not as though he was a man of negligible abilities, after all, for his works testify quite to the contrary. Nor can it be that he was an insignificant person, for he was invited into the company of those who in that case would not have paid him such attention; he held positions of authority in the nascent organization of anthropology, and in the intellectual affairs of his home town; and he was, it is said, a man of some presence, and thus all the more unlikely simply to have been overlooked.

It is true that he is described as having been unusually retiring, unassuming, and inconspicuous, but these characterizations relate to a period, in Chicago, when in some regards his life had evidently not gone well. He had sustained, it is thought, a shock so severe as to induce him to leave England for the United States, at the age of fifty-four, and to spend the last twenty or more years of his life in Chicago, exiled from everything that had previously framed his existence and given him position and security in society. This drastic change in his affairs is tantalizingly obscure, and no estimation of his character can be well founded so long as we remain in utter ignorance of the reasons for which he made such a consequential move. What is plain enough, however, is that the effects were grave and perhaps traumatic. He left behind in England, and was never (so far as we know) to see again, an eight-year-old daughter, his only child and the sole surviving embodiment of a marriage that had been cut short after only ten years. He abandoned a solicitor's practice in which he had been a partner for seventeen years, and a profession in which he had pursued his career for thirty years, by a removal to a country where his legal qualifications and experience counted for nothing. He separated himself, too, from all of the trusted stays and familiar settings that had made up his social world; his friends, colleagues, and relatives; the intellectual circles of anthropological London and literary Hull, and the environments of his upbringing. A wrench of this kind, and one made at his age, cannot have been brought about from any trivial impulse; and we can only conjecture, not knowing at all what it might have been, that the cause had personal effects which marked his demeanour in the Chicago period. If, as it seems, he never went back to England, his daughter, and his previous mode of life, this cannot have been by reason of any absolute impossibility of a practical kind, for despite his poverty his return could doubtless have been managed somehow. Instead, his long and complete exile appears rather as a further indication that the cause of his emigration was so powerful, and its effects so persistent, that he either did not want to return or could not bring himself to do so.

These years must have been trying, to say the least, and they may well have proved dejecting. Wake probably reached Chicago in 1890, but it was not until 1895 that he had a reported connection with the Field Museum, and three more years were to elapse before he was formally appointed to a position in it. For the length of nine years, therefore, he had no professional status and possibly no regular occupation. The only hint of the shifts to which he may have resorted in order to make a living is that in 1897 he was listed as a journalist.[21] Admitted, he had formed some kind of anthropological associations by 1893, when he helped organize the International Congress of Anthropology, and in doing so had made some acquaintance with such eminent

[21] This is possibly one reason that he was included in a social directory of Chicago (rather as his literary record may account for his presence in *Who's Who in America*). In this connection, incidentally, a local investigator might be able to find in the Chicago newspapers of the day some signed contributions by Wake and thence some indication of his circumstances.

figures as Franz Boas and Otis Mason, but these involvements make it only the more striking a fact that he was not better taken up by the anthropological community. He was not appointed to a university position of any kind, and it was to be some years before he was given a position in the Field Museum. Of course, appointments are not always that easily arranged, and by 1894 Wake was already fifty-nine years old and not far from a normal age of retirement. In these circumstances it might even appear a sign of consideration that he was given any anthropological employment at all.[22] This would certainly be a practical view to take, but it does not diminish the disparity between Wake's attainments and the minor situation to which he had to accommodate himself. By 1890 he had nearly fifty publications to his credit, including five books and culminating with the achievement of *The Development of Marriage and Kinship* (1889); so that by these tokens alone, quite apart from his former directorship of the Anthropological Institute of Great Britain and Ireland, he might have attracted greater regard. Yet in the end he gained a meagre subsistence as a recorder, clerk, or 'preparator' in the Department of Anthropology at the Field Museum, a menial position that he held until his death.

On the other hand, these signs of neglect and decline may also be taken as a reflection of a change of character in Wake himself. Perhaps by this point, after the precipitating shock and its train of consequences, he was so much cast down and withdrawn into himself that his known and published achievements could do little to counterbalance whatever minor impression he may have made. Certainly, although he published twenty-six articles in the twenty years between his arrival in New York and his death in Chicago, and although he displayed in these his customary competence and eclectic interests, he brought out no major or remarkable work.[23] Even an obituary notice, furthermore, was to hint at

[22] It is not at all sure, for that matter, what consideration most of us could hope for today if we were down and out and thrown on the mercy of our profession.

[23] His central interests—as displayed in his privately printed *Geometry of Science* (1904) and *Vortex Philosophy* (1907)—were in any case becoming less conventionally anthropological and, understandably ('As we grow older / The world becomes stranger . . .'), more metaphysical.

a lack of independent intellectual vigour, and at a subordinate role. Starr, who had had Wake's collaboration for some time in the editing of the *American Antiquarian*, found only these dampening words to write about Wake's capacities in the Chicago period: 'He was a careful reader and was an admirable compiler and organizer of notes from reading. He has done much work of that kind for others to use, both inside and outside of the museum.'

The biographical record of Wake is in general obscure and perplexing, and in the end pitiable. We cannot guess at his moral deserts, and it would be impertinent to form even a speculative judgement of the propriety of his conduct when he left England and committed himself to the hard course that he then endured. But he contributed substantially to the inception of organized social anthropology, he made (in the *Development*) a theoretical advance in the study of marriage and kinship which commands continuing respect, and he earned thereby a secure place in the history of the subject. He was a man of considerable capacities and admirable accomplishments, yet during his life he did not receive the recognition that a longer view can more readily accord him. He died alone, in penury, and was to be almost entirely uncommemorated. Misprized in his own time, he has deserved far better of posterity than the fragmentary reconstruction of his life that is to be composed inferentially from these sparse records.

Wake's merit of perpetuity proves still to elude acknowledgement, and a cloak of new neglect can conceal his presence even in a setting where he is known to have been active. There has latterly appeared[24] a historical paper on the origins of the Royal Anthropological Institute, a long and admirably detailed account based on a minute perusal of a large body of literature and manuscript sources (Stocking, 1971).[25] It describes with patient care and in intriguing detail the doings and communications of a great many persons who were involved in the constitution of the Institute, its formation under the presidency of Sir John Lubbock,

[24] In September 1971, and thus four years after the resuscitation of Wake's name attempted in the new edition of *The Development of Marriage and Kinship* (1967; see editor's introduction).
[25] Cf. Needham, in Wake (1967), pp. viii–ix.

the disputes over the notorious house list of 1872, and the secession of a body of protesting members in order to establish the London Anthropological Society. The story is related with such scrupulous attention to particulars, and with such a command of the material evidence, as to persuade us that we possess in it a comprehensive and definitive relation of the events in question and of the men who were responsible for them. At no point whatever is there any mention of Charles Staniland Wake.

BIBLIOGRAPHY

BURROW, J. W., 'Evolution and Anthropology in the 1860's: The Anthropological Society of London, 1863–71', *Victorian Studies*, 7 (1963), 137–54.
—— *Evolution and Society: A Study in Victorian Social Theory* (Cambridge University Press, Cambridge, 1966).
BURTON, ISABEL, *The Life of Captain Sir Richard Burton*, 2 vols. (London, 1893).
Debrett's Peerage, Baronetage, Knightage, and Companionage (London, 1964).
DUNCAN, WILLIAM, *Life of Joseph Cowen* (London, 1904).
EVANS-PRITCHARD, E. E., *The Sanusi of Cyrenaica* (Clarendon Press, Oxford, 1949).
—— *Essays in Social Anthropology* (Faber and Faber, London, 1962).
—— *The Azande: History and Political Institutions* (Clarendon Press, Oxford, 1971).
HITCHMAN, FRANCIS, *Richard F. Burton, K.C.M.G.: His Early, Private, and Public Life . . .* , 2 vols. (London, 1887).
HOCART, A. M., *Kings and Councillors: An Essay on the Comparative Anatomy of Human Society*, ed., with an Introduction by Rodney Needham. Foreword by E. E. Evans-Pritchard (Classics in Anthropology, University of Chicago Press, Chicago and London, 1970).
HUTCHINSON, HORACE G., *Life of Sir John Lubbock, Lord Avebury*, 2 vols. (Macmillan, London, 1914).
JONES, EVAN ROWLAND, *The Life and Speeches of Joseph Cowen, M.P.* (London, [1886]).
McLENNAN, J. F., *Primitive Marriage: An Inquiry into the Origin of the Form of Capture in Marriage Ceremonies* (Edinburgh, 1865). (New edition, edited with an introduction by Peter Rivière, University of Chicago Press, Chicago and London, 1970.)
RIVIÈRE, P. G., ed., see McLennan (1865).
S., F. [FREDERICK STARR], Obituary notice: Charles Staniland Wake, *American Anthropologist*, 12 (1910), 343–4.

STISTED, GEORGIANA M., *The True Life of Capt. Sir Richard Burton* (London, 1896).

STOCKING, GEORGE W., 'What's in a Name? The Origins of the Royal Anthropological Institute (1837–71)', *Man*, N.S. 6 (1971), 369–90.

WAKE, CHARLES STANILAND, *The Development of Marriage and Kinship* (George Redway, London, 1889).

—— *The Geometry of Science* (privately printed, Chicago, 1904).

—— *Vortex Philosophy: The Geometry of Science* (privately printed, Chicago, 1907).

—— *The Development of Marriage and Kinship*, ed. with an Introduction by Rodney Needham (Classics in Anthropology, University of Chicago Press, Chicago and London, 1967).

—— ed., *Memoirs of the International Congress of Anthropology, Chicago* (Chicago, 1894).

[WAKE, HENRY THOMAS], *A Memoir of a Branch of the Wake Family of Northamptonshire and Elsewhere, from 1666 to 1860* (Hudson Scott, Carlisle, 1861).

[WEST, JAMES H., ed.], *Sociology: Popular Lectures and Discussions before the Brooklyn Ethical Association* (James H. West, Boston, Mass., 1890).

WRIGHT, THOMAS, *The Life of Sir Richard Burton*, 2 vols. (London, 1906).

APPENDIX A

Wake's Bibliography

There are two titles to be added to the list of Wake's publications (Wake (1967), pp. xliii–vii):

1884–5. 'Cottingham Castle and its Lords', *The Hull Quarterly and East Riding Portfolio*, 1, no. 2 (April 1884), 45–8; 1, no. 4, 167–70; 2, no. 1 (1885), 3–7.

1910, 'Unity or Plurality of Mankind?', *American Antiquarian*, 32 (April, May, and June), 65–76.

Ancient Symbol Worship, by H. M. Westropp and C. S. Wake, which appeared originally in 1874, has been republished in New Delhi in 1970.

It accords with the trend of the present paper to explain, incidentally, the reason that Wake's paper 'Musical Tone and Colour' (1896) was not adduced in the introduction to the new edition of the *Development*, in spite of its attractive combination of topics (cf. Scriabin), and that particulars of its pagination were not supplied in the bibliography where it was listed (Wake (1967), p. xlvi). The volume of *Music* in which it was contained, entered in the British Museum Reading Room catalogue and the only copy traced in the United Kingdom, had been destroyed by enemy action in the Second World War.

Mr. James Urry has discovered, from the register of papers submitted to the Anthropological Institute, that the referees for Wake's articles in the *Journal* (he published thirteen there between 1872 and 1884) were usually E. B. Tylor and Sir John Lubbock (personal communication, November 1971).

APPENDIX B

Wake's Addresses to the British Association for the Advancement of Science

Miss Margaret E. Kenna has very kindly drawn up the following list, taken from 'Transactions of the Sections', of papers delivered by Wake to the British Association for the Advancement of Science:

'On the Antiquity of Man in relation to Comparative Geology', 1866, p. 97.
'On Initial Life', 1869, p. 151.
'On the Race Affinities of the Madacasses', 1869, p. 151.
'On the Mental Characteristics of the Australian Aborigines', 1870, p. 157.
'On the Physical Characters of the Australian Aborigines', 1870, p. 157.
'On Man and the Ape', 1871, p. 162.
'On the Origin of Serpent Worship', 1872, p. 198.
'On the Origin of the Moral Idea', 1874, p. 158.
'On the Predatory Races of Asia and Europe', 1875, p. 179.
'On the Primitive Human Family', 1878, p. 592.
'On the Polynesian Race', 1879, p. 390.
'On the Origin of the Malagasy', 1880, p. 620.
'On the Papuans and the Polynesians', 1881, p. 696.
'On the descendants of Cain', 1883, p. 563.
'On the Polynesian Race', 1883, p. 573.
'On the Race Elements of the Malagasy', 1884, p. 922.
'On the Origin of Totemism', 1887, p. 906.

APPENDIX C

Wake's Form of Will

'Memorandum as to Distribution of Effects of C. S. Wake For Mr. Van Nostrand, 5553 Drexel Av., Chicago.

Photograph of Japanese Commissioners and Mr. Skiff, etc. at Field Museum of Natural History for Miss Watson, Field Museum. Also Holy Bible and New Testament and two volumes of Mr. Dorsey's diary (albums) and 2 oil paintings. Also Machine for whirling spirals and two spiral for use by it [*sic*] and patent right.

C. S. Wake, February 26, 1910.

If my daughter predeceases me I give all the residue of my estate to said Miss R. J. Watson.
Oil paintings (in cardboard box) and pyrographic box for Wm. Chumfert and oil colors and view   John Ion
Water color box and tubes for John when old enough to use them

C. S. Wake

Oil painting of bridge in Jackson Park for Miss Maud Oliver.

C. S. Wake.'

APPENDIX D

Letter of Administration of the Estate of C. S. Wake

138	Bound books @ 10 cents each	$13·80
1	Lot of miscellaneous current literature: 'The Strand', 'Open Court', 'Monost', 'Journal of the Anthropological Institute', etc.	1·00
1	Portfolio containing charcoal sketches by C. S. Wake	·25
	Oil paints, palette, brushes, etc.	1·50
1	Lot of unfinished manuscript	1·00
18	Canvas frames	2·50
1	Pair shears with paper cutter in leather case	1·00
1	Set shirt and cuff buttons	1·00
1	Trunk	1·00

1	Suitcase	·50
1	Student's lamp	1·00
1	Table	·50
33	Book plates	no value 00·00
24	Zinc etchings	no value 00·00

Total $25·00

Index